A PRICE BELOW RUBIES

"Delve in it and
continue to delve in it,
for everything is in it"

(Pirkei Avot, 5:26)

A Gift From

THE AVI CHAI
FOUNDATION

5766

2006

A PRICE
BELOW
RUBIES

༂჻ᕁᐟᕁ჻༂

JEWISH WOMEN

AS REBELS

AND RADICALS

NAOMI SHEPHERD

HARVARD UNIVERSITY PRESS
Cambridge, Massachusetts

Copyright © 1993 by Naomi Shepherd
All rights reserved
Printed in the United States of America
Second printing, 1994

Library of Congress Cataloging-in-Publication Data

Shepherd, Naomi.
    A price below rubies: Jewish women as rebels and radicals/Naomi
Shepherd.
      p.   cm.
    Includes bibliographical references and index.
    ISBN 0-674-70410-X (cloth)
    ISBN 0-674-70411-8 (pbk.)
    1. Women, Jewish—Biography.   2. Jewish radicals—Biography.
3. Women radicals—Biography. I.Title
DS115.2.S55   1993
305.48'8924—dc20   93-24117
                                      CIP

CONTENTS

ILLUSTRATIONS

Maps (*Martin Gilbert*)

Rosa Luxemburg, 1919 (*The Mansell Collection*)

Anna Kuliscioff (*British Library*)

Bertha Pappenheim (*Wiener Library*)

Bertha Pappenheim postage stamp (*Wiener Library*)

Manya Shochat (*National and University Library, Jerusalem*)

Rose Pesotta, Puerto Rico, 1935 (*New York Public Library*)

Rose Pesotta addressing the Montreal garment workers, 1936 (*New York Public Library*)

The Cradle of Jewish Women's Radicalism

The Pale of Settlement: Russian Jews were confined to this area by laws of 1795 and 1835. By 1897 there were more than five million Jews in the Pale.

SWEDEN

St. Petersburg

Baltic Sea

BALTIC PROVINCES

LATVIA

Riga

Moscow

LITHUANIA

Kovno

Vilna

Vitebsk

R U S S I A

GERMANY

Grodno

Minsk

Mogilev

Bialystok

WHITE RUSSIA

Warsaw

Lodz

Siedlce

POLAND

Zamosc

Derazhnia

VOLHYNIA

Zhitomir

Kiev

Fastov

Kharkov

UKRAINE

GALICIA

AUSTRIA-HUNGARY

BUKOVINA

Czernowitz

Kishinev

BESSARABIA

RUMANIA

Odessa

Melitopol

Sea of Azov

Simferopol

Black Sea

BALKANS

Adrianopel

Istanbul

GREECE

Salonica

ANATOLIA

TURKEY

Adriatic Sea

Aegean Sea

0 kilometres 250

0 miles 150

© Martin Gilbert 1993

The Palestine of Manya Shochat

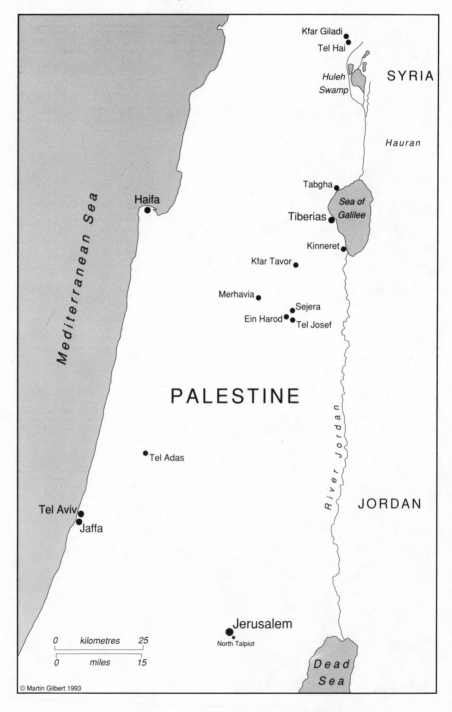

Kfar Giladi
Tel Hai
Huleh Swamp
SYRIA
Hauran

Tabgha
Haifa
Sea of Galilee
Tiberias
Kinneret
Kfar Tavor
Merhavia
Sejera
Ein Harod
Tel Josef

Mediterranean Sea

PALESTINE

River Jordan

Tel Adas

Tel Aviv
Jaffa

JORDAN

Jerusalem
North Talpiot

| 0 | kilometres | 25 |
| 0 | miles | 15 |

Dead Sea

© Martin Gilbert 1993

Rose Pesotta's America

Anna Kuliscioff and Bertha Pappenheim's Europe

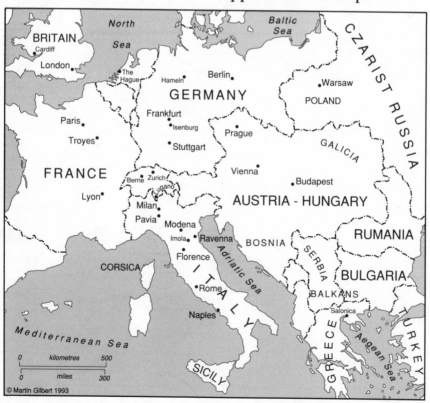

*To the memory of
Yehuda Layish*

ACKNOWLEDGEMENTS

I should like to thank the following for their help and advice during the writing of this book: Professor Ezra Mendelsohn, Professor Jonathan and Dr Edith Frankel, Professor Chedva Ben Israel, Professor Israel Kolatt, Professor Avraham Grossman – all of the Hebrew University of Jerusalem; Dr Tal Ilan; Dr Saul Stampfer; Dr Chana Safrai of the Judith Lieberman Institute and the Catholic University of Amsterdam; Professor Moshe Mishkinsky of Tel Aviv University; Dr Michael Heymann; Dr Vivian Lipman, of the Jewish Historical Society of Great Britain; Professor William Fishman, of St Mary's College, London; Dr Ada Rapoport-Albert, of University College, London; Dr Paula Hyman, head of Jewish Studies at Yale; Harriet Feinberg and Dr Hilary Marland for their information on Aletta Jacobs. Archivists and librarians I should like to single out for thanks are: Edith Wynner and Richard Salvato, consultants on the Rosika Schwimmer and Rose Pesotta Papers respectively at the New York Public Library; Dr David Doughan, the omniscient librarian at the Fawcett Library in London; the staff of the Tamiment Library, New York University, of the National and University Library of Jerusalem, of the Public Record Office, London, and of the Sterling Library, Yale. Dr Martha Bickel assisted me with translations from Russian and German, and Carrie Freedman with translations from Yiddish. Professor Chimen Abramsky of University College, London, applied a brake to my wilder theories, suggested recondite sources, and read the final typescript for errors. Martin Gilbert edited the entire book with patience and his usual scrupulous attention, for which I am infinitely grateful, and provided it with maps.

Particular thanks are due to Zohar Melamed for his skills with the computer, to David Gilbert for his help in an emergency, and to Phyllis Viski for secretarial assistance.

My husband, Yehuda Layish, who died suddenly in the prime of life a few months after this book was completed, read the manuscript as my most perceptive critic. Every idea in the book was discussed with him, every moment of excitement during its writing shared with him. He combined the traditional protectiveness of the Jewish husband with the comradeship of the modern Israeli. It is to him, in love and gratitude, and in deep sorrow, that it is dedicated.

A PRICE BELOW RUBIES

INTRODUCTION

'**M**y father was a small, sickly, grey-haired Jew with lively, kindly eyes. I can picture him bending all day long over huge ledgers in which he counted up the profits of his masters, lumber merchants, who were also his distant relatives and 'benefactors' for whom he worked as a bookkeeper at forty rubles a month. In the evenings and far into the night, he would also bend over no less voluminous books ... in which he vainly sought the meaning of life ... My mother ... was illiterate ... interested only in narrow, material family questions, and her husband's soaring into the clouds often aroused her to the verge of frenzy. The inevitable wrangle usually ended with father taking his 'holy' book under his arm and escaping into the next room, slamming the door behind him. The lock clicked, and through the keyhole one could see his shabby figure bent again over the Talmud ... Mother often wept bitterly; I pitied her, but my sympathies were with father, even though I had long ago lost faith in the holiness of the Talmud, and my belief in God had vanished.'

This is not the first chapter in a nostalgic memoir of life in a Jewish township of Eastern Europe, but the opening of a book entitled *Twenty Years in Underground Russia: Memoirs of a Rank and File Bolshevik.*[1] There is barely a subsequent mention of the author's parents. As usual in revolutionary memoirs, there is virtually no reference to her private life. The fact of her marriage to a fellow revolutionary is only revealed when she casually mentions a meeting with her husband on his way to exile in Siberia.

The author, Cecilia Bobrowskaya, was one of the second generation of Jewish women radicals. Her background was typical of thousands of such women who joined revolutionary movements, Russian and Jewish, between the 1870s and 1917. She lived in a small town in the Russian Empire inhabited mainly by Jews, with 'more tailors and shoemakers than there ever could be buyers', and she was mainly self-educated in Russian classical and revolutionary literature. In the winter of 1894, until fired for her radical activities, she went out to work in a lace factory, where illegal 'workers' circles' gathered. She then went to Warsaw to study and 'agitate' among Polish and Jewish workers. This began her career as a revolutionary.

The passage I have stressed carries within it the central theme of this book. Not all the fathers of Jewish women radicals studied the Talmud; some also had a secular education, like the first generations of the Eastern European *maskilim*, the children of the Jewish Enlightenment. But Jewish women had all been excluded from that intellectual inheritance which was the mainstay of Jewish life, while much of the responsibility for family and communal survival had been placed on women's shoulders. From about 1870 the radical ideas current in Eastern Europe were immensely seductive for young Jews of both sexes. But the limitations accepted almost unquestioningly for so long by Jewish women now intensified their motives for rebellion, just as their practical energies, approved by tradition, sought fresh outlets.

The sources of Jewish radicalism have been examined by Jewish historians; but women have not been treated separately from men, as has been the case for Russian revolutionary women and European socialist women. Feminist historians know little of Jewish history; Jewish historians have shown little interest in Jewish women in the modern period until recently. It has been generally assumed that Jewish women had the same motives for rebellion as the men, or, that their loyalty to the Jewish community was more important to them than the desire for greater independence as women. As serious research on the Jewish family, that much praised and much sentimentalised institution, is only now beginning, there has been no basis to challenge that assumption. A further problem is that so many of the outstanding women radicals disclaimed their heritage and disassociated themselves from other Jews—a fact which has not encouraged Jewish historians to accord them serious treatment.

Jewish historians have, however, noted the emotional aspect of women's participation in revolutionary movements, as if men's commitment was always intellectual, and have made critical reference to the many cases of conversion.[2] In a cooler vein, the Marxist historian Isaac Deutscher defined Jewish radicals who abandoned the community in a famous phrase as 'non-Jewish Jews'; many of the women would correspond to that definition. But no historian has thought to ask why Jewish women among the radicals were often tormented by their Jewishness. The words 'neurotic', 'hysterical', or 'temperamental' very often appear in Jewish historians' accounts of radical Jewish women. That their problems were as much circumstantial as emotional is not considered.

Certainly the nature of women's Jewishness—apart from the fact of their birth—is often hard to define precisely, for reasons discussed in the first part of this book. But even those women who disclaimed all interest in Jewish politics, like Rosa Luxemburg or Emma Goldman, the two most celebrated women radicals, are identifiable as Jews; those who know little of Luxemburg's critique of classical Marxism, or of Goldman's brand of anarchism, know at least that they were Jewish. This is not just a matter of formal 'origins'. 'Non-Jewish Jews' like Rosa Luxemburg or Leon Trotsky were often being less than frank in claiming amnesia about their early lives. The Jewish radicals, men and women alike, came from Jewish communities which until late in the nineteenth century had lived lives totally separate, as regards religion, language, social customs, and economic occupations, from the majority populations in the countries in which they lived. These communities lived according to a code which today would be comprehensible only to scattered orthodox groups in the Diaspora and the religious population of Israel. This code had elements particularly unacceptable to those women who sought independence and a new relationship between the sexes.

Judaism, a religion and also a complex legal and social system affecting every aspect of everyday life, was the central and most powerful force in the lives of these communities, from which almost all radical women came. Those who know only the vestigial form of Jewish life in the West can have little sense of what it meant to be a member of those communities, and still less what it meant to be a Jewish woman living in one at that time. At the beginning of the revolutionary period in czarist Russia, for a woman to join a radical movement meant challenging the family and community to which she belonged. The records and formal histories of these movements, with the exception of the Jewish socialist party, the Bund, tell us little about their women members, but a number of memoirs and biographical sketches remain. Further evidence of the women's lives may be buried in archival material in Russia and Poland only now being mined. But the evidence already at hand indicates that just as the experience of men and women in traditional society was different, their attraction to revolutionary ideas was based on different motives.

While radicalism among Jews was still a novelty, habits of religious training among the men were carried over into secular politics, especially among the 'half-intellectuals', the name given the many radicals who had been schooled in rabbinical dialectic and were now drawn to the theology of Marxism. Bobrowskaya recalls that, in the workers' circles, political arguments with a Russian Gentile instructor often became religious disputes. But most Jewish women, by comparison, whatever their origin— whether in the homes of the *maskilim* or the orthodox—had little or no Jewish intellectual training, and whatever they had acquired was at second hand. They did not know the Hebrew (which they usually could neither read nor write) of more than a few basic prayers, or the Aramaic terminology of the Talmud. They were barred (or 'exempted', as Talmudic scholars have it) from taking part in learned arguments. By contrast, there is much evidence that they were increasingly hungry for secular education.

Throughout the nineteenth century, the mother tongue of most Jews in the Russian empire was Yiddish; only three per cent gave Russian as their native language in a census carried out in 1897. Only a small minority of women over the age of forty, according to Jewish research statistics, had learned to read Russian by the end of the nineteenth century, and most were thus 'illiterate' like Bobrowskaya's mother. This did not mean, however, that they could not read Yiddish, written phonetically in Hebrew characters. There was a dramatic rise in the ability to read Russian, at this time, among younger women who were still Yiddish speakers. About a third of adolescent Jewish girls in the towns, and a quarter in the country, could now read Russian. While their reading skills in Russian were still inferior to those of Jewish men, they were still more than three times higher than those of women in the Russian Orthodox population, most of whom belonged to the peasantry.[3] Both this, and the fact that so many now worked in the artisan trades and industries in the towns, meant that it was far easier for them to be exposed to revolutionary literature than it was for the female population of Russia at large—despite their relative lack of learning within their own religious culture.

Anna Heller was a Jewish socialist leader, daughter of a family whose members, as so often happened in Jewish communities, were mill owners, brewers, lumber merchants, bailiffs of large estates—middlemen between the landowners and the peasantry. Briefly enriched during the nineteenth century and then impoverished as Russia freed the serfs, introduced punitive laws for the Jews, and industrialised, many such families produced radical children. Heller was one of the very few Jewish women who wrote, in Yiddish, a brief record of her life, before dying in a Soviet prison. Heller recalled that, as a devout small girl, she was reproved by her father for excessive piety as she garbled the Hebrew prayers. She retorted: 'Anyway I don't understand a word I'm saying', and was slapped for her impertinence.[4]

Jewish women had far less to discard, doctrinally, than men. Moreover, the lure of secular literature, which was more accessible to them than it was to men, proved to be much greater. Though Jewish tradition excluded women from the scholarly élite, it loaded them with responsibilities which far exceeded those borne by women in the corresponding merchant or artisan classes in non-Jewish society at this period. In traditional Jewish society, women—whether wives, mothers, or even mothers-in-law—were often solely responsible for the economic support of the scholarly aristocracy, and thus exposed to the world outside the Jewish community. In the famous Bashevis Singer family, where the father was a Hasidic rabbi, the remarkable (self-taught, and learned) mother of Israel Joshua Singer and Isaac Bashevis Singer gave birth while on a business trip on behalf of the family.[5]

In Eastern Europe in the nineteenth century, women in the Jewish working class formed a quarter of the entire work force. Even this figure is probably an underestimate, as so many women took work home.[6] Like the responsibilities of motherhood for the previous generation, wage earning now began at puberty. The young girls—seamstresses or workers in tobacco factories and the soap and sugar industries run by Jews in the north-western provinces of the Russian Empire—were hungry for learning. Russian working-class women, by comparison, who were mainly peasant in origin and totally subordinate legally, socially, and economically to their menfolk, were far less politically articulate.[7]

Esther Frumkin—probably the greatest of Jewish radical women journalists after Rosa Luxemburg but little known, as she wrote in Yiddish—describes in a memoir that at home it was only after their fathers had fallen asleep that 'one would read by the covered light and swallow ... the holy, burning little letters ... How many tragedies they would suffer at home if it became known that they were running around with the "brothers and sisters" ... how many insults, blows, tears! It did not help. "It attracts them like magnets", the mothers wailed to each other.'[8] One set of 'holy books' had taken the place of those others that the girls could not read. If the girls 'swallowed' Marxist doctrine so fervently despite the penalties involved, asking questions in the circles rather than arguing, it was very probably because, unlike their brothers, they had not been trained in dialectic.

The potential for rebellion, the desire for radical change among Jewish women, was all the stronger as they glimpsed for the first time the chance to rid themselves of traditional disabilities. Jewish men, too, sought to escape the domination of young lives by their elders—some historians, indeed, have seen the spread of the Enlightenment in Eastern Europe as the result of the 'youth culture' which followed an unprecedented leap in the Jewish birthrate during the nineteenth century—but the impact of the new ideas on women was even more devastating. It led them into political activity; it also encouraged them to seek a relationship with men hitherto unknown in Jewish society, one based on shared intellectual interests.

Jewish women's participation in revolutionary politics from 1870 onward is notable by any standard. In Czarist Russia, Jewish women in the earliest revolutionary groups, including those which resorted to terrorism, ranked second in numbers only to those of Russian women. Historians have noted this fact without trying to explain it. The leading authority on women's history in Russia during this period, Richard Stites, suggests only that 'the Jewish family was even more despotic than the Russian'.[9]

In fact, many of the fathers of those Jewish women who figure in Czarist revolutionary records in the last thirty years of the nineteenth century, and who belonged to the tiny, privileged merchant class allowed to reside in the great cities of Russia, were exceptionally indulgent towards their daughters and encouraged their higher education (even when this meant sending them to Switzerland for university studies). Even more striking (in the context of the allegedly 'despotic' or patriarchal families which are supposed to have alienated their daughters) is the fact that, as in the case of Bobrowskaya, radical Jewish women had a complex and often intimate relationship with their fathers, against whom they rebelled but whom they also wished to emulate.

The second group of radical Jewish women appeared in the Pale of Settlement, those provinces of the Russian Empire—mainly in the north-west—to which the majority of Russia's Jews were confined between the first partition of Poland in 1722 and 1917, when all restrictions on Jewish territorial settlement were abolished. Both middle-class and working-class Jewish women were among the small group of founders of the Jewish socialist party, the Bund, which inspired both admiration and hostility among the Russian social democrats. Several of the Bund's leaders, subsequently, were Jewish women, many active jointly with their husbands. The Bund, though a minority political group, had a large female membership, and its teaching cadres were packed with privileged women who took on themselves the education of working women, both in general studies and in Marxist doctrine. This was in striking contrast with the non-Jewish Russian populist and Marxist women of the intelligentsia who took it on themselves to educate the Russian women workers. Heirs to the feminist leaders of the 1860s, they stressed the importance of basic literacy and vocational rather than political training. Nor was their attitude towards egalitarianism between men and women workers as pronounced as that of the Bundist women.[10]

The importance of the Bund in Jewish women's lives was not just a matter of political belief. For the first time ever in Jewish community life, women now participated in public activity on equal terms with men. For the early revolutionaries of the Jewish élite, like their Russian populist counterparts, radical politics had meant a solitary life away from family and community, their sole allegiance to a small and endangered group of revolutionaries. This was not the case with the Bundist women. The notion of Jewish nationality was central to Bundist beliefs, and their radical activities were organised within the community.

But taking a stand against religion—for the Bund was strongly anticlerical—involved clashes with the women's families. Moreover, because it meant young men and girls studying together, usually after working hours, and taking part in political activities with no parental supervision, it flew in the face of tradition. The same was true of Zionism. Joining a Zionist youth movement was in many ways a more total rebellion than joining the Bund, as it ended in a complete break with the family through emigration—at this early stage an emigration only of the young.

However, not all Zionists were socialists and, even among the socialist pioneers, the process of reforming and changing Jewish life as it had existed for millennia in the Diaspora was more apparent than real. The earliest pioneers, of whom women were about one-third, left their families behind them in Eastern Europe and with them, as many women hoped and expected, the inequality of the sexes. Just as revolutionary women of the period believed that socialism would solve the problem of women's liberation, Zionist women, during the early period in a frontier society, were confident that building a society from scratch, without the older generation, would ensure them equality with men. They struggled to share the 'productive' manual tasks that conferred status, such as building and work in the fields. A small group even tried, though on a temporary basis, to establish all-women communes, when they found that in the early collectives they were usually relegated to what had always been woman's work: cooking, laundering, the care of infants and children, and, later, teaching. Ironically, this kind of work carried even less social status in the pioneering Zionist community than it had in the Diaspora. Many Zionist pioneer women ended up, to their bitter disappointment, working as domestic help to middle-class women in the new Jewish towns of Palestine—work which immigrant Jewish women in the West often refused to do. Only a handful of exceptionally ambitious and gifted women were to play a formative political role in the new Jewish state.

The remaining manifestations of Jewish women's radicalism were mainly offshoots of the movements in Eastern Europe, transferred to Western Europe and the United States with the mass immigration that began in the 1880s. Jewish socialism gradually petered out in this very different political climate, though Jewish women played an important part in the anarchist circles of the West during the early years of the century. They were also prominent in pacifist activities before and during the First World War.

Finally, a significant group of Jewish women were pioneers in the trade union movement in the United States until the 1930s. The economic exploitation of Jewish women in the industries of the main American cities was dismayingly reminiscent, on a larger scale, of what had happened in Eastern Europe, with additional friction between Jews of different origins: German Jewish Americans were often the employers, Eastern European immigrants were usually the employees. Thus, given Jewish women immigrants' political consciousness, it was not coincidental that Jewish women led the fight for unionisation, strike action, and protest against conditions in industry during the first third of the twentieth century.

At this point, however, the limits of Jewish radicalism began to be evident in what was one of the most mobile and successful immigrant communities in the United States. As the Jews moved into the American middle class, the Jewish family reasserted itself. The élite of religious scholars had diminished to a small group; those who headed the Jewish social hierarchy were now businessmen and professionals—as in Western Europe. Women left the workplace at marriage and returned to the home, where they assumed a new importance as domestic guardians of Jewish tradition (something which had happened much earlier in Western Europe); but it was a tradition by now considerably attenuated. The mainspring for rebellion had lost its tension.

Historically, then, radicalism among Jewish women, which had always clashed so emphatically with the conventional image of the Jewish woman, was limited both by political and by social developments. The Jewish women in the earliest radical groups, like their non-Jewish counterparts, were doomed. Many died, either in prison or by their own hands, and others fled from the Russian Empire or the Soviet Union. Most Bundist women who did not emigrate perished in the Holocaust. Politically organised women in socialist and Zionist movements played a part in the inevitably limited but none the less remarkable episodes of resistance to the Nazis. The Zionist women pioneers did not achieve the complete equality they sought, both because the economic facts of state-building and the importance of the army in the life of the country militated against them—and also because the Jewish family, from which the women pioneers had taken a prolonged holiday, reasserted its power. In the United States, as Jewish immigrants moved from the American working class into the middle class, women either became housewives (with fewer economic responsibilities than in the past) or competed for the professional opportunities open to those who now qualified for an education. With the passage of time, some have become radical feminists, or—when they remain observant Jews—campaign for change in Jewish law. But this is in a very different era.

The disintegration of the socially autonomous Jewish society of Eastern Europe in the nineteenth century meant the end of what had been a clearly defined Jewish class structure, though one which did not correspond to the Marxist pattern. Today, Jewish radicalism looks historically limited, the product of a very particular period in Jewish history. How much of it was intrinsically Jewish? And in what way were its ideas particularly appealing to women?

Jewish radicalism borrowed heavily from current political ideas in the host countries; but the Jews also had their own 'class struggle' and, perhaps even more important, a clash between the generations. The older, privileged minority, and the religious leaders, tended to be loyal to the regime, while their educated children became radical leaders. The rank and file of radical Jews came, however, from the poorer artisan class. Privileged Jewish girls who had enjoyed a secular education became the mentors and teachers of these working-class women. Jewish women radicals resemble other socialist women of the period in that they subordinated their own separate needs and interests to the founding of a new, just society; but they also had to fight a battle of their own against class differences within Jewish society, differences which had been codified in Jewish law, were still part of the fabric of Jewish communities, and affected women more than men. Men continued to exclude women from public life, and the education of sons was considered more important than that of daughters, even when the rabbinical law which had made these customs mandatory no longer held sway over the community.

Jewish women traditionally possessed a worldliness and energy often absent among the scholarly élite. In Eastern Europe, women active in economic life had mixed freely with non-Jews in the marketplace. In Western Europe, by contrast, women of privileged families who no longer worked were often educated in non-Jewish schools and acquired middle-class secular culture, in the nineteenth century, with more ease than their husbands, who in most cases had abandoned Jewish scholarship for commerce, as entry to the professions was limited.

Those Eastern European women who managed to challenge the Jewish tradition which excluded them from public affairs, and who had often shared economic responsibilities with men, found it easier to throw themselves into political life than home-bound middle-class Jewish women in the West. That is why most of the women described in this book came from different areas of the Russian Empire. Radical Jewish women in immigrant communities who migrated to the West, and who clamoured for the destruction of existing institutions in the new country, often embarrassed the older established Jewish women, who distinguished themselves in ways that fitted Jewish tradition—in welfare work and in charitable and educational activities. Such work squared well with their assimilation into the Western middle class.

Between the mid-nineteenth century, when the ideas of the Enlightenment finally reached the Jewish masses, and the 1930s, when radicalism among Jews was itself in decline, Western and Eastern European Jewries became two very different societies.

Jewish women rebels in the West, who played a leading part in the battle for women's suffrage, pioneering work in birth control, and pacifism in the First World War were usually those who had turned their back on the Jewish community altogether. A notable and particularly interesting exception was Bertha Pappenheim, founder of the Jewish women's feminist movement in Germany, who led the campaign against Jewish prostitution (a feminist issue throughout this period, though not one which interested the radicals in particular). Pappenheim, working inside the Jewish community and an observant Jewess, was deeply critical of the established Jewish leadership and the rabbis and headed the campaign against Jewish traffickers in the trade in women and girls. Though not a political radical, she was an outspoken rebel against the Jewish woman's limitations in traditional society.

Jewish prostitution, which was widespread in Eastern Europe and became internationally notorious because of the flourishing nineteenth-century white slave trade, was the result both of the gradual disintegration of Jewish communal and family tradition, preserved almost intact since the Middle Ages in Eastern Europe, and of the terrible poverty of Eastern European Jews towards the end of the century. It became an issue thrust on the attention of middle-class Western Jews by Pappenheim and a few women like her, and galvanised them into largely unsuccessful action because it laid the Jews all over the world open to anti-Semitism.

Jewish women radicals and rebels, then, were strikingly prominent in the cause of political and social change between 1870 and the 1930s across the widest possible spectrum. While Russian radicalism was a forcing house for women's activism, Jewish women carried its principles beyond the frontiers of Russia, across Europe, and even to the United States. The explosion of energy and initiative among Jewish women was ignited at a particular moment in history and was extinguished, or spent, within a few generations.

The character, personal histories, and achievements of the women I have chosen to describe can only be fully understood in terms of the Jewish tradition against which they were in full or partial revolt, as it affected Jewish life right up to the last third of the nineteenth century in the Jewish communities of the Russian Empire and parts of Central Europe—though it was already in decline, to various degrees, further West.

We have only one reliable source—the rabbinical responsa—for the history of Jewish women between medieval times and the Enlightenment; and we do not know how Jewish women in traditional communities in the mid-nineteenth century felt about their lives before the emergence of radicalism. We have only the fictional (or autobiographical) work of the male *maskilim*, or secular intellectuals. There are a very few autobiographies written by women, to which I shall make reference. Many autobiographical sketches by Jewish women born in the latter part of the century, mainly unpublished, were written in the United

States, in Yiddish, during the first four decades of the twentieth century and are only now being thoroughly studied. The vast majority of the Jewish women who wrote memoirs during the modern period, it should be noted, were or had been political radicals.

I have therefore chosen to write the rest of the book, after the opening section, as a composite biography, rather than to attempt, with the present rather meagre sources—only in the Bund records are there reliable statistics of women's participation—a full history of all those Jewish women involved in movements for political and social change during the period. Communist functionaries like Ruth Fischer of the German Communist Party or Ana Pauker in Romania have not been included; nor have outstanding but solitary figures like Olga Benario, the German wife of the Brazilian radical Luis Carlos Prestes.

Instead, I have selected mainly those behind whom there was a large group of politically active women—also described in summary: Bundists, Zionists, and Jewish women workers in the United States during the first decades of the century. I have also devoted space to Rosa Luxemburg and Emma Goldman, because they are the best-known Jewish women radicals of the period, though examining them from a slightly different angle to that adopted by their biographers. The tragic Eleanor Marx, whose only rebellion against her domineering father was her identification with the working-class Jews of the East End, has been so thoroughly portrayed in the biography by Yvonne Kapp that there is little to add. Golda Meir, Zionist leader and Prime Minister of Israel, is not included as her career reached its climax after the Second World War and so beyond the period surveyed. I have indicated in Chapter 7 why I did not choose her to represent the pioneering radical Zionists whose origin was in Russia.

Joseph Conrad wrote of his white-haired woman revolutionary in *Under Western Eyes* that 'she might have been Jewish'; Solzhenitsyn, in one of the final chapters in *August 1914*, describes what seemed to him the archetypal Jewish prerevolutionary family in which the parents were pro-Czarist, the children—the

daughter in particular—student rebels. Jewish women revolutionaries appear sporadically in period literature, and their
heirs have even made an appearance in the films of Woody Allen,
in whose Jewish families of the 1930s there is always a stubborn,
anachronistic radical or Bundist unmarried aunt. The figure of
the Jewish woman rebel is noted but not explained. I have not
tried, however, to attribute specific aspects of these women's
ideas too closely to their Jewish origins. In an otherwise distinguished article on Rosa Luxemburg, one historian comments
that the ethical content of her thought was 'unconsciously
moulded by generations of rabbinical learning and the spirit
of biblical humanism'.[11] No woman was ever 'unconsciously
moulded' by a tradition of which she was ignorant, though many
rebelled against what they had seen and experienced of women's
life as dictated by a tradition of which they were an integral part.
The reader will judge, from the evidence I have assembled, in
what way the fact that they were born into Jewish communities,
at a time when life there was still influenced by tradition, affected
their way of thinking.

Political radicalism went together with a rejection of orthodox
Jewish values, and in this sense, perhaps, these women were
rebels twice over. As one Yiddish poetess was to write:

Within me has burst my grandmother's sense of modesty
Revolt burns in me like effervescent wine.
Let good folk curse and hate me,
I can no longer be otherwise.[12]

1

A FOOTNOTE TO HISTORY

᠁ᢋᡃᢋ᠁

Women in Jewish Society before the Enlightenment

There is no history of Jewish women. In all the historical literature produced since the end of the eighteenth century, women are a footnote to the story of Jewish survival. Apart from the women of the Bible, they are largely nameless. Between the fall of the Second Temple in AD 70 and the French Revolution, only a few women were celebrated in Jewish writings. Bruria, the wife of the second-century Talmudic sage Rabbi Meir, was both famed and notorious for her learning and sharp tongue, though what was recorded of that learning, by others, is meagre. In seventeenth-century Germany, Esther Liebmann carried out financial transactions with her husband, and after his death became a Court Jew with access to German princes. Spanish and Italian Jewry at the time of the Renaissance was distinguished by a series of wealthy and influential female patrons of the community, most notably Donna Gracia Nasi, the Marrano banker's wife who used her money and influence to promote the escape of Portuguese Marranos (or clandestine Jews) to Italy, and literary ladies, of whom the best known was Sara Coppio Sulam, a Venetian poetess who engaged in theological debate in verse form with Catholic dignitaries.

Others were minor figures, rabbis' wives of whom little is known beyond their names and the bare outlines of their lives. The evidence that remains of women's lives in traditional Jewish society until the nineteenth century is like period furniture around a static figure in an ethnographic museum. Only a very few recognisable individuals stand out. The autobiographical memoir of Glueckel of Hameln, a seventeenth-century woman trader and contemporary of Liebmann, the only surviving testimony of its kind, was published two hundred years after her death. Among Eastern European Jewry there is a solitary, ambivalent female figure among the 'wonder rabbis' and mystics of the nineteenth century: Rachel Werbermacher, the Maid of Ludmir. From the end of the eighteenth century, however, when the social and religious traditions preserved almost unchanged since the Middle Ages were gradually discarded, first in Western and much later in some parts of Eastern Europe, Jewish women become visible and audible in history across a wider spectrum.

During the nineteenth century, two attempts were made to write a popular history of Jewish women, putting together the heroines of the Bible, the rabbis' and the bankers' wives, and any Jewish woman contemporary who had achieved celebrity. The pitfalls were obvious: one of these books begins with the biblical Sarah and Miriam and ends with Mrs Friedlander, the American golfing champion of the 1890s. Behind the attempt to work the sparse sources into a historical narrative was a genuine dilemma. Both books were essentially apologetic works, written by women who were successful writers: the assimilated, if devout English Jewess Grace Aguilar and the German convert to Judaism Nahida Remy.[1] Both justify Jewish practices to a Christian audience and betray unease about the way women figure in orthodox Judaism. Their separate ways of looking at women's history reflect their very different backgrounds and also the thirty years which elapsed between the appearance of the two books. Aguilar's book indicates the ambivalence towards their religion of the assimilated Sephardi élite of England, which sought acceptance by the Anglican middle class; the other, more 'scientific' approach was that of the liberal (in religious terms) German Jewish intellectuals among whom Remy moved. Both were painfully conscious of their disadvantage, as women, in writing about Jewish tradition. Both were concerned not just to produce a list of those Jewish women named in the Bible and rabbinical writings but to establish women's contribution to the survival of the Jewish people. They did so, moreover, in an age when the family had become the focus of middle-class Protestant piety (which put Jewish tradition in a favourable light) and when women's rights as individuals, as potential equals to men, had become a subject of popular debate.

Grace Aguilar, an English Jewess of Spanish descent, was a novelist whose most popular work, *Home Influence*, went through forty-one editions after the first in 1847. It is set in a middle-class Anglican household and exemplifies what historians have called the nineteenth-century 'feminisation of religion':[2] sanctification of the domestic female virtues—care of the home, maternal dedication, and charitable good work—the 'religion of the heart rather than the mind'[3], a phrase to which Aguilar returns frequently. That the author was a Jewess posed no problem: even those Victorian Christians who affected to deplore the Jews' preoccupation with money admired their exemplary family life.

Nahida Remy, by comparison, was clearly influenced by the Science of Judaism, the secular study of Jewish religion and history which had flourished in Germany since the beginning of the century. She tried to put the ancient Hebrews into the context of the study of ancient Semitic religions, and contrasted Jewish and Christian attitudes towards marriage and celibacy. If Aguilar was concerned to represent Jewish women as possessing all the virtues of the homebound Victorian churchwoman, Remy, reflecting the current feminist debate in Germany on work and female dignity, advised Jewish women to improve their educational status and find a useful occupation, while praising, without explaining, the industry of Jewish women in the orthodox communities of Eastern Europe.

But in other ways, the two women were grappling with the same problem. Both were concerned with the inroads on the Jewish communities of England and Germany by conversion to Christianity: Aguilar, in her uneasy references to 'the fearful apostasy of Israel' and Jewish women's ignorance of their own history, Remy, in her chapter on 'The Apostates', the celebrated Jewish bluestockings of the Berlin salons (Rachel Varnhagen and others) at the end of the eighteenth century, whom she seemed uncertain whether to claim for their brilliance or deplore because of their defection—a familiar dilemma for Jewish historians.

Both, moreover, were defensive about the position of women in Jewish society, and explicitly or implicitly criticised rabbinical law and orthodoxy. Aguilar had dedicated her previous book, *The Spirit of Judaism*, also a work of apologetics, to 'women, mothers and daughters in Israel', arguing that rabbinical tradition itself, with what she called its 'abuses, iniquities, idle fables and spiritless and uninspired customs', and with those 'oriental' prayers and rituals which excluded women, was leading to conversion.[4] Remy preferred to ignore the subject of orthodoxy almost entirely, giving prominence in her history to Jewish women on the fringes of scholarly life: printers, teachers, and contemporary Jewish women in German intellectual life.

Both authors had to concede the facts of women's segregation in the synagogue, the absence of ceremonies celebrating their birth and maturity, and above all their ignorance of their own religion and history.[5] Aguilar confesses that she herself, like all Jewish women, was not sufficiently familiar with the tenets of her own religion and tradition to write with real authority on her subject: 'It is expecting far too much from human nature to believe that we can feel as Jews only because we are born such.'[6] A few years earlier, the leading French Jewish journal had published a controversial letter from a young woman complaining about her ineligibility to be counted in the *minyan* or minimum number of Jewish men required for a service to take place, and of what she felt was her humiliating segregation in the women's gallery in synagogue. Such customs, she lamented, 'are not consonant, in my view, with the sophistication of French culture, and our progressive and civilising conduct.'[7]

Very little has been added to the early nineteenth-century biographical history of Jewish women, as it emerges in Aguilar's and Remy's accounts, in the hundred years of scholarship that has elapsed since their work was published. Archaeologists have unearthed references to Babata, a Jewish businesswoman of the Second Temple period who appears to have engaged in much independent litigation;[8] papyri, inscriptions on tombs, and other epigraphic material have been scoured for references to women as 'leaders', 'mothers of the synagogue', or 'elders' during the Graeco-Roman period in Italy and the Near East.[9] The medieval Geniza manuscripts, which give so richly detailed an account of Jewish life in twelfth-century Egypt, tell of a woman broker who went into business with a partner and was apparently wealthy enough to purchase her own rather unorthodox marriage dispensations.[10] English and French social historians have established the existence of women financiers like Belaset of Wallingford and Licoricia, widow of David of Oxford, who were active in the thirteenth century in England, and a network of Franco-Jewish women usurers, working from home, who provided separate, domestic loans—parlour usury—for the wives of those medieval nobles who were already borrowing from the Jewesses' husbands.[11] In Italy, women signed their names as printers and publishers to rabbinical works, usually apologising in advance that 'as they were only women' there were bound to be mistakes. Women engaged in business and acted as financial agents for their husbands, even going unescorted to markets and meetings;[12] and several women were named as ritual slaughterers, admitted to the post when they could show that they understood the technique and had proved that they would not faint.[13] Lists have been compiled of rabbis' wives who had acquired learning and who even had passed *pitkaot*—notes with suggestions for amendments of learned interpretations of the Law—round the kitchen door, as it were, to their husbands sitting in conclave.[14]

The criterion for the preservation of women's names, and the very choice of names gives some idea of their status in Jewish society at different periods. While in the Second Temple period women were often commemorated on their tombstones as the 'daughters and wives of' particular men, rather than by their own names, rabbinical dynasties often led back through the woman's family, hence the survival of their personal names. Women were more likely to be given names popular in the country they lived in, rather than biblical names, indicating their greater closeness to the secular world and the fact that they were not related, as were the men, to the Hebrew literary culture of study. In the twelfth-century Geniza documents of the Jewish community of Fustat, a suburb of Cairo, no biblical names at all for Jewish women have been found. Women in this community were often given Arabic names synonymous with victory, over-coming, and domination—whether in compensation for their actual inferior status, or perhaps to protect them during child-birth.[15]

What is notably absent is women's testimony about themselves. Among the rabbinical élite and merchant class in medieval Europe, many women were literate not in Hebrew but in the vernacular in which commentaries to the synagogue services were written. Though thousands of letters were found in the Geniza, many from women, there is no evidence that they were actually penned by women but rather by male scribes. Nor is there a single learned ruling by a woman which has become a part of the rabbinical commentaries.[16] Practically the only uncontestable authorised writings by Jewish women, between the sixteenth century and the Enlightenment, are the *piyyutim* and *tehinot* (*thkines* in Yiddish), personal poems and prayers penned by women which are concerned, naturally enough, with problems of everyday life—requests for a gentler and kinder husband, or an alleviation of poverty, or relief from overwhelming household chores—as well as indications of their participation in and attitude towards synagogue services.[17]

What biographical data there is, however, underlines the sturdy and prosaic character of the archetypal Jewish woman: a tough bargainer, a good business woman, a manager, an organiser, a materfamilias. What is notably absent, apart from the roll-call of martyrs, is the heroic and romantic figure of the Jewess as reflected in Christian art and poetry—a figure based on the legends of the Old Testament and developed in almost total ignorance of Jewish law and tradition. The noble Jewesses among the medieval Worthies, and in later literary tradition, particularly in Romantic literature, are often juxtaposed with the evil male Jew, the wicked usurer. In architecture, there is the forlorn symbolic figure of Synagoga, blindfolded, ignorant of the faith, carved over the lintels of so many medieval churches and facing the proud Ecclesia.[18] When Aguilar and Remy drew a straight line from the female figures of the Bible to contemporary Jewish women, as popularisers of Jewish history do even today, they were echoing, consciously or not, the Christian perception of Judaism. Both saw a Judaism based on the Old Testament, in particular the ten commandments and the moral lessons of the prophets, not on what appeared to them as the archaic legislation of the Pentateuch. Yet rabbinical law, based essentially on that very legislation, decided women's status in Jewish society since Talmudic times, and reinterpreted the Bible in a way that was entirely alien to Christian tradition.

Women as portrayed in the Bible had little relevance to Jewish society as it developed in exile (the Diaspora or Dispersion), with its small, powerless communities. But it would be a mistake to attribute the virtual absence of Jewish women from history entirely to the patriarchal bias or misogyny of the rabbis. It can be most simply understood by imagining European history without Christianity (no women's orders or celibate life, no separate status for single women); without a ruling class or royal families (hence no queens or royal marriages); no feudal nobility (hence no ethos of chivalry); no national rebellions headed by dynastic or popular figures (no Boadicea or Joan of Arc); but rather an uninterrupted religious and social tradition stretching from the early centuries of the Christian era until late in the eighteenth century. The unique structure of the Jewish communal hierarchy meant that rabbis and scholars were the spiritual and intellectual élite, sharing communal leadership with the merchants and financiers, those Court Jews or *shtadlanim* who represented the community with the ruling powers. Women shared in the distinction of belonging to rabbinical families but were never scholars in their own right; though they might sometimes participate in their husbands' commercial and diplomatic activities, and though from the Middle Ages onward concessions were made in rabbinical law to allow them to carry out financial tasks for the community, they could not be communal leaders. Almost all those women whose names have survived were those who lived on the borderline between Jewish communal life and the wider host society: as Court Jews who shared their husbands' privileged position, or as educated women versed in contemporary literary fashions, often influenced, more notably than their husbands, by the manners of the host society. In those Jewish communities where the influence of the surrounding society was minimal, as in the smaller towns and villages of Central and Eastern Europe from the Middle Ages to the late nineteenth century—communities dominated by the rabbis—women are historically faceless.

Why is the Christian archetype of the heroic Jewess so misleading? Most of the great biblical women figures belong to the period when the Jews existed as a political entity, and particularly before the first exile in 587 BC. They were important not for any minor role they may have played in their religious cult—there were no Jewish priestesses—but rather as secular figures: queens, tribal leaders, prophetesses (the prophet could be a lay figure). These were women who were described as capable of killing an enemy, planning a battle, and handing down a judgement. When the Bible was reinterpreted by the rabbis, they tried to argue that even in ancient times women were merely the power behind the throne, or, in Jewish terms, conformed to the Psalmist's comment that 'the King's daughter is all glorious within', a saying frequently invoked to condemn women's participation in public activities. But no one who reads the Bible critically can accept such a description of Deborah, Miriam, Jael, the matriarchs, or the heroic Esther and Judith.

Influenced by nineteenth-century anthropologists from Bachofen onward, and affected by these images of female leadership, the biblical scholars of that period sometimes speculated about the existence of a primitive early matriarchy. But the fact that in rabbinical law Jewishness is transmitted through the mother and not the father is not a sign of female importance or power. In fact, one of the curiosities of Jewish history is that it began as a patrilineal society (one in which lineage is reckoned through the father) in which women were celebrated in tribal history, and then became matrilineal in the post political, rabbinical age (from the second century AD onward), during which women had no public role whatever and became increasingly anonymous. In Judaism, unlike in other ancient social and religious systems, the matrilineal principle refers only to descent and carries with it no advantage to the women in legal terms: family status, kinship, and succession are all determined through the father.[19]

The reason for women's prominence in the biblical narrative is probably linked with the nature of Jewish life in its tribal period and during the pre-exilic kingdoms. The findings of archaeologists and anthropologists suggest that the society which produced the creation myth was one in which women's power in the community was considerable because they played an important part in the rural economy, in which Adam not only delved but cooked and where Eve not only span but gathered the harvest.[20] The rabbinical sages and early Christian fathers writing a thousand years later introduced into their work the patriarchal bias of what is now called, rather misleadingly, the Judaeo-Christian tradition.[21]

What is now known of the multiple authorship of the Bible suggests that the authors known to scholars as J and E began setting down the ancient myths and historical narratives before the Assyrian conquest and that the J text in particular is concerned with the stories of individual women and sensitive to their predicaments, at a time when noblewomen probably had greater status than the ordinary man in the street. The powerful priesthood, after the restoration to Palestine, was responsible for the compilation of the detailed laws in which women are treated as chattels and inferiors and in which all women, for the purposes of Pentateuchal law, are classed with children, slaves, or sexually impaired men. Female authorship has been speculatively advanced for the J version of the Pentateuch and the Song of

Songs, the only passage in the Bible written from an explicitly feminine and erotic viewpoint.[22] But many rabbinical sources condemn Eve, and the Song of Songs is almost always interpreted allegorically in Talmudic exegesis, as in Christian theology.

Early Judaism did not exclude women from participation in the cult; women were present in the Jewish assembly which received the Law from Moses in the Sinai, in public meetings where the Law was preached, and in annual festivals as singers and dancers. However, when Cyrus restored the Jews from Babylonian exile to Judaea in 538 BC, the laws governing Jewish social behaviour, many of which had been codified and revised in exile, began to restrict women's role in worship and in the propagation of the faith. As the old rural society was succeeded by a more sophisticated urban polity centring on the hierarchy of the Temple, the differentiation between the sexes in the observance of the cult became more clearly defined.[23] Women participated in certain cult-linked crafts such as the weaving of curtains for the Temple and the sewing of the priests' robes.[24] With the re-establishment of Temple worship in Jerusalem, they took part in all but the actual sacrificial rites, prepared offerings and tithes, and joined in assemblies of worship, possibly in separate groups or *chavurot*; and some Pentateuchal laws excluding women from Temple rituals were modified *leruhan shel nashim*—'because women wanted it'.[25] Though the priesthood was uniquely male, it was not celibate, and the priests' wives were a powerful social group. Older women, often widows, could become patronesses of synagogues, were responsible for the distribution of charity, and were charged with the washing of and mourning for the dead. Most significantly, in the early synagogues, which also date to the Second Temple period (from the return from Babylon to the fall of Jerusalem to the Romans), when the scriptures were read, cyclically, to congregations of Jews, women were among the public readers of the Torah—a custom which was gradually outlawed by the Palestinian sages who succeeded the political rulers as leaders of the nation.[26]

Nevertheless, the elaboration and revision of the purity laws both in exile and during this period, while they applied to both sexes, ensured that women lived in periodic seclusion for the length of their reproductive lives. The blood and menstruation taboos which were the legacy of primitive Judaism had become connected with the belief that idolatry and offences against Pentateuchal law, among them sexual impurity, had caused the first exile. Women were subsequently to be segregated and separated from men, both at worship and in the home at times when they were menstruating—though this segregation also meant that women, during their childbearing career, had a week's leisure each month while others cared for their husbands and prepared the family's food. Ezra's ban on intermarriage and the expulsion of foreign wives meant further discrimination against women in the pursuit of endogamy: keeping marriage within the community. All these customs became central to Jewish family and communal life over the ages and persisted well into the nineteenth century in all but the most assimilated Jewish homes.

The marriage and inheritance laws which evolved from the original Pentateuchal code ensured that the Jewish woman was under the control either of her father or of her husband. Men alone were entitled to sue for divorce; women inherited property only when there were no male heirs. Only in Jewish settlements remote from the influence of the teachings of Ezra and Nehemia, such as the military colony of Jews at Elephantine, on the Nile, set up under the Persian rule of Egypt, had women enjoyed greater freedom.[27]

The Mishnah, the Jewish legal code which evolved towards the end of Jewish political independence and was formally compiled during the second century of the Christian era in Palestine under Roman rule, treated unmarried girls and married women as their fathers' and husbands' wards; but it also protected them more effectively from exploitation and abuse. The frank celebration of women's sexuality recorded in parts of the scriptural canon was reinterpreted, and the abuse and victimisation of women which was also part of ancient Hebrew life was corrected. Men did not have the power of life and death over their wives, as in early Rome, but had to submit complaints before the courts. Widows and divorcees could testify before the courts, dispose of property, and conduct financial affairs on their own, instead of returning to their father's or brother's custody, as was the situation under Roman law during this period.[28] Barbaric customs like the adulterous woman's ordeal of drinking bitter water seem to have disappeared from Jewish life even before the Dispersion.

Women had no place, however, in the new and comprehensive system of education, introduced in the Second Temple period, which cut across class distinctions to bring the Law to all members of the Commonwealth, the Jewish polity in Palestine, so called from the Hasmonaean period onward. The institution of the synagogue evolved as part of the effort to convene Jewish communities regularly to hear the reading of the Law. Archaeological evidence suggests that in the earliest synagogues there was no separate women's gallery, just as the so-called 'women's court' in the Temple was open to men as well. If in synagogue it took some time to evolve the *ezrat nashim* or separate gallery for women in communal prayer, from the very outset women were excluded from the *Bet Midrash* or study room of the synagogue.[29] There is no doubt that in this and early Talmudic times there were exceptional women, whose names have been recorded, who acquired knowledge of scriptures and even of the Talmud. But they did so privately, either because they had fathers or husbands who encouraged it or because they managed to listen in on male debates. There is also some very scant evidence that, as in later periods, women of the ruling class were accorded secular education.[30]

Towards the end of the Commonwealth period, there were still examples of independent female activity in religious life. Women were prominent in the role of missionaries and disciples among Jesus's Jewish followers, and during the first century AD there were women among the Therapeutae sect, ascetics like the Essenes, who appear to have worshipped and studied in separate but equal assemblies. Thenceforth, however, women were to play a separate and far more passive role in the cult, but a strong material and supportive role in the Jewish community.[31]

With the fall of the Second Temple in AD 70, the codification of Jewish law entered its most intensive phase. The Mishnah legal code (the word means 'repetition') was based on the various rulings set out in the Pentateuch—which for rabbinical teaching was by far the most important part of the Bible—but was also influenced by the early Midrashim, exegetic and homiletic teachings which had evolved in the preceding centuries. Successive commentaries made up the Gemara, or Completion, and the whole was called the Talmud, completed by the sixth century. Rabbinical law, or *halacha*, is based on this foundation.

THE SAGES AND THE HEROINES: BIBLICAL WOMEN REINTERPRETED

There is no better illustration of the rabbinical view of women than the way in which, in the Aggada (the narrative, homiletic, or folkloristic part of the Talmud), the sages referred to the lively female figures in the Bible. Clearly they had to be tamed and domesticated, though they had to be accepted as figures in holy writ. So in keeping with the general Talmudic system, which interpreted the ancient myths in the light of subsequent Jewish mores, these reinterpretations display a paternalist condescension, together with some apprehension of women's intelligence and sexuality.

The story of Adam and Eve, with its suggestion that the woman's intelligence was superior and, in one of the twin versions, that she was created as man's equal (so that some biblical scholars have suggested that it might have been written by a woman), posed difficulties of many kinds for the rabbinical interpreters of the scriptures when they tried to assimilate it to the later criteria of domestic Jewish morality. One suggestion was that while archetypal woman had greater *bina* (or *da'at*), native intelligence, than man, Adam was directly responsible to God, while Eve was responsible to Adam and therefore unable to conceive of the full implication of her disobedience.[32] Perhaps as the creation story refers to mankind as a whole and not to the origins of the Jewish people, it evokes the full force of the rabbis' criticism of the female sex.

One of the very earliest Midrashim or rabbinical homilies, a genre which goes back to the Babylonian exile, deals with the creation of Eve from Adam's rib—'not from the head, lest she be vain, nor from the eye, lest she be a flirt, nor from the ear, lest she be an eavesdropper, nor from the mouth, lest she be a gossip, nor from the heart, lest she be prone to jealousy, nor from his hand, lest she be thievish, nor from his foot, lest she be a gadabout'.[33] Midrashic literature also develops a legend absent from the Bible: that Adam, parted from Eve, encountered a 'Lilith' figure or demon, the female alter ego, childkiller rather than mother, destroyer rather than creator of life, seducer of man, possessor of an aggressive sexuality.

In rabbinical lore, matriarchs, prophetesses, and heroines are all cut down to size.[34] The female prophetesses were not the equivalents of Isaiah, Jeremiah, or Ezekiel, who arose at a time of national crisis to rally the nation. Rather, biblical women provided critiques of specific incidents, and perhaps were acclaimed as prophets in recognition of their qualities of leadership. Miriam challenges Moses' exclusive right to speak in the name of the Law, for which she is stricken with leprosy. But the Talmud refers to her chiefly as a prophet of fertility, who reminds both her father, Amram, and Moses of their duty to procreate.[35] Hulda, the most important woman prophet, is consulted by Josiah to 'enquire of the Lord' concerning the discovery of the book of Deuteronomy, and prophesies God's ultimate judgement on the Jews. While her female quality of compassion is her qualification for intercession with the king, according to the rabbis it was 'as a reward for her husband's good deeds' that she became a prophet at all.[36] The other women prophets are praised for their conventional virtues, modesty, obedience, and industry, but reproved for speaking out of turn or competing with men.

The militant heroines, who used their combative intelligence and their sexuality to deceive enemies and potential fathers of their children, could scarcely be recommended as models to the domesticated Jewish women of the later era. The one woman who was obviously a political leader, Deborah, took part in the strategic planning of the war against the Canaanites and had the authority to summon Barak, the Jewish warrior, from the north. She also sat in judgement, solely a male prerogative by Talmudic times. So the rabbis criticise Deborah for her effrontery in calling Barak to her side, rather than going to his aid, and suggest that it was for this impertinence that she was given the derogatory name of 'bee', as Deborah means in Hebrew.[37] They also insist that, rather than being indoors with a man (which in the rabbis' view could have only one meaning), she handed down judgement in the open air, sitting under a palm tree.[38] It was even harder for the rabbis to accept the seduction of the enemy by Jael and Judith. In the Bible the killing of the Canaanite leader Sisera by Jael heralds the decline of Israel's chief enemy and introduces forty years of peace. But having defined woman strictly in terms of her biological role, the rabbis' chief interest is to exonerate their female ancestors from licentiousness. Examining the biblical text closely, the rabbis conclude, on rather sparse textual evidence, that Sisera had intercourse with Jael seven times before she finally killed him. This troubles them so greatly that in three separate commentaries they argue that she 'felt no pleasure' during the encounter.[39] In the case of these seductive heroines, as in that of Tamar, whose fornication with her father-in-law ensured the continuance of the House of David, they can only conclude: 'a transgression performed with good intent is more meritorious than a commandment performed with none.'[40]

Another problem for the rabbis was how to write about the cases of intermarriage in the Pentateuch and the Hagiographa, evidence that what had become one of the major rabbinical sanctions was not in operation. Given the rabbis' entire lack of interest in chronological history, it is not surprising that they do not argue, apropos of intermarriage, that in ancient times Jews practised exogamy.[41] But what they do is to justify, post factum, the marriage of Ruth the Moabite to Boaz (they maintain she went through conversion ceremonies) and the marriage of Esther to the Persian Gentile Ahasuerus.

The discussion of Esther's intermarriage is a prime example both of Talmudic dialectic and of the rabbinical ideal of woman. Mention of the story of Esther comes into a general debate on the justification of evil deeds performed in a good cause. The rabbis begin by arguing that the capital crimes of incest or murder can never be justified even to save life—in Jewish ethics the highest virtue, and one which overrules many negative commandments. The discussion turns to women, and to the question as to whether a betrothed maiden should be slain rather than be violated. A participant in the discussion asks: 'But did not Esther transgress publicly' in marrying a Gentile? To which the fourth-century Babylonian sage Rabbi Abaye answers, 'Esther was merely natural soil'—in other words, the passive object of the king's embraces.[42] Like most of the heroines in the Hebrew Bible, Esther is an intelligent woman who displays initiative; yet here, as in the case of Jael, she is represented as essentially passive. In many rabbinical sources, woman had no will independent of man; as one sage comments: 'A woman before marriage is a shapeless lump, and concludes a covenant only with him who transforms her into a useful vessel.'[43]

PROTECTED INFERIORS: WOMEN IN RABBINIC JUDAISM

Rabbinical law, *halacha*, defined women's status very clearly. It is based on commandments or *mitzvot* relating both to specific beliefs (such as the observance of monotheism) and to social conduct. In Judaism, the community is all important, the individual bound by a complex pattern of instructions relating to worship, family relations, sexuality, economic life, proper behaviour between Jews and their fellows, Jews and non-Jews, and even their food and clothing. The survival of the Jews as a distinct people with a particular relationship to God and particular duties imposed on them by this relationship is basic to the faith. The responsibilities of men and women in this covenant are entirely different, as the law makes clear.

The Talmud is written in the form of an oral debate around the Mishnah by the sages, with numerous digressions, including passages of narrative and homily (the Aggada). It is possible to make out a case for a fundamental Jewish misogyny by collecting the derogatory references to women scattered through the Talmud, while a feebler apologetic can be produced by quoting the sages' not infrequent praise of virtuous and supportive wives. What is probably more significant, in judging the status of women in Jewish law, is the structure of Talmudic dialectic, which makes it clear that the normative Jew is the male; women are discussed in a highly selective manner. The Seder Nashim—the seven orders of the Talmud related to women's affairs—deal with betrothal and marriage, divorce, the vows a woman may make and their viability, suspected adultery, levirate marriage, and the applicability of the Nazirite laws to women.[44] (The complex rituals surrounding menstruation are dealt with under the different rubric of purities, which also deals with other sources of pollution.) One contemporary scholar has argued that the Mishnah deals with women only at those moments when they pass from the tutelage of one man to another, characterised as 'moments of transfer' or instability in society.[45] A feminist scholar has elaborated this concept to argue that women are 'chattels' when their biological and sexual role is at issue, but 'persons' when considered in their own right, as single girls over a certain age, widows, and divorcees.[46]

Rabbinical law is paradoxical. On the one hand, it is governed by the original code which cannot be altered, and on the other, it is open-ended, never completed, endlessly reinterpreted. The rabbis never actually changed Pentateuchal law, or eliminated it, as it were, from the statute books. Pentateuchal law in its original form was handed down, orthodox Jews believe, directly from God. Some aspects might be temporarily in abeyance in exile, such as the suspension of the laws regulating Temple worship, or agriculture in the land of Israel. Sanctions like the implementation of capital punishment for severe offences were impossible to carry out where the power of life and death was in the hands of non-Jewish rulers.

Thus, the rabbis related to women essentially as protected inferiors. While Pentateuchal law relates to women essentially as chattels, the property of fathers or husbands, Talmudic or rabbinical law recognises their individual nature and responsibility for their actions. Of the 613 Pentateuchal commandments codified and interpreted by the rabbis, there are laws which apply equally to both sexes, most specifically those which forbid misbehaviour and carry a penalty—the 'negative laws'—and the positive laws, which are interpreted as having a different application for men and women. This is not only so in the case of gender differences, like the purity laws, but also in the case of laws which are differentiated by being 'time bound', such as those enjoining worship at fixed times. Such laws are optional for women, since their domestic duties are assumed to take precedence over ritual piety. Only men are enjoined to procreate (perhaps because women are seen as essentially passive objects in reproduction). Other laws, sentimentally seen as marking out a special place for women in Jewish ritual, have, however, ambivalent overtones. While in the Second Temple period women played an active role in Jewish worship, there are only three precepts specifically incumbent on women in the Mishnah: *challot*, a law relating to the sacrifice by burning of the tenth part of the dough used in baking, a relic of Temple rituals; *niddah*, the complicated rituals surrounding menstruation, designed to keep menstruating women and the polluting influence they carried away from men; and the lighting of the Sabbath candles, a uniquely female duty in the home. In the context of Talmudic exegesis, it is notable, however, that all three of these precepts are linked with the notion of an original female sin and guilt dating from the creation.[47]

Rabbinical law modified and humanised the Pentateuchal laws on marriage considerably. Whereas a man could betroth a woman in biblical times by purchase, sexual intercourse, or 'deed', rabbinical legislation ensured that men could not buy women (or sell them) and could not force their sexual acquiescence or gain rights by sexual intercourse; a complex set of rabbinical ordinances also safeguarded the woman's property and ensured her maintenance. The basic obligations of the man in Jewish law, which were to provide the woman with food, clothing, and sexual relations, developed into a contractual partnership in which the man was entitled to administer and control his wife's property and enjoy her earnings and in return was obliged to provide for her materially at least in the manner to which she was accustomed before marriage, if not to better it. The evolution of the ancient marriage contract, or *ketuba*, in Talmudic times indicates to what extent Jewish women were now protected. The contract became the woman's guarantee against desertion (as Pentateuchal law allowed a man to divorce his wife 'according to his wish'), specified the sum which would have to be paid to her in the case of a divorce, and ensured that in the case of all but the most serious offences on her part, the property she brought with her to the marriage remained her own.[48] Women were unable to inherit directly from their fathers or husbands while there were male heirs; but again, rabbinical law ensured that these heirs provided for the widow and daughters.[49]

While marriage was made more stable and women more generously treated, the rabbis also, however, perpetuated a number of archaic Pentateuchal laws related to marriage, the relic of Judaism's tribal Semitic culture. Chief among them was levirate marriage, which ensured that the property of a dead man remained in his family after his death, by making it obligatory for his brother to marry his widow, though a ceremony could dissolve this obligation. The rabbis retained the laws relating to the priestly sect (the Cohanim, whose names indicated that they were the priests' descendants), for whom certain marriages were banned. Both these rulings limited the range of marriage options for men and women alike and complicated the process of match-making. The rabbis also introduced another regulation which penalised only women. This was the concept of the *aguna*, or 'anchored' wife, who when widowed could not remarry unless she could prove her husband's death—which in subsequent ages, when Jewish scholars, artisans, and pedlars were often absent from home for many months, even years, was often impossible. All these rulings held good for as long as Jewish life was dominated by religious law (or well into the nineteenth century in most of Jewry) and are still in force in orthodox communities and in Israeli law today.

Perhaps the most important modification in the marriage laws, and hence in the status of Jewish women, introduced by the rabbis in the Middle Ages, related to the practice of polygyny, the right of a man to take more than one wife. As the biblical narrative indicates, this was common practice in ancient Jewish society, particularly when the first wife was barren. The foremost reason for marriage was procreation; procreation was a commandment (for men) in Jewish law, marriage was not a sacrament, and rabbinical law allowed a man to divorce his wife after ten years if she had not produced children. How widespread the practice of polygyny was has not been established, but the attitude towards it clearly varied widely in different areas of Jewish settlement and was influenced by both dynastic and economic considerations.[50]

Cases of polygyny in European Jewish society survived into the Middle Ages, and sporadically until very recently, in those Jewish communities which lived under Muslim rule; but in the eleventh century it became the subject of a special ruling attributed to an Ashkenazi sage, Rabbi Gershom of Mainz, though he probably formulated a rule adopted in earlier medieval Germany and France. An Ashkenazi Jew, if he wished to take a second wife, now had to apply for permission to not fewer than one hundred rabbis from three regions and three different communities, who would have to convene and agree together to the dispensation—obviously making it impossible.

The other important ruling attributed to Rabbi Gershom, but already in effect in Western Europe by the early Middle Ages, was that a man could no longer divorce his wife without her consent. This was also departure from tradition, as the Talmud allowed him to do so with or without her agreement. The monogamous norm prevailing henceforth in Ashkenazi Jewry, and the modification of the divorce laws, both favoured the woman. So did other European rabbinical rulings in the Middle Ages, which lifted a number of limitations imposed on women under Talmudic law, perhaps under the influence of the surrounding culture, but certainly in view of their growing importance to the economic life of the community.[51]

WOMEN'S LABOUR AND THE CLASS FACTOR IN RABBINICAL LAW

The Mishnah treats in some detail the work women did in the first centuries of Talmudic debate and also makes it clear that women's obligations differed according to their social class. 'The work women must perform: grinding corn, baking bread, washing clothes, cooking, suckling the child, making the bed ready and working in wool. If she brought two bondwomen, she need not even cook or suckle her child. If three, she need neither make [her husband's] bed nor work in wool. If four, she may lounge in an easy chair.' Rabbi Eliezer, who was notably critical of women in other contexts, dissents. Even if the wife had a hundred bondwomen, her husband should insist on her knitting, at least, as 'idleness leads to unchastity'.[52]

That women could be a separate source of family income (beyond the matter of their dowry) is also clear in that the marriage laws specify that the husband has a right to the woman's earnings, though some interpretations allow her to keep her income and spend it on household necessities. Although some authorities refer to the desirability of beauty in a woman, it is clear that the idea of a woman as a mere ornament to her husband's household is as rare in ancient Jewish law as the idea of woman as an intellectual companion is absent in later additions.

In the economy of Talmudic times, women's range of work was obviously restricted. At the same time, women were explicitly forbidden to represent their husbands in court, to be accepted as witnesses in legal actions, or to act as executors. The Talmud also specified that a husband was not responsible for his wife's commercial dealings, and, by analogy with a master's slaves, for any damages which might result from her actions.[53] Moreover, since her property was always held in trust by her husband, she could scarcely be an independent party to a lawsuit.[54]

By the Middle Ages, however, the situation was changing. Even in the community portrayed in the Geniza documents, where women were often segregated in the family home, there was a wide range of women's activities: marriage contracts were explicit on the question of whether the wife could keep what she earned. In twelfth-century Egypt, Jewish women worked as midwives, doctors, seamstresses, and spinners, and their produce was often marketed separately by women brokers. Literate women taught small children.[55]

In Europe at this time, the Jews became prominent in trade and banking, in crafts, where they had their own guilds, in real estate, and as agents for Christian landlords, though there was no Jewish peasantry. The Jews' overlords sanctioned the existence of rabbinical courts, but Jews also appeared in local courts on business matters.[56] In medieval Germany and Italy there were so many women in the wealthier merchant class and scholars' wives who were in business on their own account or as agents for their husbands that the rabbis of various communities exchanged learned opinions as to whether women's legal disabilities might not be removed altogether.[57] This did not happen, but dispensations were granted—'in the interest of the marketplace' in cases where women could be held responsible for debts, to contract on their own account, and to appear in court, as allowed by French and German law at that time.[58]

The basic problem was that under Jewish law, a woman's property was administered by her husband until his death or until she was divorced through no fault of her own, and thus she could hardly incur debts on her own account. This was sometimes circumvented by having the husband waive his rights to her property.[59] The entire debate drew attention to women's lack of legal status in Judaism, but it also underlined another factor: that dispensations could be issued to allow Talmudic law to be bypassed indicated the class element in the Jewish legal system.

As Jewish society developed from the Talmudic age onward, a complex social hierarchy evolved ranging from the rabbinical élite, through the merchant and artisan classes, to the *amei ha'aretz*[60]—the poor and ignorant. A second-century Midrash (homily) on the ideal choice of a husband for a well-born girl lists the following: a scholar, a man of standing in the community, the head of a synagogue, a charity treasurer, an elementary schoolteacher—but not an *am ha'aretz*. The social standing of the scholar was unique to Jewish society; and a tradition developed that outstanding scholars married into wealthy families. The dowry assumed an additional importance in that it was frequently the starting capital of a learned family; the women in families of scholars might, moreover, become the main, or even the sole, breadwinners in the family. Thus the more elevated the woman's social status, the more likely it was that she was contributing to or even earning at least part of the family's income. If women's labour was recognised as desirable from early Talmudic times in the poorer classes, economic responsibility for women in the privileged classes also had a long Jewish pedigree. The idea that working cast doubt on a woman's respectability only appears to have entered Jewish social life from the time when the Jews began to merge with the European bourgeoisie in mid-nineteenth-century Western Europe.

THE RABBINICAL VIEW OF SEX AND WOMEN'S STATUS

It is impossible to say whether the increasingly repressive Jewish sexual ethic developed from the segregation of women or vice versa; but to judge by rabbinical writings, the exclusion of women from the most important male precincts, in the synagogue and the school, appears to have intensified the apprehension of their sexuality, rather than neutralising it.

Rabbinical law legislates exhaustively for the control and domestication of sexuality, both of men and of women. As procreation is one of the basic commandments, incumbent on all men (a man who is sexually maimed is not a full Jew and is barred from aspects of the ritual), sex is mandatory and one of the three basic duties a man owes his wife. Celibacy is condemned. But sexuality is also dangerous in that it can lead a man into forbidden unions and distract him from the fulfilment of the commandment to study. Chastity in marriage is thus the ideal.

The rabbis extend and expand every ruling on sexuality in Pentateuchal law with a zeal that, to anyone outside the system, looks like an obsession with the subject. Early marriage is recommended as a way of anticipating the sexual urge. The appearance of puberty is watched for and every aspect of behaviour relates to the preservation of female modesty—for instance, even daughters are not to join their fathers in public once the girl enters puberty.[61]

The menstruation laws are also extensively elaborated. Whereas Pentateuchal law ordained that a woman should not have intercourse during her menstrual period, women requested, and the rabbis granted, a checking ritual to ensure that a full seven days had passed after the period had ended, and before she could take the ritual bath which preceded intercourse. The law specified what household duties a woman could perform during menstruation and which were banned to her.

The Mishnah specified not only when sex was legitimate but set a recommended norm for its frequency. Taking its cue from the passage in Exodus which warned a man that taking a second wife did not exempt him from his sexual duties towards the first, the Mishnah set down how often a man should have intercourse with his wife, according to his occupation. Men who were independent should do so daily; labourers, twice a week; ass drivers, once a week; camel drivers, once a month; and sailors, once every six months. Students were allowed to absent themselves for thirty days at a time. Women were enjoined to allow their husbands two weeks' latitude if the man had taken a vow of chastity.[62] The rabbis were scholars legislating for all sections of the community; the sexual regime they established for their own class is distinctly less demanding. At times the rabbis appear to deplore the very necessity for marriage: 'If one has to study and marry a wife, he should first study and then marry. But if he cannot live without a wife, he should first marry and then study'; according to one sage, a wife could be a 'millstone round the neck' of a scholar.[63] The command to procreate is too obvious to be mentioned, and thus whenever the subject of marriage for the scholarly élite comes up, it is axiomatic that the purpose of marriage is to work out the sexual urge—to 'avoid sinful thoughts'. However, as if to remind scholars that sexual intercourse is a religious duty, they were recommended to have intercourse on the Sabbath Eve.[64] On days of contrition—fast days—sex is taboo. Husbands were advised to console wives in mourning for other relations in this way.

As in all patriarchal religions, there is a clear double standard respecting sexual offences. Adultery by a man was condoned if the woman was not married to another—in which case it was an offence. In a woman it was always cause for divorce. While the rabbinical view of rape hovered between regarding it as an act of violence, an offence against someone else's property (the man's), and a sexual offence in which the woman might have some complicity, it follows Pentateuchal law in viewing homosexual rape as more serious than the rape of a woman.[65]

One aspect of the rabbinical view of sexuality was particularly striking in that it affected all relations between men and women in the community and prejudiced any chances women might have had of participating fully either in the communal leadership or in the brotherhood of learning. Women's dangerous sexuality was always interpreted as a threat to the seclusion and dedication of the study house.

There is a very particular ambivalence about sexuality deep in the discussions of sex in the Talmud and the commentaries: a man is enjoined to have intercourse for procreation; to satisfy his wife, performing his marital duty; if she is pregnant, for the good—at certain times—of the foetus; to ensure his own health and relieve sexual tensions. Women exist, in the words of one rabbi, 'to bring up our children and keep us from sin'.[66] Notably absent from the discussions of sex is the frank statement of male desire: to copulate for one's own pleasure is sinful. On the other hand, woman's sexuality and desire, and man's obligation to have sex to please her, is constantly stressed.[67] Though passive and forbidden to initiate sex, women are the main beneficiaries of sexuality, in the rabbinical view; they even prefer a virile to a wealthy man.[68] The corollary to this view is that all women are regarded as sexual threats and predators. The very clear ambivalence about men's sexuality in rabbinical Judaism—the view that sex is an irresistible urge, to be severely curbed and disciplined—means that the element of licence is transferred to women.

Women are an omnipresent sexual threat. Any woman talking to or having any social contact with a man is a potential seductress; the only reason for any woman's presence in the company of a man not her husband is her desire for intercourse. Hence the unintentionally comic scenarios in the Talmud in which sexual intent is read into the most innocent situation, women's desire for copulation constantly assumed.[69] The fact that most of these scenarios presuppose, logically, the presence of a priapic male in the vicinity indicates that the rabbis' real concern is the uncontrollable sexual urge of the man; but the responsibility is transferred to the woman. Hence, for instance, she is not allowed to read or recite before men, because her voice is sexually provocative, nor, of course, to sing in synagogue.[70] All prohibitions on women's full participation in worship, like their eligibility for any public office (save those tasks explicitly delegated to women and carried out in women's company), relate to what is called *kvod hatsibur*, or public decency.

In medieval times, the dualism that had first entered Judaism with the Greek writings of Philo Judaeus, the first-century Alexandrian philosopher, but was later developed in mystical, particularly kabbalistic thought, complicated the view of women's sexuality still further. Thinking about the soul and the body as two separate entities invariably classed women as corporeal, material objects, and men, who alone were capable of study, hence of reason, as the spiritually endowed.[71] Though not explicitly barred from study in theological terms, women in Judaism, unlike in Christianity and Islam, did not play a notable part in mystical movements. This, though *kabbala*, the esoteric teaching of Jewish scripture which developed into mysticism, introduced into Judaism the notion of a feminine element in God himself. In kabbalistic belief, sexual intercourse itself became a mystical union. The man, who represents wisdom, copulating with the woman, who represents instinctual intelligence, achieves knowledge.[72] At the same time, however, Jewish mysticism stressed the demonic potential of women. It has been argued in passing that this constitutes 'a problem for the psychologist and historian of religion alike'.[73] Readers of the fiction of Isaac Bashevis Singer, who came from a Hasidic (pietist, mystical) background, will recognise the theme. Moreover, individual kabbalistic prayers said by men are preoccupied with eroticism and reveal a fear of sexual inadequacy, while in those said by women, eroticism is totally excluded and sexuality is related solely to the desire for conception.[74]

Ironically enough, despite the fact that Jewish women's sexuality was so feared and repressed, women's sexual attractions were in fact almost totally irrelevant to their biological role in Jewish society. All women—at least in a community that was not entirely bankrupt—could expect to marry, and were matched with men whose place in the social hierarchy was suited to their own. Marriage was arranged between the parents, and often the young couple did not meet until the betrothal. Romantic love was unheard of. A couple who were sexually incompatible could divorce, though a woman's refusal to have intercourse with her husband had to be excused by good reasons—his physical repulsiveness or practising a trade which had unpleasant side-effects, as with tanners. Otherwise she was termed a 'rebellious wife' and her *ketuba*—marriage contract—did not protect her.[75]

Perhaps the most far-reaching interpretation made by the rabbis in Pentateuchal law, however, where women were concerned, was one which limited the commandment to study, vital to the preservation of Judaism, to men.

A Price above Rubies?

In the classic verses in the Proverbs describing 'a woman of worth'—perhaps the single most definitive prescription in Jewish literature for the perfect woman—her industry as wife and mother is praised, and so too is her wisdom, or *chochma*. The portrait begins: 'A woman of worth who can find; for her price is far above rubies.' Rubies, *peninim* (better translated as precious stones or jewels, for the Hebrew word also refers to pearls), is a metaphor for wisdom both in Proverbs and in the book of Job.

'Wisdom is better than rubies'; 'the price of wisdom is above rubies.'

Here, as so often where women are concerned, a reading from the biblical text alone as a guide to Jewish tradition is misleading. There are two notable rabbinical interpretations of these verses, often quoted in the commentaries and rulings (responsa), and neither expounds on female 'wisdom'. One comments that it is the woman's task to work hard and look after her family so that her husband and sons can study the Torah. The other argues that the 'woman of worth' is in fact an allegory for the Torah itself.[76] The reason for these interpretations is that wisdom, in Judaism, is never instinctive, the result of experience, but the reward of prolonged study, acquired by a devotion to religious studies. As such, it cannot be a female quality. The word more usually employed in rabbinical literature to describe women's 'wisdom' is not *chochma* but *bina*, intelligence. The Talmud remarks that the essential characteristic of *chochma* is intellectual subtlety—something particularly to be deplored in women.

The prime legal reason for women's exclusion from the commandment to study is that the Pentateuch does not explicitly instruct them to teach the Torah to their children, as it does to men.[77] The Pentateuchal injunction to all Jews to teach their sons the scriptures is interpreted as 'exempting' women from the process altogether, although this is not a 'time bound' commandment, like others from which women were 'exempt'. The Talmud makes a number of references to the rationale behind women's 'exemption'. There are two early and different opinions quoted in the Mishnah, attributed to the rather misogynistic Rabbi Eliezer and to the more moderate Ben Azzai, who was one of the few bachelor scholars recorded in Jewish history. Eliezer attacks the very idea of women learning the Torah as they will make 'licentiousness' of it (*tiflut*; sometimes translated as 'nonsense'). When approached by a learned woman seeking exegesis of a particular law, he told her curtly to get back to her spinning wheel.[78] Other references to women versed in scriptural learning are similarly dismissive. Ben Azzai, however, argues that a woman needs to be taught sufficient Torah to understand those laws which apply to her, in the interest of the fulfilment of the law itself.[79]

Since the time of the Second Commonwealth, study had not been the sole privilege of scholars.[80] Thenceforth almost all male Jews who were literate, whether in the merchant or the artisan class, felt it their duty, like Cecilia Bobrowskaya's father, to fit a few hours study of Talmud into their daily lives. Women had no such obligation. The question was not whether women should be kept in total ignorance, but what was the minimum knowledge they needed in order to function in the Jewish community.[81] Most post-Talmudic rabbinical commentators argued that women should know just enough Jewish law to conform to the purity and the dietary laws and to observe Sabbaths and festivals, but should have no access to Talmudic dialectic or later mystical traditions. Maimonides, writing in the twelfth century, brought various elements in the argument together thus:

A woman who studies Torah will be recompensed, but not in the same measure as a man, for study was not imposed on her as a duty, and one who performs a meritorious act which is not obligatory will not receive the same reward as one upon whom it is incumbent and who fulfils it as a duty, but only a lesser reward. And notwithstanding that she is recompensed, yet the Sages have warned us that a man shall not teach his daughter Torah, as the majority of women have not a mind adequate for its study, but, because of their limitations, will turn the words of the Torah into trivialities ... This stricture refers only to instruction in the Oral Law. With regard to the Written Law, he ought not to teach it to her; but if he has done so, it is not regarded as teaching her wantonness.[82]

This, then was the core of the rabbinical view of women's study and one which influenced actual practice in Jewish communities from the Middle Ages onward. Women did study Written Law (the Pentateuch) but not the Oral Law (Talmud). They were encouraged to acquire, in the vernacular, potted versions of the simpler points of exegesis; towards the modern era small girls even attended the first Bible class (*cheder*) together with the boys. But the moment they reached puberty, the entire question of contact between men and women made learning problematic. The Ashkenazi Sefer Hasidim, a thirteenth-century text, recommends that a man should teach his wife and daughters basic commandments; no other man could be trusted with teaching females, as his carnal desires might overcome him.[83] The authoritative sixteenth-century Shulhan Arukh by Joseph Karo argues that women will only pervert the interpretation of the Torah (that is, Talmudic learning), although they could not be discouraged from studying the Pentateuch.[84] So, in addition to the fact that they are not expressly enjoined to study (the legal objection), there is the assumption of their mental inferiority, and this combines with the practical problem of their threatening sexuality.

It is in the link between the 'exemption' of women from study (and hence from membership of the Jewish élite) and their distracting sexuality that rabbinical law departs most strikingly from Graeco-Roman culture and its attitude to women. The assumption of women's inferiority as a sex, the absence of women from positions of power (save in the ruling classes—when the Jews were a political entity), and the glorification of women's self-sacrifice or martyrdom are common to all three ancient cultures. But there could be no rabbinical parallel to Plato's (admittedly exceptional) proposal in his model government of the Republic of equal education for women, so that they might be guardians of the ideal state (to say nothing of the wisdom of Diotima); or to Plutarch's advice to educate women in geometry and philosophy, so that they might be equal partners with their husbands.[85]

Only in the medieval classic of Jewish mysticism, the Zohar, is there a description of a separate Paradise for women where, no longer hampered by their domestic duties, they can occupy themselves with prayer, study, and contemplation; but even in the popularised versions of this theme in Yiddish literature, written by men, women are still both segregated and inferior to studious men.[86]

The fear of women's sexuality, a common Christian theme and one clearly inherited from Judaism, had no place in Greek culture, though double standards of morality existed in all ancient societies.

The Jews prided themselves both on their learning and on their sexual morality, and on both scores regarded themselves as superior to other ancient cultures. The Jewish family, essential to Jewish survival, demanded women's total devotion to the home, and self-abnegation in both the intellectual and sexual spheres. The dietary and purity laws were communicated from mothers to daughters as a matter of tradition; these laws ensured that the women kept a home in which men could safely eat what they had prepared and that women were 'permitted to men' at the correct time of the month.

There is none the less some record, though meagre, of learned Jewish women. One fifteenth-century woman, the mother of Rabbi Israel ben Pathia Isserlin (her own name has not been recorded), even went so far as to invent her own variation on the woman's daily prayer 'Blessed be thou, Lord of the Universe, who hast created me according to thy will' (the male equivalent is 'who hast not created me a woman'). The rabbi's wife's version ran 'who hast not created me a beast'. Perhaps the most celebrated of these women was Rivka bat Meir Tiktiner, of sixteenth-century Prague, who preached (to women) in Yiddish and wrote a moralistic work on the teaching of children. Other women were recorded as having preached from behind windows or curtains, like the daughter of the twelfth-century Samuel Ben Ali of Baghdad.[87] Dulcie, daughter of Eliezer of Worms—commemorated in a famous poem by her husband after she was murdered by marauders—is supposed to have held public discourses on the Sabbath.[88] The daughter of the famous medieval sage Solomon Yitzhaki of Troyes (Rashi) was also learned, as was a Rhineland woman known by the nickname of 'Mrs Scholastica' at the period of the First Crusade. It is also during this period, especially in 1096, that the references to women as martyrs who preferred death to conversion, even killing their own children, enter Jewish history.[89]

Until the late medieval period Jewish women were probably better versed in their own religion than their Christian counterparts, if always within all-women schools or groups.[90] In Italy, where the community was long established and cultural assimilation was widespread, women were accustomed to giving elementary instruction in reading and writing to children of both sexes; in 1495, a Talmud Torah (seminary) for girls was established in Rome, probably the first girls' school of its kind. In Renaissance Italy, too, there were many women scribes and printers, a famous translator, Deborah Ascarelli, and, in the sixteenth century, the most famous of Jewish poetesses, Sara Coppio Sulam.[91]

Sulam, the wife of a rich Venetian merchant, had friends among the intellectual élite of both Jewish and non-Jewish Venice. She carried on a four-year correspondence, partly in sonnet form, with the Genoan poet and philosopher Ansaldo Ceba, which ended when he failed to convert her to Christianity. She conducted another learned debate with the Bishop of Treviso, but was endangered when he accused her publicly of denying the doctrine of the immortality of the soul. Her vulnerability to flattery, however, and a weakness for superstitions made her prey to thieves and tricksters, who robbed and exploited her. Her skilful parrying of her Catholic debating partners was, according to her contemporaries, almost certainly due to the learned assistance of Leone da Modena, a Talmudic scholar and philosopher who was among her closest friends;[92] even the most sophisticated of Renaissance Jewish women could scarcely carry on a learned battle of wits on the basis of the religious knowledge permitted to a woman. Nevertheless, her closeness to Modena suggests a remarkable intellect.

JEWISH WOMEN AND THE SOCIAL CONTRACT

If Jewish women were, in the Talmud's words, 'a nation apart', they were bound, in the network of rabbinical law, very closely to the entire community through the marriage bond; and the manner in which Jewish life was organised by the Middle Ages sealed the contract. Marriage was the only possible destiny for a woman; no laws relate to her save regarding her eligibility for marriage and her rights during and after marriage, whether as divorcee or widow. Marriage was not a sacrament; it was just a private affair between a man and a woman. Yet rabbinical law defines, in great detail, the different laws applying to marriage between different members of the community, as well as the circumstances under which divorce and remarriage is possible, and it is made clear that infringements of this law can bring disaster on the community as well as the people intimately involved.

Many of the laws regarding consanguinity and forbidden unions have parallels in other Semitic religions. But one does not: the particular laws governing the marriage of men belonging to the priestly sect—identifiable by their names (these families were required to keep detailed records). Although there was no Temple and no function for the priests, their survival symbolised the survival of the monotheistic theocracy, even in exile. Levirate marriage, similarly, was a relic of tribal society which commemorated Jewish history by keeping property within the husband's family.

The divorce laws, too, make it clear that a man was under an obligation to divorce a wife who had infringed the law not only for his own dignity but for the good of the community as a whole. The reasons for a man to seek divorce were not just sexual offences by the woman, like adultery or refusal to have intercourse with her husband, but also the failure to bear a child after ten years of marriage (preventing the husband from fulfilling his communal obligation of reproducing), and any transgression against Mosaic law or tradition.[93] Medieval commentaries added that if a man compelled his wife to transgress against the sexual taboos, she could demand a divorce.[94]

To what extent rabbinical law was actually observed, and the varying status of women in different communities, can be inferred from two sources: one, the medieval commentaries which reflected changing views of the Talmud; and the second, perhaps more revealing, the responsa—rabbinical answers, or rulings, to questions posed in particular periods and communities, which indicate, like case law, how far various rabbinical dispensations modified the original command.

To take two dramatic examples: Jewish women's life in medieval Islamic society and in medieval Europe followed rather different patterns. Maimonides, in his great commentary on the Mishnah, advocates the virtual segregation of married women in the home, recommending that visits to family or women friends should take place no more than once or twice a month. Here, as in his views on polygyny, the influence of Islamic culture is obvious.[95] Although passages in the Talmud suggest that wife-beating was considered a criminal act, it seems to have been common in Muslim Spain in the eleventh century. In medieval Europe, where the rabbis generally opposed it as 'the way of the Gentiles', the punishments administered to wife-beaters in Germany were particularly severe, possibly because of women's importance in commercial and financial affairs and also because of the particular respect in which the Ashkenazi Hasidim of Germany held women at this time.[96]

In the Middle Ages Jewish communal life was almost entirely autonomous, and the community had the power not only to observe but also to enforce rabbinical law. The support of weaker members of the community was ensured through taxes; hence the community could educate even the poorer Jewish boys and marry off the poorer Jewish girls. Charitable institutions were highly developed; collection of funds was often in the hands of older women, a communal and practical task that was to persist.[97] The social ideal was one of mutual responsibility, particularly important in view of the instability of Jewish life and the constant dangers of expulsion, punitive taxation, and physical persecution.

The community had the right to invoke sanctions against those who infringed rabbinical law. The rights that could be withheld included admission to the synagogue, the right to Jewish marriage and burial, and even the right to live within the area assigned to the community. At worst, an offender could be excommunicated. From the Middle Ages onward, both marriage and divorce in Europe were public affairs; where Jewish marriage had been a secular transaction, it was now, by analogy with Christian practice, performed by a rabbi in a special celebration.[98] The guilty parties in divorce were often subjected to public humiliation.[99] Because celibacy was regarded as both unnatural and antisocial, communities sometimes threatened bachelors with corporal punishment, fines, and even excommunication, though this custom does not seem to have survived beyond the seventeenth century.[100]

Communal supervision was omnipresent in the sexual life of men and women. The purification rituals were carried out at public baths financed by the community, which was also responsible for seeing to it that the poor as well as the rich could fulfil the menstrual ceremonies. For instance, in seventeenth-century Lithuania, female supervisors appointed by the Jewish councils were enjoined to provide poor women with fine white linen undergarments on which bloodstains would be clearly visible, so that they should not 'become impure unawares.'[101] Matchmaking became the province of a special group of professionals who travelled between communities seeking the correct partner for members of a specific class.[102]

From the Middle Ages onward, women aquired most of their knowledge of Jewish law and of their place in Jewish society from popular works of rabbinical exegesis which began to appear in the Diaspora vernaculars, for the use both of uneducated men and of women. The most widely read works were those in Judaeo-German, which later developed into what is now called Yiddish. Moralistic works like the *Brantspiegel* (The Burning Mirror) and *Lev Tov* (The Good Heart), published at the end of the sixteenth century, taught women domestic virtue in a style clearly influenced by similar Christian chapbooks intended for literate women. The Ma'aseh book, a collection of moral tales and parables taken both from the Aggadic or narrative and folkloristic portions of the Talmud and from the Christian folklore of central Europe, is an intriguing mixture of Jewish and non-Jewish sources (there are echoes of the literature of chivalry, but nothing to evoke the idea of courtly love). To the extent that the Jewish community encouraged the publication of this 'women's literature' in Yiddish, it deterred women from competing in what was seen as the man's unique preserve, Talmudic study, at the same time assuring them that their ignorance was no barrier to their piety.

In the second part of the eighteenth century, kabbalistic mysticism, which had first evolved during the Middle Ages, revived among the Hasidic Jews, in whose beliefs pietism and mysticism mingled. Hasidism, during this later period seen by some scholars as the orthodox response to the challenge of the Enlightenment, did not improve women's situation in tradition-bound communities. Hasidim tended to congregate in the academies of charismatic rabbis, leaving their wives for weeks and months, even on Sabbaths and festivals—when the family would normally have been together—and women were even further excluded from the intellectual and spiritual centre of men's lives.[103]

However, it has been noted that as much kabbalistic literature was translated into Yiddish, to which women had access, some Hasidic authors at this time relate more seriously to women in their writings, and there are even some supplicatory prayers which were probably written by women. They might make use of kabbalistic symbolism in these prayers, though they showed little knowledge of kabbalistic theology.[104]

By far the most important book in the vernacular for the uneducated Jew (the *am ha'aretz*) and for women was *T'sena Ure'ena* (Come Out and See), first published at the end of the sixteenth century. This book was made up of discourses on selected topics or passages from the weekly synagogue reading of the Pentateuch and the complementary passages from the Hagiographa. The book summarised or quoted early Midrashim, Talmudic sources, medieval commentaries, and comments on moral behaviour by contemporaries. Some Hebrew passages were included, to help women with a rudimentary knowledge of the language to orientate themselves in the synagogue service (where the book was sometimes read to them by the *sogheren*, the female *répétiteurs* who sat in the women's gallery), but it was also a book to be read and studied at home. Yiddish scholars maintain that the production and success of this book (which went into thirty editions within a century and, subsequently into over two hundred further editions over the next two hundred years) suggests a wide readership, and accompanied a 'revolution in the educational system' in central European Jewry, particularly as regards the education of girls.[105] Yiddish was sometimes known as the 'women's language'.

From this time onward, women had access to literary and ethical tracts of all kinds. Among Hasidic Jews, there were many bookish Jewish women who could not compete with men but tried to imitate their culture. But women's books make it plain what they were told to think about Jewish tradition and their own place in it. When *T'sena Ure'ena* is compared with the one surviving memoir written by a woman who lived about a hundred years after its first appearance, a striking contrast emerges between Jewish women's energies and talents, on the one hand, and male prescriptions for their behaviour, on the other.

T'SENA URE'ENA AND GLUECKEL OF HAMELN

It is not difficult to re-create the atmosphere in which women listened to *T'sena Ure'ena* in the women's gallery. There are numerous exhortations in the text to women: to preserve decorum and to keep their voices low while praying, lest they distract the men and inflame their sexual desires.[106] In order to make the contents of the Torah readings more accessible, commentary on the biblical narrative is in some ways similar to that of the medieval morality plays: that is, it assumes familiarity with the characters, and submits them to criticism.

In keeping with the tone of the Talmud, T'sena is packed with the anachronisms which indicate the rabbinical lack of interest in chronological history, but which must have made the readings far more vivid to their hearers. It also domesticates the Bible. The commentary deplores the savage maltreatment of women, emphasising that all Israel was ashamed of the mass rape of the Levite's concubine, that Abraham was 'embarrassed' by Lot's fornication with his own daughters, and informs its readers that if Jephtha did indeed sacrifice his own daughter, he was not a pious Jew.[107] Even the matriarchs are reproved when they are 'too curious to learn secrets' (Sarah), jealous (Rachel, Leah), lazy and indolent, or simply—a cardinal fault—too talkative.[108] Miriam the prophetess, in this version of events, plays on the timbrels after the crossing of the Red Sea in order to drown out the sound of women's voices—which would have been sexually disturbing to the Israelite leaders.[109] When the Torah reading from Exodus refers to the prohibition on lighting fires in the Tabernacle, women are warned not to discuss their cooking in synagogue.[110]

But T'sena is not simply a patronising but good-humoured version of Torah for women and ignorant men. There is no real dialectic of the kind that exercises men's minds in the Talmud. It reminds women constantly that their subordinate role in the community is based on rabbinical texts and interpretations of the Torah, and that their piety consists of helping husbands and sons to study.

In the mirror of T'sena, Jewish women are at their best the geniuses of home and Sabbath, possessed of great strength in their own domain; at their worst, they are witches versed in the magical arts, accessible to Satan: the resurrection of the dead is only possible in their presence.[111] The child is affected by the mother's behaviour, and her good and bad deeds are inherited. Running right through this popular work, moreover, is a pervasive reminder of female guilt.

The theme of guilt, of the possible effects of the failure to observe the law, is present everywhere in Jewish teaching. But whereas the Talmud reverts time after time to the notion that all the terrible vicissitudes of Jewish life are to be attributed to some fault in the Jews themselves, T'sena blames women not only for those various female complaints with which Eve is burdened in Genesis but also for the subsequent sufferings of the whole people. Women's piety can avert or diminish death and suffering in childbirth. But nothing can wipe out their collective responsibility for sin. If all Jews are guilty, women Jews are more guilty than others.

The theme of women's guilt pervades the entire book. Women walk behind the dead at funerals 'because they brought death to the world'. Women bleed because they spilled the blood of men. Women separate the *challah* (dough) offering because they separated Adam from the world to come. Women light candles on Sabbath because they extinguished the light of Adam's soul.[112] As the synagogue reading describes the making of the eight-branched candlestick, a Midrashic exegesis is recalled which teaches that women light candles on Sabbath eve because Satan was created together with the woman, and the candle drives Satan away.[113] Satan is scarcely present in the Old Testament, but women are quite often involved in references to his power in rabbinical literature. The sacrifice after childbirth is also expiation for Eve's sin. That daughters of priests prepare the dead for burial is explained by the fact that Eve brought death to the world. Women are recommended to weep copiously on the Day of Atonement. Women are enjoined, in T'sena, not to inflame men's lust, to lower their provocative voices, to keep their skirts tucked round their ankles (like Ruth who, the commentary says, gleaned corn this way). However, the general comments on sex, discussed as a gloss on the injunctions against incest in Leviticus, with reference to 'cleansing the system' through sex, appears to be addressed to the unlettered men for whom T'sena was also originally written.[114]

T'sena also explains women's segregation at prayer and the reason for their exclusion from learning. In the commentary on the giving of the law to Israel at Sinai, women, says T'sena, had the Torah presented to them separately, 'as they lacked the understanding to receive the whole Torah at once'.[115]

Women 'assist in learning' by bringing children to school. And the pious Jewish woman prays that she will give birth to a Talmudic student. When the passage in the synagogue liturgy is read accompanying the replacement of the scrolls in the Ark, 'The Torah is a tree of life to those who cleave to it', the amendment for women and the ignorant reads: 'The Torah grants long life to those who support it, even if they are not capable of learning themselves.'[116]

Women are pious, in this view, not because they study the Torah but because they enable their husbands and sons to study.

The mention of the building of the Temple by Solomon, and the sending of men to cut wood for a month at a time, reminds the rabbinical author that a man is allowed to stay away from home studying at a seminary for a month at a time. If he wishes to stay longer, he has to ask his wife's permission. She should agree, for 'it is as if she herself had learned'. A pious Jewish woman is pious, in fact, by proxy.[117]

The Torah (Pentateuch) is read cyclically every year from beginning to end in synagogue, and so was *T'sena Ure'ena* by the female leaders in the women's galleries of the European synagogues, and at home. A rare memoir by a Jewish woman, generally used for the information it conveys about women as traders and businesswomen in seventeenth-century Germany, indicates the effect of the constant reading of women's literature like T'sena and the Ma'aseh book on an intelligent and independent woman.

Glueckel of Hameln, a well-born woman of the merchant class, wrote her memoir, for her children's edification, at the end of the century in which T'sena first appeared.[118] It was kept in the family and published two centuries after it was written. Because it is a unique record of a Jewish woman's life in the pre-modern period, it has been in print ever since. Popular modern editions generally omit the rather tedious passages in which Glueckel repeats the message of the moralistic literature she read, but curtailing the moralising lessens the contrast between Glueckel's strength of character and her dutiful inferiority.

The chief historical interest of the memoirs is undoubtedly the description of the precariousness of Jewish life even among the merchant élite: the crippling taxes imposed without warning on Jewish communities, the price of their residence on sufferance in a given princely territory; sudden banishment; and the more general perils of European wars, plagues, and social upheavals. But it is the independence of spirit manifested throughout the book (the men of the family all appear to have been of far less character and less resourceful in business) that makes Glueckel's acceptance of her formal limitations as a woman even more striking for the modern reader. Glueckel shared her first husband's work as a dealer in jewellery as well as giving birth to fourteen children; when widowed, she went into business on her own.

Like most Jewish women until late in the eighteenth century, Glueckel was betrothed at twelve and married at fourteen. She refers to her two-yearly pregnancies with some humour (her first child is born in her mother's house as her mother also gives birth, and there is a mix-up with the babies). The Talmud and responsa make it clear that while twelve was the earliest legal age for betrothal, girls were sometimes betrothed even earlier. Until late in the eighteenth century in middle and Western Europe, and a century later in Eastern Europe, the young people spent the first years of marriage in their parents' or in-laws' homes, preparing themselves for economic independence.[119] Glueckel's memoirs describe a family life almost entirely devoted to the hazards of producing children and keeping them alive, and the anxiety of providing so many children with dowries or, in the case of boys, money for the marriage contract. 'We should, I say, put ourselves to great pains for our children, for on this the world is built, yet we must understand that if children did as much for their parents, the children would quickly tire of it.'[120] This central preoccupation of Jewish family life survived not only Glueckel's lifetime but even the abandonment of many of the other teachings of rabbinical Jewry. It is only in order to provide dowries and contract money that Glueckel enters into a second marriage in her fifties—a marriage which was clearly a disaster socially and financially but for which she sacrificed the little capital which remained to her, as well as her independence in her own household. She uses a very telling image to describe how the bonds she accepted willingly in her happy first marriage were resented in her second: 'The golden chain is turned to iron bonds and fetters.'[121]

Yet even in the first marriage, there is a contrast between Glueckel's share of her husband's emotional and economic life and her exclusion from his spiritual life, most movingly expressed in her description of her quandary at his deathbed: 'Whereat I said to my husband, "Dearest heart, shall I embrace you—I am unclean?" for I was then at a time I dared not touch him. And he said, "God forbid, my child—it will not be long before you take your cleansing." But, alas, it was then too late.' When her husband is asked whether he has any practical last wishes about his estate, he answers, 'None, my wife knows everything. She shall do as she has always done'; but then, as he feels the end approaching, Glueckel with her children are 'thrust by main force from the room', so that he can die in what she calls 'purity and holiness'.[122]

There is also a contrast between Glueckel's own good sense and practicality and the repetition of the superstitious folktales which have obviously been her reading matter; and between her personal sense of enterprise and the pervasive sense of woman's inherited guilt. Saving her pregnant daughter from a panic crush in a synagogue, she finds time to worry that the women's head coverings have slipped and their hair is loose about them;[123] and she is convinced that her reversal of fortunes, towards the end of her life, is somehow the result of sins she cannot even identify.[124]

THE ENLIGHTENMENT AND THE TWO JEWRIES OF EUROPE

Until the last part of the eighteenth century, the Jewish woman's life throughout Europe was essentially the same, in most respects, as it had been in Glueckel's time. Each generation of parents assumed the burden of marrying off the next, providing dowries and financial support for their children during the period when they were apprenticed either to rabbis, merchants, or artisans, for a future in learning or in commerce. Although in theory, under rabbinical law, a girl when she reached the age of twelve and a half was considered an adult and could refuse the partner her parents had chosen, in practice the exchange of financial guarantees by the contracting parents meant that breaking an agreement already made was costly and would ensure maximum pressure on the recalcitrant child. It was not only the uncertainty of economic life that led fathers to marry off daughters at the first opportunity (in medieval and late medieval times, landowners could confiscate an unmarried orphan's property). The dowry was also investment for the new couple's future. Most Jews in commercial or artisan employ, and all scholars, needed financial assistance.[125]

Talmudic legislation on marriage pronounces clearly against marriage for money alone. But the economic exigencies of Jewish life meant that no woman could marry without a dowry, and even the Talmudic scholar was not a good match if he was very poor. Few married outside their own class. Clearly the worst off, in this arrangement, as they could not rise by diligence in learning, were girls of poor or undistinguished families, who often worked as domestic servants in the houses of wealthier Jews. The councils who levied graded taxes on all members of the community, and ran a highly developed social welfare system, provided for the marriage of such girls.

But responsa from Eastern European sources in the seventeenth century indicate that the council might limit the number of marriages annually according to the resources of the community, lest the poor and their children become too great a burden.[126] Gradually the economic factors which ensured the physical survival of the community became more important than the Talmudic teaching which, while recognising class differences, tried to ensure that all had an equal chance of fulfilling the commandments connected with marriage. The role of the match-maker, whose work was guided by social and economic considerations, and who travelled from one community to another seeking appropriate connections between well-to-do families, grew in importance. And as time passed even rabbinical students were married a few years later, nearer economic independence.[127] There was no question, obviously, of adolescents choosing their own partners, though in some communities they were allowed to meet before betrothal.

From the end of the eighteenth century, the growing emancipation of the Jews of Western Europe—the right of residence in the larger cities, physical emergence from the ghetto, admission to the professions and schools, even if under a quota, and the expansion of the mercantile élite—all led to a weakening of communal and rabbinical authority. In country areas the communal and rabbinical authorities were strongest; in the cities, to which the Jews graduated in ever larger numbers, their influence waned. Fewer Jews devoted themselves entirely to Talmudic study. Jewish tradition was increasingly celebrated in the home; and the domestic piety of the women thus assumed a new importance.

While during the first half of the nineteenth century in Germany, for instance, women were still active as traders, pedlars, and general amanuenses to their artisan husbands, the assimilation of the Jews into the German commercial middle class meant that their labour was henceforth exclusively domestic; and after mid-century the Jewish husband did not allow his wife to work outside the home if he could help it. The dowry, in the marriage transaction, was now more important than the woman's earnings.

At the same time, all over Western Europe, the Jewish birthrate began falling, several decades before a similar process began, in the 1870s, in middle-class Christian society. In some cases this can be attributed to a later marriage age, as the system of dependence on parents lessened, but wherever early marriage continued, while the birthrate shrank, it is clear that some form of birth control was adopted—a flagrant offence against rabbinical law, save in a very few specific cases.[128] The retreat from the workplace, a slightly later marriage age, and a lower birthrate now heralded an important change in Jewish women's lives in Western Europe, just as growing independence of the young from the elders and the decline of rabbinical authority meant a very different kind of Jewish society.

In Eastern Europe, in contrast, the medieval pattern of traditional Jewish life continued almost uninterrupted until late in the nineteenth century. This was particularly true in the Russian Empire after the consolidation of its gains in Eastern Poland at the end of the eighteenth century, where restrictions on Jewish life and outbursts of anti-Semitism alternated with semi-liberal legislation aimed at discouraging the Jews from pursuing their separate existence. In almost every respect the lives of Jews in

Eastern Europe differed from those of Jews in the West. Instead of gravitating to larger towns, the great mass of Jews lived in villages and small market towns (*shtetls*), where they acted as middlemen between the landed gentry (often absentee landlords, as whose agents the Jews collected rents and sold the tenants' produce) and the peasantry; the local Jewish council and the rabbis were the ultimate authority.[129]

It was rare for Jews to appeal to the civil authorities against rabbinical ruling. But one such case, in early nineteenth-century Poland, concerned an extraordinary woman, Ernestine Potowski. The daughter of a Polish rabbi, she had appealed to a local secular court against her father's decision to marry her off and to confiscate property inherited from her mother (to which under Jewish law she was in fact entitled). She won her case. Later she crossed Europe on the proceeds of an invention of a natural deodorant and was among the first supporters of Robert Owen in England, one of whose followers, a jeweller named William Rose, she married. The couple then emigrated to America, where Ernestine Rose became one of the first American feminists and a signatory to the famous 1848 Seneca Falls 'Declaration of Sentiments', a statement of women's grievances modelled on the Declaration of Independence.[130] Rose can rightly be called the first Jewish feminist.

Even when Czar Nicholas I issued an edict in 1844 forbidding the Jews administrative autonomy and transferring many of the duties of the Kahal or communal leadership to municipal authorities, the rabbis' authority still held good, and in practice Jews preferred to take their grievances to their own courts. The Kahal still assessed and collected taxes, provided recruits for the Czarist army—for service which could last between the ages of twelve and twenty-five—and upheld rabbinical law in their courts. The traditional pattern of Jewish domestic life continued until mid-century. Scholarly Jews continued to leave practical life to their wives. Women continued to help their husbands and often ran enterprises like mills and breweries single-handed. The Jewish birthrate rose steadily from the end of the eighteenth century onward; until the late nineteenth century there was little emigration. Many authorities believe that the two maverick trends in Eastern European Jewry—the Hasidic movement, with its pietist and mystical beliefs, and the appearance of the rebels against orthodoxy, the *maskilim* (those with a secular education), were the direct result of the appearance on the Jewish scene of unprecedented numbers of rebellious adolescents who resented the tyranny of their elders.[131]

It was the male *maskilim*, initially a small minority influenced by eighteenth-century Western European ideas, who first protested against the treatment of women in Jewish society, as part of a general revolt against orthodoxy. They rebelled against the perpetuation of the scholarly system which, in their view, by sequestering so many young men in Talmudic academies, prevented the Jews from becoming a 'productive' element in modern society. Furthermore, when they looked around them at the outside world, they saw that in other societies adolescence was a time of emotional growth and economic training, not of premature exposure to sexual experience and the burdens of family life. In a further rebellion, they protested against the entire network of matchmakers and the dowry system, which made marriage into a commercial transaction with women as the chief commodity, and against women's function in marriage, which they saw at best as servitude and at worst as making women into what one irate writer, Moses Leib Lilienblum, described as a man's 'chamber pot'.[132]

But, ironically enough, what the early *maskilim*, influenced by their reading of Western literature, wanted for their women was not greater freedom but conformity to the women's middle-class existence in Western Europe of the nineteenth century—a chaste, private life with the partner of their own choice, and the confinement of women to the home. They were against the employment of women in commerce and trading. In other words, these enlightened young Jews who had experienced their own mothers and mothers-in-law as a dominant and domineering force in the family were actually trying to deny women power, even as they idealised the free choice of partners available in the outside world.[133]

Save for a very small minority of rich merchants' wives and daughters, the Jewish women of Eastern Europe were not to attain the middle-class security of those in the West. Precisely at the time when Jewish women were conforming to the housebound life of the middle-class women of the West, the Jewish middle and artisan classes in Eastern Europe were declining into dire poverty. The freeing of the serfs in 1861, the redistribution of lands, and the laws prohibiting Jewish residence or purchase of property in large areas of the Russian countryside sent the Jews into the towns, where the rising birthrate had already contributed to overcrowding and poverty. While a small minority of Jewish manufacturers profited from the industrialisation of the urban centres, the mechanisation of labour put the mass of Jewish artisans out of work. Women were now to work in greater numbers, at more menial tasks, and under more pressure, than ever before, not only after marriage but before it—in factories, workshops, and at home. Privileged women who had achieved an education were swept up in the political debates then dominating the Russian intelligentsia.

Jewish women both in Western and in Eastern Europe were among the first to take advantage of the new educational opportunities open to post-Enlightenment women. From the mid-eighteenth century, prosperous Jews in Western Europe who could afford to hire private tutors had their daughters taught French and Italian as forms of accomplishment.[134]

Some precedent for this can be found in Jewish history. Secular learning was not forbidden to Jewish women, and there is evidence that even in rabbinical households women read literature and secular philosophy in eighteenth-century Germany, Italy, and England. The daughters and wives of wealthy but unlettered Jewish merchants held court at the short-lived but famous salons which brought together German and French scholars, the impoverished German aristocracy, and intellectually curious Jewish women at the turn of the nineteenth century in Berlin and Vienna. This was a period when the rights of women and Jews, as two oppressed groups, were being discussed throughout Europe.

But the enlightened daughters of the German and Austrian Jewish élite were interested in neither issue. It has been suggested that while Jewish men raised on the rationalist philosophy of the Talmud were drawn increasingly to the anticlerical and rationalist ideas of the eighteenth century, the women, with no such background, were swept away by nineteenth-century romanticism and by Christian dogma. Romanticism, in the long run, was detrimental both to women and to Jews, and political developments in Germany, which resulted in the dominance of the Protestant middle class, put an end to the phenomenon of the Jewish women's salons.[135] For a short time, women in the Jewish élite became a majority among those marrying out of the faith, trading their substantial wealth for social status.[136] But most Jewish women opted for a secure place in middle-class Jewry, in which their piety—the celebration of Sabbaths and festivals in the home and the cult of scriptures rather than the study of Talmud, a Judaism hitherto regarded as superficial and elementary, suitable for children and the unlettered—became the norm.

Reform Judaism, which evolved in early nineteenth-century Germany, held rabbinical conferences in the 1840s which recommended that women should participate in the commandments related to specific times, such as synagogue prayers; should participate in religious education; and should be counted in a quorum.[137] Eventually, in Western Europe and the United States, Reform Jewry did away with many aspects of orthodoxy, but it never gained a foothold in Eastern Europe. The Jews of the West came to resemble their middle-class Gentile neighbours, with religion becoming largely a private affair, community life a matter of synagogue attendance and welfare. The result was a new consciousness, as Grace Aguilar observed, of the archaic, 'oriental' dissonances of Jewish orthodoxy.

In Eastern Europe, however, the orthodox pattern of domestic Jewish life continued uninterrupted. In some middle-class families there might be minor concessions to modernity—in dress, for instance, or in the practice of young couples meeting before the marriage. Pauline Wengeroff, the author of one of the very rare autobiographies written by Jewish women, describes how she and her fiancé were able to become acquainted, at least superficially; but he too was chosen by her parents.[138]

In all but the most privileged families, the only escape for a young woman was by acquiring a trade or profession. An exceptionally interesting Yiddish memoir written by Puah Rakowski, who pioneered the first secondary schools for Jewish women in Warsaw in the last decades of the century, begins with her childhood and unhappy first marriage, and subsequent escape from her family.[139]

Rakowski was born in Bialystok in the Pale of Settlement in 1865 to a fifteen-year-old mother. She could trace her lineage back to Rashi (the medieval sage Solomon Yitzhaki of Troyes) through thirty-six generations. Her maternal grandmother ran a water-powered flour mill and was known for her commercial talents; first married at twelve and divorced at fifteen, she married twice more, each time outdoing her husband in practical and business matters. Rakowski's father was a *maskil* merchant who knew Russian and German and had studied science and book-keeping. Like many little girls of such a background in the nineteenth century, Rakowski studied in the *cheder* or Jewish Bible class with little boys for a few years and then attended a private school for girls, where she learned Russian. As a child she was intensely pious, but her avid reading of Russian literature made her want a further education.

At this point, however, her parents arranged her marriage, at twelve, to a cousin. Rakowski describes herself as 'totally indifferent' to her coming marriage, absorbed in reading and writing poetry. Her fiancé, meanwhile, was bought out of his contract by an aunt, who was a higher bidder, for her own daughter, and Rakowski was betrothed and married to another—or 'led to the slaughter'. Her caustic comments on her husband make it clear that the marriage was a sexual and emotional disaster. By the age of twenty she had two children. Fortunately, her husband was constantly away on business, and Rakowski left her small children with her mother and went off to study midwifery, one of the few professions open to women, though she had to threaten suicide before she obtained her husband's consent. Determined to be independent, she set up a millinery workshop for herself and other struggling women. At the age of twenty-six she got her divorce—this time by threatening that she would convert to Christianity—and was able to begin an independent life as a teacher in Warsaw.

The memoirs of Jewish radical women show that such rebellions often occurred in the families where the father already had some secular education and allowed his daughter secular schooling, only to rein her in by an arranged marriage at puberty. As Rakowski points out, it was both the example of her strong and independent grandmother and the knowledge from her reading that a different way of life existed which encouraged her to strike out on her own. The younger Rakowski children followed her. One sister became a Zionist, one a socialist. Her two youngest brothers were anarchists; all had their spells in prison.

Jewish women, by Rakowski's time, were ripe for rebellion. Christian patriarchal values were not wholly abandoned by the women revolutionaries from Russian Orthodox homes, but transmuted.[140] The same was probably true of the Jewish women, with the difference that it was not doctrine which was abandoned—since of that women had little knowledge—but custom and tradition. The Jewish woman had for centuries combined assertiveness and self-abnegation; this made her an apt recruit for radical activities, which demanded practical initiative together with an at times masochistic readiness for self-sacrifice. Although these qualities also appear among non-Jewish women in the revolutionary Russian subculture of the time, in the case of the Jewish women they are clearly linked with the rejection of specifically Jewish family ties and woman's time-honoured role in the community.

Jewish women's closeness to, but exclusion from, a powerful tradition of learning, and their exposure, by contrast, to secular literature, made them particularly sensitive to the appeal of new ideologies. In the case of Jewish working-class women in radical groups, the passion for learning marks them out from their counterparts in Russian and Polish revolutionary movements.[141] For the newly emancipated middle-class Jewish women, the

Jewish sense of guilt, of misfortune as punishment, even more powerful in the rabbinical view of women than in that of men, re-emerged in the guise of the general feeling of privileged Russian women: that their advantages had been won at a cost to the poor and oppressed. Given the Jewish women's image as protected inferiors in rabbinical law, they could hardly have been inspired by the sense of woman's moral superiority which was part of the religious background of their Russian Orthodox counterparts.[142]

Political activity not only meant assuming public roles, which women had always been denied in rabbinical tradition; it was also a commitment which would demand a heavy price in their private lives, as the biographical sketches which follow will show. Breaking with tradition very often meant a formal break with the family and a renunciation of the protection the community offered the married woman. But even when it did not, the breach with the past was irrevocable, and most of these women were conscious that they had finally severed the 'golden chain', with both its rewards and its restrictions. What they sought was an emotional and intellectual partnership of equality with a man— a totally new concept in Jewish mores, and one which often proved hard to achieve.

In 1919 the radical Yiddish poetess Kadia Molodowski wrote a poem 'Froyen Lider' in which she summed up the price of the abandonment of tradition. In this poem, the rebel mourns the generations of women who preceded her, those who suffered their restrictions (the reference in the second verse is to the *aguna* or anchored woman who cannot get a divorce as her husband is missing) in near-silence, and expresses perfectly the mingled compassion and hostility with which Jewish women in the age of rebellion looked back at the lost world of their mothers.

> The faces of women long dead, of our family,
> Come back in the night, come in dreams to me saying,
> We have kept our blood pure through long generations,
> We brought it to you like a sacred wine
> From the kosher cellars of our hearts.

And one of them whispers:
I remained deserted, when my two rosy apples
Still hung on the tree
And I gritted away the long nights of waking between my
    white teeth.
I will go to meet the grandmothers, saying:
Your sighs were the whips that lashed me
and drove my young life to the threshold
to escape from your kosher beds.
But wherever the street grows dark you pursue me—
wherever a shadow falls.

Your whimperings race like the autumn wind past me,
and your words are the silken cord
still binding my thoughts.
My life is a page ripped out of a holy book
and part of the first line is missing.[143]

2

SINGING FOR THE REVOLUTION

Anna Kuliscioff and Other Early Radicals

In the year 1876, three young Russian revolutionaries—two girls and a man, all wanted by the Czarist police—took refuge in Kharkov. They were penniless, living on what they could earn from odd jobs as shoemakers, actors, and scribes who penned petitions to the authorities for illiterate peasants. The two girls, moreover, had beautiful voices and, by singing in a public park, found that they could earn just enough to keep the trio alive.[1]

One of the girls, Anna Moisevna Rozenstein Macarevich, was a Jewess from Simferopol in the Crimea. Her father was a Jewish 'merchant of the first guild' entitled from 1859 (four years after Anna's birth) to live anywhere in the Russian Empire. This made him one of only five hundred Jewish merchants who enjoyed such a privilege.[2] Inspired by the ideas of Lavrov and Bakunin, she had abandoned a brilliant academic career in Zurich to join a populist revolutionary group. The young Russian nobleman she had married at eighteen had now been in prison awaiting trial for over two years. Bakunin, to whom she had appealed in vain to support a wild scheme to rally the peasants around a false czar, had just died in exile in Bern. Only chance had preserved her, so far, from the fate of almost all the outstanding Jewish women revolutionaries of this and the following decade: imprisonment, madness, or often death by suicide.

Anna Rozenstein had been raised, like these other women, in

the comfortable and protective home of a well-off and semi-assimilated merchant family, with private governesses and tutors for foreign languages. Such families, continuing the tradition of secular education for privileged Jewish women and hopeful that intellectual accomplishments would help their daughters to advantageous marriages, supported their ambitions and financed their studies abroad. The aim of most Jewish girl students was to become independent with the help of a diploma, even if they toyed with the fashionable radical ideas current among the intelligentsia of Moscow and St Petersburg. But a notable few were to join the first women revolutionaries, together with women from the Russian gentry whose families were so different from their own.

Only a generation or two separated girls like Rozenstein from women who entered arranged marriages at puberty, whose education ended with the Bible class, and whose awareness of politics was limited to constant apprehension that their husbands or sons would be removed by the next military draft or that they would have to move house as a result of anti-Jewish legislation. No woman could have symbolised more dramatically the over-turning of that Jewish tradition which ordered the covering of women's hair and pronounced their voices invitations to sin than Anna Moisevna Rozenstein Macarevich, as she stood in the park in Kharkov, her thick plait of blonde hair hanging on her shoulders, singing for the revolution.

Rozenstein's luck was to hold, and in the following year, even before her husband was condemned to five years of forced labour, she left Russia, to which she never returned. Her sympathies developed through support for Italian anarchism to Marxist socialism; she became one of the clearest voices of the radical conscience of Italian social democracy. Henceforth she was to call herself Anna Kuliscioff (Kulisceva—a woman from a far-off Eastern land), a dominant woman in the Italian Socialist Party, contributor to the influential socialist review *Critica Sociale*, leading socialist feminist, and lifelong partner of Filippo Turati, founder and unchallenged leader of the Socialist Party until 1912 and thenceforth head of its reformist wing. While her life developed in exile—and Kuliscioff was always to retain an outsider's critical acumen, though she was accepted and even cherished by the Italian Socialists—most of the other outstanding Jewish women who had played a part in this early stage of the Russian revolution were dead or silenced.

Anna Kuliscioff alone, among an assembly of Jewish women of extraordinary talent and courage, was able to realise her potential to the full. The other revolutionaries of the first two decades of rebellion in Russia can be seen as dedicated and brave, or naïve and suicidal; they had no time to develop further.

'The revolution awakened, among Jewish girls from comfortably off families, a burning desire for higher education and independence, and this shook the very foundations of Jewish traditional life, far more seriously than the educational development of the male intelligentsia.'[3] This is how the Jewish contemporary historian Elyohu Cherikover introduces the couple of pages dedicated to the Jewish woman's role in the populist and terrorist early phases of the Russian revolution. He goes on: 'The Jewish woman devoted herself to the revolutionary movement with special fervour and took part in all its aspects—from cultural work among the Russian masses, propaganda among the peasants, and exhausting physical work in the factories, to even anarchist and terrorist activities.' Cherikover devotes little space to detailing these activities; instead, he emphasises that Jewish women severed their ties with their families more completely than the men. 'The revolution changed the entire character of the radical Jewish woman, much faster, and probably more deeply, than it did that of the Jewish man.'[4] With that he abandons the subject, only to return to women later in the context of the conversion of many Jewish revolutionaries to Christianity. In discussing male populists' conversions, he suggests that this was part of the Jewish ambition to enter more fully into the soul of the Russian people, and particularly that of the peasantry, whom the populists believed to be the moving force in any future revolution. Once women became involved, however, conversion 'took on the aspect of an epidemic'; and the main cause was intermarriage. The detachment from the family tradition was more pronounced for women than for men, and when a daughter of Israel left her family and entered the Russian radical camp, parents who were afraid for their religion often sat *shiva* (the seven-day mourning ritual) for her.[5]

The fact that families sometimes went into mourning for radical daughters, and not for sons, and that they were 'afraid for their religion' (that is, for the continuity of Jewish survival) indicates the particular responsibility of girls in the Jewish family. While girls of Russian Orthodox origin also joined the radicals in defiance of their parents, the Jewish girls were rejecting not only their class and family, but also the demands made on them by their (frequently persecuted) community. The ceremony of mourning also suggests that it was the families who rejected the girls, rather than the opposite. Strictly in terms of rabbinical law, intermarriage of girls was, in the short run, less damaging than that of men—as all children of Jewish mothers are Jews. But they had broken the chain and were doubly treacherous, for their parents' generation was loyal to the Czarist regime, by which they had benefited. This did not mean, however, that they always severed their ties with their families entirely. The case of Anna Kuliscioff indicates the opposite.

Women's conversion out of conviction, conversion in order to marry, and marriage to a Christian without conversion all meant rejection of Jewish roots. The fact that women frequently converted in order to marry in Russia itself—civil marriage did not exist at this time—should be balanced against the fact that many of these marriages were fictitious, enabling women to live independent lives, and that in Russia at this time marriage was the only way (providing the husband agreed to give his wife total liberty) to release a girl from the legal control of her family before the age of twenty-one. Most of the girl rebels broke away when they were students.[6]

The observation that the desire for education and independence by girls 'shook the foundations of traditional Jewish society' more than the original rebellion of the *maskilim* is more significant. The real problem was that once the principle of free choice, in private life as in education and in politics, became dominant, it overruled previous religious and ethnic taboos; to dedicate oneself to a cause conflicted with loyalty to one's own family or faith: in Judaism, one and the same loyalty. There is no indication that the girls converted from any interest in Christianity—as had been the case with some of the German Jewish women intellectuals at the end of the previous century. Conversion, in Czarist Russia, did not guarantee the end of legal or social discrimination; the sole reason motivating the radical girls' conversion, as far as one can ascertain, was the desire to free themselves from parental authority. This was particularly notable in the families who, because of their financial or academic achievements, had worked their way out of Jewish segregation.

Among the young Jewish intelligentsia of the merchant class, who had grown up in families which had often become isolated—both in terms of place of residence and occupation—from the Jewish community with its restrictive and protective institutions, there was little sense of Jewish solidarity. For girls with no Jewish knowledge, no social or religious bond could compete for the attractions of the new revolutionary creed. Again, Jewish girls' motivation was dissimilar to that of their Russian Orthodox counterparts. The notion of the moral superiority of women, enhanced by learning, which was central to the flowering of radicalism among daughters of the privileged Russian classes, was totally absent in Jewish tradition. If it existed among Jewish women radicals, it was as the result of their partial assimilation.[7]

Cherikover and other historians note that the male populist *maskilim* were quite frank about their sense of alienation from the Jewish community. But many of these men still had intellectual ties to Judaism; some had even been *yeshiva* students (members of Talmudic seminaries).[8] It is not surprising, therefore, that the women, almost all of whom were daughters of wealthy parents in the large Russian cities, merchants and not scholars, who had no such ties, should have felt themselves even freer to adopt the new revolutionary creed.

Most of the the outstanding Jewish women among the populist revolutionaries of the 1870s and the terrorist groups which followed them—a doomed generation—came from what Jewish historians describe as *balabatishe*—well-off, respectable families, daughters of those successful Jewish merchants and professionals whom the czarist regime had allowed to settle in the larger Russian cities, or girls who had somehow made their way out of the Pale of Settlement. Such families did not resemble the 'despotic' Russian Orthodox families against whom so many of the Gentile women revolutionaries rebelled. Nor had Jewish society been influenced by those cultural changes in European Russia which had produced a feminism more vigorous than any other in Europe at this time, and which culminated, in this otherwise backward society, in an unparalleled demand for women's scientific education during the second half of the century.[9] The Jewish attitude towards daughters combined the protective paternalism of tradition with encouragement of women's accomplishments in the style of Western Europe.

But the admission of Jewish girls from these families to Russian secondary schools, when these were opened to all classes in the 1860s, and the omnivorous appetite of educated Jewish girls for Russian literature, produced a small but pioneering cadre of young Jewish girl revolutionaries during the 1870s and 1880s. While the Jewish populists never exceeded, in the movement, their proportion in the population as a whole (about four per cent), the number of Jewish *women* who fought Czarist rule was out of all proportion to their numbers. With the exception of Rozenstein, the women were not leading figures, like the Russian Orthodox women Perovskaya or Figner. What was remarkable was the price they paid, particularly in the last stage of Czarism. Between 1907 and 1911, of the 72 political prisoners in the Mal'tsev (Siberia) women's prison, 23 were Jewish. By comparison, 37 of the prisoners were Russians (categorised separately from Jews). Only 14 of the prisoners came from the gentry; most were petit bourgeois, of whatever nationality.[10]

Exposure to literature and to political ideas acted on young Jewish women like pure oxygen, and was just as dangerous. By this time, the literacy rate of Jewish women in Russian had passed that of the general population, and girls whose grandmothers had not even been able to read the Hebrew script of Yiddish, let alone Russian, were now so soaked in the culture of the intelligentsia that they considered themselves capable of taking the message of populism to the Russian Orthodox peasantry.

The pamphlet that Anna Rozenstein took abroad with her in 1876 rejected the Western European ideas which both Jewish *maskilim* and liberal Russians had taken as the basis for reform so far and argued that Russians 'should liberate themselves from the influence of Western ideas and shape their actions according to the ideas and customs of the Russian people, rooted in Russia during a long historical process—that is, simple forms of communal organisation like those existing in peasant communities, and the grassroots rebellions raised by wandering bandits':[11] a process in which the Jews had played no part whatever and which, moreover, had contributed nothing to Jewish emancipation.

There is little in any of the historical evidence about the radical women to suggest that they felt particularly discriminated against as Jews. Yet anti-Semitism was rife among the Russian peasants. Isolated incidents suggest, however, that they did respond when they felt their Jewish honour was challenged: **Lev Deich**, one of the early revolutionaries and the first chronicler of the Jewish contingent, describes how a radical Jew, among several—including a woman—exiled to Siberia for their participation in a demonstration on the Kazan square in 1876, was reviled as a *zhid* (yid) by a district officer of the czarist police. The man swallowed the insult, but a Jewish woman boxed the officer's ears, earning arrest and further exile but boosting her comrades' morale.[12] A more tragic incident concerns the Jewish student **Prescobia Bogoraz**, who converted in order to contract a fictitious marriage with a Christian comrade and joined the terrorist People's Will movement. Put in charge of the printing press, Bogoraz found to her consternation that she had been handed a pamphlet inciting the peasants to anti-Jewish pogroms—for some populists believed this to be a useful way of arousing rebellion against the czar. She protested but was overruled by Sergei Degayev, the committee member who was eventually unmasked as a police provocateur. Bogoraz was later denounced by Degayev and died in prison.[13]

But there is no evidence that sentiments of solidarity with their oppressed people motivated the Jewish girls who joined the early revolutionaries. They were, on the contrary, very conscious of belonging to a privileged sector of Russian society, and were anxious to discard those very privileges which their families had only so recently obtained; what is striking is their feelings of guilt at belonging to that very class into which these families had so laboriously climbed. They were even more anxious to discard traditional motherhood and domesticity. Their rebellion reached its apex when, in the cause of revolution, they even abandoned their studies.

Quite often Jewish girls embarked on their education with the full support of their wealthy and well-established, hence semi-assimilated families. The cases in which a struggle is recorded are of girls who came from 'petty bourgeois' families, those in which Jewish orthodoxy was still observed, early marriage favoured, and higher education for girls discouraged. The custom of giving girls private tutoring from an early age—common to wealthy Jews, the gentry, and the Old Believers—qualified them to compete successfully at the gymnasium level, where they often carried off medals, and from the 1870s put them in the running for the very first university classes for women in Russia. This, despite the fact that from 1887 there was a quota system for Jews in the gymnasia and universities: 10 per cent in the Pale of Settlement, 3 per cent in Moscow and St Petersburg, and 5 per cent elsewhere.[14] Those women who came from the Pale of Settlement had to overcome the obstacles to their residence elsewhere in Russia.

Both Gentile and Jewish girls contracted fictitious marriages, but whereas in the case of Gentile girls this was often because their landowner parents did not wish them to study, for Jewish girls it was a stratagem to escape from the Pale. Other stratagems were bribing landlords and janitors, or even, as a last resort, enrolling with the police as a prostitute in order to receive the yellow ticket which gave women the right of residence in the larger cities like Moscow and St Petersburg.[15]

Jewish women radicals nevertheless figure among the very first students at the special medical and paramedical training courses for women opened in the 1870s in St Petersburg. One of the four first Jewish women, of a total of 89, to qualify (as a midwife) from a training course was **Anna Epstein**. By the end of the decade 169 Jewish women, of a total of 796, had attended the more demanding medical courses.[16] But Epstein, like many radicals who enrolled, did not go on to deliver babies; instead, she went back to her native Lithuania and joined a group of Jewish revolutionaries, all former rabbinical students, who were occupied in smuggling subversive literature across the western frontiers of the empire, a task in which the Jews were particularly experienced. About a third of all cases of smugglers apprehended at this time were Jews, who had long played a major role in outwitting the customs and financial officials of the czarist regime. Later, Epstein became one of the emissaries between exiled revolutionaries in London and their Russian comrades.[17]

But middle-class Jewish girls were far more gently nurtured and probably less capable of coping with the outside world than their trading, peddling grandmothers had been. Their Bundist, Zionist, and Bolshevik successors, most of whom came from traditional Jewish backgrounds, emerge by comparison as much tougher. The populist girls' attempts to harden themselves, both physically and emotionally, were all the more difficult.

From the 1870s, many Jewish girls were sent to receive higher, and expensive, education in Switzerland, then the powerhouse of Russian radicalism in exile. Zurich was then the only place in Europe where Russian women could qualify as doctors. The upbringing the Russian women students had received enabled them to study in foreign languages, but the impression they made on their male colleagues was of shy, polite young ladies, most of whom, in the words of the Georgian populist Dzabadari, 'could not yet have entered so-called "society"'.[18] They were also sexually puritanical (possibly for fear of getting pregnant) and tried (but failed) to convert the Russian men students to the idea of revolutionary celibacy.[19]

The Russian-born **Rosalya Idelson**, the Jewish librarian at the Russian students' library in Zurich, decided to set up an all-woman debating club, the Woman's Club for Logical Speech, which would give them confidence in public speaking. (It is remarkable that in the revolutionary history of this period there were more women capable of planting a bomb than making a rousing speech in public.) Idelson herself gave the first lecture, on the theme of suicide ('a psychopathological phenomenon of social origins', of the kind that would disappear in a just society). The club foundered as many women felt that an all-woman group contradicted the idea of sexual equality.[20] Idelson's lecture was to be grimly illustrated by the suicide of all too many young women revolutionaries who proved unable to stand the strains of interrogation, imprisonment, and separation from their comrades, though it is notable that these women seldom figure as informers.

Idelson, who was one of the first educated Jewish girls in Zurich, wrote contemptuously of the Swiss students that 'they were not yet ready to part with their precious ideal of woman—an obedient, industrious servant, tidy cook, solicitous nurse, wet-nurse, fecund she-cow and so forth. As you know, all these delightful qualities are usually implied by the sonorous and silly word femininity'.[21] Idelson came from Vilna, traditionally the bastion of the Jewish Enlightenment in the Pale of Settlement. She was neither an extreme radical (her second husband, Smirnov, was one of the chief supporters of the moderate populist Lavrov) nor, like the rest of the revolutionary women, a feminist in the modern sense. But in the traditional Jewish context she could scarcely have been more of a revolutionary.

Idelson was a courageous political journalist, one of the exile circle which enabled Lavrov to control the leading revolutionary journal *Vpered!* (Forward!). This provided a platform for Jewish as well as general radical ideas. Idelson, too, had made an early, fictitious marriage with a Jewish student in order to win freedom from parental control and, with the help of another revolutionary, financed her own medical studies in Zurich, where she met and married Valerian Smirnov. Later she returned to Russia on several dangerous missions for the journal. She abandoned political life only when in her late thirties she became a mother. Eventually she became the wife of a Soviet general.[22]

The professional training Jewish radical girls acquired was not always put into practice; if they had not gone to university to learn revolutionary theory, they quickly picked it up, and many were caught in a dilemma regarding their new-found education. The Bakunin wing of the populists in particular did not believe that intellectuals were superior to the peasantry. Some girls got this message even before they began their studies; Lev Deich, their contemporary, records the case of **Felicia Sheftel**, a young girl who had not even completed her studies at the gymnasium in Zhitomir. Though she had only a few months left before she graduated, she wanted to join the revolution straight away; 'every missed day was a criminal loss to the fulfilment of the happiness and wellbeing of the deprived masses.' (Not only schoolgirls but the populist leaders of this time believed that the millennium was round the corner.) Deich succeeded in persuading Sheftel to finish school, at least, but two years later she was arrested and exiled to Siberia. When Deich last met her, she was a faded, subdued woman married to a man far her inferior in intelligence and ability, who had helped her to escape from exile and whom, Deich notes sadly, 'she obeyed absolutely'.[23]

Political debate seduced other girls from their studies. Anna Rozenstein, who had entered the Zurich polytechnic to study technical sciences, is said to have torn up her student's card in a symbolic gesture of rebellion against study as a privilege.[24] It was more than ten years before she was to resume her studies, in medicine, in Italy. For many who had completed their studies, revolutionary life was far too demanding for them to practise their profession, though scores of Jewish graduates of the women's medical courses, like **Dora Aptekman**, who studied at Zurich, went on to practise as a doctor.

If Rozenstein was, in Cherikover's words, the 'first Jewish woman conspirator', another Zurich student, **Beta Kaminskaya**, from a merchant's family in Melitopol, whose mother had died when she was young and whose father indulged her every whim, was the Jewish girl who first took literally the command to 'go to the people'—to arouse the new working class, many of them former serfs, to revolution and to expose the iniquity of their rulers and employers.

In 1873 the czarist government ordered the girl students abroad back to Russia, in what was the first such decree addressed to women, warning them that delay would result in their exclusion from further studies or occupation.[25] On their return, the little group of radicals to which Kaminskaya belonged began to infiltrate factories in the Moscow area, disguised as peasants; she was the first woman to make the attempt.

From four in the morning, for fifteen hours at a stretch, in the Moscow winter, Kaminskaya worked with the peasant women sewing rags together in a heavily guarded factory where they slept on filthy mattresses alive with bedbugs and lice and ate thin soup and bread. Not only were the conditions such that Kaminskaya, a healthy if diminutive girl, was a physical wreck within weeks, but the illiterate women who were the objects of her propaganda were unresponsive, wanting no more at the end of their working week than a meal and a few hours with a man. Kaminskaya and her comrades eventually succeeded in forming a few small circles of workers (all of whom were men), to whom they distributed propaganda. But the group—about fifty strong and historically notable as the first revolutionary organisation to comprise intellectuals and workers—was detected by the secret police within months, partly due to the carelessness of one of the workers, and all its members were rounded up and imprisoned by the autumn of 1875. They remained in jail until their trial in early 1877 (the famous Trial of the Fifty) which demonstrated, *inter alia*, the ineptness of an imperial regime challenged by a handful of students.

Kaminskaya was not among the defendants. She had gone into a clinical depression while in jail and was released into the care of her father, who throughout had demonstrated his support and devotion. At home she quickly recovered her strength but was soon off again to 'join the people', apprenticed to a shoemaker in St Petersburg. During this period she learned of the case in preparation against her comrades. She relapsed into such guilt-ridden melancholia that she was soon home again in her father's care; though she was watched, Kaminskaya managed to get hold of a box of matches, with which she succeeded in poisoning herself.[26]

The failure of the campaigns of the populists among the peasants and workers, who were largely indifferent to their activities, and the continuing crackdown on the rebellious students eventually led the young revolutionaries to terrorism: assassination attempts, first by members of the People's Will militant group and later by the terrorist Social Revolutionaries against the Czar and key figures in his entourage—in particular the SR's Combat Section, in which many Jewish women were involved. Those in both groups included: Gesya Gelfman, in the assassination of Czar Alexander II in 1881; Sofya Ginsburg, in the attempt to assassinate Alexander III in 1891; and Dora Brilliant, in the assassination both of the Minister of the Interior, Plehve, in 1904, and of the Grand Duke Sergei at Yakutsk in 1905.

Gesya Gelfman was probably the only woman among the early revolutionaries who was not from an assimilated family and was not a student (there were a number of Jewish men of this kind, particularly in the more militant groups). Her fate was all the more tragic in that she appears to have been caught between two worlds. According to a Russian source, she fled her petty bourgeois, orthodox family on the very eve of an arranged marriage, distressed by the rituals of preparation (shaving of the head and ritual bath).[27] She joined the People's Will (a terrorist offshoot of the Land and People populist movement), whose executive had taken a vow to assassinate the Czar in 1879 and finally succeeded in doing so in the spring of 1881. Gelfman was not a member of the executive; she looked after the apartment where the explosives were hidden. Her comrades refer to her as a gentle, vulnerable person. Almost immediately after the murder she was arrested, and when she was refused a visit by her lover, she revealed that she was pregnant. It was for this reason alone that she was not hanged with the other conspirators, who included the intrepid non-Jewish Sofya Perovskaya. Her baby was taken from her at birth and died almost immediately in a foundling hospital; she herself died five days later.[28]

The other women were active terrorists, and reckless. **Sofya Ginsburg** came from the same Jewish landowner background as the Rakowski and Bronstein (Trotsky) families. She finished school in the year of Alexander's assassination and, after failing to break into the quota in Petersburg, studied medicine in Bern. She then joined the populist group following Lavrov and Tikhomirov and had ties with the Polish proletariat rebels, with whom Rosa Luxemburg, a few years later, began her revolutionary career. While in Switzerland, she had learned to make explosives; and while in exile in Paris, her fellow conspirators decided to send her back to Russia to reorganise the People's Will, which had disintegrated after its leaders were executed. But by this time the Czarist secret police was far more adept at infiltrating the student groups, and Ginsburg was inept as a plotter; she left pamphlets to be scattered after the assassination in a shop in Kharkov. Arrested and sentenced to death—which was commuted to life imprisonment—she committed suicide in prison.[29]

Dora Brilliant, whose end was identical to Ginsburg's, was a Social Revolutionary—the most extreme and fanatical of the early revolutionary movements. She too came from a wealthy merchant family, also described as orthodox. Boris Savinkov, the ringleader of the group, records in his memoirs both her cool handling of bombs and her anguish at the thought of how they were actually to be used. Her statements at her trial also show that, like her fellow intellectual terrorists, she both courted death and danger and shrank from actual killing and the guilt it induced. If Katayev, the assassin of the Grand Duke Sergei, hesitated to throw a bomb, at the risk of his own life, lest it harm innocent bystanders, Brilliant both wanted to participate in the assassinations and yearned to die herself. The need to give one's own life in exchange for that of the victim was a form of secular expiation. For those who had rejected religion, the court of appeal had become that of history.[30] In the case of girls from orthodox merchant families, it seems likely that the traditional guilt of women was amplified by guilt at the privileges their class had won.

What was remarkable about these young Jewish women terrorists and marked them out from their Menshevik and Bolshevik successors was their indifference to revolutionary programmes. They were totally involved in the act of destruction, obsessed with the value of their own deaths. In this they were very similar to their non-Jewish Russian counterparts. However, purification through terror—martyrdom or immolation in prison—appears to go back in Russian tradition to the self-burning among the Old Believers, among whom women too had played a leading role; this was something totally alien to Jewish tradition. While the Jewish girls often committed suicide when their mission failed, their Gentile comrades thought that their very overt melancholy was a reflection of the 'centuries of Jewish suffering' in their dark eyes.[31] For those girls who had come from orthodox families, the inheritance of female guilt, and the female martyrdom and suicide revered in Jewish history since the period of the Crusades, was more likely to have been the origin of their desire for self-sacrifice.

However, these women did nothing to improve the lot of the Jews. The murder of Alexander II was followed by a series of restrictive laws against Jewish residence in the countryside, calculated to appease the peasantry; coincidentally, it reduced still further the participation of Jews in populism in that it also prevented their membership in the (generally anti-Semitic) *zemstva* or locally elected organs of self-government which the populists so admired. These measures were not opposed by the radical intelligentsia, for whom the peasants came first. They were followed by state-backed pogroms, aimed to let off more subversive steam. Eventually, most of the intelligentsia was also denied residence in the great Russian cities: Moscow itself was closed to Jews in 1891.

In 1918, the 28-year-old Jewess **Fanny Kaplan** performed one of the last acts of protest of the Social Revolutionaries Combat Unit section. Kaplan had been born in the Pale, educated at home, and remained in Russia when her father, a teacher, took the rest of the family to the United States in 1911. She had joined an anarchist group in 1906 and was arrested after a bombing incident in Kiev. Amnestied during the 1917 revolution, she decided that Lenin was a traitor to the socialist cause and tried unsuccessfully to kill him. She was shot without trial two days after the attempt.[32]

The revolutionary creed swiftly devoured the early Jewish radicals, save for Anna Kuliscioff, who, as a historian of her new country put it, 'managed to survive, intact, every possible political experience and the most destructive adventures'.[33] Like all the other Jewish women who joined the earliest revolutionaries, she retained no link with her own community, though she intermittently expressed sympathy with persecuted Jewry.

When **Anna Kuliscioff** fled Russia, she was still a follower of Bakunin, who preached the doctrine of international anarchism, the total abolition of the state, as against what he saw as the authoritarian dogma of Marx. His ideas were most popular in France, during the Commune, though his attempt to organise an uprising in Lyon in 1870 had failed. So it was to Paris that Kuliscioff went in late 1877, after working for a time in the British Museum as the anarchist noble Kropotkin's secretary. Among the anarchists exiled in Paris she re-encountered the Italian disciple of Bakunin, Andrea Costa.[34]

Costa, despite the collapse of his own anarchist uprising in Bologna in 1874, was a natural leader, a fiery orator, and Kuliscioff found in him a kindred spirit and the man who elicited her first great passion. His attraction to her was even more predictable. Every memoir of the young Kuliscioff mentions her luminous beauty. Lev Deich describes her as blonde and blue-eyed, with thick, wavy hair and very white skin; she had a natural elegance that made her look older than her age—remote from the familiar portrait of the Russian *nihilistika* whose cropped hair and black clothes proclaimed her contempt for society and conventional femininity.[35]

Costa wrote of the winter evening in Paris when he fell in love with Kuliscioff, who had come to visit him in the florist's shop where he worked in the Rue d'Aboukir: 'You took off your hat, revealing your broad, white forehead, and smiled at me; your blonde hair shimmered in the candlelight.'[36] But the intellect and fierce will beyond that broad white forehead was eventually to baffle and defeat Costa. 'It's your head, that terrible little head of yours which is hostile to me,' he was to write.[37] Anna, for her part, came to realise that her lover, for all his libertarian ideas, was as jealous and narrowly uxorious as any bourgeois husband.

The lovers spent only a few months of their five-year liaison together, as they were pursued by the government and police of every European country to which they fled. Anna had evaded capture in Russia; the chief of the czarist police in Kiev recognised her in the street, but her air of aristocratic self-possession confounded him. He did not arrest her.[38]

The French, Italian, and Swiss police were less gallant. The anarchist community in France—at this stage hovering between the early idealism of Proudhon and the later philosophy of violence—was a small group of intriguers, with the police on their heels. Kuliscioff was soon arrested, and was set free only by the personal intercession of Turgenev, who was fascinated by her despite his unwillingness to alienate the Russian ambassador in Paris. Expelled from France, she and Costa renewed their activities, and their liaison, in Italy, where she was again imprisoned in 1879, charged with plotting against the state, tried, and acquitted. The two fled this time to Lugano, where they attempted to set up an anarchist journal, the *International Socialist Review*. For the third time in two years since leaving Russia, Kuliscioff was arrested and jailed. When they were finally at liberty and together, Costa had to return to Italy to continue his political work.[39]

At some stage during Kuliscioff's anarchist adventures, she had become convinced of what she was to later call the 'nihilist metaphysics', the 'artificiality', of anarchist philosophy.[40] It was during their liaison that Costa, the most thoughtful of the Italian anarchists, came to substitute scientific socialism, or Marxism, for his previous creed—what one historian has called a 'spectacular conversion' which led to the first emergence of organised working-class protest in Italy.[41]

By the time of her trial in Florence in 1879, Kuliscioff defined herself not as an anarchist, or even an internationalist—the accusations levelled against her—but as a Russian revolutionary socialist. In her own defence, she insisted that the International had never penetrated Russia, where political conditions were quite different to those of Western Europe. 'Internationalists cannot make revolutions to their liking, because it is not in the power of individuals to create or provoke revolution; only the people can do so ... socialists must take part in popular movements ... but cannot create them on their own. The revolution must begin with the people.' For instance, the Italian grain taxes had evoked spontaneous protest. 'Socialism must be ready to take control of such protest, to channel instincts and feelings latent in the people, into socialist political forces.'[42] In other words, Kuliscioff's political thinking had already evolved from the utopian creed of the populists and anarchists to belief in a socialism which would evolve according to the different economic and political circumstances in each country, based on the needs of the masses.

In 1881 Costa founded the Revolutionary Socialist Party of Romagna, whose platform combined the idea of parliamentary reform together with the gradual education of the proletariat, within the framework of the existing political institutions. Costa himself became the first socialist deputy in the Italian parliament, as representative for Ravenna. The philosophy behind this party was clearly aimed at the Italian anarchists but was heavily influenced by Marxism, ten years before the *Communist Manifesto* was even translated into Italian; Costa had read Marx in French translation.

Anna's experience in populist Russia and her transition to Marxist socialism may both have influenced Costa's thinking. But their love affair, perhaps artificially prolonged by so many dramatic separations (as Anna's letters show she suspected), came to grief as soon as they were able to live together. Anna's determination to pursue an independent career clashed with

Costa's need for a supportive and domesticated woman.

At first Anna deferred to her lover's every wish. 'We are separated not by a whim, but by the very reason for, the essence of, our life,' she wrote, when Costa left her in Switzerland in 1880. 'I would never want to be an obstacle to your necessary work in Italy.'[43] But Costa did not reciprocate by encouraging her to study and continue her own political activities. Instead, he insisted that she isolate herself from her old comrades, go nowhere without him, and see no other man. He termed her ambitions 'the false independence and false dignity of a woman'.[44] Her Russian comrades were horrified by her attempts to conform to his idea of her as a bourgeois madonna (he addresses her in letters as '*vergine mia*') and by her longings for a child as the 'fruit of their love'. 'It must be the climate affecting you,' wrote her friend Elena Kovac from Russia.

But Anna, too, longed for stability and domesticity, and—as her subsequent letters to others also prove—had no wish to remain a 'wandering Jew', 'though many of my friends think I need tempests and adventures'.[45] She agreed to care for Andreino, Costa's son by an earlier mistress, and he persuaded his parents of Anna's innate respectability. The lovers contemplated a ménage in Costa's home town, Imola, together with his parents. This was also to include Anna's mother. This lady, under the influence of her two rebellious daughters, had actually left her 'despotic' (as Anna calls him) husband and fled to Odessa to her second daughter, Adele. 'She has nothing now, cares for nothing save our approval for what she has done—just imagine that!' wrote Anna to Costa.[46] But the despotic merchant Rozenstein went on remitting funds to his womenfolk, and eventually for Anna's illegitimate child, whom he adored. Anna continued to meet her father regularly in Europe until the end of his life.

Reunited with Costa in 1881, Anna conceived the child she desired and gave birth in Imola at the end of that year to a daughter, Andreina. (Both his children, interestingly, bore Costa's first name, but later Anna called her daughter Nini and Ninetta.) Despite her affection for Costa's parents, however, Anna was soon deeply unhappy. She had not escaped the embrace of Jewish custom only to find herself in a far more repressive Catholic home. Re-exiled from Italy with a nursing infant at her breast in 1882, Anna began her medical studies in Bern, against Costa's wishes. When eventually she was granted permission to live in Italy, she returned there to live and to study alone.

The letters exchanged during their liaison tell a story of a woman torn between her passion for a man and desire for a home and family, and her recognition that he would not or could not accept her as an equal, denying her that partnership which was not only her ideal but an absolute necessity in her emotional life. 'I must live with you or die,' she wrote from Switzerland in 1880. 'I left everything for you—mother, friends—I'm alone and have only you ... I could have acted differently.'[47] At first, when he expresses jealousy, she loses control completely: 'I worship you like a god ... I would let you slap me if you wished.'[48] And in 1880: 'I want to take you away from your beautiful country ... I feel what only a mother or a lover can feel. You are mine, I don't want them to take you away again ... I love you with a passion I don't want to analyse ... I belong to you entirely.'[49] Yet the woman who could write this withdrew, with great dignity and sorrow, from her lover when she realised that while he shared her passion, he would not share his active life with her.

Costa's few attempts at a reconciliation were half-hearted and clumsily sexual. Anna was not to be moved. 'Real love grows and develops only when two people are morally and intellectually as one,' she insisted.[50] She found what comfort she could in her child and the strength to complete her studies alone, graduating from the University of Pavia as a doctor of medicine in 1885. The partnership she had failed to achieve with Costa she found, in that year, with the young Milanese lawyer and poet Filippo Turati.

Kuliscioff had by now formed a friendship with one of the first Italian feminists, some twenty years her senior, Anna Maria Mozzoni. For an emancipated Russian woman intellectual, Italian women looked like an oppressed nation. Italy was one of the most backward of European countries at this time where women's education was concerned; women were subordinate to the family and the dictates of the Church. At the time of Kuliscioff's arrival in Italy, Mozzoni, with other upper-class Italian women from the industrialised north, was engaged in a battle for the admission of women to the universities and of qualified women to the professions. It was Mozzoni who introduced Kuliscioff to Italian feminism, which had begun to develop ten years before her arrival in Italy. But what was chiefly to concern Kuliscioff was the conditions of the women in the working class—those women whom she was to know intimately as a doctor—and the relationship of socialism to women's emancipation.

Mozzoni also introduced Kuliscioff to Turati. They were to form one of the most important partnerships in European socialist history, a union commemorated in a voluminous correspondence (in Italian, their *Carteggio*) spanning a quarter of a century, which is remarkable both as a historical document and a record of an amazing meeting of minds, the rarest of political dialogues, which only ceased with Kuliscioff's death in 1925.[51]

The correspondence, which began when both were imprisoned in Milan in 1898, continued between Anna in Milan, where she worked as a doctor, a journalist, and a political organiser—and later as the editor of a socialist women's journal—and Turati in Rome, where until the Fascist regime banned the Socialists from the Chamber of Deputies in 1925, he played an active part in Italian politics. Kuliscioff, though she often represented Turati in party forums, never followed him about the country. Hence the comprehensiveness of the correspondence, which details every incident in politics save when the couple attended the same conference or were at home in Milan together.

'Our letters are a conversation at a distance; ideas, feelings, plans, meet in them as if the space dividing us was suspended, as if we had one mind, one soul. What marriage could ever rival such a complete and perfect identity as ours? A pretty woman might appeal to you—make you feel younger—I can see you laugh—but ... our total union exalts me and comforts me like a great moral victory we have won together,' she wrote Turati in 1907.[52] She continued to give and expect such total commitment all her life. There is little reference to Jews or her Jewish background in the letters; yet this definition of her 'total union' with Turati expresses perfectly the personal aim of the Jewish women rebels in their relationship with men: a union which clearly was the antithesis of that of their parents. 'Ideas' precede even 'feelings' as bonds uniting a man and a woman.

Kuliscioff's happiness with Turati was all the greater for her disappointment with Costa. To one of the leading Italian radicals, Napoleone Colajanni, she wrote shortly after meeting Turati, who had visited her as part of a scheme to help Russian liberals in jail: 'The harmony between high intelligence and feeling is very rare, and this is Turati's unusual gift. The embittered soul is comforted encountering a nature like his, and begins to be resigned to the human race, which is in the main a very ugly species.'[53] A few years later, in a lecture on the subjection of women, she made a rare personal reference to her own past: 'The experience of many women who have tried to break away from the traditional feminine role, and above all my own personal experience, have taught me that while many generous men, thinkers and scientists, will make every effort to solve complex social problems, this is not so where men's privileges with respect to women are concerned.'[54] It is very clear from the correspondence that while Anna appreciated Turati's great sensitivity of character, and his rigorous mind (the two qualities which meant that he was to be regularly upstaged by socialists with greater mass appeal), Turati acknowledged Anna's superior strength, her political acumen, and—though she was only three years his senior—her maternal protectiveness where he was concerned.

Soon after setting up house with Anna, Turati became a convert to Marxism. He left the democratic centre of Italian politics and joined the recently established Italian Workers' Party, made up chiefly of men in industry and agriculture who had gained the vote in the suffrage reforms of 1882. These artisans and peasants now protested against the conditions in northern Italian factories and against middle-class interference in workers' politics, and above all claimed the right to strike and to form unions.

If Costa had been able to arouse militant workers to action in the Romagna while acting as first socialist deputy in Parliament, Turati's first steps in politics, as a middle-class intellectual spurred by Kuliscioff into joining a working-class party which explicitly rejected his class, were less certain. His chance came when, in 1889, the Crispi government dissolved the Workers' Party. Turati and Kuliscioff now founded the Milan Socialist League, a group made up of workers and liberal intellectuals, something which had happened earlier in Russia but which was an entirely new departure in Italian political history.

The League formed the basis of the Socialist Party which was to be established four years later. While the local anarchists put up a fight against this new alliance, there was a stormy session in which Anna took part; and when she nominated the four men who were to lead the party, her resolution was passed by a two-thirds majority.[55] In November of that year Turati was elected to a position in local government, the first political appointment of his career, and in January 1891 the couple founded the famous journal *Critica Sociale*—ostensibly a review of both cultural and political affairs, but in essence an attempt to sketch and discuss a new socialist ideology based on Marxist theory.

Kuliscioff and Turati frequently wrote the leading articles together—those signed TK—but even when she did not sign her name, it was often Kuliscioff who suggested subjects for articles and with whom Turati discussed every move.[56] In the sixth number of the journal, the couple set out the aims of Italian socialism: the socialisation of industry, control of industry by the workers, universal suffrage, and the abolition of the army among them. This ideology was anti-chauvinist—in keeping with their belief that the Italian Risorgimento had been a bourgeois movement; anti-authoritarian; and in favour of the equality of the sexes, since Kuliscioff was an ardent disciple of August Bebel, who had introduced the 'woman question' into Marxism, believing that the working class and women were two subject peoples whose liberation would coincide.[57]

Perhaps the greatest weakness of the League was that it represented chiefly the intellectuals and the industrial working class of the Milan region. Turati was never quite to overcome his privileged origins as a socialist leader. Kuliscioff, the letters indicate, kept the aim of the class struggle before him, the vision of the ultimate socialist revolution. This made her very popular with the more militant wing of the party, particularly Arturo Labriola, the syndicalist socialist from Naples, who in 1893 wrote to Engels: 'In Milan there is only one man—and she is a woman.'[58]

As a southerner, familiar with the serf-like poverty and feudal oppression of Italy south of Naples, Labriola was nearer Kuliscioff's revolutionary ideas.[59] It was the tragic predicament of the Sicilian peasantry which finally provoked Turati into assuming a more dynamic and less purely intellectual role in Italian socialism, barely months after the foundation of the party.[60] The prohibitive price of grain in Italy, the result of a protectionist government policy which profited the northern industrialists, had already reduced the peasantry in the far poorer southern regions to near-starvation; small landowners were also hit by the collapse of the banks following the withdrawal of foreign investment. Both these and the disastrous military adventure in Abyssinia led to the uprising in Sicily at the end of 1893, in which desperate peasants, helped by city intellectuals, staged widespread strikes and riots. They were organised in what were called the *fasci*, part mutual-aid societies, part peasant leagues, by socialists and intellectuals—a tradition later to be debased by the followers of Mussolini. In January 1894 the prime minister, Crispi, called in the troops and violently suppressed the strikers and rioters, causing many deaths.

The newly created Socialist Party was immediately in crisis. One wing dissociated itself from the *fasci*, but the other, including both Turati, with Kuliscioff, and Labriola, supported them.[61] *Critica Sociale* acclaimed the uprising as a sign of the revolt of the working classes against their oppressors throughout Italy. This stand confirmed Crispi's fears of a countrywide insurrection which could tear Italy apart. The next number of the journal was seized, as were many pamphlets, and the Socialist leaders were menaced with prison.

Kuliscioff, on behalf of the party, wrote to Engels in London in one of the most significant exchanges in modern revolutionary history. She defined what was happening in the north, too, as 'a state of siege' and anticipated that Turati would be put on trial, with the possible 'trifle' of a ten-year or more sentence. What were the socialists to do? 'The party has barely been born and certainly one cannot speak of a socialist revolution in a country which is two-thirds medieval, and in which the peasantry lives in conditions similar to France at the Revolution.' She described two trends in the party: one gradualist, hoping for a slow process of reform, the other seeking to exploit the uprisings among peasants, the unemployed, the starving, and those bankrupted by the government's policies. She made it clear that she herself thought the party should lead the 'rebellious masses' or at any rate take part in the disturbances, which were spontaneous (unlike those of the anarchists, she stressed) and 'the organic product of an historical period which is now coming to an end'. Turati added only a very characteristic footnote to this letter, saying that there were two opinions not only in the party, but in every one of its members.[62]

Engels' celebrated response (addressed to Turati) advised the socialists to work together with the bourgeois parties, the radicals, and the republicans, for an eventual overthrow of the government, while retaining their own independence.[63] This was a policy which Turati was to follow consistently; in the short term it did not protect the party from persecution by the government, but it won Turati popularity as a martyr, enlarged the Socialists' following, and made him the dominant figure in socialist politics for nearly two decades. In the long run, however, it turned the more fervent revolutionaries in the party against him, and from 1912 restricted his effectiveness to the much smaller circle of 'reformist' socialists who never had the electoral power to block the rise of Fascism.

Kuliscioff's role in all this was complex and difficult; intensely loyal to Turati, she was by political temperament impatient with compromise and suspicious of the attempts of the liberal Giolitti, prime minister during most of this period, to woo Turati away from the socialist camp. The Socialist Party was dissolved and went underground. At the local government level, the Socialists formed alliances with the bourgeois parties, which gave Turati a power base from 1896. Though no trade union movement as such yet existed in Italy, the movement had a solid organisational base among the workers in the local Chambers of Labour, a long-established local tradition. But once again the government's protectionist policies led to widespread poverty and famine, this time also in the north. The Socialists encouraged a popular uprising in Milan in May 1898, and again the army was called in: tens were killed and hundreds wounded. This brutal repression included the arrest and trial of all the socialist leaders: Turati was sentenced to twelve years in prison, Kuliscioff, as a fellow 'subversive', to two years.

It was then that the great correspondence between the two began; rather typically, Turati's imprisonment (the first in his life) led to a depressed reconsideration of his fitness for active politics. Kuliscioff's courage, however, heartened him. She insisted that no special amnesty be requested for herself. 'If I had to gain my freedom at such a price, I would be so humili-ated, so diminished, so disgusted, that freedom, the love of my dear ones, the affection of good friends, would mean noth-ing to me,' she wrote to a colleague.[64] Already frail from the effects of previous imprisonments, she was now suffering physically from the effects of sleeping in chill cells and liv-ing in darkness for eighteen hours a day. Turati's mother appears to have looked after Anna's daughter while she was in prison.

The arrests, predictably, benefited the Socialists and Turati in particular, and public indignation led to their release after only a few months' imprisonment. It was again typical of the difference in their personalities that Turati shrank from being re-elected on a wave of public sympathy. Kuliscioff thought this sentimentality. She told him sharply that he was spoiled: 'You were born wearing a shirt, while I am naked as a newborn chick.' He answered meekly, 'You are all resolve, I all indecision, and this is why I need you.'[65]

During the last years of the century, while Turati functioned as a member of the Milanese local government, he and Kuliscioff used their influence among the working class in the Milan region to organise mass rallies intended to draw the Italian Parliament's attention to the industrial hazards affecting women and children. Sometimes there were as many as three hundred such rallies on the same Sunday.[66] This was the first direct attempt by the working class in Italy to influence legislation.

In the general elections of 1900, the Socialists increased their parliamentary force from 15 to 32 deputies, with Turati as unchallenged leader of the party. Between this period and the Libyan campaign in 1912, Turati (with Kuliscioff as both his chief supporter and his most acute critic) advanced steadily towards power, chiefly through a series of accommodations with the liberal leader Giolitti. But Kuliscioff saw very clearly the obstacles facing Italian socialism and the shortcomings of its intellectual 'reformist' leadership, which was not always in touch with working-class problems. On the other hand, government repression of strikes in the industrial north, and of peasant uprisings in the south, undermined Turati's plans for many parliamentary reforms; his opposition to using the weapon of the general strike, for instance, lost him the support of the radical socialists, and his antimilitarism detracted from his popularity among Italians smarting from Italy's weak international status.

Kuliscioff was far more aware than Turati of the dangers of seduction by Giolitti. She helped him refuse a place in government in 1903 and in 1911, when the astute liberal leader tried to split the socialist movement.[67] While the couple frequently disagreed on tactics, Kuliscioff admired Turati's sensitivity, his revulsion at what he termed the 'anarchist instincts' of the Italian masses, as well as his superlative powers of analysis and idealism ('None but you has the ability to sound chords in my soul I had thought were long since severed,' she wrote in 1906).[68]

In the mid 1890s, Kuliscioff was still a militant revolutionary;

but her subsequent correspondence with Turati reveals a growing awareness of the perils of social upheaval, a wariness of socialist promises that could not be fulfilled, and an increasingly clear-eyed view of the real motives and potentialities of the 'masses'. In 1899, at an international socialist congress in Rome, she wrote of the participants: 'I swear that there is nothing worse than Jacobin extremists. Great violence, great intemperance, an appetite for bombast—and underneath it, nothing but wretched triviality and personal pettiness.'[69]

Kuliscioff brought to her critique of Italian politics not only her experience in Russia (she remained in touch with old comrades like Vera Zasulich, the terrorist from the impoverished nobility who had shot at a brutal Czarist governor in 1878 and was acquitted) but also developments in English socialism and, in particular, German social democracy. Italian politicians and the press, she pointed out in 1900, were completely mistaken where Russian politics was concerned. The day of student rebels, such as she had been, was over. 'It is no longer the idealistic bourgeoisie which is at war with Czarism.' During the twenty years since she had left Russia, the country had become an industrial power, while remaining, in the political sense, 'semi-barbaric'. The Russian bourgeoisie, she wrote, was content with the absolutist regime which granted it every legal and material benefit. Hence, the European 'spirit of '48' was irrelevant. What she feared now was a bloody upheaval by the new urban proletariat, led by the déclassé bureaucracy, petite bourgeoisie, and sons of clerics, something which could only be prevented by international support for reform in Russia by European socialists; but she despaired at their lack of understanding.[70]

While urging Turati to increasingly radical policies, Kuliscioff doubted the capacity of the Italian Socialists to take power. 'If we study revolution, we may see that in good faith or in bad, the people [are] always deceived. The masses, moreover, will only move if you appeal to their real interests.' If socialism could not promise them public control of the means of production, they would fail to win support. Most astutely, Kuliscioff predicted that in a semi-feudal society like that of Italy, the peasantry in particular could only be recruited if they were promised individual, not collective, land reform. 'What better guarantee of freedom' than the exercise of that freedom? If the working class did not know how to use the vote in their own interests, abstract ideas of freedom had no value, she wrote.[71]

Kuliscioff was to have no sympathy for and no illusions about the Bolsheviks. In March 1917, after the Czar's overthrow, she glimpsed the liberation of Russia of which she had dreamed. 'I'm in ecstasy from yesterday evening,' she wrote to Turati in Rome, 'as if I were in Petrograd with the revolutionaries.'[72] She hoped the March revolution would encourage German socialists, and looked forward to enlightenment all over Europe. But her horror at the 'terrorist dictatorship' of Lenin in October meant that, almost alone among Western socialists, she knew the revolution had been betrayed.[73]

Immediately after the Bolshevik revolution, in a rare reference to the fate of the Jews, Kuliscioff rejoiced at the Balfour Declaration promising a national home to the Jews in Palestine. She was furious that the Italian Prime Minister Orlando, in his inaugural speech on foreign policy, had referred to Palestine only as 'The Holy Land of the Sepulchre', without mentioning 'the people persecuted in almost all of Europe, which will finally have its own place of refuge from all pogroms, including those carried out by the Russian revolutionaries'.[74] She had no illusions on that score either.

As opposed to her private criticisms on socialist policy in general and Turati's relations with the liberal governments with which the socialists were in opposition, Kuliscioff only challenged Turati in public once—over women's suffrage and the party's lackadaisical support for what she regarded as a major issue.

In 1890, the year in which Clara Zetkin, the German socialist feminist, founded the famous women's paper *Die Gleichheit*, Kuliscioff made her first appearance on a public platform on the question of feminism. In a long lecture which drew heavily on current ideas in sociology and anthropology, but was primarily influenced by Marxist theory, Kuliscioff made clear her differences with the middle-class feminism of Mozzoni and her followers.[75]

Kuliscioff argued trenchantly for women's civil and political rights, appealed for equal pay, and protested against women's exploitation both by their employers and their husbands (in Italy at this time, women constituted 60 per cent of the Italian industrial labour force). While Kuliscioff echoed the current optimistic belief of socialist feminists that industrialisation was making women the social equal of men, she was already aware that across the social spectrum, from doctors and lawyers to the working-class husbands who believed their wives would 'settle down at home' as soon as they had earned a little more money, men feared women's competition and would not support their struggle. She even argued, rather ahead of her time, that women should be paid for housework as an occupation rather than receiving handouts from their husbands.

However, whether from her experience as a doctor among the working women of Milan or from comparing Italian and Russian women, Kuliscioff never saw women merely as victims of the system. Women's fear of change, she thought, made them essentially reactionary and conservative, unsuited to that full partnership with men which was both her personal and social ideal. She deplored more than all else the lack of solidarity among women of all classes.

Many of Kuliscioff's early articles in *Critica Sociale* are devoted to the problems of recruiting women to socialist activities. In Zetkin's Germany the Social Democrats were a legal party, and the unions solidly based; yet even there many women feared and discouraged their sons' and husbands' involvement in left-wing politics and held them back.[76] In Italy during the last decade of the nineteenth century, with the Socialists intermittently banned or condemned as subversive, it was no wonder that many working-class women, as Kuliscioff complained, hid the party's invitations from their husbands and found ways of keeping them at home.[77] She opposed the election, in 1892, of a 'token woman' put up by one of the early syndicalist groups, before women were given equal conditions at work.[78] And she attacked, with just as much vigour, the middle-class feminists who feared that socialist ideas would destroy the family, as those men who opposed women's participation in politics.[79]

The ideas on women's liberation which Kuliscioff had brought with her from revolutionary Russia were sometimes a political embarrassment to Turati. Marriage in Catholic Italy was indissoluble, but under the influence of ideas infiltrating from Western Europe the idea of a 'limited marriage' (*matrimonio a termine*) for a trial period was discussed by Italian liberals and socialists.

Kuliscioff attacked this in *Critica Sociale* on the good Marxist grounds that it was not the form of marriage that was important but its economic basis—that when a woman was economically independent, and the couple functioned on equal terms, 'people could live together without a formal wedding ... and so much the better for them; and then it would occur to no one to subject to formal control such intimate relations, which concern only two people making their own free contract.' She admitted it was too early for such free unions in Italy, as marriage was meanwhile the only legal form of protection for women who, if abandoned without an alternative source of income, would have no claim on their partners.[80] Turati could not let this pass. He added a disclaimer, on behalf of the party which, he hastened to add, was not actually recommending 'free unions' as part of its political programme.[81]

In Kuliscioff's private life, however, her ideas were very different where her own daughter's future was concerned. Andreina was to marry, in 1904, into a highly conventional Milanese Catholic family—not only with Kuliscioff's assent but to her infinite relief. Kuliscioff's letters show that Andreina's irregular status, the sense that her own early freedoms had been at her daughter's expense, had caused her remorse and anxiety about the girl's future. Andreina was, she acknowledged, a placid, home-loving girl with no political views—and she did not force her own ideas on her. 'Anyway, there must be a law of balance in the universe ... I rebelled against everything and everyone. I suffered greatly, I sacrificed the best years of my youth. Now my daughter, in recompense, will respect all the laws and all the conveniences.[82] Kuliscioff became the adoring grandmother of Andreina's children, though she deplored her too-frequent pregnancies, remarking that whether a husband strayed or was faithful, the woman always paid the price.[83]

Meanwhile, in Andreina's childhood, Kuliscioff played a leading part in rallying working-class women, in advance of the local elections of 1897, to support Socialist candidates, as only they would introduce legislation protecting women in industry and in the northern countryside, where in the rice-fields they were attacked by leeches and malaria, and whose children, as she knew well, suffered from anaemia, rickets, and malnutrition. She led the Socialist women's lobby for an eight-hour working day, equal pay for equal work, freedom for women to market their own produce, and maternity leave in all sectors of women's employment. As she was later to remind Turati, women responded and were among the Socialists' most energetic propagandists and campaigners.[84]

The reforms Kuliscioff formulated were part of the programme approved by the Sixth Socialist Congress in 1900. In 1901 the party presented a law in Parliament forbidding the employment of women under twenty and female labour in unhealthy and dangerous work, as well as night work. The first Italian laws protecting working women were passed in the two following years, though maternity benefits were only fully granted in 1910. Kuliscioff always maintained that these laws had not been promoted by the state but were passed under pressure from the Socialists, prodded by the women's section of the party. Kuliscioff herself had been largely responsible for framing the laws—probably her main contribution to Italian politics and social welfare. In 1912, inspired by the example of Zetkin, Kuliscioff founded the Italian women's socialist organisation and its journal, *La Difesa delle Lavoratrici*.[85]

In the following two years Kuliscioff found herself in public conflict with Turati over the issue of women's suffrage. Unlike Turati, who was concerned chiefly with local issues, Kuliscioff was keenly aware of feminist developments in other parts of Europe, in England, Germany, and Finland in particular, where the battle for women's suffrage was carried on primarily by middle-class feminists but where women played an important part in the local Socialist election campaigns—something Italian women had ceased to do, disillusioned with the Socialists, over the previous decade. Now, a strengthened Italian Socialist Party was preparing to do battle over the suffrage issue—for men but not, as in Austro-Hungary or in Germany, on behalf of women as well. Why, she asked, were the Italian Socialists so cautious? The reason was that they believed that they were on the verge of pushing through an extension of the suffrage to illiterate males, and thought campaigning for women's suffrage, in Catholic Italy, would compromise their chances of success.[86]

Kuliscioff, though reluctant to attack Turati in the pages of the journal they had edited together for over a decade, now tore his arguments for 'gradual progress' to pieces. If women were 'absent' from politics, as he argued, were illiterate men more 'active'? And if they were, it was the fault of the Socialist Party's neglect. In a series of articles, she defended Italian women against his criticisms, and in so doing presented a very subtle argument, for a Marxist, and one which could only come from a woman exceptionally responsive to the devout, working-class women with whom she came into daily contact. It was no good, she argued, to complain of the passivity and conservatism of Catholic women who, at work, were little more than enslaved animals, when religion was their only form of idealism and source of comfort. Marriage and maternity had alike disappointed them. But what had the Socialists given women? What had the Socialist Party done to prove, towards women, that it was less deceitful than religion, less clerical than the priests?

In 1912 the Socialists succeeded in their battle for the extension of male suffrage, at the cost of a failure on another front which turned out to be far more important—their opposition to the Libyan war. Giolitti extended the franchise to those who had fought for Italy solely because they had been soldiers. As Kuliscioff wrote bitterly, women had only the privilege of bearing soldiers to lose them in wars—and not thereby to win the right to vote.[87]

In Kuliscioff's lifetime, the struggle for women's suffrage in Italy was unsuccessful.[88] Within the Socialist Party, however, Turati yielded and scheduled an amendment to the motion in Parliament. This, saying simply, 'Women have the right to the vote,' was defeated on May 15, 1912, in the Chamber of Deputies by 209 to 48. Of the supporters, 27 were Socialists. The male suffrage reform bill was passed by an overwhelming majority, 294 to 62, in June. Italian women were not to get the vote until after the Second World War.

To the end of her life, Kuliscioff felt that even those Italian Socialists most sympathetic to the issue of women's suffrage undervalued women's (extraparliamentary) contribution to the party. Her feelings were expressed in a letter written to Turati in May 1923, after she had read the text of an address he had given to the Eleventh Conference of the International Women's Suffrage Alliance in Rome the previous day. She was, by now, too ill to leave Milan, and she was pleased to have participated in the conference if only through him, she told him. But she would have written the speech differently. He should have acknowledged the role socialist women had played in 'raising the moral and intellectual level' of socialist politics, as well as promoting legislation for their own rights. 'The best advice you could have given women of all classes,' she said, 'would have been to tell them to carry on their struggle inside . . . Parliament.' This would 'have been a sign of recognition of the influence women can exert on politics, even where they are still excluded from the political arena.'[89]

Kuliscioff had escaped the destruction of her ideals in Russia; but for the rest of her life she had to exert her brilliant mind only through her partnership with an active politician, in a country where women's rights were still not granted, and where she and other socialist women were unappreciated. Despite her willingness and pride, as she often wrote, to act with and through Turati, the note of bitterness is frequently audible.

Turati had written to Kuliscioff, at the beginning of 1913, that it was her 'Slav tendency' to take political developments too seriously.[90] What troubled her most was the threat of war, which she saw looming over Europe from the end of 1912, and in the Italian context, the rise of Mussolini, who had capitalised on the Socialist Party's opposition to the Libyan war in order to win the editorship of the Socialist Party daily, *Avanti!*, which he was to use as a power base.[91]

The Italian Socialist Party was the only one in Europe to oppose the war as a matter of policy. Kuliscioff saw, far more clearly than Turati, however, that sooner or later political realities would force Italy into the war, and that continuing Socialist opposition would compromise the party's future 'for twenty years'.[92] Although Turati realised that Mussolini's 'simple-minded' theories appealed to the Italian masses, he underestimated the Fascist leader's cunning and was unable, as Kuliscioff suggested, to rally the party's leadership against him and eject him from *Avanti!*. Mussolini was thus able to outflank the reformist leadership and gain immense personal popularity as a former pacifist who now, with d'Annunzio and other Irredentists, espoused the cause of war under a nationalist banner. At the end of 1915 Mussolini was expelled from the Socialist Party; but the party came out of the war divided and unable to use its considerable electoral strength, boosted by a new system of proportional representation, to take power—as Kuliscioff continually urged between 1906 and 1920.

Though Kuliscioff was so heartened by the March 1917 revolution in Russia, she agreed with Turati that an uprising in Italy in mid-war, in imitation of the Bolsheviks, would be disastrous.[93] But during the post-war period, when what the country needed was a politician able to carry out substantial reforms without destroying the existing political framework, she regarded Turati's hesitations as disastrous. Both had opposed violence during the left-wing factory seizures of 1919.[94] But whereas Turati limited his activities to proposals for legislation, Kuliscioff saw that it was only as a political leader that he could appeal to the imagination of the dispossessed and the unemployed both in industrial and in rural regions.[95] In February 1920, she wrote: 'You [the reformist Socialists] want reform, but you don't want to make the effort to grasp power now the time is ripe. The maximalists [in the party] want communism and a proletarian dictatorship, but can't even exploit local uprisings to carry that out. Both of you share the same lack of will power, for which you blame one another. Programmes alone are not enough; they must be put into practice.'[96]

Once again, her revolutionary past came to the fore when she urged him 'to form a programme of action in Parliament and as an agitator, dealing with leading questions amid the working class.'[97] But Turati believed this to be impossible. He knew that she compared Italian Socialists unfavourably with the achievements of the revolutionaries in Russia, but he could see all too many reasons not to act as she advised. If the Socialists took power alone, he said, the middle classes, alarmed by the frequent strikes and uprisings, would suspect the Socialists of 'bolshevism', the masses would demand the moon, the West would try to starve out Italy as it had Russia, and 'our people are incapable of the sacrifices the Russians have made.'[98]

In her letters, Kuliscioff tempered her criticism with compassion. But as Turati delivered speeches in Parliament in favour of reforms no one was to introduce, Kuliscioff was not taken in, as he was himself, by the warm reception he received.[99] Unable to seize power, which he said would result in 'shooting or being shot', Turati found it temperamentally easier to end his days in politics as leader of a liberal opposition both to Fascism and to the extremists in his own party.[100] The one thing Turati or Kuliscioff only contemplated at the last moment was the total overthrow of Italy's fragile liberal democracy. Even as late as the spring of 1923, with Mussolini the head of a government with a socialist opposition, Kuliscioff still believed that the fate of the Fascists would be that of the revolutionary socialists in Italy: they would be 'pacified' and 'absorbed' into the liberal–clerical centre.[101]

Perhaps as a woman whose youth had been spent fleeing or being expelled from one country after another, even Kuliscioff was reluctant to see that her refuge had become a trap. But by July 1923, when Fascist thugs staged demonstrations in

Parliament itself, Kuliscioff was reading the signs correctly. 'Today I too believe that we must pack our bags and go into exile.'[102]

Within a few months the 'second wave' of Fascism that Kuliscioff had been expecting took place. There were indications that Mussolini and the Italian trade unions were coming to terms; Mussolini's proposals for an automatic two-thirds majority for the party with the largest number of votes threatened Italy's democracy. Turati, in despair, planned to step down in favour of Matteotti as head of the reformist Socialists.

The murder of Matteotti in June 1924 and the succeeding crisis in the Italian Parliament probably provided the opposition with its last chance to save Italian democracy from Fascism. Kuliscioff believed, rightly, that the opposition should stand its ground. But, as Italian historians have noted, she was in Milan and thus far from the realities of everyday politics. Turati, on the other hand, was convinced that Mussolini had gone too far and that he could 'smell the death' of the Fascist government. He anticipated that the powerful industrialists would abandon Mussolini, and was led astray by the sudden popular acclaim for himself, the result of revulsion at the Matteotti murder.

Kuliscioff did not believe the regime would fall of its own accord. 'The opposition bloc must not allow the favourable moment to pass,' she wrote urgently to Turati on June 19, 1924.[103] In the event, the opposition, including the Socialists, acted in precisely the opposite manner. They walked out of Parliament in protest, leaving Mussolini in control of the field, and while they pondered whether or not to return, Mussolini acted, taking over the War Ministry, suppressing the opposition press, and sending the Socialists into hiding.

But Anna Kuliscioff did not have to pack her bags again. She died, at the age of seventy, in December 1925, the year of Mussolini's triumph, leaving Turati a virtual recluse in their home in the Galleria Emmanuele in Milan. A year later he was smuggled out of Italy and became the symbol of Italian liberalism in exile, dying in Paris in 1932 at the age of seventy-five. His heir was Andreina Gavazzi Costa, the daughter of Costa and Anna Kuliscioff.

Kuliscioff's funeral, in Milan, was one of the last flickers of light of Italian socialism before the dark night she had predicted. Large crowds of intellectuals and working people followed her cortège to the cemetery; on the way, they were attacked by Fascist thugs. The Italian historian Salvatorelli wrote of this outrage: 'Fascism committed far worse crimes; but perhaps none marked, more inexorably, its irrevocable immorality.'[104]

EIGHT CANDLES ON THE CHRISTMAS TREE

Rosa Luxemburg as Woman and Jew

Rosa Luxemburg, the most famous and intellectually the most gifted of all the Jewish women revolutionaries, is a difficult and controversial historical figure to define. Was she primarily one of the greatest of Marxist theoreticians, the most brilliant of polemicists?[1] A pacifist whose main contribution to revolutionary theory was that the threat of war could consolidate internationalism?[2] An economist who was the first to apply Marxist theory to imperialist capitalism?[3] The first 'European', or essentially a moralist whose impact on practical politics was minimal?[4] The debate continues.

Rosa Luxemburg was a Polish Jewess inspired by the revolutionary ferment of the last years of the nineteenth century, during which she came to maturity. Most of her political life was lived in Germany during the heyday of pre-First World War socialism. She was therefore in a unique position to read lessons on social democracy to the Bolsheviks, as in her famous controversy with Lenin, and she brought revolutionary passion from her Polish–Russian background to the far more sedate, bureaucratic socialist parties of Europe, as in her battle against European reformists of Marxism and in her acid critiques of the German Social Democrat (socialist) Party. Intensive biographical research has revealed that for twenty years she was the main link between Western European socialism and Eastern European revolutionary groups, often in so conspiratorial a fashion that neither side knew of all her activities. Finally, as one of the leaders of the Spartacist (German communist) uprising in Berlin in January 1919, which was brutally suppressed by the military with the connivance of the Social Democrats, she was murdered, together with her colleague Karl Liebknecht. This martyrdom made her posthumously into a heroine of German socialist history, though Luxemburg disliked Germany (while admiring its culture) and was, during her lifetime, one of the most hated figures in German politics and in Social Democratic circles—hated as a woman, a Jew, and an 'Easterner'.

But the difficulty of distinguishing the mythical from the real historical figure of Luxemburg pales besides the problem of assessing what one historian has called the 'elusive Jewish component' in her character and political creed.[5] Luxemburg herself was unequivocally hostile to all attempts to link her beliefs to her Jewishness, just as she was determined, from the very outset of her political career, to avoid involvement with the 'women's' section of the Social Democrat Party.[6] At least two Jewish historians have attempted to see in her political philosophy a 'universalist' message which has its origins in the Judaism of her rabbinical ancestors (some fifteen generations of them on her mother's side);[7] and one feminist historian has even attempted retroactively to make Luxemburg into a militant feminist before her time.[8] These arguments are all too easily demolished. To suggest, therefore, that Luxemburg's identity as a Jewish woman had direct implications for her political beliefs is to court ridicule.

None the less, it is worth examining very closely both what she herself wrote about herself and her family and about the Jews in general, and to compare this with what is now known about her origins and her oblique and difficult relationship with the Jewish socialist party (the Bund). Rosa Luxemburg's passionate and total hostility to nationalism, in particular that of Poland, and her fanatical idealisation of the working class, have puzzled all those who have studied her writings because there is a strongly irrational element in both. There is some evidence that both these aspects of her political thinking were influenced by her Jewish background, in particular her early life and even her sex, though this link has nothing to do with the supposed 'universalism' of her rabbinical ancestors, and is even further from any general feminist theory.

Rosa Luxemburg was born in the small Russian-Polish town of Zamosa in 1870 and spent the first nineteen years of her life with her Jewish family, mainly in Warsaw. She was sent by her parents to a Catholic high school, and biographical memoirs written shortly after her death by her German colleagues give the impression of an assimilated and cultivated family with very few ties to Judaism.[9] This was indeed the impression that Luxemburg herself tried to convey, and only recently has it been demonstrated, with the publication of a series of family letters, that it was far from the truth.[10] To begin with two tiny but early points in her independent life: Rosa Luxemburg changed her name, on leaving Poland, from Luksenburg to Luxemburg, which sounded somewhat less Jewish and more 'international'—thereby eliciting the ironic question from her sister Anna: 'Is that how you spell your name now?'[11] Elzbieta Ettinger, the biographer who has concentrated almost exclusively on Luxemburg's personal life, has discovered that the story of Luxemburg's being smuggled out of Poland under the straw in a peasant's cart by a friendly priest, who believed she wished to marry her Christian lover—a story repeated by almost every previous biographer—has no basis in fact: she had a valid passport, which she used to leave Poland. The romantic priest story, a literal flight from her Jewishness, as told to one of her earliest biographers and colleagues, appears to have originated with Luxemburg herself.[12] Like so many other Jewish revolutionary women, Luxemburg did contract a fictitious marriage to a Gentile for political purposes—in this case to become a German citizen—but the couple parted on the steps of the registry office in Basle. The important liaison of her life was with Leo Jogiches, a Jew whose origins were similar to her own, whose revolutionary political career began in Jewish socialist politics, and who never seems to have had the problems with his Jewishness that were so evident in Luxemburg's case. Their intimacy owed much to these similar origins, just as her failure to bend him to her will in their life together is strikingly reminiscent of many post-Enlightenment families. Other Jewish male *maskilim* had similar problems in their relations with dominating, maternal women.

Even the first collections of her own published letters indicate a more traditional Jewish family background than Luxemburg cared to admit to. In the famous letters written from prison during the First World War to Karl Liebknecht's wife, Sonya, there is the much-quoted reminiscence of childhood: 'My mother, who besides Schiller, thought the Bible to be the source of divine wisdom, stubbornly believed that King Solomon understood the language of birds. At the time, I grinned at this motherly naïvety with all the superiority of my fourteen years and a modern scientific education.' Now, Luxemburg writes, watching birds from her prison, she understands the wisdom of her mother's teaching.[13]

Lina Luksenburg, Rosa's mother, was brought up in a rabbi's family. Her brother was also a rabbi, and women in such families customarily read Yiddish (a language Rosa affected to despise, though she obviously knew it fluently). The reference to Solomon is to be found in *T'sena Ure'ena*. Biographers and analysts of Luxemburg's thought, occupied with more important matters, have failed to note that in the Bible there is no mention of Solomon's 'understanding the language of birds'. This is a piece of pure rabbinical folklore, which first appears in the Midrash Tanhuma (fourth-century) commentary and is repeated in the rabbinical exegesis of the Song of Songs.[14]

There are very few references to Lina Luksenburg in the letters; in one instance Rosa wakes at night calling for her mother in what was obviously a rare moment of weakness (mentioned in a letter to Jogiches, with whom she was much franker on family matters).[15] Most of her references to her parents, in letters to others, are wry or ironical, a mode which veils her intense ambivalence about the family and about ties that she was never able entirely to break but clearly resented. Yet to sentimentalise her relationship with her family is totally to misjudge her character.

The references to Lina in the family letters during her final illness and death sketch a portrait of a Jewish woman totally dedicated to her family, self-sacrificing, pious, and home-bound[16]—the model of the post-Enlightenment Jewish woman as the Jewish *maskil* wanted to see her, and the antithesis of Rosa Luxemburg's own model of the socialist woman, as much a product of fantasy as her idea of the proletarian male.[17] Rosa Luxemburg's own personal life was cultured middle class: her ideal was a home and children, a few congenial friends, the occasional visit to the opera, and a regular summer holiday in a rural setting. Her cultural preferences were similarly conventional; she admired in a painting by Le Brun 'the whole sophistication of pre-revolutionary France, a truly aristocratic culture with a light touch of decay' (she was excited by the noble German pedigree of Hans Diefenbach, the young admirer of her last years). She paid much attention to the furnishings of the various lodgings in which she lived, and to her dress; and while she prided herself on her strong sexuality ('I have enough temperament to set a prairie on fire'), she was just as decorous in public as her female ancestors. She confessed that 'female eroticism in public has always been embarrassing to me', mischievously quoting the famous retort of the Social Democrat Auer to the revisionist Bernstein in a very different context: 'One doesn't say things like that, one does them.'[18]

The family letters recently published indicate that Luxemburg's family was by no means remote from other Jews or from tradition. The Luksenburg children had Hebrew as well as Polish first names (though we do not know Rosa's). The letters refer, without explanation or a gloss for Rosa, to the family saying *kaddish*, the prayer for the dead recited regularly in the synagogue during the weeks following Lina's death, though there is some confusion as to two different prayers—the *kaddish* said only by men, and *el moleh rahamim*, permitted to women as well. These prayers were said, in Rosa's absence, on her behalf as well.[19] She obviously became desperate at the news of Lina's death and in her letters threatened suicide. She was not alone at this time, as her family supposed, but on holiday with Jogiches, who deliberately held up the visit of a friend bringing the news of her mother's death (it is not clear whether he knew the reason for the visit) so that she could finish the article she was writing.[20]

Yet remorse had no effect on her behaviour, as she neither visited her family to comfort them (they thought it was she who needed comfort) and later very grudgingly spent two weeks with her father, after a ten-year separation.[21] He continued to urge family responsibilities and chores on her. She corresponded fitfully. His last letter to her reproaching her for 'complete indifference' to family matters—'An eagle soars so high he loses all sight of the earth below ... I shall not burden you any more with my letters'—makes painful reading.[22]

She was far away in Paris when her father died in Warsaw, some months later, in September 1900. In a letter written during the First World War in a style part sentimental, part ironical, to Hans Diefenbach, she recommends him to spend time with his dying father, lest he regret it later. In this letter, written from Breslau jail, she writes, 'Even if you can't help a sick person, it helps you to be near him. Your presence alone will do the poor man good and if you don't, you'll be angry with yourself for every hour you haven't given him. I was not so fortunate.' At that moment, she goes on, 'I was taking care of mankind's urgent affairs and making the whole world happy', at a congress of the International where she was meeting with 'Jaurès, Millerand, Daszynski, Bebel and God knows who else'.[23] 'Meanwhile the old man couldn't wait any longer, he probably told himself there was no use waiting ... so he died.'[24]

There is a striking similarity between the wording of this letter and that of her famous letter to Mathilde Wurm, a Jewish Social Democrat friend, written a few months earlier, also from prison. 'Why do you come to me with your special Jewish sorrows? I feel just as sorry for the wretched Indian victims in Putamayo, etc. ... I cannot find a special corner in my heart for the ghetto. I feel at home in the entire world wherever there are clouds and birds and human tears.'[25] Here the identification with people far away, her internationalist sympathies, and her feeling 'at home' in the whole world resembles her claim to have been 'making the whole world happy' rather than dealing with the special sorrows of her family.

To Rosa Luxemburg, Jews meant the family, and family obligations; her memories of her early youth; and her contacts with the Bundist Jewish socialists. Although her relations with her brothers and sister were more relaxed than those with her parents, Luxemburg was intensely ambivalent towards her entire family and found their affection for her oppressive; it is hard not to link this with her attitude towards her fellow Jews in general. Ettinger, the only biographer who notes the ambivalence, suggests that it may be connected with her physical disability, a slightly dislocated hip that was misdiagnosed in childhood and caused a permanent limp, which she may have blamed on her family (her elder sister also limped).[26] Her exemplary physical courage was related, as it often is, to impatience with disabilities of all kinds, in herself and others, and she was exceptionally insensitive to Jewish disabilities—in all senses.

Her limp apart, she appears to have had a happy early childhood; her father, who was not well off, bought her the best education available. But her parents' very Jewish anxiety about her marriage prospects must have been particularly galling, since she attempted for years to domesticate Jogiches. She lied to her family consistently about her relationship, pretended to have married him, and forced his co-operation in this charade.[27] In many letters she refers to him as her 'husband', herself as his 'wife'. Despite the fact that she scarcely saw her parents from the time of her departure from Switzerland in 1889, she never severed her ties with the family, deceived them to please them, and tied herself up in knots of guilt about them.[28] The greatest Jewish woman revolutionary never came to terms with the full implication of her rebellion in terms of the Jewish family.

Letters recently published also show that Luxemburg's father Elias tried to get Jogiches, as bridegroom apparent, to contribute to the dowry of his older daughter Anna, for whom he thought he had arranged a marriage through the good offices of the Jewish community. So much for the assimilated Luksenburgs, cut off, as so many biographers have insisted, from other Jews.[29]

There are other indications that Luxemburg knew more about Jewish tradition (via her mother, in all probability) than she wished to admit, though this knowledge was muddled and superficial, in the way it often was for Jewish women. In 1900 (the year in which her father died) she refers to the philosophy of someone she calls Ben Akiba. 'My discussion with Karl [Kautsky] naturally dealt with the general situation in the [Social Democrat] party [opportunism], its future, and the tactics to be pursued ... his [K's] ideas can be summed up in the saying of Ben Akiba: 'Everything has always existed, so there's no point in worrying about it, material progress leads to socialism, so everything will be all right—and so on and so forth.'[30] There is no one in rabbinical tradition called Ben Akiba, only Rabbi Akiva, who was anything but a quietist or an opportunist; he confronted the Romans and refused to abandon his beliefs even under torture. Possibly she (or her mother) had confused him with Ben Sira, the second-century Jewish sage whose great homiletic work is indeed written in the spirit she suggests. As she displays no interest in Jewish history apart from the Bible—while in prison she asked for the French (Catholic) version to be sent her[31]— the reference is probably linked to her mother's repetition of Jewish folklore and rabbinical parables, the kind of traditional Jewish female moralising which the young rebel could only have found irritating.

Two days later Luxemburg was still pondering on 'Ben Akiba'. This time it was in a letter to the Kautskys, making the same point, and she adds, 'I hate this sort of philosophy.'[32] What she really hates, it seems, are her mother's pious reassurances and acceptance of fate, as graphically described in her brother's letters, and Anna's letters, in which they tell her how her mother accepted the torments of terminal cancer with resignation, as 'God's will'.[33] That was certainly not Luxemburg's way.

Perhaps the most revealing letter as regards her half-dormant Jewish family memories is that written to Sonya Liebknecht from Breslau prison, dated December 1917. Luxemburg, who had

Rosa Luxemburg, 1919.

Anna Kuliscioff.

Bertha Pappenheim's passport
photograph.

A 1954 German postage stamp portraying
Bertha Pappenheim. The caption reads:
'Bertha Pappenheim—Helper of Mankind'.

Manya Shochat.

Rose Pesotta, Puerto Rico, 1935.

Rose Pesotta addressing the Montreal garment workers, 1936.

attended a Polish Catholic school of the kind which accepted very few Jews, invariably celebrated Christmas, something Jogiches, who gave fewer signs of having conflicts about his Jewish family, had found absurd (when she sent him a copy of Strauss's *Leben Jesu*, he mockingly sent her a Molière play).[34] Now, in her letters from prison, she refers to *Die Heilige Nacht* rather than the more prosaic *Weinacht Abend* (Christmas Eve), and about the second Christmas she had spent in prison she writes: 'The Christmas tree this year is rather inferior to the one I had last year. I don't know where I'm going to put the eight candles I bought for it.'[35] Eight candles are those a Jewish family needs on the last night of Chanuka, the Maccabean Feast of Lights which generally takes place near the date of Christmas (the Jewish date and its relationship to the Gregorian calendar vary). Luxemburg was obviously unaware of the significance of what she had written.

Luxemburg would not have been the only little Jewish girl to envy her schoolfriends' Christmas tree and to compensate herself for its absence in the family home when she grew up. Given her Catholic schooling, there is nothing unnatural in her use of Christian imagery, as when, describing to Sonya a holiday in Corsica, she notes how the peasants she saw while out on a walk looked like the Holy Family, and Corsica a place where 'the Bible and antiquity were still alive'.[36]

But another reference in the letters to her relations with Christianity is more complex. Writing to Hans Diefenbach again from prison during the First World War, she recommends that he read Hauptmann's novel *Emmanuel Quint*. Here we have an intriguing glimpse of the confused way in which Luxemburg saw herself, her great ego but muddled identity. 'I was caught, among other things, by a problem in reading the book, which I haven't encountered in any other work, but which I feel so deeply in my own life. That is, the tragedy of a man who preaches to the masses and who finds that every word of his becomes "*vergrobert*" (coarse) and "*erstarrt*" (stiff) as it leaves his mouth, becoming a caricature in the brains of listeners. And the preacher is bound to this caricature, surrounded by his disciples, by their ugly shrieks, as they shout, "Show us the miracle. You have taught us. Where is your miracle?"[37] Here Luxemburg sees herself as a preacher (Quint is a Christlike figure, an innocent). In another letter, however, she compares the trials of socialist leadership to those of Moses, another physically flawed leader whose message was at first rejected. The 'miracle' was of course internationalism, and the mob had jeered at her in 1914, when the Second International disintegrated under the nationalist pressures of the World War I.

It is also notable that on the rare occasion when Luxemburg—who was a stickler for getting facts right—refers to Jews with any sympathy, she gets the facts wrong. In her study of the Russian writer Korolenko she remarks that he 'naturally' protested during the Beilis ritual murder trial of 1913; she calls Beilis a 'Kishinev' butcher, confusing this Kiev brick factory official with the notorious Kishinev pogrom, which took place in 1903.[38] She uses the Kishinev pogrom, still confused, as a metaphor for the hysterically chauvinist atmosphere in Germany in early World War I in the famous 'Junius' pamphlet: 'The atmosphere of ritual murder, the Kishinev air that left the policeman at the corner as the only remaining representative of human dignity.'[39] Even more telling is the fact that in an article she wrote, on the one occasion when she referred in passing to the pogrom which she herself experienced as a child of eleven in Warsaw in the year 1881, she again got the date wrong.[40] The pogrom lasted three days, during which time thousands of Jewish homes were damaged and several people killed; the street where the Luksenburg family lived, Zlota Street, was one of those where the mob rampaged. Ettinger, the only biographer to stress the impact of the pogrom, believes that this was the origin of Luxemburg's fear of the mob, which surfaces in a number of her letters.[41]

But the impact of the pogrom, of which Luxemburg never expressed a single personal memory, on her intellectual life may have been more complex. That year, 1881, was the year of the pogroms in Russia, the outburst of anti-Semitic passions which followed the murder of Czar Alexander II. In Poland, most of this news was censored. The authorities tried to give the impression that through the industrialists they were trying to discourage the workers from similar anti-Semitic demonstrations. On the other hand, they collected knives and other potential weapons from Jewish households, suggesting that it was the Jews who were preparing for violence. The Warsaw Jewish community was asked to show restraint by the chief of police, and notices repeating this were posted both in Polish and Hebrew throughout the Jewish quarter of the town (on the edge of which the Luksenburgs lived).[42] Throughout the year, however, there were anti-Semitic incidents, and it is inconceivable that they were not discussed in the Luksenburg household. The previous autumn, Rosa had entered the first class of the state school, the Russian gymnasium for girls, where there was a quota—meaning that she had to score particularly high marks to be admitted. Students were separated for religious instruction according to their creed. As an adult, Luxemburg was to tell the ten-year-old daughter of a political colleague: 'At your age I didn't play with dolls, I made the revolution.'[43] Though this was typical Luxemburg irony, she was certainly acutely aware at that age of her situation as a member of the hated minority.

The pogrom began on Christmas Day, 1881, the sequel to a panic in a Warsaw church during which many were suffocated. Provocateurs took advantage of the situation to suggest that Jews were responsible. Gangs of thugs burst into shops, synagogues, and Jewish homes; one man who attempted to defend a synagogue was killed. Most Jews barricaded themselves in their houses. For three days troops who were called in arrested Jews but did nothing to stop the hooligans, who were criminals and thieves and prostitutes known to the police. The chief of police went on holiday on Christmas Eve and returned after the pogrom was over.[44]

The Polish press played down the pogrom and attributed it to provocateurs and foreigners; joint Christian and Jewish groups from the clergy and intellectuals volunteered to help the Jewish victims. The most detailed account of the pogrom is to be found in the diplomatic reports of Baron Brenner, the Austro-Hungarian consul in Warsaw, who confirmed that the pogrom appeared to be carefully organised, that the police had stood by, and that the perpetrators were known criminal elements in the city. He added, however, that 'the workers, but for a small minority, did not play any part in the disturbances, though the authorities gave unlimited license to the crowds for two whole days, thus encouraging the success of the pogroms.'[45]

Moreover, the press, having deplored the violence, insisted that only assimilation by the Jews could prevent such events from recurring; for many Polish intellectuals, the pogrom was an expression of Jewish–Christian rivalry to be solved only by the Jews abandoning their traditions and assimilating. Warsaw had a large traditional and orthodox Jewish community, mostly Yiddish-speaking artisans, whose families lived as they had done since the Middle Ages. Jews like Elias Luksenburg, the *maskil* whose Judaism was attenuated in the style of the Jews of Western Europe, were in a minority.

As Ettinger points out, it is inconceivable that the pogrom and its aftermath did not leave a lasting and decisive mark on the highly intelligent and sensitive girl who lived through it. It is at least worth considering whether it may not have had two further results beyond the obvious fear of mobs that threatened Jewish lives and destroyed their homes. First, there is the identity of the pogromists and the exoneration of the working class: Luxemburg's idealisation of the 'workers' (both men and women) may well have dated from this event. Second, the suggestion that, by assimilating, the Jews could prevent the repetition of their persecution may have affected the girl's thinking. This belief, after all, underlies much of Luxemburg's critique of Jewish politics. (At a more trivial level, it may even be connected with her demonstrative celebration of Christmas, a form of protective colouring?) Among Jewish revolutionaries, Luxemburg was the most critical of her own people, descending, at times, to merciless abuse of other Jews (most freely in Yiddish, and in her letters to Jogiches).[46] For this as well as her apparent indifference to German anti-Semitism and—for instance—the Dreyfus case, she has been bitterly criticised by many Jewish historians. But the pogrom, at such an impressionable age, may have influenced not only her attitude towards Jews in general but other aspects of her political philosophy.

Luxemburg's internationalist beliefs, or rather her belief in the solidarity of the international working class—a belief that was to be so cruelly shaken at the beginning of the First World War—may thus well have had their origins in this early experience of 'special Jewish sorrows'. That her apparent lack of sympathy for Jewish problems was not a necessary corollary of inter-nationalism is clear if one compares Luxemburg and the Russian Marxist Martov, the Menshevik leader who shared many of her internationalist ideals yet retained his interest in and compassion for his fellow Jews.[47] It has been suggested that the reason for the difference was the political environment in which the two functioned, and the fact that the Russian intelligentsia was far more sympathetic to the issue of Jewish rights than the Poles. Even where Polish socialists condemned anti-Semitism, they refused to see the Jews as a separate group (as they had at the time of the pogrom) and insisted on 'cultural assimilation'.[48] The radical faction headed by Luxemburg and Jogiches, the SDKPiL or Polish Social Democrats, believed that the Jewish workers organised in the framework of the Jewish socialist party, the Bund, would gradually lose their separate identity and merge with the Russo-Polish working class which would triumph in the revolution. Thus for a while, the two radical leaders held meetings with Bundist leaders, though Luxemburg's attitude towards them cooled notably after the Bund formed its own political organisation in 1897.[49]

Luxemburg's uncompromising stand against all nationalisms, including that of Poland, was shared by virtually none of the leading socialists of her time. Her hostility to Jewish nationalism was two-faceted. She rejected Zionism as just another form of European nationalism. But her attitude towards the future of the Jewish minority in the Russian Empire was more complex. Like Lenin, she argued that the Jews of Russia were not a nation. But she did not share his view that there were two Jewish cultures: one progressive and revolutionary, the other traditional and conservative. She denied the Jews a national identity on cultural grounds, and this denial coloured both her relations with the Bund and her writings on the national question.

The Jewish socialist Bund might have been a natural ally for the SDKPiL, the tiny Polish Social Democrat Party that was competing for votes with the main Polish Socialist Party, as Jogiches appeared to believe in the early years of the century. Luxemburg herself deplored the Polish socialists' anti-Semitism and intolerance towards the Bund, which she put down to their 'social patriotism'—a form of nationalism that would not tolerate the principle of self-determination for other groups.[50] But this did not mean that she would herself agree to even a tactical alliance with the Bund. During her student days in Zurich, she had kept away from other political exiles—whether from caution or diffidence is uncertain. But in Jogiches' company, she certainly knew Bundist theory and its leadership. Her hostility to the Bund had complex origins, as is clear from an incident just before the 1905 revolution.

The SDKPiL were now for the first time not a tiny band but growing. The Polish Socialist Party (PPS) by then was only slightly larger, and the Bund as large as both, with about 35,000 members.[51] The three parties vied for the Polish radical workers' allegiance. The Bund, which was constituted of many Jewish groups within the Pale of Settlement, particularly in the north-west provinces, and of which the Polish Jews were only one element, had refused to support the idea of Polish independence at its party congresses in 1899 and 1900. In the summer of 1905 Jogiches—now estranged personally though not politically from Luxemburg—tried to negotiate an alliance between the Social Democrats and the Bund. This evoked a particularly violent reaction from Luxemburg. 'I do not agree to any alliance with the Jews. Of course fight together but march separately. This rabble needs us, we don't need them.'[52] The fact that the 'rabble' were among the first to use the strike weapon (which Luxemburg regarded as vital to the class struggle) in the Russian Empire, and that in 1905 the members of the Bund outnumbered the Russian Social Democrats three to one, is disregarded.[53]

Was this just, as has been argued, because Luxemburg was perfectly consistent in her opposition to all forms of nationalism, the Jewish version included? It is not possible here to analyse all the contradictions in Luxemburg's arguments against nationalism. Clearly, she underestimated its force, particularly among the working class she idolised, and she was bitterly disillusioned as a result. But to look more closely at her arguments in so far as they relate to the Jews is to see what George Lichtheim has called her 'intellectual perversity' at its most naked.

From 1895 Luxemburg wrote frequently on 'the national question'.[54] Two main assumptions are present in her arguments. The first is that national and socialist aspirations are incompatible, as the first is always bourgeois. Here, where Poland was concerned, she differed from Marx (on whose theories she always tried to improve), who saw Polish nationalism as a possible source of rebellion against Czarist autocracy. She continued to hold this extreme view during the revisionist debate in Germany and elsewhere. The second assumption concerned the concept of national self-determination in the context of the Russian Empire. All parts of this huge entity had to move into social revolution together; national separation was retrograde. The proletarian (that is, industrial) revolution was the basis of revolt (that Poland was economically ahead of Russia meant for her that it could spearhead the revolution).[55] The much-discussed principle of self-determination, in her view, was a tactical and intellectual concession to the bourgeoisie; she believed that Polish socialists should content themselves, like other peoples under domination, with a joint proletarian revolution with the workers of Russia.

The biographer who first linked this view with Luxemburg's origins as a member of an underprivileged minority is Paul Froelich, a Jew and an ex-communist who knew Luxemburg personally.[56] Clearly the commitment to internationalism by Jews (and there were many so committed besides Luxemburg, though perhaps none more eloquent or forceful) had much to do with the fact that modern nationalism, in Eastern Europe, was generally hostile to Jews. But Luxemburg's arguments are more complex than this suggests.

In her articles Luxemburg comes back repeatedly to the question of how and why nationalism must be identified with the bourgeoisie. Here she specifically deals with the question of culture and its role in nationalism. She examines the Russian Social Democrats' programme of 1905 (she is writing post-revolution) and argues that point 9, 'that all nationalities forming the state have the right to self-determination', is striking because it has nothing 'specifically connected with socialism nor with the politics of the working class'.[57] Equality before the Law (without distinction of sex, religion, race, or nationality), linguistic rights, and local self-government were not (in her words) sufficient in the eyes of the authors of the programme to solve the national question. She does not argue that such differences are not important, or do not exist; indeed, she quotes Kautsky (at this stage her ally) on how, in Austria-Hungary, the different nationalities should be federated. Political programmes, she writes, have to provide practical and feasible solutions to social and political problems, as everyday guidelines, to lead the working class and to separate revolutionary from bourgeois and petit-bourgeois politics—this, while taking the different cultural characteristics of separate countries into consideration. But where the Jews are concerned, she first defines them as a separate national group like the rest and then tries to argue that their particular characteristics as a nation are culturally invalid.

After discussing Polish nationality in the western provinces (those where the Poles were seventy per cent of the population, and 'the decisive element in the sociocultural development of the country',[58] she goes on to the Jews. Whereas the Poles' demographic strength entitled them to self-government, the same, she said, was not true of the Jews. (Fifty-eight per cent of the urban population of Russia in 1897, the year of the founding of the Bund, was Jewish. Most of this population lived in the Pale of Settlement.)

Her argument should be quoted in full:

Jewish national autonomy, not in the sense of freedom of school, religion, place of residence, and equal civic rights, but in the sense of the political self-government of the Jewish population with its own legislation and administration, as it were parallel to the autonomy of the Congress Kingdom, is an entirely utopian idea. Strangely, this conviction [that of the Bund, in other words] prevails also in the camp of extreme Polish nationalists, e.g. in the so-called 'Revolutionary Faction' of the PPS [the main Polish Socialist Party], where it is based on the simple circumstance that the Jewish nationality does not possess a 'territory of its own' within the Russian Empire. But national autonomy conceived in accordance with that group's own standpoint—i.e. as the sum of freedoms and rights to self-determination of a certain group of people linked by language, tradition and psychology—is in itself a construction lying beyond historical conditions, fluttering in mid air, and therefore one that can be easily conceived, as it were, 'in the air', i.e. without any definite territory. On the other hand, an autonomy that grows historically together with local self-government, on the basis of modern bourgeois-democratic development, is actually as inseparable from a certain territory as the bourgeois state itself, and cannot be imagined without it to the same extent as 'non-territorial' communal or urban self-government. It is true that the Jewish population was completely under the influence of modern capitalistic development in the Russian empire and shares the economic, political and spiritual interests of particular groups in that society. But on the one hand, these interests were never territorially separated so as to become specifically Jewish capitalist interests; rather, they are common interests of the Jewish and other people in the country at large. On the other hand, this capitalist development does not lead to a separation of bourgeois Jewish culture, but acts in an exactly opposite direction, leading to the assimilation of the Jewish, bourgeois, urban intelligentsia, to their absorption by the Polish or Russian people. If the national distinctness of the Lithuanians or Bylorussians is based on the backward peasant people, the Jewish national distinctness in Russia and Poland is based on the socially backward petite bourgeoisie, on small production, small trade, small-town life, and—let us add parenthetically—on the close relation of the nationality in question to religion. In view of the above, the national distinctness of the Jews, which is supposed to be the basis of non-territorial Jewish autonomy, is manifested not in the form of metropolitan bourgeois culture, but in the form of small-town lack of culture. Obviously any efforts toward 'developing Jewish culture' at the initiative of a handful of Yiddish publicists and translators cannot be taken seriously. The only manifestation of genuine modern culture in the Russian framework is the Social Democratic movement of the Russian proletariat which, because of its nature, can best replace the historical lack of bourgeois national culture of the Jews, since it is itself a phase of genuinely international and proletarian culture.[59]

Before trying to analyse this astounding farrago, it is worth noting that Luxemburg particularly hated Jews as translators. In a sense, she was herself a translator, of one political tradition to another, living between worlds. Many Jewish *maskilim* and intellectuals did not like reading Russian or German works in Yiddish, though the Bundists 'went to the people' in that vernacular. But the contempt for Jewish translators is, as far as I know, particular to Luxemburg: note her letter to Mathilde Jacob written in 1915. 'I read your copy of *Anna Karenina*. The translation is hair-raising. I doubt whether there are better. Whatever translations I have read from Russian literature were always sheer trash, because these translations are usually the work of Russian starvelings of the Mosaic faith who, as such, imagine that they know German but who are completely uneducated in the literary sense.'[60] She criticised the great Yiddish writer I. L. Peretz for having 'the effrontery to insult Heine' by using German words. In fact, one of the first translators of Marx from German into Russian (four chapters of the second translation of *Das Kapital*, in 1896) was a Russian Jewess, Evgenia (Zhenia) Hurvich, later a member of the Bund. Jewish women translators played a very important part in the diffusion of Marxist culture in Eastern Europe.[61]

With regard to the Jewish question and nationalism, Luxemburg makes several shrewd points. One is that extreme nationalists concur with those (not the Bund itself) who think the Jews should have a separate territory. The right-wing Poles did not disapprove of Zionism; nor, later, did the Nazis. It was a liberal, not a right-wing, belief that the Jews should be able to enjoy equal rights in all countries with regard to education, religion, civic rights, and so on, without a separate territory. Western Jewry based all its policies on this assumption. What Luxemburg completely overlooks is that in Eastern Europe this belief simply did not apply. The entire history of the Pale of Settlement in the nineteenth century, of repressive laws, of quotas (to which she belonged in her Catholic school in Warsaw), and of anti-Semitism in general made it impossible. She does not do as anti-Semites do and blame Jewish separatism, the very fact of a different religion and a different history, for anti-Semitism: she is too much of a liberal for that. Instead, she argues that Jewish history, religion, and so on is not really a valid culture. She admits that the Jews see themselves as linked by a common language, tradition, and psychology, but she insists that such people are 'floating in the air'. The choice of phrase is significant: in Yiddish, *luftmenschen*, or people without an occupation, is disparaging in a very Jewish way.

As a good Marxist, believing that society had to progress through bourgeois capitalism to proletarian socialism, Luxemburg argues that if the Jews were really a separate nation they would have an attachment to a particular territory. This puts her in awkward company, so, she continues, the Jews are part of Russia, in particular the intelligentsia which has abandoned its Jewishness and joined the Russian bourgeois class. This, she knew, was a tiny minority of Jews like herself. The others were not part of the proletariat but the petite bourgeoisie, the class which, as Peter Nettl has remarked, was for her the 'intellectual rubbish bin of history'.[62] To this rubbish bin she consigned the mass of her fellow Jews.

Luxemburg was not the only Jewish revolutionary to note that Jewish society did not fit the classic Marxist pattern, or to express hostility to their beliefs. Chaim Arlosoroff, who like Luxemburg had benefited from both Eastern and Western European culture, observed that the Jews were neither, in the main, bourgeois nor industrial workers but impoverished artisans.[63] Yet his main point was that the mass of Jews were poor, and that Jewish employers and workers were not very far apart in terms of income, privilege, or class. But Trotsky expressed his feelings about Jewish society in similar terms to Luxemburg, as did Alexander Helphand (Parvus), one of Luxemburg's ideological mentors.

At the time these revolutionaries were writing, the main difference between the Jewish and the non-Jewish industrial proletariat in the Russian Empire was that the first was more literate, better organised, and more active in labour disputes. Jews hostile to their own traditions would not acknowledge this, and Luxemburg argued that Jewish culture (of which, unlike Trotsky, she was largely ignorant) did not exist. Luxemburg dismissed Yiddish, spoken by the vast majority of the Jews of Poland, a language with a long history and literature of its own. Her conclusion, or 'solution' to the Jewish problem, therefore, was that the Jews adopt the culture of the Russian proletariat.

Luxemburg's hatred for the Bund now becomes much clearer. Here was a socialist movement at that time also dedicated to internationalism. Yet because of a strong Jewish identity, which she could perceive but not share, because she had only experienced it tangentially, it was politically independent.[64] Luxemburg, by contrast, preferred to repeat Marx's definition of the Jews as a sickness inherent in bourgeois society, 'the spirit of huckstering and swindle which appears in every society where exploitation reigns'.[65]

Marx, in London, at the end of his life, subscribed to a paper which could have told him about Jewish socialism in Eastern Europe.[66] But in the main his life was lived very remote from Jews and their affairs. Luxemburg, however, had had numerous direct contacts with the Bund in the 1890s and knew how similar their aims were to her own, but also that they refused to deny their Jewishness. She was caught in the dilemma common to so many other emancipated Jews, unable to deny their Jewishness entirely for reasons of moral integrity (she was persistently identified and attacked as a Jew) but equally unable to ally themselves to specifically Jewish organisations and aims for fear of being driven back into the society from which they had escaped. This dilemma was intensified by the fact that she was a woman.

In the first of the five articles on the national question, Luxemburg states: 'If we recognise the right of each nation to self-determination, it is obviously a logical conclusion that we must condemn every attempt to place one nation over another, or for one nation to force upon another any form of national existence. However, the duty of the class party of the proletariat to protest and resist national oppression arises not from any special "right of nations", just as, for example, its striving for the social and political equality of sexes does not at all result from any special 'rights of women' which the movement of bourgeois emancipationists refers to.'[67]

There is nothing particularly remarkable about the fact that Luxemburg makes one of her very rare references to the subjection of women in the context of the oppression of nations. This had been a commonplace of Marxist rhetoric since Bebel published his famous *Woman and Socialism*; in fact, it was one of the ways in which countless socialist leaders managed to pay lip service to women's rights without doing anything about furthering their suffrage. What is striking is that there is an implied link here between Jews and women as two groups subjected to 'social inequality and social domination'. As Luxemburg was keenly aware of the problems of being both Jewish and a woman, but determinedly refrained from making a point of either to avoid confinement to a sexual or racial ghetto, the parallel is camouflaged.

The 'bourgeois emancipationists' to whom Luxemburg is referring were those middle-class women's movements in Europe whose goal was first and foremost women's suffrage—known to German revolutionary socialist women as the *Frauenrechlerinnen* (women's righters). These movements were violently opposed by revolutionary women on the grounds that they made women's political and juridical rights, under the existing social order, their goal, while detaching them from other basic social issues. The subject divided socialist women themselves, with those who supported the reformists, or 'revisionists', believing that an accommodation could be reached across class lines, while revolutionaries like Luxemburg did not.[68]

It was only in 1915 that Luxemburg finally overcame her dislike of middle-class feminists sufficiently to agree to attend the Women's Peace Conference in The Hague—though she was prevented from doing so because she was arrested and imprisoned for her antiwar stance a few days earlier.

This did not mean that women like Kuliscioff and Luxemburg did not support those who urged the socialist parties of Europe to back suffrage for women; it did mean, however, that they saw the issue as part of the class struggle and that it was working women's rights which preoccupied them.[69] It has been seen that Kuliscioff was disturbed by the possibility that a selective franchise might be extended to privileged women alone, and urged the Italian socialists to follow the lead of the German Social Democrat Party, in which women workers played an important— if still supportive—role at election time. But while Kuliscioff had a keen sense, probably from her work as a doctor among the working class of Milan, not only of women's suffering but of the practical and psychological obstacles to their participation in politics, Luxemburg—knowing very little of the working class in general and working women in particular—idealised proletarian women just as much as she did proletarian men.

Luxemburg wrote very little about women, but a brief article in her friend Clara Zetkin's women's socialist journal, *Die Gleichheit*, on proletarian women is significant:

For the propertied bourgeois woman, her house is the world. For the proletarian woman, the whole world is her house ... Bourgeois women's rights advocates want to acquire political rights in order to participate in political life. The proletarian women can only follow the path of the workers' struggles, the opportunity to win a foothold of real power through primarily legal statutes.

In the beginning was the deed for every social ascent ... The ruling society refuses them [women] access to the temple of its legislation ... but to them the Social Democrat Party opened wide its gates.[70] [The biblical wording towards the end is intriguing.]

In fact, the history of women's socialism in Germany shows that Luxemburg was entirely wrong in her generalisation about those women who were members of the Social Democrat Party at this time. Most were the wives of SPD men (unmarried working women were notably uninterested in political action). Their interests were overwhelmingly domestic—that is, the issues which preoccupied them were those which affected their families directly. And the SPD in general was concerned with the solidity and integrity of the family as part of its political organisation, and not in 'widening the horizons' of its female members.[71] Clara Zetkin herself noted these very points.[72]

Although Luxemburg subordinated the question of women's rights to the general revolutionary struggle, like most leading socialist women at this time, it would not be true to say that she was indifferent to the issue. She was responsible for introducing Point Ten into the SDKPiL's programme at the beginning of the century, which specifically demanded the abolition of all laws discriminating against, and full political freedom and equality for, women.[73] On at least two occasions, Luxemburg spoke out for women's suffrage: the first was when, in March 1902, the Belgian socialist leader Emile Vandervelde came to an agreement with the Belgian Liberals for parliamentary action in favour of equal suffrage, but for men only, and on the expectation that the Catholic Clerical Party would try to disrupt this alliance by proposing votes for women. Like Kuliscioff, Luxemburg was indignant that male socialists assumed that women were less 'ready' for the vote than men. But her arguments were rather different. It was not only, she wrote in an angry commentary on the Belgian socialists' decision, that proletarian women had much to contribute to 'the agitational work of Social Democracy'. 'In its political and spiritual life, too, a strong fresh wind would blow in with the political emancipation of women, which would dissipate the stagnant air of the present Philistine family life, that so unmistakeably colours our party members, workers and leaders alike.'[74] (The socialist–liberal alliance failed, in the event, to convince the Belgian Parliament on the suffrage issue, and also did not back up its arguments with the strike weapon, thence earning Luxemburg's further scorn.)

Luxemburg again made her point about the proletarian women in a speech she made to the Second SPD women's rally in Stuttgart in 1912. Here she rephrased the accepted Marxist view, from Bebel onward, that economic independence was essential to women's emancipation and their participation in the class struggle. 'Female education and intelligence,' she said, 'have become necessary for the economic mechanism itself. The narrow, secluded woman of the patriarchal "family circle" answers the needs of industry and commerce as little as those of politics.' The SPD and the unions, she maintained, had 'lifted the women of the proletariat out of their stuffy, narrow existence, out of the miserable and petty mindlessness of household managing' ... and socialism had brought about 'the mental rebirth of the mass of proletarian women'.[75] Hence the argument that they now deserved socialist support for the suffrage.

The view of women in the context of the discussion of nations struggling for autonomy, and the idealisation of working-class women, are linked to the idea that it is essential to free women altogether of their traditional role in the home, on the assumption that this was what working women wanted, or rather ought to want.

There is a striking parallel between what Luxemburg wrote about Jews and what she now wrote about women—not about the bourgeois women, whom she dismisses in a contemptuous aside, but about those very women whom she idealised as part of the proletariat. Jews are all petit bourgeois with a 'small-town' mentality and limited horizons. Women in the home similarly are bound to the 'petty mindlessness' of home life. First, it is necessary to change the mental habits of both groups. Second, neither have a valid culture; both are to become part of a greater, more important movement for the general good of the revolution.

It is thus worth examining the parallels in Luxemburg's own life between the limitations she overcame as a Jew and those she overcame as a woman.

Luxemburg arrived in Berlin as an obscure economics graduate from Zurich in 1899, at the age of nineteen, and, offering as her qualifications her expert knowledge of Polish economics and the Polish political scene—as well as her opposition to Polish nationalism, which suited the Germans very well—she was soon sent off to agitate among the Silesian miners. In terms of Russian, or rather Russo-Polish, politics she was not unique as a woman agitator and activist: she befriended and feuded with many others.[76]

Luxemburg never intended to be a mere agitator, however, and referred to her Polish campaign for the German SPD as her term 'in the desert'. What she was interested in doing was improving on Marxist theory and influencing the main policies of the German SPD. As she was very critical both of socialist bureaucracy and of the German trade unions, she rapidly made herself extremely unpopular—all the more so because she was a woman in German socialist politics, where, unlike the situation in Russia, they played only a supportive role. In both countries, moreover, she was viciously attacked as a Jew; and even within the German SPD, where vulgar anti-Semitism was taboo, she was abused in private conclaves by many of her colleagues.

Luxemburg's way of dealing with both these problems was to turn her back on them and—almost always—to refuse to be drawn. Moreover, she resented attempts made on her behalf to defend her. When she was attacked as a Jewess at the time of the Morocco crisis in 1911, and a colleague, Konrad Heinisch, came to her help openly, she sent him a blistering letter: 'Since 1898, I have been unceasingly vilified personally and most viciously, especially in the south [of Germany, where anti-Semitism was most pronounced] without ever responding with a single word or sentence. Silent contempt is my reaction, prompted—aside from personal pride—by a purely political consideration: all these personal insults are simply manoeuvres to direct attention from the political issue.'[77]

This was not only Luxemburg's stand when she was attacked as a woman and a Jewess; it also governed her silence on persecution of the Jews in general. Only where anti-Semitism could be shown to obstruct socialist interests would she confront it directly—as in the Dreyfus case, where (as Dreyfus belonged to a class she despised) she dealt with the subject only in so far as, in her words, it exposed the old enemy of the working classes—militarism. She writes not a word about the persecution of the man on account of his race.[78]

On the one occasion on which she reacted to anti-Semitic slurs against her in Poland, in the Polish socialist press, her argument was that these slanders, which she termed a 'literary pogrom', were aimed, in essence, against socialism. She reserved her criticism for the 'progressive' or liberal Polish press rather than for the Polish socialists who had accused her, and her party, of trying to Russify Poland, together with the Bund.[79]

All this does not argue 'Jewish self-hatred', as has been maintained. To deal with these insults in the widest intellectual framework—even if inconsistently—was the only way that she could deal with them at all. This, after all, had been the way in which Jews had dealt with anti-Semitism since the days of Moses Mendelssohn, in the belief that anti-Semitism was simply a rational error, or, as she put it, 'the common banner of political backwardness and cultural barbarism' which would be corrected when the Enlightenment was complete, or when society reached its revolutionary apotheosis.[80]

Luxemburg's life as a woman was at least as problematic as her life as a Jew. Her complex relationship with Jogiches was very far from the socialist (or feminist) ideal; it was he who financed her life for years, often criticising the way she spent his money, while refusing, most of the time, to live with her, and—since her domestic idyll was impossible for him, given his essentially solitary character—denying her the child she badly wanted. For years he was the referee and judge of her political writings, whose approval she consistently sought. In her mature years, she tried unsuccessfully to dominate and domesticate him. This led directly to the breach between them.

Unlike Kuliscioff and other Jewish women revolutionaries, Luxemburg was very careful to preserve an appearance of bourgeois 'respectability', agreeing to Jogiches' condition of absolute secrecy about their liaison; the same applied to her later affairs. This may well have reflected her Jewish family upbringing as well as her vulnerability as a public figure. Since she did not preserve his letters as he did hers, it is impossible to assess the character of Jogiches, the arch-revolutionary, the male *maskil*, of whom there are very contrary accounts. But he was certainly the only man to elicit her total commitment, to the point of subordinating her personality to his: 'Now I am I, since I am free of Leo,' she wrote when after fifteen years their intimacy ended. Certainly her subsequent sexual relationships, first with the young Kostia Zetkin and later with Paul Levy, as well as her literary dalliance with Hans Diefenbach, never rivalled the intensity of her liaison with Jogiches. Her fundamental problem with men was that she tended intellectually to overshadow everyone around her. She believed that only Jogiches' obstinate determination not to yield to her (what she called his 'inability to love') prevented them from constituting the perfect emotional and intellectual match, an ideal very similar to that of Kuliscioff, who was more fortunate in every sense.

It is possible that the murder of Rosa Luxemburg had a greater impact on her image in history than the ideas she espoused in her lifetime. Together with the murder of Liebknecht, it deprived the radical Left in Germany, and perhaps in Europe as a whole, of its intellectual leadership; it also discredited the Social Democrats who connived at it. It earned Luxemburg mythical status. The question is, however, why she did not choose to flee Berlin when she saw the revolution was doomed, and live to fight another day.

The simplest answer is that she would not abdicate her influence precisely at the moment when she expected the masses to rise, at the war's end, and rebel against their bourgeois leaders; and she was encouraged when mass strikes and working-class uprisings began all over Germany in early November 1918. There was also her joint responsibility with Liebknecht, whose impetuosity had triumphed. Yet it soon became evident that the SPD's leaders, now the rulers of Germany, would tolerate no Soviet-style revolution, and the army signed a new oath of loyalty to Germany's new government. By January 8, 1919 she was already advising a tactical retreat for the Communists, of which the Spartacist League under Liebknecht and Luxemburg was one faction. As the uprising collapsed, Jogiches and Luxemburg together forced Liebknecht to resign from the Revolutionary Commission—which meant removing the Communists completely from the other disaffected SPD elements in the revolt. Other revolutionary leaders, in similar circumstances, fled into exile and waited for a more auspicious period in which to take power. Luxemburg was already disillusioned with the international proletariat, which had split along nationalist lines during the war. Why then did she court almost certain death by remaining in Berlin?

All her life, Luxemburg had had a horror of the mob; this was, perhaps, the reverse side of her idealisation of the abstract working class she never came to know. She had made great efforts, from the outset of her political career, to overcome this fear: by standing on platforms above the crowds, winning their applause; and of course by participating in the 1905 revolution, in Warsaw, where her efforts were soon cut short by arrest and imprisonment. Her fear, eerily foreshadowing her violent end, was graphically described in a letter written to Luise Kautsky in 1917: 'Do you know what thought obsesses and frightens me? I imagine that again I must enter an overcrowded gigantic hall, the glaring lights, the ear-splitting noise, the mass of people pushing against me ... and I feel an urge to suddenly run away! I have a horror of crowds.'[81] This was a fear which it was essential for her to combat, as a political personality who overcame the obstacles of her race, her sex, and her physical disability by her ability to argue, her dazzling skill in dialectic, and her determination to best her opponents—something which had been a challenge since her schooldays. At this stage, she could no longer afford to doubt the German proletariat's capacity to 'learn from history', despite all the evidence—clearer daily—that it was fragmented, disorientated, and incapable of following her leadership.

There is also a chilling quotation from Luxemburg's letters which has a disturbing echo of the women revolutionaries, and the Jews among them, in the People's Will and the Combat Unit of the Social Revolutionaries in Russia who committed suicide more than three decades earlier. To Sonya Liebknecht she wrote, in February 1917: 'I hope to die at my post, in a street fight or in prison.'[82] This is surprising, since Luxemburg had always shared, with the Warsaw positivists who were her earliest intellectual influence, the attitude that romantic self-sacrifice was absurd nonsense and that a prudent retreat in order to function more effectively was more useful—especially for the brains of the movement—than death on the barricades.

In a letter to Adolf Geck, an SPD colleague who had lost his son in the war, Luxemburg foretold the circumstances of her own death 'perhaps by a bullet of the counter revolution'. There is no need, however, to attribute clairvoyant powers to her, and she certainly underestimated the hostility towards her among her former SPD colleagues.[83] When Luxemburg was taken under arrest, on the night of January 15, 1919, to the military headquarters of the right-wing Frei Corps, at the Hotel Eden, she was expecting to be imprisoned for yet another spell; she took with her a small suitcase and a copy of Goethe's *Faust* as reading matter.

Nevertheless, Luxemburg's letter to Geck, which speaks of the death of a son in war as a sacrifice, is a strange one for the greatest of pacifists. Her final taunting words to the government which claimed to have restored 'order' in Berlin were an open challenge to her murderers.[84] Was it simply impossible for her to be faced with the evidence that the 'proletariat', idealised since childhood, was not behind her? Or did the woman who had rejected or suppressed all the associations of her Jewish childhood and youth and struggled hopelessly with their conflicting demands on her as daughter and woman ultimately seek, if in a very different context, the personal 'sacrifice' expected of the Jewish woman, implicit in Jewish tradition?

4

THE DOUBLE REBELLION

Esther Frumkin and the Women of the Bund

S oon after the Bolshevik revolution of October 1917, a campaign was launched against the Jewish religious establishment
in the Soviet Union. At first it was mainly a war of words, the
communist press in Yiddish thundering against Jewish cleri-
calism. Later, synagogues were picketed and noisy demonstrations
were held outside synagogues and study houses on the Day of
Atonement; administrative measures were taken to close down
the *kehillot* (councils), synagogues, seminaries, and even the
elementary schools, the *chadarim*. The larger synagogues and
Batei Midrash, houses of study, were turned into communist
cultural and recreational centres.[1] The driving force behind this
campaign was the Jewish Section (*Evsektsia*) of the political
education department of the Communist Party, staffed entirely
by Jewish communists.[2] One of its most notable propagandists
was a woman, Malka Frumkin, better known by her revolutionary
pseudonym Esther.[3]

Soviet law forbade the teaching of religion, but in practice the
battle against the religious establishments in the Soviet Union
during the first decade of communist rule waxed and waned,
influenced by factors such as relations with the West and the
policy of the Communist Party towards the peasants. Orthodox
Jews resisted the communist attacks stoutly, and many Jewish
schools and seminaries went underground. The final phase of

persecution, the arrest and punishment of rabbis and religious teachers, was the work of the secret police[4] (in this organisation, too, there were many Jewish leaders and officials). But the Jewish Section had served the Communists' purpose of attacking Judaism without exposing the Bolsheviks to the accusation of anti-Semitism. It was a tragic irony that the woman who was so prominent in the campaign against orthodox Jewry was deeply committed to the preservation of Jewish identity and culture under communism—but waged her battle against the rabbis with a fervour her contemporaries noted but were unable to explain.

In 1923, during the second and militant phase of the anti-religious campaign, Frumkin published a brochure entitled *Down with the Rabbis*.[5] The title, not her own, was taken from placards carried by Jewish communist youth when demonstrating in Jewish townships and quarters of the Russian cities: 'Down with the Rabbis and the Priests.'[6] It was an axiom of the Jewish Section that the Jews could serve as examples of anticlerical fervour to their Christian counterparts, and Frumkin herself continued to argue, correctly if dangerously, that the Jewish socialists had a revolutionary pedigree longer than that of the communists, even if they were 'latecomers' to the Bolshevik revolution.[7] By this stage, in 1926, Frumkin had twenty years' experience behind her as a teacher and political journalist in the ranks of the Jewish social democratic party, the Bund; yet she had also played a leading part in the dissolution of that party and its merger with the Bolsheviks, who until then had enjoyed little support from the Jewish population of the Pale. The theme she now stressed, in her work as Commissar for Political Education and later as a university teacher, was that it was possible to create a new, secular Jewish culture based on the Yiddish language and the restructuring of Russian Jews into one proletarian class. Both these ideas had been current in Bundist circles from early in the movement's history; but the form they assumed in Esther Frumkin's thinking—tortuous, often paradoxical, but always fervent—was entirely her own.

Frumkin had achieved leadership status in the Bund, and her loyalties were first and foremost with her own people. But the

October Revolution destroyed the Bund, and Frumkin, however reluctantly, joined the ranks of the Bolsheviks. No woman was more admired or more hated by Jews under the first phase of Soviet rule; no woman in Eastern Europe achieved such stature in Jewish politics. Frumkin's physical fate was, like that of her fellows in the Jewish Section, to be purged from the Communist Party under Stalin and to spend her last three years in a forced labour camp. Where the Jews were concerned, her scarcely less tragic fate was to be expunged from the commemorative histories of the Bund and to be remembered by historians chiefly in the context of the work of the Jewish Section.[8] Yet few Jewish revolutionaries had attempted more ardently, or with more intellectual virtuosity, to reconcile her pride in her Jewish origins and her wide Jewish culture with her belief in the aims of the revolution.

In no field of Jewish politics, even among the Zionists, were Jewish women to achieve the importance they enjoyed in the Bund. At successive Bund conferences they were prominent both among the intelligentsia and the working-class rank and file; they made up a third of the Bund membership at the height of its influence among the Jewish public; and they were active both in organisational and teaching roles—though, with the exception of Frumkin, not as theoreticians—throughout the brief lifetime of the movement, from 1897 to 1921.[9] When the authorities arrested most of the male leadership in 1898, women stepped in and held the movement together. Women's participation in the Bund not only marked their first appearance in Jewish political life; it also recognised their new roles as educators and as wage-earners in Jewish cultural and economic life, both of which involved them from the outset in the class struggle in the Jewish community of the Pale of Settlement.

The Bundist women are the best documented of all groups of radical Jewish women. There were of course many also attracted to both the Menshevik and the Bolshevik parties. A number of remarkable women figured in the leadership of the Menshevik social democratic party which was subsequently eradicated by

Lenin. Most notable of these was **Eva Broido**, born in 1876, a member of the Menshevik Central Committee and Secretary General of the Menshevik Party during the February revolution of 1917.

Broido's father is described in her memoirs as an 'unworldly Talmudic scholar' incapable of supporting the family. Her mother ran the family timber business and farm single-handed, in the Lithuanian province where Broido was born. Eva attended the local *cheder* with boys, who treated her as an intruder. Fluent in Yiddish, Hebrew, and Russian, she later taught herself German, from which she translated several Marxist classics circulated secretly among the revolutionaries—among them Bebel's *Woman and Socialism*, which greatly inspired her.

Unlike the populists, Broido, who had been raised in the heart of the countryside, had no romantic notions about the peasantry and sought fellow socialists among the Jewish urban intelligentsia. At fifteen she was already working in a chemist's shop in town and studying pharmacology. Mismatched while still an adolescent, she eventually left her two children with her mother and joined other Jewish rebels in St Petersburg, where she met the Menshevik Mark Broido. The couple were married while in prison for their political activities. Repeatedly imprisoned and exiled to Siberia, Eva along with her husband and children left Russia after Lenin seized power. She returned alone to Russia during the Stalinist period, in 1927, on a mission for the Mensheviks in exile, was arrested after six months of journeying, and, when she could not be broken during the preparation for the Menshevik 'show trials' in 1931, was exiled to Tashkent and Siberia. She was not heard of after 1937.[10]

The women in the Jewish intelligentsia which founded the Bund were similar in some ways to those early revolutionary Jewish women who had joined populist and other revolutionary fractions in the 1870s and 1880s. Their grandfathers were often Talmudic scholars, their grandmothers breadwinners: fathers were usually merchants, *maskilim* who combined some Jewish learning with secular culture.[11] Most, however, came not from cities like

Moscow and St Petersburg, where the Jews were a small and restricted élite, but from the great Jewish centres in the Pale of Settlement, from Lithuania, Latvia, and White Russia. These daughters of the bourgeoisie recruited and educated a much larger group of women: the workers in the Jewish urban working class. The Jewish workers, towards the end of the nineteenth century, were craftsmen and apprentices, salesmen, factory workers, porters, and domestics, and they made up fifteen per cent of the five million Jews in the Russian Empire; even during the Bolshevik period they constituted about one quarter of the Jewish population. While from the earliest revolutionary period non-Jewish Russian women who helped found the co-operative '*artels*' also taught working-class women at 'educational Sundays', the origins of this relationship were quite different.[12]

The women in the Bundist rank and file were members of that Jewish working class whose roots had been in the craft industries for centuries. The earliest phase of Jewish labour activity began in the guilds, the *khevres*, where dissatisfaction with the employers often took the form of protest in the synagogue—for Jews a social as well as a religious meeting place and a traditional place for demonstrations, where they might block the access to the Scrolls of the Law to those who refused them better pay. But the guilds were conservative, their members orthodox, and either excluded women from active membership or relegated them to auxiliary groups dealing with women only, as in the burial societies or the female barbers' guild in Grodno. On occasion, women may have formed their own rival organisations; there is record of a guild of women tailors in Mogilev in the first half of the century.[13]

A later phase of labour organisation, also originating in artisan groups, though not in direct descent from the *khevres*, was the emergence of the *kasses*, mutual help funds accumulated by workers during periods of unemployment (or later, strikes). These developed into embryo trade unions.[14] Here, too, the older men objected to women's participation, both for economic and for social, traditional reasons, and in those tailoring establishments where women worked as assistants, relations between the sexes were bad.[15] But with the influx of so many Jews from rural areas after the restrictive 1882 May Laws, thousands of young women began working in the workshops and small factories which were set up in the cities in the second half of the century: unmarried girls of poor families who were forced to seek work outside the home, and were drawn into the sphere of workers' activism from the very outset of Jewish socialist politics. The first stage of women's organisation was, again, to evolve a separate body; the women's tailors *kasse* in Vilna celebrated its tenth anniversary in 1899.[16] Eventually the women, too, were organised as contributors to, and beneficiaries of, the *kasses*, and it became clear that there was to be no sexual division in a movement which took its ideology from the far more emancipated society of Western Europe.

By the 1880s the conditions under which an entire working population of women functioned were in themselves reason for revolt. There were hundreds of unmarried Jewish women employed in the hosiery factories in Vilna, and a labour force consisting mainly of women and children worked long hours— sometimes seventeen or eighteen hours a day—in the cigarette and match factories of the north-west Pale, where many developed lung diseases. By the end of this decade, young girls became particularly good recruits to groups in Minsk and Vilna trying to organise strikes for better working conditions and health care facilities. One of the first labour leaders was a woman in Kovno known only as 'Liza the Tailor'.[17] In the Minsk sugar refineries (one of the few industries in which Jewish manufacturers were prominent), Jewish girls were working a twenty-hour day at the turn of the century.[18]

The first stage of Jewish socialism in the Pale was the educational work by the intelligentsia, those middle-class Jews who had acquired a higher education. They set out to introduce selected members of the working class organised in 'circles'— which in effect became revolutionary cells—to a programme of basic studies, in the hope that this cadre might become politically active in the Jewish 'street'. These educational schemes attracted, as teachers, those Jewish girls of merchant families who had studied in the special courses now open to women in Russian universities, or who had at least attended the Russian state gymnasium or secondary school for girls. The Jewish middle-class women of the Bund had no counterpart in non-Jewish circles in their fervour to recruit working girls to the revolutionary struggle.[19] They gathered around them those working girls who were hungry for knowledge, but they had little understanding at first of the dire poverty in which the girls lived. Pati Srednitskaya, later the wife of Arkady Kremer, one of the founders of the Bund, discovered that the girl who came to the door of her house selling sauerkraut was eager to study, but she was taken aback when the girl's mother demanded payment for the time her daughter was wasting when she could have been earning her living. She only consented to her daughter's studies when Srednitskaya convinced her that it would improve the girl's marriage prospects.[20]

The workers' circles organised by the intelligentsia from the 1880s taught not only basic subjects like Russian language, mathematics, and geography but also Darwinism and Marxism. Eventually, if the students succeeded, they were given copies of the classic pamphlets of Russian socialism and radicalism.[21] Obviously this demanded a degree of literacy in those selected for instruction, at a time when the spoken language of a large majority of the Jewish proletariat was Yiddish; a persistent minority of the men and an even greater number of women were illiterate in Russian, and less than a tenth of Jews studied in Russian schools.[22] Although some of the girl workers were from Russian-speaking middle-class families who had been impoverished after the May Laws, many others had little knowledge of the language. There was at this time a growing tendency among the more ambitious workers to study Russian on their own; but what undoubtedly made the middle-class women good teachers was that many of them knew Yiddish, a language in which, towards the end of the nineteenth century, an increasing number of Jewish women were literate. It was easier to read Yiddish, which is spelled phonetically in Hebrew script, than Hebrew, which is written without vowels; and there was by now an entire women's literature made up not only of the medieval tracts and *T'sena Ure'ena* but a flow of romantic novels translated from German, which were very popular among Eastern European women at this time. The first task of the women teachers was to encourage the girls literate in Yiddish to learn to read and write in Russian.

The working girls eagerly seized on the socialist tracts they were given, though they had to hide this subversive literature from their parents, who were afraid of all illegal activity and even more afraid of their daughters' association with young men in the circles after working hours. Esther Frumkin, in a retrospective article, described her early circle teaching among the Jewish women factory workers in Minsk thus:

> I see them now, crate makers ... soap workers, sugar workers ... pale, thin, red eyed beaten, terribly tired. They would gather late in the evening. We would sit until one in the morning in a stuffy room, with only a little gas lamp burning. Often, little children would be sleeping in the same room and the woman of the house would walk around listening for the police. The girls would listen to the leader's talk and would ask questions, completely forgetting the dangers, forgetting that it would take three quarters of an hour to get home, wrapped in the cold torn remnant of a coat and through deep snow ... With what rapt attention they listened to the talks on cultural history, on surplus value, commodity, wages, life in other lands.

Recent research suggests that these Jewish women workers were far more interested in study than their Russian counterparts, and it is difficult not to link this with their attempt to rival the culture of their menfolk.[23]

But not only was it a far cry from *T'sena Ure'ena* to the *Communist Manifesto*; the pupils of the circles had difficulty applying Marxist theory to the community in which they lived. Martov, the social democrat and Menshevik leader who was at this time teaching circles in Vilna, writing of his work with one of the women workers' groups, recalled that the Marxist definition of the bourgeoisie, powerful but lacking in spiritual belief, did not correspond in the least to the women workers' knowledge of the orthodox, hard-working, and well-educated merchants or master craftsmen who were their employers. 'They could not see this petit bourgeois class as one which was powerful, dominated society, controlled the people, and what appeared in the Manifesto appeared to them to belong to some imaginary country.'[24] Martov, who was to become a Menshevik, not a Bundist, leader, none the less realised as early as 1895 the need to 'fit our propaganda and agitation to the masses . . . to give it a more Jewish character'.[25] Thus many of the Russian Jewish intellectuals, who had abandoned the language of their fathers, now turned back to Yiddish as a political instrument, and a flourishing Yiddish political press emerged, and with it the Jewish woman journalist, a new figure in Jewish society. *Kol Ha'Mevaser*, the Yiddish supplement of the Hebrew weekly *Ha'Melitz*, published in the 1880s, was the first newspaper to appear in Yiddish, and it had women correspondents.

A major breakthrough in the Jewish socialist movement, and perhaps for the Social Democrats in Russia as a whole, began in the early 1890s, when the leadership decided to move from the cultivation of an educated cadre of worker pupils to agitation among the masses—the recruitment of a Jewish proletariat. This led to the widespread use of the strike as a revolutionary weapon, pioneered by Jewish workers. One of the first signs of this change was an illegal celebration of May Day by Jewish workers in 1892 in the woods outside Vilna, at which four speeches were delivered, two of them by women. It has been observed that 'the very participation of the women workers, and even more significantly, the fact that they delivered speeches, is a proof of the importance of the women workers during the first days of the [Jewish socialist] movement, on a scale unknown in the Russian workers movement and even in the more developed Polish movement.' According to contemporary witnesses, the women workers formed one half of the workers' circles, and perhaps even a majority. The texts of the speeches were smuggled abroad to Switzerland

and published in 1894 by Leo Jogiches, in the SDKPiL party journal which he and Rosa Luxemburg edited.[26]

Thus, not only did Jewish women's political activity break with Jewish social tradition; it also set a precedent for revolutionary activity among women, at the formative stage of socialism—a double rebellion.

The women speakers at this historic meeting in 1892 were both seamstresses—one of the more respected and better-paid crafts. Seamstresses were apparently the largest group among those attending the circles.[27] Immediately clear, in both speeches, is the influence of Marxism and international socialism, and a class consciousness which transcends Jewish allegiances. The first speaker, **Fanya Reznik**, began by saying that this, the first May Day celebration by Jewish workers, was 'unlike the other holidays we celebrate', which were 'holidays for the rich, who are not interested in whether their poorer brothers celebrate or not'. In fact, traditional Jewish society involved the provision of festival fare, by the wealthier members of the community, for the poor; but this, of course, smacked of charity, not egalitarianism.

Deploring the situation of the Russian workers compared with those in the West, Reznik condemned the duty of military service, 'which serves to protect the employer class against their enemies'; it was well known that the poorer members of the Jewish community bore a greater burden of military service than the merchant class. Her main appeal was for the spread of the *kasses*, the mutual help funds, which would give the workers the courage to strike even at the risk of their jobs.

After arguing for a twelve-hour day, Reznik suggested that the time saved should be used for study, 'in order to dispel the darkness of our present environment'. The Enlightenment had now reached Jewish workers, men and women alike.

The other speaker, **Yelena Gelfand**, explicitly referred to women's participation in the demonstration as equals, here indicating that where Jewish socialist women were concerned, they were in the mainstream of Marxist revolutionary tradition. 'The woman question is not a separate issue, but part of the great socialist question.' Economic independence of the man in the family, said Gelfand, was not sufficient. Working women, exploited by their employers, had fallen victim to capitalism, whereas the lower salary they were paid had undermined men's economic security; this though the working woman 'is not inferior to men in her working ability or intellect'. Women's interests were not separate from those of the whole proletariat, and they would only achieve real freedom in a socialist society.[28]

Reznik and Gelfand were socialists working within the Jewish community. But there were other Jewish women who inspired non-Jewish working women to participate in illegal union activity. Ten years after the 1892 meeting, several Jewish knitters who had come from the Pale of Settlement to St Petersburg inspired an exceptional group of stocking knitters to form a union of machine knitters. Although four of these eleven migrants founded the union, the first executive committee was all male. But in 1903 a Bund veteran, **Elena Isakovna Gasul**, joined the committee. This union's aim was not only to unionise but to break down sexual segregation; however, it was soon incorporated into a larger textile union.[29]

By the time of the founding of the Bund in 1897 in Vilna, the Jewish workers had modified their internationalism to accommodate a movement with a Jewish ideology. In the two-year battle to decide Bundist policy, which was to end with the victory of those advocating a widely based Jewish proletariat and an end to the élite of the circles, it is recorded that women in particular backed those in the leadership who thought that education should precede revolution and who accused the intelligentsia of betraying the working class.[30] This may have been because the main role of middle-class women in the leadership was as teachers, while working women saw no way to escape their exploitation other than by education.

It was often those women workers who had graduated from the circles who were most active as organisers and agitators. At the first clandestine meeting of the Bund leadership, two of the seven delegates were women, both workers. These were **Maria Zhaludskaia**, a seamstress, and **Rosa Greenblat**, whose main contribution to the debate was that the Bund should publish basic philosophical studies like Engels and Feuerbach, rather than propagandist material.[31]

But however strong the desire to teach and be taught among the women—something which may well have emerged from the general educational deprivation of women in a traditional Jewish society that highly valued education among men—what was most remarkable was the organisational energy of the Jewish working woman. **Sara Fuks**, a leading Bundist who committed suicide at the time of the Bolshevik revolution, after being accused of counter-revolutionary activities, had written a little earlier that the new leadership in Jewish society had arisen from the workers themselves, and not from the bourgeois intelligentsia. This happened rarely in non-Jewish women's worker society, drawn from the Russian peasantry. A striking exception was the Brus'nev organisation, led by two women of peasant origin, Karelina and Boldyreva; it was crushed by the police in 1892.[32]

There are many examples of Jewish women Bundists of working-class origin: Maria Zhaludskaia, for example, had wanted to study to become a pharmacist or midwife while working, but within months as Martov's pupil she decided to renounce her educational plans for socialism and joined a tailors' trade union. She was described by a contemporary as 'intelligent, a belligerent person with a tough character, difficult to get along with, with the coarse face of a village peasant and a hoarse voice, but with a warm personality'.[33] Like many working-class Jewish women (and very unlike the gently nurtured revolutionaries in Zurich who had found public speaking so onerous), she thought nothing of jumping on a tree stump in an illegal gathering in the forests and rousing the crowds with her oratory.[34] When the Vilna Bundists decided to organise cells in other cities in the Russian Empire, she was sent to Warsaw and, after the arrest of the original Bundist leadership, played a leading role with her husband, Taras Katz, in the reorganisation of the Bund. She was twice arrested and sent to Siberia but the details of her later life and death, as in so many of these women's biographies, are unclear. One version has it that she retired from political life in

1908. Another, that she disappeared in the first purges of the Stalinist era, twenty years later.[35]

Maria Zhaludskaia's fellow organiser, at the second Bundist conference in 1898, was **Zivia Hurvich**. The conference was attended by four women out of the thirteen participants, at a time when the original, mainly middle-class leaders had been arrested. Hurvich was the daughter of a tavernkeeper and a glovemaker. She too was active as an agitator and helped organise an underground printing press in Lodz and workers' cells in a number of Russian cities. Repeatedly arrested and exiled, like so many Bundist women, she continued to defy the Czarist police by returning to her illegal work. She was last heard of when she joined the Menshevik internationalists during the 1917 revolution.[36]

Anna Heller, one of the middle-class Bundist women leaders, and one of the few to leave at least a partial memoir of her work, asks, in an article written much later, in 1942, why so many women took part in the dangerous illegal work: among the activists, she mentions in particular Sara Fuks and **Esther Riskind**. When speaking on a platform in a labour market in Bialystok, Riskind was accidentally killed by a police bullet aimed at an anarchist bomb thrower. The daughter of a Hasidic family, she had run away from home, like a number of other Jewish revolutionary women, on the eve of an arranged marriage. Heller maintains that Riskind 'carried her Hasidic (pietist, mystical) fervour into the socialist movement'.[37]

Anna Heller, herself one of the most notable women in the movement, suggests that the dominant reason for women's courage was the readiness for self-sacrifice.[38] But her own memoir, which covers only a part of her political life, suggests other motives. One was something common to Jews and Christians alike in the wealthier middle class: a feeling of guilt towards the peasantry. In the case of the Bundists, social awareness gradually extended to their own underprivileged working class. Heller was brought up in the Grodno district of Russian Poland in a family of estate administrators, one of the most common occupations for better-off Jews, who acted as tax collectors and administrators for absentee landlords. Like Emma Goldman, who was roughly her contemporary, Heller was the daily witness of the peasants' poverty and suffering. Later, she taught in the circles in Vilna.

Heller resented the fact that her brothers received a higher education while she was expected to marry. Influenced by the heroine of Chernyshevsky's novel *What Is To Be Done?* she decided to acquire a trade as seamstress, midwife, or dentist; against some parental opposition, she finally chose the last and became a young recruit to the Bundist founding generation in Vilna. Revolutionaries in hiding would often arrive at her clinic, their faces swathed in bandages to evade the police.[39]

Heller and her husband were arrested in 1902 and sent to Siberia, where they were among those political prisoners who took part in the 1904 Siberian revolt, the Romanovke uprising. She helped fortify the building in which the fifty-seven rebels barricaded themselves, obtained food, medicine, and weapons, and improvised a red flag to fly from the building. When, after seventeen days, the rebels—six of whom were women and nine of whom were Bundists—surrendered, the women and men were separated, and the women were told they would be given only prison sentences while the men would be shot. Heller, speaking in the name of all the women, demanded to be judged equally with the men and given equal sentences. All were sentenced to twelve years' hard labour but were released under amnesty during the 1905 revolution. Like most Bundists, Heller was disillusioned by the Bolshevik revolution, but she remained active in educational work and social welfare for the Jewish working class in Vilna. Arrested after the Nazi–Soviet Pact, she died in a Soviet prison in 1941.[40]

Zhenia Hurvich, a Vilna woman intellectual who belonged simultaneously to the Bund and the Russian Social Democrat Party—something which was rare for a Bundist—and had helped translate the second volume of *Das Kapital* into Russian, was saved by this distinction from exile to Siberia but not from dismissal from the Marx Engels Institute during the Stalinist period.[41]

While Jewish women in the traditional community had sacrificed themselves for the family, Bundist women sacrificed their chances of a family life. A life on the road, in prison, or in exile made marriage difficult, childbirth unlikely. Of those who did marry, several, like Srednitskaya, Heller, and Zhaludskaia, had political partnerships with their Bundist husbands, but few are recorded as having children. A notable exception is **Liuba Levinson**, one of the most dashing women in the Bund leadership, wife of a Bund leader, who after many years in the movement, her health already damaged by prison, gave birth to a baby during one of her spells in exile. She took the child to New York to leave in her sister's care, intending to return to revolutionary work in Russia; but, weakened by illness, she collapsed in her bath and drowned.[42]

Most Bundist women who survived bolshevism in Russia died in the Holocaust. The last days in the life of **Pati Srednitskaya**, one of the first women teachers in the circles—who survived her husband, Arkady Kremer, 'father of the Bund', by many years— were spent in the Vilna ghetto when it was overrun by the Nazis. Her first concern was to salvage what she could of a Jewish library destroyed by German soldiers; her last effort was to rally other ex-Bundists around her. An eye-witness account describes how she told these women, as they faced the Nazi firing squad: 'Let us all sing "The Oath" [the Bundist anthem, which has echoes of Jewish tradition], and then we shall not be so afraid.'[43]

It was at the moment when the Bundist policy of educating a worker élite gave way to that of creating a Jewish proletariat, in the mid 1890s, that **Esther Frumkin**, then an intelligent adolescent in a Minsk gymnasium (secondary school), developed an interest in Jewish politics. No less fervent a socialist than Luxemburg, no less a believer in the class struggle, her family background and environment made her concern herself first and foremost with her fellow Jews and to try and reconcile the multiple contradictions, which she saw no less clearly than Luxemburg, between capitalist society as Marx saw it and Jewish society in the Pale of Settlement.

Frumkin was born Malka Lifschitz in 1880 (ten years after

Luxemburg) into a wealthy merchant family in Minsk, where more than half the population of the city was Jewish. Her grandfather was a rabbi, her father well-versed in both Jewish and secular culture. Her parents wanted their three daughters to have a thorough education in both traditions. By the time she went to the Russian gymnasium, Frumkin was fluent in both Yiddish and Hebrew, in which she could read the Bible, and was also familiar with such classics of modern Hebrew literature as *Ahavat Zion* by the first Hebrew modern novelist Avraham Mapu, who wrote of Jewish historical subjects in a style borrowed from French romanticism. In adolescence she was influenced by the Russian novelists and the ideas of the early revolutionaries. She could not ignore the fact that beyond her comfortable middle-class home were the sweatshops, the pedlars, and the still more pathetic hordes of unemployed Jews of Minsk. Here—even to judge from the numbers of those officially applying for Jewish charity at festivals—about a fifth of the Jewish population lived in poverty.[44] The sight of Jewish women standing at the threshold of the homes of wealthy families at holiday times was to Frumkin not the opportunity to distribute charity, the traditional role of Jewish women, but a sign of public humiliation.[45] If Bundist and Menshevik women like Heller and Broido, raised in the countryside, were aware first of the plight of the Russian peasant (though in Broido's case without feeling involved), Frumkin's social consciousness was aroused by that of poor urban Jews.

While still at the gymnasium, Frumkin came under the influence of a student who was later to be the first to carry Bundist ideas to the immigrant Jews in the United States: Avrom Valt Lessin. Like Martov, and unlike the first Bund leadership, Lessin did not believe that classical Marxism could be applied directly to the Jewish class structure in the Russian Empire or that the Bundists could create an exclusively proletarian party. The true distinction in Jewish society, he argued, was not between employer or employee but between the rich minority and the poor majority. The Bundist aim, he thought, should be to unite all the impoverished sections among the Jews to fight for the basic political rights of the whole Jewish people, in a movement which would be not only socialist but also nationalist.[46] Although Frumkin was later to abandon social democracy for bolshevism and to use increasingly tortuous arguments to justify the dictatorship of the proletariat, she was never quite to abandon the claim that the new Jewish proletariat would be a restructured, reborn nation, and not only part of the Soviet working class. There was in this argument something of the romanticism of a Mapu, as well as the pragmatism of a Lessin.

While still an adolescent, Frumkin taught a women's circle in Minsk. At the age of seventeen she went to attend higher pedagogic classes in Petersburg, where she studied philology and Russian literature, as well as teacher training, and became well-versed in Marxist literature.[47] Her knowledge of philology was later to enable her to make a spirited defence of Yiddish not only as an instrument of propaganda but as a modern language with a respectable linguistic pedigree, while her training was to enable her to teach not only in a Minsk vocational school for women tailors but later in life in the communist university for foreign students. She was fluent, eventually, in six languages.[48]

In 1900 Frumkin returned to Minsk and to her family. She was never one of those revolutionaries who turned their backs on family and children, and within a couple of years she married an engineer, a fellow Bundist, and in the following year gave birth to her only child, a daughter. But the marriage was to be tragically short. Boris Frumkin had been imprisoned two years earlier, had contracted tuberculosis in prison, and, despite medical treatment in Switzerland, died the year after his daughter's birth. Thenceforth, and despite successive periods in prison and exile during which her daughter lived with Frumkin's parents, Frumkin kept house for a growing family of children—her little girl, the child of her wet-nurse, and, after the death of Frumkin's sister Gitte, two nieces. As a teacher, and even in her later university work, she was said to take a personal and almost maternal interest in all her students. During the First World War, while exiled in Astrakhan, Frumkin made a second marriage—to Rabbi Wichmann—which lasted only a short time. It was not, a friend commented, 'a marriage of equals'; but she signed herself, subsequently, in private communications, with both her husbands' names. The choice of her pseudonym, Esther, is a parallel to her given name Malka (queen). Tall, with intense dark eyes and an impressive speaking presence, she managed, in her maturity, to dominate political platforms, and was the only woman to play a policy-making role in the Bund leadership. Little more is known about Frumkin's private life, but, according to what she wrote in early articles about the Jewish home and the role of the mother, it is clear that she was far from being antagonistic to Jewish family tradition, and it is not difficult to imagine her, in a different age, as a powerful *rebbitzen*—rabbi's wife.[49]

Frumkin was sufficiently well known to the Czarist police as a subversive to be arrested, for the first time, during the elections to the First State Duma (the lower House of the Russian Parliament) in 1906.[50] The exact cause is unknown, but the background can be reconstructed. After the 1905 revolution, and the Czarist October Manifesto granting a semblance of liberalism to the regime, the socialists emerged cautiously from the underground, as it was now legitimate to carry on trade union activities and openly to publish newspapers.[51] Frumkin, who in her student days had published a number of articles and translations, became a frequent contributor to the Yiddish socialist press, under her pseudonym. Socialist journalists trod a very fine line between acceptable criticism and subversive propaganda, and it was actually in the office of one of the Yiddish papers that she was arrested for the second time, in October 1907.[52] She had already written articles stating openly that the new Czarist reforms were insufficient and that only a socialist revolution would sweep away social injustice, including discrimination against the Jews.[53]

While the established Jewish leadership—the merchants and middle-class professionals—had flocked enthusiastically to organise representatives to the first Duma, the socialist parties, knowing that few of the workers who supported them had the franchise, decided to boycott the elections.[54] In a blistering article on the Jewish election committees, Frumkin described the rabbis, lawyers, and doctors gathered to exchange favours and discuss political horse trading with the Russian and Polish parties as being without a thought for the Jewish working population. She accused them of representing only the wealthy seat-holders in the synagogues, the master artisans in the *khevres*; they talked of democracy, because it was fashionable, she wrote, but the beadles in the synagogues did not even consult the congregants when choosing candidates for election. Yet they had the affrontery to argue that the Bund was a class party which represented only the workers. They promised the Jewish electorate an end to pogroms and military service, but she predicted that they would not fight for their people in the Duma. In fact, there was very little the twelve Jewish representatives in the first Duma (five of them Zionists, who in any case saw no future for the Jews in Russia) could do against powerful anti-Semitic elements like the Union of the Russian People, who produced the notorious forgery, the *Protocols of the Learned Elders of Zion*.[55]

Frumkin frequently attacked the traditional Jewish concept of Klal Yisrael—the alleged solidarity according to which the Jewish community was supposed to function as an integral whole, each Jew protecting and supporting the other. Klal Yisrael was a fiction, she alleged. Apart from the socialists, each artisan and professional group looked after its own. The rich could escape abroad, the lawyers and doctors could find work outside the Pale, and the daughters of the wealthy could study outside Russia. Real solidarity existed only among the socialist workers.[56]

The traditional Jewish leadership, the rabbis and the community leaders, were made up of the most conservative elements in both the old religious élite and the new professional class—neither of which were concerned with revolution. The first sought to retain their ancient privileges and the second to further their careers. Yet because of their manifold disadvantages under Czarism, they were drawn to alliances with the Cadets, the liberal party which sprang up after the 1905 revolution, and the labour, peasant-based Trudoviki Party. These parties were committed to full citizenship for all minorities, but their main constituency was the anti-Semitic peasantry. This earned the Jews who joined them the contempt of the Bund.[57]

Frumkin's thinking, as expressed in her political articles and speeches, gave a totally different turn to traditional concepts like Klal Yisrael. She carried on imaginary dialogues, in her articles, with familiar Jewish figures, rabbis, shopkeepers, artisans, to whom she tried to prove that the interests of the workers were also those of the Jewish people in Russia as a whole—all, that was, but for the tiny minority, the wealthy bourgeoisie. While agreeing that the Bund was part of the international working class, she pointed out, in an article also published in 1906, that the orthodox, independent small artisan, who mistrusted the Bundists—those socialist Jews who observed no commandments and did not believe in the Messiah—would actually profit from the Bund's demands to do away with the military service, particularly prolonged for the poor, to use public funds for slum clearance and other social reforms, and to grant the Jews access to the mining and other industries from which they were at present excluded. The Bund backed cultural autonomy, she reminded them, and the recognition of Yiddish as a national language. But perhaps her strongest argument was that the Bund alone had organised self-defence units against the pogromists, that they had done away with traditional Jewish passivity, the sycophantic stand of the rabbis and the wealthy towards the Czarist rulers and oppressors.[58]

Even at this early stage in her career, Frumkin was already advocating the establishment of Yiddish schools; her concept of a Jewish proletariat, and her argument that Yiddish teaching was the way to inculcate socialist values in Jewish children, were inextricably linked in her political philosophy.[59]

In this she was speaking for many of her Bundist colleagues. In her brochure on the Jewish Folk School, she painted a vivid picture of the Jewish town in the Pale in which no Jew needed a word of any language but Yiddish to lead a full working and cultural life. 'The Jewish worker [in Vilna] spends his whole life in a Yiddish-speaking environment; in the quarter in which he lives, the courtyard of his building, everyone speaks Yiddish: the milkman, the tailor, the shoemaker, the artisans in the workshops. In the national schools [where Russian was the language of instruction] the pupils spoke Yiddish in recess. Jewish businessmen did business in Yiddish. Yiddish was spoken in the Jewish hospital. There was a flourishing Yiddish press and theatre. As the community had grown, so had the use of Yiddish. Charitable institutions, credit facilities, even the emigration bureau used Yiddish as the lingua franca.'[60]

There were, however, no Yiddish schools—a striking exception. Jewish education meant education in Hebrew, in the *chadarim* and *yeshivot* (Talmudic seminaries). Frumkin pounced on this fact and made it her task to urge the case for Yiddish education for the Jewish masses. But here, her political and cultural ambitions were to clash.

For years the intellectuals had referred to Yiddish as the 'jargon', as the language of political propaganda used in order to reach the Jewish 'masses'. However, there was a problem in the choice of Yiddish as the language of political instruction. If the Jewish masses were to become part of the Russian revolutionary movement, it could only be by abandoning their traditional occupations in the *shtetl* and becoming assimilated into the Russian economy. In doing so, they would increasingly need to use the Russian language with their comrades and colleagues and eventually abandon Yiddish, the language which expressed perfectly the way of life of the *shtetl* based as it was on Jewish autonomy and rabbinical law and family custom. (By contrast, Hebrew was the language, at prayer, of those who saw themselves as a spiritual élite among a mass of semi-barbarians.) The probable decline of Yiddish, in this process, was something Frumkin could never bring herself to contemplate; theoretically, she could envisage total assimilation, but she could not accept it. There was a passion, partly that of a professional linguist, in her love of Yiddish; but it was also the core of her political philosophy. This was, in effect, to make 'the women's language' into 'the folk language'—the language of the people.

The use of Yiddish was thus, for Frumkin, the cornerstone of the Bundists' claim to represent the Jews of the Russian Empire. Yiddish was, moreover, almost as important to the identity of the Bund as their Jewishness itself.

The Bund was not against the Jewish faith. The Bundists regarded religious belief as a private matter; but they had rejected all the apparatus of religion, both because they saw much of rabbinical law as archaic and superstitious, but also because the conservatism of the rabbis, and their passivity in political terms, offended them. Bundists were also against the tradition according to which the rabbis and the wealthy merchants represented the Jewish community with the authorities, in the framework of the *kehilloth*, the Jewish community organisations, which even after their autonomy was abolished in 1844 had continued to serve as intermediaries between Czarist authorities and the Jewish communities for such purposes as tax collection and military recruiting. But the one element of traditional Jewish life in Eastern Europe that the Bundists, by the early years of the twentieth century, did not want to change was the use of Yiddish, the vernacular which had survived not only as a Jewish lingua franca but because Hebrew was not to be used for everyday, secular matters.

Initially, it had been hard for those Jewish intellectuals who were half divorced from their background by their education to reach the masses. Some had to relearn Yiddish in order to communicate with them. But once adopted, Yiddish became not only linguistically but politically respectable. The Bund maintained that while the Jewish socialists were part of the international working class, they also represented a potentially autonomous political entity, one with its own history, culture, and society, distinct from the rest of the peoples of the Russian Empire. The intelligentsia debated endlessly the question of how the Jews might claim, save in terms of a shared religion, that the Jews were a separate 'nationality', when they had no territory like the other national elements in the empire.

Yiddish, the Bund could justly maintain (and this was Frumkin's chief theme), was the language of the people, and the Bund's use of Yiddish legitimised its claim to speak for all Jewish workers in the Russian Empire. This made up for the paucity of actual numbers. For even at the height of its influence at the end of the century, the Bund represented only a tiny minority of the five million strong Jewish population in the empire, most of them in the Pale, with some 30,000 members; even in proportion to the Jewish working class, which numbered 400,000, the Bund was a small group. The Zionists, who had the allegiance of the Jewish middle class, had ten times that number of members, though—with their eyes fixed on another country and another time—they were far less active in the Jewish street.[61] But while most Jews spoke Yiddish, Hebrew—the hoped-for lingua franca of the Zionists—was spoken, outside the syna-gogues, only by a minority.

The debate among Jewish intellectuals over the actual status of Yiddish did not become fully politicised until the Yiddish Language conference of 1908 in Czernowitz (Bukovina) during the period of Esther Frumkin's political exile from Russia. This conference was called by literary figures in the international Jewish community in order to give respectability to the language, and recognition to Yiddish studies and the new Yiddish literature in which distinguished writers like I. L. Peretz, Shalom Aleichem, and Mendel Mocher Seforim had already produced master-pieces.[62] It was the Czernowitz conference, which Esther Frumkin attended as the Bundist delegate, which made her internationally famous in Jewish circles and added to her growing reputation as a leading Bundist orator. A critical scholar has observed that by politicising a cultural conference, Frumkin virtually perverted its aims and destroyed any possible consensus between its participants.[63]

Her first challenge to those present was to attempt to change the proposed definition of Yiddish as *a* language of the Jewish people to *the* language of the Jewish people—a proposal which brought her into headlong conflict with the great Yiddish writer I. L. Peretz, who found himself honour-bound to acknowledge the supremacy of Hebrew in Jewish culture.[64] At the third session of the conference, Peretz proposed the formation of a worldwide Yiddish literary and cultural organisation, based on Czernowitz, which would legitimate Yiddish as the national language of the Jews everywhere, establish societies for its promotion, set up libraries, textbooks, and model schools, and encourage publishers, writers, and teachers to disseminate its literature.[65]

The proposal was attacked by the Zionists, whose aim was of course to revive the use of Hebrew as a spoken language, rather than one of prayer and study; and, also by Frumkin, on behalf of the Bund, because she saw Yiddish as the language of the Jewish working class and believed that its promotion on an international scale would weaken the Jews' class consciousness. This stood the conference on its head, and thenceforth the entire debate was coloured by Jewish politics. Despite Peretz's recognition of the cultural treasures of Hebrew, he too defined Yiddish as a language which would serve as a bulwark against assimilation, the language of a Jewish renaissance; the Zionists saw it as the language of exile. But Frumkin continued to define Yiddish as the instrument of an Eastern European Jewish revolution alone, and would not compromise with what she termed 'general Jewish politics'—that is, of the Diaspora as a whole. She opposed, and helped defeat, Peretz's proposal for a central organisation, and when the conference discussed setting up schools and libraries on a worldwide scale, she resigned in protest from the conference.[66]

In 1909, after studying for a while in Vienna, Frumkin returned illegally from Austria-Hungary to Russia, and between this time and the Bolshevik revolution lived underground. She was arrested for the third time in the autumn of 1912, imprisoned for four months and sent into exile to the Arkhangel'sk district of Siberia. All that is known about her wartime activities is that with the Czarist police on her heels, she travelled between Minsk (where her daughter was living with her parents), Romania, and the Astrakhan province of Russia, where she worked in an orphanage and contracted her short-lived second marriage.[67] It was at this time, before she took up her political career, that she wrote a number of articles in Yiddish and in Russian, spelling out in greater detail her ideas on the Yiddish 'folk school' and how it was to contribute to the evolution of a Jewish proletariat.

In Frumkin's writing at this period, there is no visible conflict between her affection for the culture based on religious customs in the home and her passion for socialist reform. Unlike most of the Bundists, she expressed, at this period, no hostility towards religion. Her enemy was, on the contrary, that middle-class intelligentsia which was not only a class enemy but a cultural one: an enemy that was prepared to jettison, with Yiddish, all its Jewish customs and to assimilate into the Russian world. Like Luxemburg, Frumkin identified Judaism with the family and with rituals and traditions centering on the family. But far from rejecting the family, she argued that 'national education was only possible when the family was the nucleus of the nation'.[68]

The Jewish bourgeoisie, Frumkin maintained, had deserted the nation and were reading Yiddish authors in Russian translations. (Luxemburg had objected to the contrary procedure.) She accused the bourgeoisie of celebrating family unity on Sunday rather than on Saturday, the Jewish Sabbath; by a cruel irony, just over a decade later the Evsektsia was to try to persuade Jewish workers, in the interests of 'productivity', to make Sunday their day of rest.

However, since Frumkin was not an observant Jewess, what she was suggesting was to return the Jewish festivals to a historical, rather than a religious, context—by making them the celebrations of a new, liberated, and revolutionary Jewish nation. Again, ironically, this was precisely what was happening in the society set up by the Zionists, whom Frumkin opposed so bitterly as utopian dreamers.

The Jewish worker, Frumkin argued, had to transform Jewish holidays into national-proletarian celebrations, and religious traditions (even the recital of Jewish prayers) could be the basis of egalitarian ideals, as proclaimed by Isaiah and other Jewish prophets. This was less a socialist than a romantic vision, one that was to be cruelly perverted under Bolshevik rule.

Frumkin's idyllic picture of the Jewish home, with the mother lighting the Friday night candles, the father blessing the wine, the grandmother reading *T'sena Ure'ena*, and the Havdala ceremonies at the close of the Sabbath, ending its peace and ushering in the 'tumult of the week', was part of a political vision.[69] Such customs were, in her view, to form the basis of a Jewish proletarian society, with the worker family as its ideal, replacing that Jewish hierarchic society which had placed the rabbis and

Talmudic scholars at its apex. It is notable that such a double rebellion would have strengthened precisely those areas of Jewish life in which women had long exercised their energies and minds: the family and secular education. However, the selective Judaism that Frumkin wished to preserve—domestic celebrations, historical festivals, and the universal message of the prophets— was precisely the type of Judaism that, since the Enlightenment, had been adopted by the bourgeois Jewish society of Western Europe.

Frumkin's ideas were exceptional and controversial for a Bundist; 'national cultural autonomy', in the view of its chief Jewish theorist, Vladimir Medem, was something that could only evolve historically and might well lead to eventual assimilation.[70] But Frumkin claimed that her view, too, was 'historical'. She observed that the Jewish intelligentsia, whose opportunities for employment were limited outside the Pale of Settlement, were turning back to their own people; in the contemporary growth of Yiddish literature and culture, which was unprecedented, she also saw a sign of national consolidation.[71]

Frumkin's most influential work, her brochure on the Jewish Folk School, written in 1910, outlined her vision of Yiddish education as the key to the new proletarian culture.[72] In stressing education as the most powerful of formative influences, she was responding to the idea that had drawn most women into the movement in its earlier stages.

The educational system she had in mind was not traditional Jewish education (Jewish customs were to be something transmitted at home) but a wide general education which incorporated arts and science and stressed practical work (indicating her exposure to the Montessori system, which she had seen while on her travels in Switzerland and Austria). But also included was the work of the great new Yiddish fiction writers who were perpetuating in their novels and stories the life of the Jewish *shtetl* and its religious sects. The works she singles out for mention by I. L. Peretz, then at the height of his reputation, are two stories with religious themes.

Frumkin argued that though children would have Yiddish as

their first language, their second would be Russian—necessary in their working life if they were to break out of the petit-bourgeois artisan class and enter the Russian proletariat proper.[73] This was her solution to the contradiction in her vision. Already, and particularly among girls who were more likely to be sent to the state schools, Jewish literacy in Russian was beginning to gain on literacy in Yiddish—and this was a trend which accelerated under communism, even though Yiddish was then to be recognised as a national language.[74]

After a spirited linguistic defence of Yiddish and a denial of its bastard status (was not French a bastardised form of Latin?), Frumkin argued that the Jewish lawyers and doctors who could no longer find work in the great Russian centres were going to have to relearn Yiddish (as indeed the socialists among them had already done) in order to work among the masses in the Pale of Settlement, and that the assimilationist intelligentsia and the bourgeois would eventually have to join with the workers to create the Yiddish Folk School.[75]

The retreat of the Jewish intelligentsia to the Pale of Settlement, however, was less part of an historical process than the result of czarist discriminatory quotas; and during the Bolshevik era, on the contrary, it was those Jews who had severed their ties with their own community most completely who were to be those most influential in Soviet politics.

The February revolution of 1917 briefly lit up the horizons of the Jewish social democrats who believed that finally they were to achieve all the aims for which they had struggled: the abolition of Czarist discrimination, an end to anti-Semitism, the triumph of socialist brotherhood. Their loyalty to the revolution transcended even their previous, internationalist opposition to the war. In April many of the Bundists, including Frumkin, became 'revolutionary defencists', who believed that Russia should continue fighting in order to preserve the revolution from destruction by Germany.[76] Frumkin was made a member of the central committee of the Bund, and in May returned to Minsk to edit the influential Yiddish journal *Der Veker*.[77] But the Bolshevik revolution of October was to confront Frumkin, together with all the Bund leadership, with a tragic dilemma.

It soon became clear that the Bolsheviks would tolerate no form of socialism but communism, and no rival political organisation. The Menshevik Social Democrats and the Bundists were branded deviationists, and almost immediately the measure of free expression which had finally been won from the czarist regime in 1905 was curtailed. In November 1917 Frumkin attacked the new censorship imposed in the name of democracy and proclaimed that 'the free word lives'. In that same month she attacked the Bolsheviks openly as a minority group which was creating a dictatorship.[78] In this she spoke for the mass of the Bundists, who were social democrats by education and political outlook. Those who, like Frumkin, were to become supporters of the new regime never quite managed to live down their social democratic past, and eventually paid for it with their lives or their freedom.

Between the Bolshevik revolution of October 1917 and the final dissolution of the Bund in March 1921, when many of its leaders became Soviet functionaries in the framework of the Jewish Section, political events outside the Soviet Union—and violence, both anti-Semitic and Bolshevik, within it—conspired to drive the Bundists into the arms of the Communist Party.

The Jews were the main victims of the counter-revolutionary battles which followed on the establishment of Russian communism. In 1918 Minsk was occupied by the Germans, who were joined by White Russian reactionaries. After the Germans retreated, Frumkin was put in charge of education by the Bolshevik majority in the Revolutionary Council, and communists and Bundists together formed frontline military corps: she fought among them.[79] In this part of the empire (White Russia), where the Jews were a majority in most of the cities, they were tolerated by the revolutionaries, but in the Ukraine hideous pogroms were carried out, not only by anti-Bolshevik Russians, Ukrainians, and Polish opponents of socialism but by anti-Semitic elements of the Red Army as well.[80]

Not only were the Jews in danger of their lives during this

period of military and political flux; their economy was in chaos. It is estimated that during the years 1918–1921, seventy to eighty per cent of the Jewish population were without a regular income.[81] For Jewish politicians who felt responsible for the future of their people (the Zionists had fled abroad or gone underground) and who had links with the Bolshevik leadership, maintaining a separate political identity became increasingly difficult. When the Soviets set up a Jewish Section, one of its first tasks was to close down the Zionist schools.[82]

For the first two years after the revolution the Bund held out stubbornly against a merger with the Bolsheviks and managed to maintain its own unity. But at the eleventh conference of the Bund, in March 1919, the strains of maintaining the forms of social democracy were beginning to show. The German revolution, betrayed by the social democrats, had failed. In Poland, the Jews were mercilessly persecuted; in Russia, the Soviets had consolidated their power and were ruthlessly suppressing their opponents. The Bund was in the throes of its last ideological debate: the Left and Centre Left accepted the dictatorship of the Bolsheviks in principle, while the Right hewed stubbornly to social democracy. Still, even on the left, Frumkin and others criticised the Bolshevik terror, censorship, and other limitations on freedom. Bundist institutions faithfully and democratically represented the diversity of opinion in the party, and Frumkin asked the Bund to retain its ties with international socialism.

The breaking point came a year later, at the twelfth congress in April 1920; Frumkin, who led the left wing, demanded that the Bund ally itself openly with the Bolshevik government. This time, she made no criticism of terror and censorship, but asked of the communists that the Jewish working class be given the chance of setting up a Jewish communist organisation of its own, which would enjoy autonomous status within the Communist Party.[83] This was clearly a last-ditch argument. The socialist regime, she said, would guarantee the Jews safety from persecution, but the 'national cultural' needs of the Jews could only be provided by their own people.[84]

When it became clear that the Bolsheviks would not tolerate

any form of Jewish political autonomy, Frumkin told her fellow Bundists that only two choices remained: to join the Communist Party, or to become a small, ineffectual sect. She recommended the first, though believing that the Comintern's decision to dissolve the Jewish workers' movement was a serious error.[85] In 1921, the Bund formally disbanded itself. Thenceforth Frumkin was to concentrate all her energies on the Jewish Section (Evsektsia) in which for nine years she and a few of her colleagues attempted, as part of the political and educational work that was their brief, to destroy the old Jewish communal and religious structure, to force a secular Yiddish culture on the mass of the Jewish population of Russia, and to restructure the Jewish class hierarchy in such a way as to bolshevise the Jewish worker and eliminate the 'unproductive' small traders and artisans who had no place in a communist society. Among their more notable activities were the anti-religious campaign, the battle against Zionism, the introduction of the Yiddish folk school, and the settlement of thousands of Jews in the ill-fated Birobidjan autonomous region and in other underdeveloped parts of the Soviet Union.[86]

During most of the 1920s, when Soviet policy appeared to be favourable to ethnic pluralism, the more idealistic members of the Jewish Section could persuade themselves that they were creating a new form of Jewish economic and social life. But with the onset of the era of Stalinism, increased centralisation, large-scale industrial development, and the ruthless suppression of national and regional loyalties and traditions, the Jewish Section lost its usefulness in Communist Party eyes, and also lost its own nerve.

Even before the Comintern decided to dissolve the Jewish Section, it was being torn apart by dissent and accusations of ideological 'deviation'—not only a counterpart of what was happening in the Communist Party as a whole but perhaps a sign that the more principled members of the section, of whom Frumkin was one, knew that the hope of preserving, within the communist juggernaut, the spirit of Jewish social democracy was an illusion.

The ferocity with which Frumkin pursued the orthodox Jews of the old dispensation led Boris Bogen, an American social worker who spent time in Russia during this period, to call her 'a frenzied Medusa, whose fury was on the head of the rabbis'. Frumkin was not all-powerful; and while the local bureaucrats in the Jewish Section were often most assiduous in destroying every vestige of orthodoxy, she and her colleagues in Moscow sometimes reined them in; she is recorded as having ordered a Bet Midrash in Vitebsk returned to its students. However, there is no doubt that she concurred with communist policy. What accounts for her attacks on the rabbis, given her affection for Jewish tradition?

Frumkin had written, during that period of transition to bolshevism, that in the Bund 'We have changed our tactics, but not our programme.'[87] But if during the early days in Minsk she could identify with Lessin's critique of Marxism in the Jewish context, by 1919 she was already beginning to justify dictatorship as in her analysis of the difference between communism for the Russian and the Jewish 'masses', aware somewhere that the Jewish proletariat would have to be dominated rather than led. As early as 1914 she had complained bitterly that the Bundist plans for Yiddish education received only a lukewarm reception among the Jewish workers, and that they had less national consciousness than other groups in the Russian Empire: 'Can one say that they feel the oppression of the Russian school in a hundredth, in a thousandth degree that it is felt by the Polish and Georgian masses?'[88] In 1919, she was changing from teacher to commissar. 'On the Russian street you can speak of the Soviet regime as being representative of 90 per cent of the population. But on the Jewish street, a proletarian minority has to rule over a non-proletarian, albeit poor and toiling majority. And that is why the Jewish commissariats and Jewish sections (among the Bolsheviks) have that certain flavour of working under the masses, over the masses, but not with the masses.'[89]

Once she joined the communists, she too began to subtly rewrite the Bundist past. She translated Lenin into Yiddish and wrote, with another Jewish Section leader, Moshe Litvakow, a book on Lenin for the Yiddish reader, including a chapter dealing with Lenin's views on the Bund and its 'mistakes'. The logic of her political speeches and articles became steadily more tortuous, and while she had always favoured an almost Talmudic complexity of argument, her attempts to reconcile her Jewish identity with her role as Russian commissar led her to read into a speech by Stalin a tacit endorsement of Jewish national autonomy.[90]

Tragically, Frumkin's once affectionate loyalty to Jewish tradition now turned to a passionate hatred of orthodox Jews, in whom, because she knew their fervour so well, she recognised her chief enemy.[91] Where once she had praised the role of women in preserving Jewish customs in the home, the Yiddish communist press she controlled now attacked women in particular as a 'backward' element because they clung to formal weddings, Passover celebrations, Friday evening observances, long after their actual faith had been renounced.[92]

During this period, on a mission abroad, Frumkin became dangerously ill. Her option was either to have an operation which might save her life or to continue working to the end. Even such decisions, under the Bolsheviks, had to be referred to the party. Frumkin accordingly cabled the Jewish Section in Moscow for instructions—and, with their approval, had her operation. Her forefathers and mothers, at similar moments of choice, would have consulted the community rabbi.

In Moscow, as a commissar with administrative powers behind her, Frumkin not only presided over the dissolution of the religious schools and seminaries but, with her colleagues, was also able to finally establish a system of education in Yiddish, which was recognised as a 'national' language by the communist regime. By the end of the decade, half the Jewish children in the White Russian and Ukrainian republics were attending Yiddish schools, although elsewhere the figures were much lower.[93] But it was a brief triumph.

In 1926, while over seventy per cent of the Jews in the Soviet Union still listed Yiddish as their mother tongue, that younger generation in which Frumkin had put her hopes for a new Jewish proletarian Yiddish were already turning away from the language. By 1939 the number of Jews who knew and read their 'national' language had dropped by nearly one half.[94] The fact that the Jewish Section was ordered to operate in Yiddish proved a handicap, since it was always short of organisers and teachers who knew the language.[95]

In the schools, the reality was very far from the dream that Frumkin and other Bundists had cherished under czarism. Jewish history, like religion, was banned from the curriculum, and there was to be no synthesis of Jewish folklore and modern socialist theory, as Frumkin had envisaged it. The great Yiddish novels were taught not as literature but as satirical portraits of the Jewish folk tradition, which was held up to mockery. There was to be no higher education in Yiddish, save in teacher-training colleges, and entrance examinations to secondary schools and colleges were held in Russian; after the Jewish Section disbanded, Jewish parents who were not actually forced to enrol their children in Yiddish schools opted increasingly for a Russian education. Yiddish education remained the artificial creation of a minority, and Yiddish came to be associated, increasingly, with the culture of the backward *shtetl*, with the result that the industrial Jewish workers were not attracted to the activities of the Jewish Section. Unlike the old Bundist press, the Soviet Yiddish press—including *Emes*, the Yiddish version of *Pravda* for which Frumkin wrote regularly—had a very limited readership. Soviet Jewry in the cities was on the road to assimilation.[96]

By 1926 Frumkin was openly admitting that large-scale assimilation was inevitable; yet she still hoped for the transfer of the *luftmenschen* of the Jewish *shtetl* to the new agricultural settlements which, with help from the Soviet government and Jews in America, had been set up in Birobidjan and in the Crimea.[97] But here, too, she was to be disappointed. Those Jews who did take up pioneering farming in the Soviet empire, an enterprise which reached its height in 1930, were not the neglected petite bourgeoisie, and by the Second World War most of the farms had been deserted.[98]

Frumkin made her last speech as a political figure at the Sixth All-Union Conference of the Jewish Section and its offshoots in Moscow in December 1926. It was perhaps the most tormented argument she had yet delivered, in which she simultaneously defended the Soviet government's policy on nationalities, attacked petit-bourgeois nationalism, and argued that the agricultural settlement of large masses of Jews on Russian territory (not in one region alone but wherever Soviet development called for their participation) would actually create a Jewish nation: 'The proletarian revolution awakens forgotten peoples and tribes. It opens up a road for them to national development and consolidation, the road to national statehood.' The Jewish people, she went on, echoing Lenin, was 'not yet a nation in the strictly scientific sense of the word, since it has neither territory nor a common economic basis. But this new Jewish nation might take its place among the other peoples of the Soviet Union.'[99] This was the final, tightrope formulation of Jewish identity stretched to comply with communist demands. But even so, it was unacceptable to the Communist Party, and there were to be no further conferences of the All-Union Jewish Sections. The sections had served their purpose and were disbanded four years later.

Frumkin's last official position was as head of the Jewish Department at the University of the National Minorities of the West, dubbed the 'Little International', of which she eventually became the rector after the death of Julian Marchlewski, one of Rosa Luxemburg's old comrades. This was a centre for communist indoctrination for groups of foreign students. When it was closed down at the height of the purges in 1936, Frumkin was transferred to the Institute of Foreign Languages in Moscow. It was there that in January 1938 she was arrested and taken to prison.

Frumkin's obituaries were published five years before her death, because colleagues in exile assumed that she was dead when no news was received of her from the moment of her imprisonment until her trial in August 1940. She was sentenced to eight years' forced labour in Karaganda, in Kazakhstan, one of the grimmest concentrations of political prisoners. As she was suffering from diabetes, and was already, at sixty, a very sick woman, she was given work indoors as an accountant. Her daughter and son-in-law were also in prison. Of all the family who remained in Minsk and fell into Nazi hands, only the daughter of the wet-nurse who had tended Frumkin's own child survived.

It was said that, in the camp, Esther Frumkin was sometimes greeted by those other political prisoners who remembered her speeches in Minsk, Moscow, or elsewhere. Friends in the party worked for her rehabilitation and in 1943 she was released; but she had not received insulin for her diabetic condition and died shortly after her release in June 1943.[100]

Frumkin remains one of the most controversial figures in Jewish revolutionary history. Her career suggests that rather than trying to subordinate her Jewish loyalties to communism, she tried to reconcile communism and Jewish survival. But her assertion that the Jews would finally become a nation under communism was diametrically opposed to the Marxist belief that socialism would lead to the assimilation of the Jews into one international, classless proletariat. Even those who hated her respected her knowledge and fervour. The Medusa figure who pursued the rabbis so mercilessly was also, in her desire to preserve Jewish culture centring on the family, 'a true daughter of the Jewish tradition'.[101]

5

A RADICAL IN TRANSIT

Manya Shochat and the Zionist Women Pioneers

In January 1904 a young Russian Jewish woman with a fierce, intelligent face, thick glasses, and short-cropped hair in the style of the nihilist women of a former generation disembarked at the port of Jaffa to visit her brother, an engineer who had emigrated to Palestine a year earlier. Manya Vilbushevitz, twenty-four years old and already a seasoned revolutionary, was at that very time involved in a terrorist plot to assassinate Plehve, the Czarist Minister of the Interior. Only a frantic telegram from her brother, intimating that he was ill, had brought her to Palestine; 'I was not yet a Zionist,' she noted later. Finding that her brother was in perfect health and had tricked her to get her out of danger, she hurried back to the port. But there was no boat sailing for Europe at that time.[1] Thus pre-state Jewish Palestine acquired its leading woman radical.

As Vilbushevitz's fellow conspirators were subsequently betrayed by the notorious double agent Azev and executed, her brother's trickery probably saved her life. In 1904 she was already a controversial figure in Jewish politics in Russia. She was to be no less so throughout her life in Palestine; and where Diaspora Jewry was concerned, she never quite lived down her conspiratorial past, for in Czarist Russia, though active in Jewish self-defence, she had been a major figure in promoting police socialism and allegedly betrayed many of her former comrades in the Bund.[2] Once in Palestine, she soon began to see scope for radical change in the tiny Jewish community of Ottoman Palestine, at that time dominated by capitalist philanthropists and their settler protégés. At this time the Jews, who were still no more than ten per cent of the population, owned only one per cent of the land.

When Vilbushevitz learned that the conspiracy against Plehve had failed, her brother and his friends took her on a tour of the country on horseback. She showed scant interest in the plantations or in the little towns on the coast; but the wild territory beyond the Jordan River, particularly the sparsely settled Hauran uplands—the north-eastern Druse territory, where land already had been purchased by Edmond de Rothschild, but where no colonist had ventured—fired her imagination.

Four years after that first visit, Manya Vilbushevitz and nine other pioneers, including her future husband, Israel Shochat, set up the first farming collective in Palestine, at Sejera in the Galilee, the very first prototype of the kibbutz. This was, in her view, a pilot project for an eventual settlement drive in the Hauran. Both she and Shochat had been active in Jewish self-defence inside Russia; both had been influenced by the Social Revolutionaries, to whose terrorist wing she had briefly belonged. Manya had the greater political experience, Shochat was the more flamboyant. (Shochat's men were to ride around crowned with Muslim headdresses and hold up the Jewish wedding canopies with rifle butts.)[3] Vilbushevitz saw that whatever the financial support forthcoming from Zionist patrons in the Diaspora, only young, highly motivated people, prepared to venture beyond the coastal plain, could make extensive Jewish settlement in Palestine possible, and that only communal living could make such settlement economically viable. The Sejera collective, founded by her inspiration, was defended by civilian guards under Israel Shochat's leadership. These guards were the forerunners of the Jewish pre-state underground defence force, the Hagana.[4]

Manya Shochat, as she is known in Zionist history, belongs to that small company of pioneers, the men and women of the Second Aliya (Immigration) of the first years of the twentieth century, whose utopian socialism and conspiratorial habits both had their origins in pre-revolutionary Russia. Once the socialist parties created a countrywide labour movement, they were relegated to the margin of Zionist politics. Some of these diehard radicals returned to Russia; but the majority were brought to heel by the labour leadership under David Ben Gurion. At the height of their career in pre-state Palestine, in active middle age, people like Manya and Israel Shochat became politically obsolete. Having carried the principles of collectivism and Jewish self-defence to Palestine, they had no further historical role to play.

While Manya Shochat displayed remarkable qualities of leadership as a young woman in Russia at the turn of the century, in Palestine she was scarcely to participate in party politics. In the radical groups to which she belonged, loosely affiliated with the dominant socialist party, Ahdut Ha'avodah (later the mainstay of the Israeli labour party, Mapai), she was sometimes treasurer, sometimes envoy to Diaspora Jewry, sometimes social welfare worker. She had little patience for administrative or committee work and, with no political position, lived on as a famous anachronism. During the British Mandate, in times of civil strife, she continued to ferry arms across the Arab lines in Palestine at the risk of her life; in old age, during the War of Independence in 1948, she was twice taken prisoner and released by Arab soldiers. Her thirst for dangerous adventure and self-sacrifice indicates that she was closer to her revolutionary forerunners than to her Marxist-Zionist comrades; for a short period she had belonged to the Combat Unit of the Social Revolutionaries. As a woman activist, moreover, she was a maverick figure in Zionist history, resembling neither the stoutly feminist trade unionists who founded the General Council of Women Workers nor the few women politicians who, like Golda Meir, used that organisation as a springboard to national politics.[5]

At Sejera, Manya Shochat encouraged women to guide a team of oxen. This may have been the origin of the myth of the 'ploughwomen', as the pioneering women liked to call themselves. It is sometimes argued that the sexual equality of the Second Aliya was later squandered by the Jewish state, which reaffirmed the place of religion and the family at the expense of women's liberation. But the majority of the earliest Jewish immigrant population in Palestine (the First Aliya of the 1880s) were observant Jews; and the women who wanted to share in farming, building, and other 'productive' occupations of the Second Aliya more often found themselves cooking and cleaning for the men. Farming techniques were strange to both the young men and the young women who had come straight from their classrooms and their parents' homes in the Russian Empire to the rocky hillsides or malarial lowlands of the Galilee. But the men received professional training and tools while the women were shunted into kitchens and laundries, where they had to improvise; most of them came from comfortably off families which had employed domestic servants.[6]

The period literature is full of the complaints of young women 'whose soul yearned for the soil', and whose hands itched to 'work the land', but were barred from doing so. Photographs survive of the fortunate few who did manage to stagger along behind the plough or climb ladders with plastering trowels, wearing long, cumbersome skirts. (It is remarkable that before the 1930s few Jewish women workers except at Sejera—for Manya herself liked wearing men's clothes—thought of wearing trousers.) The work of breaking stones and preparing the land for the plough was probably beyond women's strength, but looking after animals and growing vegetables was not. When eventually a small but determined women's labour movement did form collectives, it was to work in market gardening or poultry runs, in agriculture, and in the building industry in trades like floor tiling.[7] But what really drove the women to despair was their sense of inferior status and the dismissive attitude of many of the men.

When the newcomers set up their own settlements in the Galilee, few women were accepted. Even these women were classed as 'service workers', not members, as their work was not considered 'productive'.[8] What made this all the more painful was that these educated young women had little or no experience of cooking, particularly with the meagre, unfamiliar ingredients and under the spartan conditions in which they found themselves. Perhaps remembering the food in their mothers' homes, the young men in one urban collective, dissatisfied with the fare, mocked the cooks by playing 'trains' with the uneaten food.[9]

Zionist women never achieved occupational equality in the pre-state period, even in the farming battalions which created the myth. The majority of pre-state women immigrant workers in the towns were consigned to work in domestic service, or to the same industries in which their working-class counterparts had worked in Eastern Europe—textiles, clothing, and tobacco.[10] For political and economic reasons—for experiments in sexual equality were not at the top of the Zionist agenda—the pre-state labour movement did not back the principle of equal pay for equal work and, as the feminist Ada Maimon pointed out in 1929, women workers' status in pre-state Jewish society in Palestine was actually very similar to that in England or Germany thirty years earlier.[11]

By the late 1920s, with women brought under the umbrella of the trades union movement (the Histadrut), a paternalist bias which was very Jewish was obvious. Women enjoyed a special status as 'members' wives', and housewives who did not work outside the home benefited from the social services of the Working Mothers' Organisation. Socialist women were bitterly resentful of the term 'member's wife', and maintained that they were denied equality in the labour movement. 'We are "exempted" from obligations but are accorded no rights', enjoying 'those of our husbands, expected to vote along with them, but, usually, as they decide.'[12] The 'exemption' had a familiar ring for Jewish women. It meant second-class status.

The survival of the symbol of the ploughwoman and the myth of the new Jewish woman, equal in every way to the man, is partly due to the fact that agricultural work received priority not only in the ideology but in terms of the financial support obtained from the Zionist organisations in the Diaspora.[13] For it was only in agriculture, in the new collectives or *kibbutzim*, and after a prolonged battle, that women succeeded in demolishing the domestic stereotype. Just as the kibbutz became the symbol of the reborn Jewish nation though only a tiny minority of the immigrants to Palestine settled on a collective settlement, so the image of the *halutza*, the pioneering Jewish woman, emerged from the women's struggle for equality in the kibbutzim, the rural collectives. The *poelet*—the 'working-woman', a name applied to factory workers and even originally to cleaning women in private households—had nothing like the same renown. The radical women of Manya Shochat's generation paid dearly in physical and emotional terms for winning equal status. They were rebels not only against traditional Jewish society but against the Zionists' conservatism where women and their role in society was concerned.

There were no women theoreticians of Zionism; there was no equivalent, in the Zionist movement, of a Rosa Luxemburg or an Esther Frumkin. There were no women delegates at the first Zionist Congress in Basle in 1897; most of the women present were there because they accompanied their husbands, and Theodor Herzl, though welcoming them gallantly to the congress and addressing them as 'honoured guests', also specified that they did not have the right to vote.[14]

By the second congress, a year later, there were a number of women delegates representing women's Zionist organisations in central and Western, though not Eastern, Europe; but whereas there were stormy arguments about whether the second congress's membership was democratically composed (the left-wing deputation left the congress in a huff), the 'woman question' did not arise at all. By contrast, in the Bund, created in the same year, women were active in the leadership and shared in the debates. Even during the formative years of the Zionist socialist movement in Palestine, only one woman—Rachel Yanait Ben Zvi—took an active part in political life together with the men (though there were several notable women among the right-wing Zionists) and perhaps for this reason was reluctant to ally herself publicly with the labour feminists.[15]

The Zionists may have wanted to reform Jewish society, but they were initially a middle-class movement, among whom there were many traditional community leaders and rabbis whose attitude towards women was conventionally Jewish. The main Zionist activists and theoreticians were middle-aged and middle-class, and had little intention of emigrating to Palestine themselves.[16] Among the young immigrant activists, most were students. In keeping with tradition, most women Zionists—particularly on the right, for the socialists were still in a minority—filled educational and philanthropic roles. Women made up about thirty per cent of all immigrants to Palestine in the early years of the century; but many of them had gone in order to join the orthodox communities in the holy cities of Jerusalem, Hebron, and Safed. Only a minority of young socialist women, from the first years of the century, built and farmed together with the men, expecting in this way to eliminate their traditional inferiority within the community.

Ada Maimon, the leading pioneer feminist, came from a family of rabbis in Bessarabia. Her father, she recalled, saw to it that his daughters studied Hebrew and Yiddish, and she wrote of him with affection and respect. But she attributed her militant feminism to the moment in her childhood when, like so many other girls whose youth was spent listening to Talmudic discussions from which they were barred, she asked why girls should be 'exempted' from so many Jewish duties. 'Exemption,' she concluded, was an insult, 'injustice, repression'.[17] She demanded equal employment and remuneration for women workers as a means of ensuring their equality in the new Jewish community in Palestine—an immigrant society with women from highly traditional communities, like the Yemenites, as well as women from countries undergoing social revolution. This made the task of the Zionist feminists far harder than that of feminists in any European country.

The Zionist leadership was also under pressure to show signs of economic success to its philanthropic investors in the Diaspora. Economic realities did not encourage social experiments like employing women in work usually reserved for men. But the Zionist feminists among the socialists waved aside the crude materialism of 'employers who thought only of their profits'.

'Women in other countries may ask for work which matches their physical capabilities, as they work in order to earn a living. But there is nothing creative about that. The Hebrew woman worker is creating a new society,' wrote 'Judith', one such worker.[18] Such views ensured that the Zionist feminists always remained a small élite, remote from the core of the problem, which was the status of women in the towns. Women did play a part in the growing Jewish towns; the textile and clothing industries, in which they were well represented, eventually had a growth rate above the average. But probably because of internal occupational segregation, wage differentials between men and women remained discriminatory.[19] That this state of affairs persisted throughout the pre-state period, despite the efforts of exceptional women like Maimon, was at least in part due to the isolation of the radical, kibbutz-based women from the mass of immigrant women.

The Second Aliya was made up mainly of unmarried young men and women or married couples without children who fled the pogroms of 1903 and 1905, following the October Revolution in that year. They had little knowledge of social or economic conditions in Palestine and romantic ideas of an empty country waiting for their redeeming labour. The reality was different. The established Jewish community, both the townspeople and the First Aliya colonist farmers, disapproved of the young radicals and preferred hired Arab labourers, who were both cheaper and more experienced in construction and in vineyard and plantation work. While they occasionally hired the men, they forbade their own daughters contact with the godless, free-thinking female pioneers.[20]

Unemployment among the new immigrants was so severe that women were expected to allow men first chance of work, so that the women had to compete with both Arab labour and that of their own menfolk. If socialist women workers in Russia were expected to subordinate their own ambitions to the interests of the working class, in Palestine the pioneer women had to take third place to working-class and Jewish national interests.

Women were told that they lacked the physical strength to

plough, sow, and harvest, and they were not allowed to stand guard, though they were given back-breaking and less rewarding work in the kitchens. Perhaps their bitterest revelation was that they were not really considered comrades of their men. When there were debates and arguments, they rarely took part; when the pioneers met to decide policy, the question of women's work was not discussed.[21]

In a frontier society, male strength was clearly at a premium, but there were other reasons for the dismissive treatment accorded women. The majority of the pioneering radical men came from traditional homes, and many of them had spent some years in a Talmudic seminary. Beneath an egalitarian veneer, they shared the conviction of the *maskilim* that women should support men and not challenge them. Many of the women were well-educated and accomplished, but only a minority spoke Hebrew, the language of the new country.[22]

It was not surprising, therefore, that the socialist women pioneers eventually decided that only by setting up their own farms, communes, trade unions, and eventually a separate movement in the Federation of Labour, could they redress what they saw as injustice. The beginnings were small. One of the women of the original Sejera collective, **Hanna Meizel**, a trained agronomist who had studied in Germany, secretly planted a market garden, out of sight of the main settlement in 1909, and a tiny group of women began to produce and market vegetables. A year later, when Meizel had obtained her own funds from a women's Zionist group in Germany, she set up a training farm for women at Kinneret, on the sea of Galilee.[23]

Not only were these gently nurtured, idealistic young women at a disadvantage in the early settlements where work was concerned; they had insisted that they could do without male patronage and protection, and suffered the consequences. Frequently, they found themselves alone in isolated and dangerous parts of the country when the men were away on special missions connected with Jewish self-defence, which sometimes lasted for months. The first women to give birth to children found that their responsibilities were overwhelming and that having children was initially considered selfish and anti-social. The case of **Pessia Abramson**, a member of one of the early collectives, is particularly poignant. Abramson had trained at the first all-woman agricultural school at Kinneret and worked in the settlement of Merhavia, in the Jezreel valley. She led the struggle to take women out of the kitchen and into responsible organisational work. Later she joined the first permanent co-operative settlement in Palestine, Tel Adas, with her husband. But among these pioneers, starting a family was betrayal of ideals. After bearing two babies, she was slighted by her female comrades. Weakened by childbirth and illness, unable to play her full part in the work of the co-operative, and with her husband constantly absent on missions, she shot herself.[24]

Although the Kinneret training farm did not survive the First World War economic crisis in Palestine, it formed the nucleus of an independent women's movement which lasted from the end of the war until 1927. In 1921 this movement founded the General Council of Women Workers as a separate body within the Histadrut, the Federation of Labour within whose framework the socialists became the dominant force in pre-state Jewish Palestine. It retained a measure of independence until 1927, when the Council became a social services organisation, which contributed to the welfare of working women and through whose ranks women could rise to carefully controlled leadership positions in Labour's central institutions, and eventually in the Israeli Parliament. Thenceforth women's interests were once more subordinated to those of organised labour as a whole.[25]

While determined groups of socialist pioneering women proved that in principle they could compete in almost every field with men, the ideal of full equality proved unattainable. A restricted and unstable economy and the fact that the Labour Movement was dependent on both the Mandate government and Diaspora Jewry in matters of economic planning and funding meant that the problem of women's inequality, though recognised, was shunted aside by male leaders, and women did not manage to form a political pressure group. At the founding meeting of the Histadrut in 1920 only four women out of eighty-seven delegates were present. The female labour force was then about twenty per cent of the whole. The women delegates did not represent women workers but were part of one of the political party delegations. Labour leaders, chief among them Ben Gurion, feared that women would constitute a minority faction potentially resistant to socialist hegemony within the Histadrut. Thus, after a struggle, leaders in the General Council of Women Workers came to be appointed by political factions in the Histadrut and not by the women members, as the feminists had intended.[26]

The socialist feminists were also hampered by the fact that the radicals had little in common with the mass of women immigrants in the towns. Among the women in the Palestinian Jewish community as a whole, there was little solidarity. Middle-class women who campaigned for equal rights were shunned by socialists—as in many European countries at this time.[27] Different stages of immigration to Palestine brought women who did not share the motivation of the pioneer radicals, who regarded their working lives as a temporary phase, who were reluctant to campaign for better conditions, and who hesitated to challenge the male leadership. Women of the calibre of Manya Shochat and Golda Meir had no interest whatever in feminist politics. They were reluctant to make a separatist stand and impatient with women who could not compete with men on their own terms.

Only in farming, where women made up thirty-six per cent of the work force by the 1930s (compared with twenty-nine per cent in the labour force in general), did women manage to alter the tradition of occupational segregation. There was still a distinction between male and female roles, linked to their physical abilities: women distinguished themselves, ironically, in those branches of farming for which Jewish women in rural communities had been responsible in Eastern Europe.

The pioneering women's main achievement was winning recognition of their status within the collectives. The 'working settlement population', the *hityashvut haovedet*, men and women alike, came to be seen as the Zionist aristocracy, linked to the settlement of territory whose purchase was only consummated with its cultivation, and whose cultivation was only economically viable in the form of rural collectives or co-operatives, whose members both farmed the land and defended it.

In this framework, women's potential could be more fully exploited, and this came to be recognised not only by the male settlers but—perhaps more significantly—by those in charge of investment and settlement policy in the Zionist organisation. Chief among them was Arthur Ruppin, the senior official in charge of the economic development in Palestine, who wrote in 1919 that it had been a mistake to train only men for agricultural labour, and that it was now advisable 'to attribute the same importance to the labour of women as we do to the labour of men when we select candidates for agricultural settlements.'[28]

Manya Shochat was associated both with the early Ha'Shomer (Watchman) Second Aliya group and with Gdud Ha'Avodah (the Labour Legion), a roving army of socialist labourers who made up the nucleus of a number of permanent settlements which were among the earliest kibbutzim. These were the two pioneering groups who were fervently dedicated to the principle of the use of Hebrew labour, rather than having Jewish overseers for Arab labour, and to the social ideal of the collective. In Ha'Shomer, with its emphasis on para-military activity, with a few exceptions women remained camp followers. The Labour Legion, however, came nearest of all the early Zionist ventures to giving women equality. Zionist history would be much duller without both these groups; even the most sober historians suggest that the Jewish state might not have come into existence without their contribution. Perhaps inevitably, their members remained an élite and a minority among the working population of the pre-state Jewish community, and they were frequently an embarrassment to the Jewish leadership. Their political philosophy was too utopian, or too naïve, to survive the compromises of party politics, and their dissolution marked the end of the revolutionary period in Zionist history.

By the time Manya Vilbushevitz arrived in Palestine, she had taken part in every kind of political action open to the Jews of her time in pre-revolutionary Russia; she had 'gone to the people' as an apprentice carpenter and as a volunteer worker among the peasants; she had organised educational circles among the Jewish workers of Minsk; a former Bundist, she had betrayed her Bundist comrades, in order to set up a rival trade unionist party, aided by the Czarist police which sponsored 'state socialism' in the hope of drawing the Jewish radicals away from the Bund. When her new party collapsed in the wake of repression and pogroms in 1903, she had turned to terrorism, and smuggled arms to the beleaguered townships of the Pale. She had thrown herself into each of these activities with equal ardour, conviction, and ability, and—during a lull—she had enjoyed one adventure probably unshared by any other Jewish woman revolutionary. Disguised as a man, she had taken part in one of the first Russian military journeys in a balloon.[29]

Manya Vilbushevitz was the youngest of eight children in a wealthy and educated Jewish family which owned an estate near Grodno, Lithuania. Young radical women of this generation very often abandoned the Jewish community altogether. The reason why Manya did not seems to have been that her closest early ties were with her father. Unusually in such a family, it was her father, and not her mother, who identified strongly with Judaism; he had broken away from his own very assimilated background and reasserted his Jewish roots. But he was also a Russian patriot, deeply loyal to the monarchy; it is possible that this made Manya vulnerable to the enlightened autocracy of police or 'state socialism'.

As a small girl, Manya emulated her father's piety as best she could, though not in the conventional Jewish way; she improvised her own prayers. The wide Jewish culture her father gave her, including a knowledge of Hebrew, later enabled her to make the transition to Palestine more easily than most women of her class. An elder sister, unhappily married, committed suicide. Manya, somewhat neglected by her mother, ran wild on the family estate, riding on horseback and befriending the peasant children. Like the Russian populists whom she then resembled, she soon experienced the guilt of the privileged; and like her father, she ran away from home: but in her case, it was to join the working-class Jews of Minsk.

Her three brothers, engineering students and later industrialists, had already joined the Zionist movement. At one stage Manya organised a strike in a factory run by one of her brothers where she worked as a carpenter, dressed in men's clothes. She was to benefit from her brothers' influence and wealth later in her career as a Palestine socialist.

Manya did not yet see her future outside Russia. Like many women in the Jewish radical camp, she believed her first priority was to prepare worker intellectuals who could form an enlightened revolutionary cadre; in Minsk, like Esther Frumkin, she taught the Jewish workers Russian and the rudiments of socialist theory. At eighteen she joined a small group of gentile friends on a mission to the Tartar area of Kazan, in the Volga Basin, to help peasants suffering from famine and other diseases, including syphilis. Each member took a village under his or her care, and Manya had the chance to observe how the local *mir* or commune functioned, its virtues and deficiencies, including the fact that the village elders tried to appropriate for themselves the food she distributed. On her return to Minsk she formed an urban collective, which followed the principle of 'going to the people' while living in equality. Its members were bound by secrecy and shared property, with all decisions made jointly. All these experiences were to contribute to her concept of the rural collective in Palestine.

At this stage of her life Manya's unusual abilities and political passions were exploited by Czarist forces that were trying to contain and control the radical left rather than suppress and destroy it. During the two years following the foundation of the Bund, the Czarist secret police—the Okhrana—arrested not only most of the leadership but as many Bundist sympathisers among the intelligentsia as they could lay their hands on, both in Vilna and in Minsk. In 1899 Manya Vilbushevitz was one of some sixty radicals imprisoned and kept in solitary confinement in Moscow. She was interrogated at length by Sergei Zubatov, then head of the Okhrana.

Zubatov, himself an ex-radical, believed that repression would not suffice to extinguish the revolt against social and economic injustice. At the same time, his talks with the Bundists convinced him that there was a genuine division between the Jewish intellectual leadership and the artisan rank and file who were concerned primarily with their physical and working conditions, sought legal redress for their ills, and were reluctant to endanger their position still further by open insurrection. He won a hearing, if little more, from his Czarist superiors for a policy by which an openly recognised trades union leadership, of the kind which underlay the very structure of the Bund, would be allowed to voice its grievances, suggest reforms in the terms and conditions of employment, and even stage strikes, all with the tacit backing of the authorities.[30]

There were some precedents for this combination of autocracy and licensed reform in Russian history.[31] Moreover, there was a predisposition among many of the Bundists to seek legal backing for their claims. The Jewish masses were primarily interested in bettering their working conditions and status; if that could be achieved legally, so much the better. Even at that first workers' meeting in the woods outside Vilna on May Day 1892 (at which the two women workers had spoken) the speakers had invoked an archaic law dating back to the time of Catherine II limiting the length of the working day.[32] Moreover, Zubatov's techniques of persuasion were seductive; many of the prisoners believed that he was both concerned for the fate of the Jewish workers and sympathetic to their ideals. He was most successful with the young Manya, whom he managed to convince (for she repeated this version of their encounter to the end of her life) that the proposed policy had originated with her, and not with him. She was to prove his aptest pupil, manifesting an astounding talent for leadership and organisation.[33] But he also won over mature Bundist leaders such as Alexander Chemerisky (later to be one of Esther Frumkin's colleagues in the leadership of the Evsektsia) and even to extract a confession, if not collaboration, from the redoubtable Grigory Gershuni, later a revolutionary terrorist.[34]

Zubatov's campaign scored some initial success as it came at a time when the Bundist programme of 'agitation' had not yet got into its stride and the original leadership was under arrest or in hiding.[35] In the summer of 1900 the released Bundists began returning to the Pale, where those who had been persuaded to do so by Zubatov continued to undermine the organisation from within. Despite recurrent doubts and worries, Manya continued to provide Zubatov with the names of Bundists whose plans she thought dangerous for the 'simple workers' and candidates for arrest and 're-education', though at this stage her role was not known to the Bund.[36] She also informed him that as the Zionists were opposed to political struggle and critical of democracy, they would turn the balance in the Jewish communities in favour of a pro-Czarist policy focusing Jewish discontents entirely on economic issues.[37] Thenceforth Zubatov recommended 'playing into the hands of nationalist [Zionist] aspirations' as a way of taking the revolutionary steam out of Russian Jewish politics.[38]

In June 1901 a Jewish Independent Labour party, headed by Zubatov's allies—the most energetic and influential of whom was Manya—was set up in Minsk and almost immediately came under attack from the Bund. With the help of the police, however, it began publishing manifestos, held 'legal' workers meetings (at which there were heated arguments between the Independents and the Bundists), and agitated for changes in working conditions for the different artisan groups. By August they had six craft unions in Minsk under their control and thus were winning concessions from the employers. But this involved something of a juggling act. Police arbitrators managed to convince the workers not to strike, and the employers that they had fended off the strike.[39]

In Minsk, the Independent Party succeeded in drawing away a substantial part of the Bund membership; Manya was summoned to St Petersburg and instructed by Plehve, the Minister of the Interior, to extend the party's activities to Vilna. But here the Bund had closed ranks and Chemerisky, entrusted with the job, was accused of being a police provocateur. He was also told that Manya's life was in danger.[40] Manya won the consent of Plehve for a Zionist congress to take place legally in Minsk in

1902. But time was already running out for both Zubatov and the Independents.

Manya had warned Zubatov that if he was unable to fulfil his promises—among them official recognition of the party, legalisation of the Jewish trade unions, an end to censorship—continuing repression would discredit the party Independents.

Towards the end of 1902 Manya went to Odessa to help set up the local branch of the party under the leadership of a Zionist Jew, Khona Shayevich. Here the party was only too successful in organising strikes, which in July of the following year had spread from the dockers to workers in the main industries of the city. This was too much for the authorities, who arrested and deported Shayevich to Siberia. The Jewish Independents in the Pale had already collapsed under the impact of renewed repression and the terrible Kishinev pogrom of April 1903. Soon after the Odessa strikes Plehve removed Zubatov from his post and banished him.

All Manya's rebellious ardour was now turned against the anti-Semitic minister. In her own version of her life, recounted in old age to her friend Rachel Yanait Ben Zvi, she maintained that after Shayevich's arrest she confronted Plehve, pistol in pocket, and, after making a revolutionary speech, prepared to hurl an inkpot at him, before being ejected. This event bears an uncanny resemblance both to her account of a failed assassination attempt on Zubatov's life (her pistol jammed) and to her later account of a confrontation with the Turkish governor of Jaffa, and perhaps should not be taken literally. What is certain is that her next move was to join the Social Revolutionary plotters against Plehve's life, a scheme for which she was raising funds in Berlin when summoned to Palestine in 1904.[41]

The flirtation with death which characterised the early women populists and the Social Revolutionaries was marked in Manya. One of her younger comrades in Palestine commented later: 'A certain light appeared in Manya's eyes every time she was involved in something risky.'[42] According to her daughter, she had also a history of suicide attempts (the last in her unhappy middle age), and there was no woman more feared, because of her terrorist past, among the Zionist pioneers. Ben Gurion found her so alarming that when, at a moment of political conflict he visited her kibbutz in the Galilee, he was careful not to go alone.[43]

During the next three years, during which she travelled between Palestine, Europe, the United States, and (on clandestine missions) Russia, Manya tried to win support for the idea of the rural collective, from wealthy Jewish patrons and from socialist immigrants alike. This idea was alien to both groups, for very different reasons. The rural economy of the First Immigration was that of labour-extensive vineyard and plantation farming, in the fertile coastal region. The Jewish farmers employed local Arab labour and were dependent for their basic financing and marketing facilities abroad, as they were for expert advice and supervision at home, on the staff of the Rothschild enterprise based in Paris, and later on that of the Jewish Colonisation Association (JCA). Edmond de Rothschild, first patron of Jewish settlement, had invested some two million pounds sterling in Palestine during the last twenty years of the nineteenth century, but the annual deficits persisted.[44] As a socialist, Manya rejected the colonialist pattern in which Jews had become the overseers of peasant labour, but she was aware that only economic arguments would encourage a change of policy in the Diaspora. For this to happen, the idea of the collective had to be tested. Manya needed volunteers.

Convincing early socialist settlers to break away on their own was going to be difficult. Not only were the young pioneers desperately short of work and prepared to do any kind of hired labour; the Marxist training of this generation had instilled in them the belief that socialism in Palestine should create a wage-labour proletariat that would function in the framework of intensive capitalist development.[45] The idea of self-sufficient, autonomous rural collectives appeared as a populist and utopian throwback. It was only when it became clear that a purely Marxist view of the economy ran up against theoretical and practical obstacle of Arab labour that the ideal of 'Hebrew labour' in the pre-state Jewish community was seen to be unworkable, or workable only when realised within the confines of the rural collective.[46] All her life the conflict between Jewish nationalism and the fate of the Arab working class was to remain an ideological problem for Manya Shochat, as for a small group of Zionist socialists.

In Russia, the populist students had prepared manifestos based on their statistical research among the peasants. Manya's first move in Palestine was to visit twenty-three Rothschild settlements and reach conclusions as to the reason for their economic instability. She inferred from her findings that the idealistic settlers of the First Immigration had been corrupted and dis-illusioned by their dependence on Rothschild and their Arab hired labourers.[47] There were clearly many other, technical reasons—for instance, reliance on one crop, viniculture—but the fact that the colonists had so little say in policy had also contributed to their instability. By the time Manya made her survey, Rothschild had transferred many of his functions to the JCA, whose policy was to encourage arable farming in the Galilee, which needed less initial investment and less hired labour, thus enabling the JCA to reduce both financial help and supervision. It was this switch, rather than any initial success by Manya in persuading the European financiers or Zionist bureaucrats abroad of her case, which was to make the earliest collectives feasible. Another factor was the establishment, in 1901, of the Jewish National Fund, a pre-state organisation, which purchased land in the name of the Zionist community as a whole. But new forms of settlement had still to be evolved.

It was at this early stage that Manya made contact with Israel Shochat, a socialist pioneer still attached to Marxist theory, who rejected her proposal to set up a collective. He was, moreover, involved in creating, in the utmost secrecy, his own defence corps, given the historical name of Bar Giora, the Jewish military leader in the war against Rome. Its aim was to replace the hired Bedouin and Circassian (Slavic Muslim) guards of Jewish colonies by Jewish armed horsemen.[48]

Manya next attempted to establish a pilot project by forming a carpenters' co-operative on the lines of a Russian 'artel' (a commune whose members lived and ate together), but she had a more ambitious scheme in mind—the settlement of the Hauran—and when she left to explore that region again, the 'artel' disintegrated.[49] In the summer of 1905, while on a visit to Paris, Manya extended her researches by studying French governmental materials on colonisation patterns in French North Africa. She presented herself to Rothschild and outlined her ideas for large-scale collectives, manned by pioneers, on his lands in the Hauran.

Manya appears to have intrigued the baron sufficiently to extract permission to colonise there, an empty offer since no funds were promised with it. Perhaps he recognised the self-confidence of one born to privilege—greater self-confidence than the facts justified, since at that stage Manya was a general without a single recruit behind her. Later that year, however, she was to be more successful in extracting money from him.

The 1905 revolution had taken place in Russia, but the limited concessions to the liberals had not brought much relief to the Jews. The revolution was followed by the notorious October pogroms. Jews in exposed townships, even when organised in self-defence units, lacked weapons, and a former comrade of Manya's now approached her for help. Putting aside her plans for Palestine, she returned to Rothschild for funds for Jewish self-defence in Russia. After initial hesitance, lest he complicate Franco-Russian relations, Rothschild provided her with 50,000 francs in gold, with which she purchased small arms in Liège—chiefly Browning pistols and large numbers of bullets—as well as a revolver, equipped with a silencer, for herself.[50]

Throughout most of the next year, Manya and a handful of women recruits went in and out of Russia in various disguises—she travelled alternately as a French dressmaker and as a rabbi's wife—carrying revolvers in false-bottomed suitcases ostensibly packed with the latest fashions, or with tracts for seminaries in the Ukraine. At one stage, in Odessa, she disguised herself as a maid to a wealthy Jewish family who had temporarily given over their house to a Jewish self-defence group. A young man entered the house under the pretext that he was seeking a fellow revolutionary who had gone off with his wife, but Manya, experienced by now, scented the Okhrana on her trail and shot him dead. With the help of her comrades she packed the body into one of the cases which had held the 'scriptures' and mailed it from the nearest station to a fictitious address, collapsing with fever and vomiting at the horror of the act only after the despatch was completed. The arms cache in Odessa was not discovered. Four years later, Jewish immigrants to Palestine smuggled what weapons remained into Palestine through Jaffa port, at Manya's request.[51]

Manya participated in the work of a self-defence unit during a pogrom of 1906 in Siedlce, and then, as an act of revenge against the pogroms, joined the Combat Unit of the Social Revolutionaries, changing her lodgings every night, with the secret police always one step behind her.[52] In late 1906 she left Russia for the last time.

Back in Palestine, Manya again tried to find recruits for settlement in the Hauran, but the socialist leadership was wary of her; only Israel Shochat, with an eye on deserted territory where he could train his horsemen without Turkish surveillance, was now, for the first time, attracted by the suggestion. But Manya had not yet found financial and technical backing. How important both were she must have learned from her brothers, founders of the chemical, food, and machine industries in Palestine. At the beginning of 1907, she set off for the United States, carrying letters for Judah Magnes, the American Jewish lawyer who was to work later for Arab–Jewish understanding, and Henrietta Szold, one of the first women Zionist leaders in the United States.

Despite such contacts, however, Manya's scheme appeared as unrealistic to wealthy Jews in America as it did to the veteran Zionist leader Max Nordau, whom she met later that year in Paris. Nordau told Manya bluntly to seek psychiatric care. But what she brought back from North America was the model of the Dukhobor communes in Canada. These Christian non-conformist and pacifist peasants had been persecuted by Czars and Cossacks alike; Manya had encountered them first in Kazan in 1898. Through the financial and personal intervention of Tolstoy and the British Quakers, some eight thousand Dukhobors had found homes in Canada, where Manya visited them. It is interesting that Manya found the example of these spartan Christians more suggestive than the socialist Russian Jews who formed the Am Olam farming communities in the United States at the same period—perhaps because the land owned in common by the latter was divided and farmed individually.[53]

Manya's eventual model of the collective was inspired both by the example of sharecroppers in Russia and tenant farmers in Palestine (at first she considered a collective made up both of Jews and Arabs). The role of the landlord, or property owner, was played first by the JCA and later by the Jewish National Fund. Israel Shochat provided the volunteers. Manya was able to establish a collective within the protective framework of the experimental farm at Sejera, where the JCA administrators were trying to train Jewish farmers to be self-sufficient. The more romantic vision of the Hauran was postponed for the future, though Manya never forgot it. She raised it in 1909 at the founding meeting of Ha'Shomer, the defence and farming organisation which grew from Shochat's Bar Giora; and during the 1920s, when the Hauran was already part of French Syria, she was part of a Zionist group that wanted to exchange this land for tracts in Western Palestine—land which Manya hoped might be farmed by Jews and Arabs together.[54] Political realities prevented this from happening.

Sejera, the prototype of the kibbutz, was an experimental farm in two senses; unlike the earlier training school, Mikve Israel, the instructors were not concerned with theoretical agronomy and plantation botany but practical work with field crops and stock farming, for which modern reaping and threshing machines, as well as cattle, had been brought from Europe. The second sense in which Sejera was an experiment was that it was intended to teach select groups of Jewish farmers both farming skills and self-reliance. It was the good fortune of Manya and her comrades—Israel Shochat and the band of radicals that had gathered around him—that since 1901 the farm had been run by an adventurous young agronomist, Elie Krause, who, like his predecessor Haim Kalvarisky, was not opposed in principle to the idea of collective farming or to female farm labour. After 1905 Krause encouraged girls to work not only in the dairy or chicken coop but even in the fields.[55] His chief concern—apart from the fact that his superiors in Paris were unlikely to look sympathetically on a socialist revolutionary as one of their protégés—was that the young radicals were totally inexperienced in farming and might well wreck his new machinery and mishandle the animals.[56] He thus made it a condition of acceptance that two of the collective's members should be experienced farmers of his own choice.

A further risk, of which neither Krause nor Manya had any knowledge when the collective was set up, was that Shochat had motives for responding to Manya's proposal which had nothing to do with the ideal collective or even experimental farming.[57] As in his previous enthusiasm for her Hauran idea, he was looking for a training ground for his embryonic defence force.

The kibbutz prototype was made up of eighteen members: Manya, Israel Shochat, Krause's two farmers, and Shochat's followers, who included five women. According to the contract drawn up with Krause, all the members worked in the fields and the dairy on the same terms as tenant farmers, with the use of livestock, seeds, and machinery, and gave him a fifth of the harvest. Krause gave them lectures in agronomy and insisted on daily reports on their work, but they worked without formal supervision, apart from the other tenant farmers and trainees, even eating separately in their own communal kitchen. The women were full members of the collective, though in Krause's reports to Paris he gave them men's names, as the Paris administration disapproved of employing women.[58] Manya herself worked part time in the dairy and kept the collective's books.

The risk involved in hiring Shochat soon became apparent. He was determined to oust the Circassian and Bedouin guards from the nearby villages from their traditional role as watchmen, and resorted to trickery to do so.[59] Using Jewish guards gave the Jewish settlers a sense of self-reliance as well as training in handling arms. But it infuriated the local sheikhs and led to increased friction between the Jewish farmers and the nearby Arab villages, since any Arab death at the hands of a Jew led to a blood feud. After the departure of the members of the collective, Krause prudently re-employed the Circassians.[60] It was to take several years for the Jews to assume responsibility for the defence of their own settlements.

The collective ended its contractual term of a year—it was not renewed—having made a profit, and having justified the experiment. Near the end of her life Manya was to remember that year—the year also of her marriage to Israel Shochat—as the happiest of her life. Marriage for the revolutionaries, born conspirators and adventurers both, was to mean neither physical nor emotional stability. In its early stages, Ha'Shomer lent itself out to whatever settlement needed armed guards, and the women went with them. Shochat was an emotional nomad, too, whose striking looks and swashbuckling reputation attracted many women. According to his daughter, after the first few years of marriage to Manya, Shochat was chronically unfaithful. Manya, for her part, had intense friendships with two other male comrades; but despite her innate romanticism, she was puritanical like other Russian women radicals.[61] Politically and sexually she remained loyal to Shochat, but the Shomer in its roving years was a hard environment for women.

When the Shomer held its founding meeting in 1910, Manya raised the question of women's work in the mobile collectives and warned that as women did not share in guard duty, it was important for the Shomer to settle on the land—to choose one particular site to farm. A handful of women—including Esther Becker, Zippora Zaid, and Manya herself—insisted on standing guard in the collectives, and even following the men on reconnaissance missions; but their role could only be defined in an established community.[62] The moment of truth came when the Shomer went out to its first 'conquest of the land' in the Galilee: the reclamation of land in Kfar Tabor (Dabbariyeh) bought by Jews but still farmed by its original Arab tenants; and later, when it set up a commune at Tel Adas. Here the women staged a miniature revolt. Esther Becker stood up and said that the women would refuse to cook if the men did not share the kitchen chores.[63] After a token protest, the men gave in; thenceforth men worked in the kitchen in the collectives, though women did not share men's work to the full. This is still the case in the kibbutz today.

The married couples in the Shomer had now produced five children, and women occupied in caring for their babies clearly could not play an equal part in the work of the collective as well. Manya, remembering a similar system in Russian communes, suggested that the infants should be housed together with one woman in charge. This was the system subsequently adopted in all the new collectives—the 'children's house' of the kibbutz.

By 1913 Shochat realised that the nomadic period was coming to an end and that the 'watchmen' should also be settlers, but he himself never became a farmer.[64] After a period during which, like Ben Gurion, he studied law and (covertly) Turkish strategy in Istanbul, he returned to Palestine on the eve of the outbreak of war. The couple was now living in the port of Haifa, where Shochat worked with a team constructing the Jewish engineering college, the Technion (where Manya worked as an accountant), a cover for his conspiratorial work, planning Jewish self-defence.

With the advent of the First World War, the Turkish administration ordered the Jews to turn in their arms. This was obviously the last thing that the Shomer would do. Anonymous political rivals, possibly in the Labour movement, informed on Manya as a source of information, and in November 1914 she was arrested and brought before Baha el Din, the Turkish governor of Jaffa. On this occasion, as on others, she lectured her enemy on Zionism, and—as she recalled later—hurled a dagger at him. She was charged with concealing weapons and was sent for trial by a military court in Damascus, while other Zionist leaders like Ben Gurion, Yitzhak Ben Zvi, a future president of Israel, and Shochat were merely exiled to the Turkish province of Anatolia.

Neither the Zionists nor the Turks wanted to let Manya take the stand, since she was bound to seize the occasion to make a political speech. Influential friends bribed the judges. She was condemned to exile with her husband, and her small son was sent after her. Though another child, a daughter, was born in exile, this was the last period during which the Shochats were to live together until their old age.[65]

When, following the Balfour Declaration of 1917, Britain assumed the Mandate in Palestine, the Shomer group, unlike the mainstream Jewish community, regarded the British with no less enmity than they had the Turks, and they were soon stealing arms from British depots to acquire weapons for Jewish self-defence not only against Arab attack but, ultimately, against their mandatory rulers. Manya herself organised the theft of a Lewis machine gun.

The Shomer also refused to sacrifice their independence to the dominant socialist party, Ahdut Ha'avodah, of which they were nominally members. The original labour farming union which they had helped found, Ha'Horesh (The Ploughman), was absorbed into the Histadrut in 1920. The pre-war attempt to set up a labour battalion on a wage-labour basis had broken down. But the Shomer still wanted partial autonomy in what they regarded as their special responsibility—the defence of the farmers. During the war years they had strained at the harness, eager for blood revenge when one of their number had been killed and frustrated at having to guard Jewish farms which employed Arab labour.

On his return from exile in 1918, Shochat persuaded the Shomer community to settle down. They set up a group of kibbutzim (now the basic form of Jewish rural settlement) in the northern Galilee, ostensibly to facilitate the import of scarce food to the area during the difficult post-war period, but which were to serve later as way stations for the smuggling of arms into Palestine. This part of the country, which immediately after the war was under French rule, remained particularly exposed to the hostility of the surrounding Arab villages, and the settlements had to be evacuated temporarily in the summer of 1919, after battles that claimed Jewish lives, a trauma never forgotten by their inhabitants.

From 1920, when the Histadrut established the Hagana, its defence arm, there were disputes between the Shomer leadership and the Histadrut, which thenceforth was to form the nucleus of Jewish leadership in Palestine. Even though Shochat announced the formal dissolution of the Shomer in that year, it remained a potentially rebellious element in the Labour movement for another seven years. This was both because of the presence of so many untamed Russian revolutionaries and internationalists in its midst and because Shomer members regarded themselves as far more experienced and efficient in defence matters than their fellows in the fledgling Hagana.

This view seemed justified when, in May 1921, following a left-wing Jewish demonstration, the bloodiest riots then seen broke out in Jaffa, during which 47 Jews were killed and 134 injured; 48 Arabs were also killed, most in punitive action by British troops.

The Jewish community was ill prepared to restore order or even to rescue the survivors in what was predominantly an Arab town. Shomer members entered the area (Manya was disguised as a nurse), evacuated many of the Jewish wounded, and interrogated them as to the identity of the murderers, who had been led by an Arab police officer, Tewfik Bey. Meanwhile, members of the Jewish units in the British army, without consulting their superiors, hurried to help the Jews defend the nearby settlements. It was Manya who took the decision to assassinate Tewfik in revenge, but it was some time until an actual assassin was found—Yerachmiel Luckaser, a young Shomer member. Acting under Manya's orders, he ambushed Tewfik Bey and shot him dead in January 1923.[66]

The Hagana leadership was informed of this plot, and did nothing to prevent its execution. The assassination indicated to the Labour leadership, however, that the 'former Shomer' as they were called were an unreliable element, and one likely to be blamed by the British authorities for any further acts of violence or revenge. When the Hagana itself assassinated Jacob de Haan, an orthodox, anti-Zionist Jew suspected of spying for the Arabs, some years later, it was Manya who was arrested by the British police.[67] Although she was released for lack of evidence, the suspicion that the Hagana had informed on Manya added to the by now strained relations between the Labour leadership and the Shomer. By this time, the Shomer were part of a larger and more important radical movement, Gdud Ha'avodah (the Labour Legion).

The Labour Legion was made up of young, highly motivated single people from Russia and Eastern Europe who arrived in Palestine at the time of the Third Aliya—the immigration immediately after the First World War. They had been so strongly influenced by the October Revolution of 1917 that the mainstream socialists in Palestine were as apprehensive as the Mandate authorities regarding their communist sympathies and allegiances. In fact, at the outset they had no political strategy. They were a mobile work force which focused on public and agricultural projects; the Legionaries worked under the auspices both of the Histadrut and the Mandate authorities and lived under the roughest of conditions, on the work sites, in camps organised as communes. The first such commune, which was founded in 1920, worked on building the road between Tiberias and Tabgha, on the north shore of the Sea of Galilee.

Elsewhere they built British army camps, prepared land for settlements, harvested, constructed housing projects, and even cleared land for cemeteries. Eventually Legion camps developed into new collectives, or kibbutzim, which became radical strong-holds, among them Eyn Harod and Tel Yosef, in the Jezreel valley, and Kfar Giladi and Tel Hai, in the northern Galilee. They also founded a Legion commune in Jerusalem.[68]

Women in the Labour Legion worked side by side with the men: on road work, in building, and in the fields. They were far more liberated than the women of the Second Aliya, for several reasons. By now there were work camps in Europe in which men and women trained together for pioneering labour, prior to emigration. They were a younger generation, among whom the women no longer saw themselves as 'helpmeets' but as equals; they had no hesitation in demanding their due, and even their manners were freer. To dispel the tensions of the grinding days of labour, they broke into wild dancing and singing. 'The [Second Aliya] male veterans joined in gradually but the women hesitated at first. They thought us immoral when we strolled around arm in arm with the men,' one woman Legionary, 'Judith', recalled. 'This was just a comradely gesture ... without any romantic intent.'[69] All children in the new collectives were brought up in the 'children's houses', and men took their turn in the kitchen. Paradoxically, however, the very fact of rotation of the members in all the tasks of the commune meant that women had no sooner acquired experience in the field or cowshed than they were transferred to the kitchen—and so complained that they never had time to become expert in the techniques of farming. When it came to electing representatives to the administrative and political jobs, moreover, it was the men who were more frequently chosen.[70]

Just such a community was that of the collective where Israel and Manya Shochat were members—Kfar Giladi, in the hilly reaches of the upper Galilee. Israel by now lived chiefly in Tel Aviv, from which he masterminded the Shomer; Manya spent most of her time travelling, as fund-raiser, or as troubleshooter for Shomer members all over the country; when she visited Kfar Giladi, she slept on a camp bed in the room of friends.

The Shochat children, Geda and Anna, were brought up in the children's house of Kfar Giladi. Their early life was a sad example of what happened to the children of Zionist leaders at this time. Their parents were virtual strangers; when, after the day's work was over, the other children went off for a couple of hours with their parents, the Shochat children were left alone. The boy, Geda, ran away and was found selling stolen shoelaces in Tel Aviv. At his bar mitzvah, Manya gave him a bizarre double gift: phylacteries (small leather boxes worn by Jews at daily prayers, containing fragments of scriptures) and a pistol. Many years later, after Manya's death and Geda's suicide, Anna's bitterness spilled out in a radio interview which revealed the seamier side of the Shochat's lives, their near total neglect of their children, Israel's womanising, and the despair that led Manya to attempt suicide in 1921. Kibbutz veterans recalled that when Anna was five, and ill, Manya dumped her in an orphanage in Jerusalem to receive medical care—something which explains an incident recounted in the radio interview: that later, at a social meeting with Ben Gurion, Anna told him she was an orphan. Ben Gurion responded unsympathetically: 'The country would not have existed without people like your parents.' Dutifully, Anna concluded, 'I knew that there was something more important than myself; the homeland.'[71]

The Shomer leaders were not among the founders of the Labour Legion, but they were important above all in the Legion's defence wing, which—since the Hagana was still in its infancy—greatly expanded the Shomer's network of mobile guardsmen.

From 1921 the Shomer was entrusted by the Hagana with smuggling arms into Palestine. Their main source was Austria, where there was a post-war surplus of weapons and ammunition to be siphoned off with the help of malcontent ex-army officers. The material was sent to Haifa port in every possible container, including refrigerators (new at this stage to Palestine) and beehives. One of the beehives fell and broke, spilling its contents on to the quayside. Because of the subsequently increased surveillance by the British customs and police, the main arms route then became Trieste–Beirut, from which the arms and ammunition were brought through the hills of southern Lebanon and into the upper Galilee.

These included heavier equipment which the Hagana foresaw, even at this early stage, would be needed for an eventual Jewish war with the Arabs; machine guns were concealed in cement mixers and steamrollers. Manya raised the funds for the purchase of arms; the details of her frequent journeys abroad, and the sources of funding, were mostly undocumented. Her revolutionary past now made her a problematic emissary. When she travelled to the United States in 1921 to raise funds for the newly established Workers' Bank (Bank Ha'Poalim), she found herself at the centre of a controversy. The Bundist leader Vladimir Medem published details of her relationship with Zubatov, basing his allegations on letters found in the Czarist archives at the time of the 1917 revolution by a young Bundist revolutionary, Dovid

Zaslavsky. The motive for this attack was competition for financial help from the American Jewish labour circles by Bundists and Zionists, and the socialist Zionist leadership in Palestine had no choice but to proclaim its belief in Manya's innocence and block her request for a 'trial of honour' by a labour tribunal. But the entire incident had made them wary of Manya's services, and one Labour functionary, Ephraim Bloch-Blumenfeld, told her bluntly that it had been a mistake to send her.[72]

In the early 1920s there was, as yet, no single recognised Jewish leadership in Palestine, though the labour parties steadily gained adherents, and the Histadrut—the Labour-led trade union body with its welfare and health services, loan and marketing facilities, and labour exchanges—was becoming a miniature administration. From the outset there was hostility between the radicals in the Labour Legion and the Histadrut. Labour leaders praised the achievements of the collective but recognised that the majority of the Jewish labour was not recruited to the collectives, whose members represented only six per cent of the working class. Moreover, they suspected, correctly, that the pro-Bolshevik element in the Labour Legion sought Soviet political support in ousting Britain from Palestine.

Ben Gurion, secretary general of the Histadrut, was keenly alert to the potentially subversive power of the radicals and knew at first hand the charismatic power of their leaders. He himself had worked briefly as a labourer at the Sejera farm in 1908–9. Shochat, perhaps recognising a rival, had then refused to accept him as a member of the Shomer. The two men had met again as students in Istanbul. Now Israel and Manya were prominent among those who controlled Soviet-type collectives and led what was beginning to look like an independent fighting force. They were also inspired by the conspiratorial methods of the Bolsheviks, who had shown them how a radical minority could seize power.

At this time the judicial powers of the Histadrut were still largely undefined. It was difficult for Ben Gurion to break the power of the Labour Legion as he had broken the recalcitrant members of the little communist fraction, in May 1923, by withholding Histadrut facilities.

The Legion collective settlements enjoyed the benefits of Histadrut's services, but Ben Gurion suspected that they intended to set up a rival political party, dedicated to internationalist principles, potentially sympathetic to the Arab working class and with ties to the Communist Party in the Soviet Union.

In 1923, and again in 1926, the Legion settlements found themselves in economic difficulties and turned to the Histadrut for help. To deny this to the Legion was far more difficult than to the communists, as they were perceived as Zionist trailblazers; they were also so inured to privation that it was likely that they could withstand sanctions. But by the end of 1926 Ben Gurion finally saw his chance to crush the Legion, in what became an open confrontation, following a series of dramatic incidents involving Israel and Manya Shochat.[73]

The Hagana leadership had long suspected that the Shomer was fortifying its own power centre at Kfar Giladi and possibly siphoning off some of the arms brought into the country. These suspicions were justified. Shochat was contemptuous of the labour bureaucrats where warfare was concerned, and his aim was to set up his own military school, and even an embryonic airforce. Two incidents in the early 1920s alerted the Hagana to what was going on. The head of the Hagana, Eliahu Golomb, suspecting Shomer tricks, decided to send non-Shomer Hagana members to pick up an arms consignment from Europe—this time, a hollow grindstone containing ammunition. On the winding road through the Galilee, near Kfar Giladi, their truck broke down, and after spending the night in the settlement, the Hagana men returned to find that the grindstone had disappeared. The settlers pleaded ignorance, but Ben Gurion sent for Manya. There is no record of their exchange, but the talk resulted in the Shomer people surrendering the grindstone and its contents to the Hagana leadership.[74]

This, of course, could not be brought into the open, as both the Hagana and the Legion were, though rivals, allies against the governing power, the British Mandate authorities. There followed what was known as the 'Chariot Coup', an exploit which resembled both the early Bolshevik 'expropriations' and plain highway robbery. Shomer agents ambushed a gang of gold smugglers in the Galilee, disguised as British policemen, and got away with 15,000 pounds in gold. This haul enabled them to acquire their own arms supply and—unknown to the Hagana— to stash it away in a huge underground cache built thirty feet under the cowsheds of Kfar Giladi.

The Shomer, under Shochat's leadership, had blueprints for what was becoming a private army. In April 1924 its leaders met in secret in Haifa and decided to seek training abroad, not only for army officers but for pilots—as well as planning further Shomer settlements in the Negev. Manya was part of the group, which was perhaps why the decision was also taken to form a women's legion and send them abroad for training in clandestine combat. Israel Shochat gained the ear of Léon Blum in France, then a leader of the socialist opposition in France, though no actual training facilities. These were obtained by Luckaser (Tewfik Bey's assassin) in Berlin, from which he returned to found an officers' training school in Tel Yosef, one of the Legion's settlements. It was at this point that Israel and Manya overstepped the limits of caution and played into Ben Gurion's hands.

In 1925 Israel and Manya Shochat acted as host to two communist agents visiting Palestine. Shortly afterwards, Shochat and two other prominent members of the Legion announced that they had been invited by the Soviet Co-operatives Centre to Moscow to study Soviet child care, agricultural, and other institutions. Several Labour leaders, including Ben Gurion, had visited the Soviet Union, but no one believed, as Golomb put it, 'that Shochat was the man to study farms and child care'. This was true enough; Shochat hoped the Soviets would agree to training his pilots, in return for political co-operation. In his own memoir, Shochat records his belief that the Soviets would then have supported the foundation of a Jewish communist state in Palestine.[75]

The Histadrut forbade the delegation to leave, arguing that such missions were the province of the Executive alone. Shochat defied the ruling. The visit proved a fiasco, perhaps because the communists were unimpressed by Shochat's credentials. It is also possible that they had been told that Shochat was a British provocateur. On Shochat's return, Ben Gurion commenced an all-out campaign against the Legion. Using the objection of a handful of families from the nearby settlement of Tel Hai to a merger with Kfar Giladi, he threatened to expel the members of both collectives from the Histadrut. The real reason, of course, was that he feared that the entire upper Galilee region, the main arms-smuggling route, would fall into the hands of his radical rivals. The rumour was also spread once more that the Shomer had murdered De Haan. This was too much for Manya, who wrote to Ben Gurion: 'I hadn't thought you were capable of using such means to hurt the Legion. I respected you too much as a person. The path you chose will destroy us and you. There's no forgiveness in my heart and I am breaking off all personal relations between us.'[76]

Ben Gurion chose to interpret this message as a threat to his own life. A Histadrut enquiry, at which Manya refused to testify, ended with the expulsion of the extreme left wing of the Legion membership, and its central body, the Circle, was disbanded. The Legion split. Seventy of its most radical members, led by Mendel Elkind, returned to the Soviet Union and set up a Jewish collective settlement, Via Nova, in the Crimea. This disappeared during the Stalinist era. The other members of the Circle, including Israel and Manya, were thenceforth powerless.

The last quasi-political role the Shochats played was when, in 1933, Ben Gurion appointed them to be in charge of the bodyguard 'squadrons' of the Labour sports team, HaPoel, which by then was coming under frequent attack in the streets of Palestinian towns by its right-wing rival, Betar.[77]

So, in her late forties, Manya Shochat found herself on the sidelines of political life in Palestine. In quiet times, she continued to travel on fund-raising missions, and at others, to cross the lines dividing Arab and Jewish areas of Palestine in disguise. During the 1929 civil conflict between Jews and Arabs in Haifa, she got through a British roadblock with a car full of arms by pretending to be a nurse in charge of a wounded comrade; in fact, she had slashed him and herself with a razor blade to bloody them both. When in Kfar Giladi, she worked in the kitchen and the laundry, in precisely those chores she had avoided before, perhaps to prove that she did not see herself as superior to any other member of the commune.

The principle of Hebrew labour for which the Labour Legion stood was never fully realised during the pre-state period; from the thirties onward, Arab labour was used even in the kibbutzim and the co-operative settlements, the *moshavot*, because there were too few Jews prepared to do manual labour.[78]

Politically, Manya continued to belong to that small minority which hoped, against all odds, for the creation of an international proletariat, and, in Palestine, for a 'working-class' understanding between Jews and Arabs that would transcend nationalist politics.[79] She was a sympathiser, though not a member of, Brith Shalom, the small intellectual and international Jewish group which favoured the creation of a bi-national state.[80] In 1930, she was among the founders of Ahvat Ha'Poalim (The Workers' Brotherhood), whose aim was to encourage cultural relations between Jewish and Arab workers, so that they could understand one another better and work for equal rights. Their manifesto makes it clear why she did not participate fully in Brith Shalom, as that group believed in achieving understanding through meetings with the Arab leadership. Ahvat Ha'Poalim stood for a *rapprochement* at the working-class level—joint trade unions and co-operatives, bringing Arab workers into the Histadrut (something which only happened after the foundation of the state of Israel in 1948), and propaganda and cultural work aimed at bringing the two peoples closer.[81]

But this aim, and the ideal of Hebrew labour, were essentially irreconcilable. The struggle of the Jewish workers, particularly those of the collectives, against cheap Arab labour increased the enmity between the two peoples. Moreover, the ideological debate this contradiction produced was of no interest whatever to the Arab leadership; nor was it a political issue in the Arab–Jewish conflict. The basic problems remained that of finding work for Jewish immigrants, on the one hand, and the struggle over the land itself, on the other.

Nevertheless, the question of the Arabs of Palestine and the moral problem they posed the radicals was one that continued to haunt Manya Shochat into old age. One of the few letters she left behind was written in 1959, to the then Prime Minister, her old friend and comrade Ben Gurion, two years before her death, when she was half blind and ailing. She suggested that he abolish the system of military control to which the Arabs of Israel were submitted during the first years of the State of Israel. Her letter ended: 'It is time to end this disgrace. There are, among our defence experts, those intelligent enough to find a way to combat a fifth column among the Arabs without resorting to military government.' She signed the letter with her 'love and blessing'. To which Ben Gurion replied: 'I am with you in your desire for equality and justice; the difference is in the way in which we perceive reality.'[82]

THE REBEL AS LACEMAKER

Bertha Pappenheim and the Problem of Jewish Feminism

In the year 1895 Bertha Pappenheim, an elegant and reserved single woman in her thirties, accepted the position of house-mother in a Jewish orphanage in Frankfurt—an unpaid position. Six years earlier, when she moved with her mother to Frankfurt from her native Vienna, Pappenheim, like many other well-born and wealthy Jewish women in Western European cities, had worked in a soup kitchen for immigrants from Eastern Europe. She had also organised a little nursery school, directed sewing classes (she both collected rare lace and tatted lace herself), and set up a girls' club in a poor district of the city. She attended synagogue regularly and observed all the Jewish festivals. While she had no formal higher education, she was well-read in several languages, and five years earlier she had published a book of short stories under a male pseudonym.[1]

None of this was particularly remarkable for women of her background. From the mid century, German and Austrian women of the Jewish middle class did not do paid work, though in pre-industrial Germany keeping house and preparing and preserving food for a large family was a full-time job.[2] The more privileged women were accomplished linguists and shared the pastimes of the local élite (Pappenheim was a good horsewoman). As well-born Jewish women had always done, they dispensed charity to the poor. Like their German counterparts, Jewish women were the more pious sex, and men the breadwinners; family Sabbaths and religious holidays had replaced Talmudic studies as the centre of Jewish religious life.[3] While by the mid century there were few Jewish girls with no education at all, and the wealthy merchant class even sent girls like Pappenheim to Catholic schools to acquire a secular education, few were encouraged to embark on a serious career.[4] Only Pappenheim's publication of a book was unusual, though her adoption of a pseudonym had precedents: the best-known German Jewish woman writer of the nineteenth century, Fanny Lewald, began her career at the age of thirty only after her father gave his consent to her writing; she published her first novels and stories anonymously.

But Bertha Pappenheim was not just another well-bred young woman whose literary talents were acceptable as long as she remained an amateur, and who did social work to fill in her time. In one circle she was already recognised as a woman of formidable intelligence and will-power, though one who had been mentally unstable. This was the tiny group of Viennese Jewish doctors and their wives who knew that Bertha Pappenheim was Anna O, the deeply disturbed young woman whose case history was documented in Josef Breuer and Sigmund Freud's *Studies in Hysteria*, published in the same year in which Pappenheim took over the running of the orphanage.

Breuer described Anna O as 'markedly intelligent, with an astonishingly quick grasp of things and penetrating intuition ... she had great poetic and imaginative gifts, which were under the control of a sharp and critical common sense ... bubbling over with intellectual vitality' which because of her boring domestic life 'left her with an unemployed surplus of mental liveliness and energy'.[5] The most remarkable aspect of this assessment is that it was written about a young woman whom Breuer had first encountered partly paralysed and blind and virtually mute, a 'hysterical' condition which had developed while she was nursing her dying father and which intensified after his death.[6]

Anna O became renowned in the annals of psychoanalysis not so much because of the severity of her mental illness but because, responding to Breuer's sensitive interest, she herself evolved a stratagem of survival: what analysts were to call the 'talking cure' by which repressed memories are believed to be articulated and their terror exorcised. Freud was inspired by the case, which was fundamental to his development of the psychoanalytic technique, and his first biographer, Ernest Jones, revealing Anna O's real identity long after her death, referred to her as 'the real discoverer of the cathartic method'.[7]

Both psychoanalysts and feminist writers have been intrigued by the fact that Pappenheim went on to become a leading Jewish feminist and social reformer. The intelligence, passion, and wit Breuer noticed are evident in her letters and reports—if not in her fiction.[8] Anna O has been posthumously 'analysed' by a score of practitioners in the field. Feminist writers have taken up Pappenheim no less eagerly, suggesting that her hysterical symptoms were the direct result of the frustration of a highly intelligent girl of great character, with no outlet for her intellectual talents, subjected to the enforced idleness of a privileged woman's life in *fin de siècle* Vienna.[9] But Pappenheim never underwent psychoanalysis; and we do not know what kind of therapy she was given after Breuer abandoned her case. Lacking the detachment of the trained psychoanalyst (a profession which did not yet exist), he fled in horror when his patient, whom he had thought 'cured', suddenly went into imaginary childbirth, having cast him in the role of father. Nothing at all is known about the seven years which separated his flight from Pappenheim's arrival in Frankfurt with her mother, save that some of this time was spent in sanatoria.[10] Thus it is impossible to ascertain exactly how Pappenheim overcame her mental illness.

Her lack of outlet for her intellectual capacities is surely an insufficient explanation for her breakdown. Pappenheim's complex relationship with her parents, who remained the dominant influence throughout her life in a way which was closely related to Jewish custom and family tradition, appears to have been at least as important a factor in her illness as the fantasy life she developed as a young girl (what she called her 'private theatre') as compensation for her frustrated energies.[11] At least one contradiction is outstanding. While she was aware that her activities after her parents' death (and particularly her interest in prostitutes) would have been incomprehensible to them, she continued to insist in her letters that her parents had been her inspiration and her model in life. She was, moreover, to form no relationship to replace the ties to her father and mother. Parents had been powerful figures in orthodox Jewish society when they decided on their children's future and their partners; now that marriage took place later, and boys had emancipated themselves, the greater was the emotional responsibility of the unmarried girl, and possibly the difficulty in forming other ties.

In orthodox Jewish society, social work and charity had been the occupation of the middle-aged woman whose children were grown, or of widows, ensuring that they too remained active. Now it was also that of the growing number of girls of good families who had not yet found a suitable husband. Breuer remarked on Pappenheim's strong social conscience and the fact that caring for poor and sick people enabled her to 'satisfy a powerful instinct'.[12] It was also a powerful Jewish tradition.

The best witness to the link between the sick, fantasy-ridden girl and the active, disciplined, but essentially solitary adult reformer whom she became is Pappenheim herself. She knew that she alone was responsible for her solitary life (she did not lack offers of marriage) and that her social work kept her sane. In a letter written from Palestine in 1911, at the height of her career, one of a long series written to the subscribers in her women's group, she apologised for having failed to take notes at her last port of call. 'I catch up on this duty because the word "duty" is one I like. It means a very good and necessary equivalent to my fantasy which goes on at a gallop, as if there were no duties at all. Duties which you accept of your own free will are laws you have given to yourself and are no burden. What is for you "duty" is for me "sacrifice", which consumes everything we do willingly.'[13] Pappenheim's idea of 'laws you have given to yourself' was obviously new. This was an individual response to laws handed down and ineluctable; the acceptance of duty, to the point of personal sacrifice, however, was traditional.

Pappenheim realised that her loneliness helped fuel her anger against oppression and injustice. In one particularly revealing letter, written from Warsaw in 1912, she expressed sympathy with Jewish revolutionaries: 'I have often thought that if one has nothing to love, to hate something is a good substitute. That is perhaps why I like to read the Workers' Press. They are so violent in their feeling for the masses or at least for their leaders, out of hate and yet out of love for their ideals.'[14] This suggests that, had she been born into a different Jewish community, she might well have become a radical.

Her work with immigrants from Eastern Europe, and her own journeys there, gave her a unique insight into (and perhaps a wistful envy of) the Jewish women radicals in a society so different from her own. In an essay on 'The Jewish Girl', written towards the end of her life, she described the greater maturity of the girls of Eastern Jewry: 'The misery and repression under which the Jews ... were forced to live and which made out of them pauperised and proletarian masses, influenced the Jewish girl as soon as she took wings to leave home and to join working women and students. In a highly political group, long repressed vitality found a hard won but happy freedon—the breaking of all links and forms was almost a sacred act for the individual.'[15] The word 'sacred' is significant here—as if the act of rebellion had a religious justification of its own.

The life of Bertha Pappenheim is most vividly illuminated, therefore, by seeing this feminist reformer in the specific context of Jewish women in the West in the late nineteenth century, torn between their loyalty to their traditional roles and duties and the new intellectual and practical opportunities now open to their sex. It is notable that Pappenheim was the translator of both the *Memoirs of Glueckel of Hameln* (one of her ancestors) and of Mary Wollstonecraft's *Vindication of the Rights of Woman*—a difficult and complex symbiosis. Pappenheim believed in education for women but—a hundred years later—was far less of a feminist than Wollstonecraft. She did not believe that middle-class women should become economically independent as a matter of principle, and she saw the family as a woman's first concern. She thought that even her chosen profession of social work should be performed by volunteers, rather than constitute a state service, a very traditional Jewish view. In one of several mocking obituaries for herself, she wrote, 'She was by descent and training an observant Jewess, but she believed herself separated from her roots—obviously under the revolutionary feminist influence. She was often hostile—but never denied her origins.'[16]

The leaders of the Jewish women's movements which developed towards the end of the nineteenth century in England and the United States and a few years later in Germany were solidly middle class in origin and inspiration. They tried to strike a balance between the tradition of public service by women which already existed in the Jewish community and the growing movement for women's education and emancipation in Gentile society. They were not feminists in the sense of claiming complete equality with men, though they struggled, with varying degrees of success, for representation.

In the mid-nineteenth century, both in England and America, women from the Jewish wealthy merchant class like Louisa Lady Rothschild and Rebecca Gratz were almost indistinguishable from the evangelical women who glorified family values, distributed charity, and encouraged educational reform. In the far more conservative Germany, where women had no civil rights nor the chance of higher education until the Weimar period, they had to battle far harder for representation in community organisations.[17]

Where Jewish women broke with tradition, it was in forming women's organisations which had no precedent; founding schools where boys and girls could study together; encouraging higher education for girls (in rare cases, even religious education); and, in what was perhaps the most extreme development of all, claiming the right of the single woman to independence, rather than marginal status within the society. A woman such as Pappenheim might now choose to remain single rather than enter an arranged marriage not to her liking. This was a striking innovation in Jewish life.

Jewish women tried to change the discriminatory bias against women in Jewish law, or to bypass it, with limited success. In the United States, the widespread adoption of Reform Judaism eliminated the physical segregation of women in synagogue worship and allowed girls into the Sunday school network (on the Protestant model) created by Gratz, a literary lady supposed to have been the original of Scott's 'Rebecca'.[18] In England, the women of the assimilated Jewish middle class, which regarded itself as virtually a dissenting church, set up their own benevolent and charitable societies on lines similar to those of Protestant reformers like Octavia Hill.

The 'Rothschild Houses' built in 1886 in the East End, however, indicate a certain difference. These offered an alternative to the Jewish slum, but their sponsors did not intervene in the domestic lives of the families who lived there.[19] Unlike their Gentile counterparts, the Jewish poor were usually more orthodox in the religious sense, and more tradition-minded than their benefactors, and they did not take kindly to moral lectures. However, whereas Jewish charity had demanded no equivalent of the means test, the new policy stressed the Victorian virtues of thrift and self-help.

In America and in England, two exceptional women, Ray **Frank Littman** and **Lily Montagu**, acquired a measure of rabbinical learning and even delivered sermons in synagogues belonging to the Reform and (in Britain) the new Liberal Jewish movement. Both were advocates of women's suffrage; while Littman abandoned her career on marriage, Montagu, who remained single, became one of the founders of the Liberals, organised clubs for single girls, and urged reform of Jewish law to achieve 'equalisation of women's rights in religious marriage and divorce'.[20] But traditional Judaism, even in its more assimilated forms in Britain and the United States, could admit of no radical change in Jewish practice where women's worship and religious law was concerned, even at the time when privileged women like Louisa Goldsmid, one of the founders of Girton College, Cambridge, were in the forefront of the campaign for women's education in Britain. In Germany, where the Jewish tradition of learning had become secularised—no more than ten to fifteen per cent of German Jews were orthodox by the end of the century—it was the sons in the family who were encouraged to study for professional careers, not the daughters. Pappenheim's brother Wilhelm, for instance, was sent to university, while her own education ended early—something she resented deeply.

Under the influence of local feminists, however, Jewish women formed their own community organisations. In 1893, a national Jewish women's organisation was set up in the United States whose aims were to help women study Judaism, to provide Sabbath schools for the poor, to undertake philanthropic work, and to act as a forum for the exchange of ideas.

In 1902 in England, a Union of Jewish Women was set up which performed these functions but also—following the example of the growing British women's movement—established girls' clubs and encouraged young working women to study and find work outside the factories and workshops.[21] Two years later, inspired by the example of the German feminist Helene Lange and her crusade for women's education and employment, Bertha Pappenheim founded the German Jewish Women's Movement, the Jüdischer Frauenbund, after she despaired of women enjoying administrative positions in Jewish charitable and social welfare organisations which, even when they dealt with women's affairs, were inevitably dominated by men.[22]

All these organisations, though they were influenced by Western European feminist movements in general, shied away from fundamental changes in women's positions in Jewish society. So Jewish women who wanted full emancipation joined the non-Jewish movements, where in Hungary, Austria, Holland, and Germany they led the fight for the vote. The most notable Jewish feminists were **Rosika Schwimmer** and **Vilma Glucklich**, who led Hungarian women to suffrage in one of the shortest campaigns in European feminist history (1904–1920); **Aletta Jacobs** and **Rosa Manus** in Holland; and **Anita Augsburg**, **Alice Salomon**, and the militant **Adele Schreiber** in Austria and Germany.

These women were giants in the feminist movements of Europe. Like other feminist leaders, most were hostile to radical politics; and they were not identified in any way with the Jewish communities from which they came. Socialist sympathies, and particular Jewish interests, were regarded equally as handicaps in suffragist circles, which, though not anti-Semitic, did not encourage what today would be termed ethnic pluralism. Most feminist movements, predominantly middle class, were concerned with votes for women, not with radical change; socialist feminists were a minority.

Aletta Jacobs and Rosika Schwimmer, prominent in the Dutch and Hungarian women's fight for suffrage, were both women of exceptional talent and strong personality. They were first to be close colleagues, but after a bitter feud over policy, complicated by personal animosity, severed relations completely during the First World War.

Aletta Jacobs, born in 1854 (a year before Anna Kuliscioff), was the first woman physician in Holland, as well as its outstanding feminist. Her medical activities as a pioneer of birth control (she opened a clinic for women in Amsterdam in 1882, where she dispensed contraceptive advice, and was part creator of the 'Mensinga' diaphragm) and women's doctor gradually gave way to her feminist activities; she became internationally famous when she organised the 1915 Women's Peace Conference in the Hague, which brought together women from the United States and Europe, from belligerent and neutral states alike.[23]

This was a remarkable attempt, on the part of a determined band of well-connected and distinguished women, to enlist diplomatic support for an attempt by the neutral countries (which then included the United States) to break the military deadlock in the trenches by negotiations.[24] The diplomatic records of England and France, weighed against the reports by the women peace delegates entrusted with missions to the chancelleries, suggest, however, that they were given no more than a polite hearing.[25] The chief weakness of the campaign (which has been given exaggerated prominence in feminist history in the light of contemporary women's peace movements) was not so much that it was all-woman, but that it did not at any stage appeal to, or attempt to recruit, the support of working women in the munitions factories, whose labour, at that stage of the war, was certainly more important to the politicians than the supplications of women arguing in the name of universal motherhood.[26] It is intriguing to note their firm belief that wars would end once women had the vote. The records kept by the delegates indicate that the women argued as vigorously for women's suffrage as for peace. A brave woman at the Congress who argued that most women, too, were pro-war was 'hissed'.[27]

Rosika Schwimmer, daughter of an assimilated Hungarian Jewish family, was a gifted political journalist, powerful orator, and successful suffragist leader years before she became, with Jacobs, a fervent pacifist and co-leader of the Women's Peace Movement. It was unfortunate both for the movement and for Schwimmer that in 1916 she recruited Henry Ford and his chunk of American business interests to the peace campaign.[28]

The Ford Peace Ship mission in late 1916 was ridiculed by the American press, rejected by the Women's Peace Movement, and finally ended when America broke off diplomatic relations with Germany in February 1917. The defamation of Schwimmer by her enemies in the Ford entourage as a scheming Jewess who had misappropriated Ford's funds put an end to her career in feminist circles. Her unsuccessful attempts to extract a formal apology from Ford continued for years.[29] After the war Schwimmer returned to Hungary, where she served briefly as ambassador to Switzerland under the liberal Karolyi regime— only to resign under that of the communist Bela Kuhn and to flee that of the Fascist Horthy. Though libelled as a German and a Bolshevik spy, she spent the rest of her life in the United States, as a proponent of world government. Schwimmer remained permanently stateless; her application to become an American citizen was repeatedly turned down because she would not agree, in her application forms or under questioning, to 'bear arms' on behalf of her adopted country; and during her declining years she was largely dependent on one of her American disciples.[30]

In their public lives, neither Jacobs nor Schwimmer made much reference to their Jewishness. Jacobs' autobiography ignores the fact almost entirely. But her model was her father, Abraham Jacobs, a country surgeon, an antimilitant, and a liberal, who encouraged her ambitions, not her mother, an industrious Dutch housekeeper.[31] Schwimmer, too, was raised in an assimilated family; she attended a Catholic school, sang in the Szabadka Cathedral Choir, and although the men in her family served in the officers' corps of the Hungarian army, she was chiefly influenced and aided in her career as a journalist by a feminist, suffragist, and pacifist uncle, Leopold Kutscher.[32]

The middle-class feminists' rare personal remarks about Jews, however, indicate both pride in their origins and a keen sense of the problems they produced. Writing to Schwimmer in Budapest in 1904, Jacobs said, 'We have recruited some good young workers to the suffrage movement. It is remarkable. They are always Jewish girls. With us and everywhere else, courage and spirit are found most in these girls.' But she was writing to a fellow Jewess. These were not sentiments she voiced in public.[33]

When Schwimmer gave an interview to a (Jewish-owned) American paper in 1915 on 'War and Feminism', she commented, 'I am surprised not to find more Jewish women filling the prominent place in the suffragette ranks in America. In Europe, the Jewish women have made the movement ... In some countries, for instance in Hungary, our opponents tried to discourage women's suffrage by calling it a Jewish movement.'[34] The same was true in Germany, where opponents of feminism branded it as inspired by Jews.[35]

Jacobs' chief lieutenant, **Rosa Manus**, was even more tormented by her Jewishness. She would not accept a leadership position for fear of anti-Semitic comment. To a Gentile colleague, Mia Bossevain, she complained in 1914, 'You simply don't know how dreadful it is to be born a Jewess ... nothing will ever change the world's attitude to our race.'[36] Manus was to try desperately, in the 1930s, to alert the international feminist movement to the peril of the Jews under Nazism; and the American feminist leader, Carrie Chapman Catt, tried to publicise the persecution of Jewish feminists in 1937. But when Manus was deported to a death camp by the Nazis in 1942, Catt circulated a letter to friends and acquaintances in the movement claiming that she 'was the first of us all to suffer and to die for our cause', ignoring her fate as a Jewess entirely.[37]

American feminists had turned their backs on Schwimmer in her hour of need during the Ford episode, and it was clearly in much despair that, in 1927, she penned a score of versions of a tragic letter to Ford's wife (a letter apparently never sent) in which she appealed for a public rebuttal by Ford of the libels against her. Schwimmer's mother was dying, and Schwimmer wrote that in view of the calumnies against her, her parents had begun to doubt whether the ideas of universal service to mankind which they had instilled in her might not have been less use to her than the principles of self-protection.[38] It was a question many Jewish idealists were to ask themselves during the Nazi period.

However, leading feminists like Jacobs and Schwimmer could scarcely have pursued their activities in a Jewish context. The issues of (public) birth control and pacifism were equally repellent to the Western Jewish leadership. Though statistics indicate that the privileged classes limited the number of their children, Jewish law was firmly against the idea of birth control save in cases where the mother's life was in danger and under other very specific circumstances. Though pacifism (like internationalism) was believed by anti-Semites to be supported almost uniquely by Jews, they played a very limited role in European pacifism at this time. So far from being 'internationalist', the middle-class Jews of Central and Western Europe were excessively patriotic; the right to serve in the army had been eagerly accepted as one of the benefits of emancipation. During the First World War many awards for bravery were given to Jewish soldiers in the armies of Europe, though many Jews were subsequently barred from Veterans' leagues. The pressures on Jews to prove their loyalty were overwhelming.

Thus, in promoting the causes of birth control and pacifism, outstanding Jewish women were, once more, rebels not only against convention but against the dominant beliefs of the communities to which they were bound, now, only by ethnic pride. If they were silent in public about their Jewishness, it was probably for the same reason that so many middle-class feminists, particularly in the United States, declined to acknowledge Jewish support for the feminist cause: the fear of being associated with political radicalism in any shape or form, particularly in view of the fact that Jewish women radicals were so prominent in revolutionary and anarchist movements.[39]

In England, **Rose Witcop**, and in the United States, **Emma Goldman** and **Rose Pastor Stokes**, were vigorous promoters of birth control, not in connection with the Malthusian and eugenics debates, as most birth control supporters (including Jacobs) were, but because of their socialist beliefs. Rose Witcop is a particularly interesting case; hitherto a neglected figure, she was important not only in disseminating birth control information but in helping family planning become an open issue for the British Labour Party.[40]

Witcop, who arrived in the East End of London from Russia as a child of five in 1895, began her political career as an anarchist, a member of the circle around Rudolf Rocker, the German, non-Jewish mentor of Jewish anarchist immigrants in London. Her sister, Milly, was Rocker's companion, and what he wrote of Milly (her three sisters 'went the same way', he wrote) was probably true of Rose as well: 'She had been very religious as a child ... In the Ukraine people kept the Jewish faith and practice. In London she found people for whom religion had become a dead ritual. The conditions under which she lived and worked forced her to draw conclusions which she could not reconcile with her old beliefs ... it must have been agony for her to be a divided being.'[41]

The anarchists made up the liveliest group among East End radicals and one in which women were particularly prominent. Rose Witcop entered into a free union with Guy Aldred, an anarchist, feminist, and pacifist. When he was imprisoned as a conscientious objector in 1916, Witcop ran the anarchist paper he edited, *The Spur*, for which she wrote a number of remarkable articles attacking not only the war but also those women suffragists, like Mrs Pankhurst, who supported it and who tried to win popularity for the suffragist cause by promoting war service for women.[42] She had previously also attacked, in the columns of another anarchist paper, those wealthy British Jews—the Rothschilds, Samuels, and Montefiores—who, at the time of the Beilis trial in 1913, had taken a different tone in their protest against Russian anti-Semitism to that of the Anglo-Jewish working class. She accused the financiers of helping to keep the Czars—among other capitalists—going, and thus 'with an engaging frankness, they confessed to having no quarrel with the Czar or his government.' Like all anarchist, and many socialist, Jews, she argued that there were two 'Jewish nations', 'the oppressed and exploited section, and the successful or exploiting section'.[43] The philanthropy of these Jewish leaders made no impression on her at all, and she felt no kinship with them.

After the war Witcop, like so many other anarchists, became disillusioned with the Russian Revolution—she visited the Soviet Union in 1921—and also severed her connection with Aldred, who married her, when they were already estranged, in order to prevent her deportation by the British authorities. Thenceforth her anarchist beliefs took second place to a campaign for birth control among the British working class which occupied her for the rest of her life.

From 1915 her articles in *The Spur* had shown a growing preoccupation with problems facing working-class mothers, and in particular the hypocrisy of those who urged them to bear sons only to sacrifice them in wars. After the war, her interest was the toll on female health taken by multiple childbirths and illegal abortions. She perceived that the spread of birth control centres by Marie Stopes had not solved the problem of working-class women, that the methods she suggested were not within their reach, and that her books, like others circulating, were too expensive and were targeted essentially to middle-class women. The eugenics argument that the state should limit the reproduction of the poor and disabled was also totally alien to Witcop's social ideas. Instead, she tried to popularise the work of Margaret Sanger, the American birth control pioneer whose ideas had developed from her work as a midwife in the poorer (and mainly Jewish) areas of New York. In 1923, Witcop and Aldred published Sanger's pamphlet *Family Limitation*, and were immediately prosecuted under the Obscene Publications Act. They were supported by the Malthusians, socialists, and leading feminists (including Bertrand and Dora Russell), who agreed with Witcop that 'the crime we have been guilty of was the circulation of [birth control] knowledge amongst the very poorest and the unemployed at a merely nominal price'.[44] Marie Stopes, however, inimical to radicals, refused to testify for the defence. The Aldreds lost their case, and Witcop was unable to appeal because of lack of funds. Copies of the first edition were impounded.[45]

But attitudes to birth control information on demand were changing, and this was the last trial for disseminating contraceptive advice in England; Witcop reprinted the pamphlet the following year (minus illustrations that had been judged obscene) successfully. The Aldred trial had aroused the interest of women in the Labour Party, in power in England for the first time during 1924; they formed the Workers' Birth Control Group, which now began to campaign for ministerial support for birth control instruction through state-controlled welfare centres.

Witcop, however, was not represented in this group after the first deputations to the Ministry of Health. In 1925 she opened her own birth control clinic in Shepherd's Bush—a middle-class area but one within easy access to working-class women in the East End who might have hesitated to seek advice nearer home. She ran this clinic until her premature death, after an operation, in 1932. While she may initially have been suspect for her anarchist beliefs, by the time of her death she was accepted in Labour circles and, according to her nephew, had been on the point of becoming a candidate for a safe Labour seat in Parliament.[46] But Sanger's association with anarchists like Witcop and Goldman certainly delayed her access to Aletta Jacobs, whom she admired and whose advice she sought, for years—though Jacobs softened later.

The leaders of the Jewish women's movements, even when they backed women's suffrage, were staunchly conservative, particularly where conventional family values were concerned. They put the well-being of the community, and Jewish solidarity, before feminist reform; and they were painfully conscious of anti-Semitism, believing that the way to make Jews fully acceptable in Gentile society was to adopt, as far as possible, the manners of the Gentiles, while preserving their own separate religious and family customs in the home.

Such movements tried to reconcile the Jewish notion of a separate sphere for women with the secular spirit of women's emancipation. This was a contradiction in terms; thus it seems doubtful whether they can really be called feminist.[47] However, in one sense at least they were thrust into a militant role by circumstance. Unlike their Gentile counterparts, the Western Jewish women's movements became the patrons of a working class of Eastern European origin, with whom they had little in common save their religious faith—even this practised in a different style. This involvement was to put Jewish women, with the help of a few male colleagues, at the front of the battle against anti-Semitism.

It was no accident that all the new women's organisations were set up in the decade of the greatest migration in Jewish history since the Inquisition. The target of the Western European Jewish feminists' enlightened philanthropy, social welfare, and educational work was, from the 1880s, a working-class population which was foreign and ultra-orthodox in the religious sense (thus, in Western eyes, outlandish and backward), and sometimes socially rebellious and politically radical: the immigrant Jews from Eastern Europe. But if the radical minority was to intermittently annoy and embarrass the established communities of the West, what was far more serious was that Jewish emigration on so massive a scale encouraged the breakdown of communal authority and the integrity of the Jewish family.

This encouraged anti-Semitic attacks on the one front Jews had always considered safe from calumny—their exemplary family life. It was in this battle that Jewish middle-class women for the first time publicly conducted the defence of their entire community. When eventually the Jewish women's groups of Western Europe and America were to join forces, it was in order to try to combat an evil which had its origins in the oppressed and disintegrating orthodox communities of Eastern Europe and which travelled with their emigrants: Jewish prostitution.

Because Britain led the 'vigilance' and 'purity' campaigns against white slavery, Anglo-Jewish feminists were the first to confront the problem of prostitution. The Americans were not far behind. But the German group was in some ways the most interesting. Pappenheim's Jüdischer Frauenbund was the most actively feminist of the Western Jewish women's organisations. The German Jewish community, in some senses the most assimilated of European Jewries, was also the most diehard in its stand against women's representation in communal bodies. In this, it was typically German. Germany was one of the most backward states in Europe where women's rights were concerned. But the Jewish community went beyond German resistance to women's emancipation. Even after 1918, when German women had been given the vote and were represented in the leadership of Protestant groups, most Jewish communities continued to deny women a say in communal affairs.[48] In 1919 the head of the orthodox community in Berlin, Rabbi David Hoffman, still claimed women were barred, on Jewish legal grounds, from public office, and the Frauenbund actually tried resorting to Talmudic quotations about women 'seal-bearers' in antiquity to justify their claim—unsuccessfully.[49]

In some senses, the Frauenbund was conservative. It limited its work to welfare and education. Its leadership was also strongly opposed to abortion and did not publicly advocate birth control. One reason was undoubtedly the fall in the Jewish birthrate, and another the incidence of intermarriage. But the Frauenbund was totally radical in its central concern: prostitution. Here it breached the silence and near-apathy of the official German Jewish male leadership. The men were slow to take up the challenge and when they did so, it was under conditions of near-secrecy, unlike their English counterparts.

The Frauenbund, by contrast, aligned itself publicly with international groups who were trying to combat the traffic in women. Pappenheim herself, unlike her women counterparts in England and the United States—who left work on the streets to their male colleagues—visited brothels in Eastern Europe and the Middle East and studied the treatment of venereal disease and the attitude of the local police towards pimps and prostitutes. In so doing, she frequently clashed with the male leaders of Jewish communities in Eastern Europe, and was unpopular with many in the West.

The policy of Jewish communities in the West towards the immigrant Jews was made up equally of solidarity—the heritage of communal responsibility—and the desire that the newcomers should not endanger the social standing of respectable, assimilated middle-class Jews. The ultimate expression of this fear was the encouragement of the immigrants' re-emigration, if not their repatriation. The Hilfsverein, the leading German Jewish social welfare organisation, was set up in 1901 with precisely this end in view. In England, the Jewish Board of Guardians played a major educational role from the late 1860s in providing training and education programmes for the Jewish poor;[50] from the 1880s the British and American leadership took traditional philanthropy out of the hands of the immigrant community heads and extended social welfare work to what was an attempt at mass re-education. Anglo-Jewish and American women played a central part in this campaign.

The greatest change brought about by emigration was the challenge to the authority of the rabbis and former community heads. In the Jewish township of Eastern Europe, families had turned to the rabbis for rulings on every detail of everyday life, and to the wealthy *gvirim* for intercession with the authorities. Despite the Czarist laws depriving the rabbis of much of their power, the communities had continued to seek rabbinical sanction and rulings, reluctant to appeal to the Gentile courts. Under Russian law, moreover, religious ceremonies were binding without a civil contract having been drawn up. This applied to Jewish marriage and divorce, a system which—despite the survival of discriminatory laws like that of the *agunot* or deserted wives—on the whole protected women within a stable community system.

With the expulsion of so many poor Jews from the countryside

of the Russian Empire to the cities and the consequent disintegration of so many traditional communities, however, both
the communal sanctions against sexuality outside marriage and
the family structure itself were damaged. There were brothels in
most Jewish quarters in Eastern Europe, as there were in the
host societies.

What was more serious for Jewish communities worldwide
was that Jews played a conspicuous part as traders in the
prostitution rackets of the late nineteenth century, particularly in
Turkey and South America; prostitution was officially condoned
in most of Europe at this time, and the police only intervened
in cases of violence. Outside Europe, prostitution was an open
market. Jewish middle-class communal leaders in Eastern Europe
and in Germany preferred to pretend Jews were not involved in
the traffic. The first concerted Jewish attack on the traders (rather
than on the prostitutes) came from the respectable Jewish middle
class in Britain (in Cardiff, the Welsh town where there was a
large Jewish community) and, significantly, from socialists in the
poorer districts in Warsaw, who sacked the brothels and ran the
pimps out of town.[51]

Most damaging to the Jewish reputation was the fact that, as
the anti-white-slavers soon discovered, the exploitation of Jewish
girls was made possible at least partly by the specific nature of
Jewish ritual marriage, which exposed many women and girls to
the traffickers. The simple ceremonies which sufficed to pro-
nounce a couple married in a Jewish community isolated from
the world were not recognised outside. In Western Europe and
the United States marriages and divorces had to be registered
with the civil authorities in order for women to have any legal
rights whatever. A woman abandoned by a husband had no
redress if she had no civil marriage certificate. Women who had
gone through only a religious ceremony or worse, the *stille
huppeh*—the marriage with none but the two necessary witnesses
and the most rudimentary ceremony (which in Jewish law
was still binding)—were not married in the eyes of the civil
authorities.[52]

Among the first generations of Eastern European Jews who

were newcomers to the big cities, and among immigrants, criminals took advantage of Jewish women's ignorance and their uncertain civil status. Parents entrusted their daughters to strange marriage brokers; pimps and traders 'married' a series of women and then handed them over to brothels; and the high birthrate and poverty of Jews in many parts of Eastern Europe led to girls leaving home to seek work in the cities. Many ended up in brothels. In the Jewish community as elsewhere in Victorian times, later marriage increased the number of young men seeking sexual activity with prostitutes. Finally, the emigration of thousands of men without their wives—promising to send for them later—left thousands of *agunot* who could not be formally divorced under rabbinical law, with little chance of tracing their husbands.[53]

Tragically, that carefully stratified legal system which had underwritten the Jewish family structure was undermined by the strains of emigration, community disintegration, and change. One of the strengths of Judaism had always been that it had no centralised hierarchy. The authority of the rabbi rested on the degree of his own learning, not on the fiats of a centralised ecclesiastical élite. But the consequence of this was that leading rabbis in Western communities often became social rather than theological leaders. Orthodox rabbis refused to change traditional practice even though it endangered women; and the rabbis who belonged to the community élite preferred to turn a blind eye to Jewish prostitution rather than draw attention to a scandal which might, if acknowledged, encourage anti-Semitism. While in Gentile communities church leaders often played a leading part in the fight against institutionalised prostitution and the international traffic in women, the rabbis—with a very few isolated exceptions—turned away in horror from an evil which was common knowledge in the congregations of Eastern Europe, publicised in the press of the West, and described even in Yiddish literature.[54]

The Jewish prostitute was abhorred, not pitied. The notion of the 'fallen woman' who might repent and be saved did not exist in Jewish law; there was no Magdalen figure in Jewish theology.

Girls who had 'strayed' could not be readmitted to the community. There was no provision for their children within the Jewish communal structure. Prostitutes were termed theoretically 'unclean' and barred access to the community; even in death they could not share Jewish burial.[55] In Buenos Aires, a special cemetery was established for the burial of Jewish prostitutes.[56]

The first woman to take action against Jewish prostitution was Constance Battersea, a Rothschild who learned of the Jewish prostitutes' plight in London from a Christian missionary friend who had been told, 'Our own people disown us, their Law forbids them to receive us again, and we will not enter a Christian home; we have no wish to join your church, for, however bad we may be, we will not give up our own faith.'[57] Lady Battersea, a Jew married to a Gentile, but not a convert, founded the Jewish Ladies' Society for Preventive and Rescue Work in 1885; it was later renamed the Jewish Association for the Protection of Girls and Women. This antedated any other Jewish women's association, linking Jewish and other women's movements.

Jews were undoubtedly prominent in the international traffic in women and girls between the 1880s and the Nazi period; but they were even more prominent, eventually, in the organisations which tried to combat it. Jews—in particular the women's organisations—were actively involved in intercepting prostitutes in transit; in rehabilitation and welfare work; and in framing anti-traffic legislation.[58]

But it took some time for the awareness of the traffic in Jewish women from Eastern Europe to filter through to the highly protected and respectable middle-class women of Central and Western Europe. They might have been dimly conscious that there were Jewish women among the prostitutes who worked the streets of every European capital, but only some personal knowledge of the immigrants' background could suggest the scale of the white slave traffic.

Fifteen years after Lady Battersea's revelation, Bertha Pappenheim learned, in her conversations with poor women immigrants from the East, of Jewish prostitution in Eastern Europe. In 1902 she founded a Jewish welfare society, Care for

Women, and, as its representative, attended her first conference on the traffic in women.[59] Here she learned of the scale and notoriety of Jewish participation. She knew very well the political danger of acknowledging Jewish prominence in the trade. But she also knew that to remain silent was to be guilty of complicity in what she regarded not only as an evil but as an injustice to women. Henceforth she dedicated herself not only to social work and women's rights but to trying both to understand and to combat the traffic in women—something she rightly dubbed 'Sisyphus Work'—and in doing so to resolve some of her own ambivalence towards the status of women in Jewish tradition.

Bertha Pappenheim was the youngest and only surviving daughter in an observant Jewish family whose origins, on her father's side, were in the ultra-orthodox communities of Hungary, and on her mother's the merchant aristocracy of German Jewry. For Pappenheim, the disadvantages of being a Jewish woman began at birth. Near the end of her life she was to write that the 'old Jews' offered congratulations only when a boy was born; the response to the question of the baby's sex if it was female was 'Nothing, a girl', or 'only a girl'.[60] Writing of 'the Jewish Girl', she pointed out that all the customs surrounding birth and the entry of the Jew into the covenant, the circumcision ceremony at which a boy received his name, applied only to males. Her comments on the habits of the old Jews illustrate what had happened to other orthodox practices in contemporary Germany, or what she called the 'somewhat more advanced West'. Boys were no longer sent to *cheder* at the age of three, but rabbinical students appeared in well-to-do homes, like her own, as tutors. Pappenheim commented: 'They brought a certain spirituality to the families and in return got a little culture.'[61] The phrase is typical of the ambivalent attitude of Pappenheim to the ultra orthodox, and to Eastern European Jewry among whom the old Jews' customs still prevailed.

Pappenheim respected and observed Jewish traditions, but she was certainly not an orthodox Jewess, and there is, in all her writings, the patronising attitude towards the 'uncultured'

Ostjuden characteristic of the German Jewish high bourgeoisie. Eastern Jews knew their Talmud, but they were frequently lacking in manners and secular learning; of the women, and their contacts with well-born Russian Gentiles, she wrote: 'Jewish society consists of many not very refined women and it must be difficult to deal with them, even if one does not belong to the nobility.' In her view, it was through the adoption of Yiddish, 'the women's German', that German culture had reached Eastern Europe, and in her travels in Eastern Europe, she believed that she traced 'a definitely German interest in education within Jewish womanhood' to the influence of 'German language and German spirituality'. She linked women's inability to follow the Hebrew of the synagogue, and the anachronistic nature of orthodox rituals, to the diehard nature of Eastern European orthodoxy and its resistance to change.[62]

There was no doubt in her mind that rabbinical law discriminated against women: 'The people of books locked women out of Jewish spiritual life, its sources; they were to believe and to do—without knowing why,' she commented, exactly like Grace Aguilar in England half a century earlier. Few Jewish women of Pappenheim's class and time were to attack Jewish tradition so trenchantly where women were concerned. The exclusion of Jewish women from learning was a sin, she maintained: 'The wife of the Jew was to carry bricks for family life as a beast of burden, her spirit was to remain dull.' The most famous verses in praise of women in the Bible, 'A woman of worth who can find, For her price is far above rubies,' Pappenheim termed 'a lovesong with gefülte fish'. Towards the end of her life, in 1934, she concluded that women were 'a torn thread' in Jewish tradition—Pappenheim's variation of Glueckel's 'golden chain'. The breach with tradition had been blamed on emancipation; but it was, she argued, the result of that discrimination against women which was an integral part of rabbinical Judaism.[63]

Thus far, Pappenheim was a rebel. Yet her attitude towards women's education and work shows that as the dutiful daughter, the loyal member of the Jewish community, and a woman of the German middle class, she could not stand up unequivocally for women's emancipation. She disapproved both of the Berlin salon Jewesses so renowned in German history and of these Jewish women revolutionaries of her own generation who had abandoned their communities together with their faith. Hostile to Zionism both as a patriotic German Jew and because of the antireligious bias of the Zionist left wing, she was sceptical as to whether Zionism would really afford women equality. She thought many Jewish girls who sought a university education did so for frivolous reasons, and she had no particular regard for women intellectuals, if they rejected the demands of family life. She also described the unmarried independent woman as 'a chrysanthemum born unique and without a future'. Though she, herself, remained single by choice, marriage, on the basis of free choice and equal partnership, remained her social ideal, and motherhood 'the essential goal of the Jewish woman's existence'.[64]

Pappenheim believed that gently nurtured, spoiled young women in the Jewish communities of the West should involve themselves in social work as a part of their real 'education'; this meant, for her, not book learning but the willing assumption of social duties.[65] 'To them, poverty is a street beggar or a scene in a play, sickness is disgusting, and crime is a sin. Under such circumstances we cannot be surprised when girls do not understand, or at best, feel fleeting pity for the tragedies of humanity.'[66]

It was in order to study Jewish prostitution more closely that Pappenheim set out in 1904 with a colleague, Dora Rabinowitz, to tour the Jewish quarters of the larger cities and the townships of the Austro-Hungarian region of Galicia. She was astonished to find that in Eastern Europe prostitution was common knowledge, and that the tough-minded and energetic rabbis' wives who, as she noted, had more practical knowledge of the world than their husbands were perfectly prepared to discuss it with her, even if, to avert the evil eye, they spat to one side as they did so.[67] These women, and the doctors and welfare workers she met, gave her an idea of the scope of the problem. She was immediately shown streets and brothels where Jewish prostitutes worked, Jewish traffickers combing the streets for likely recruits, and the hospitals where girls were treated for venereal disease.[68]

The conventional wisdom in middle-class 'vigilance' circles which engaged in crusades for 'sexual purity' at this time was that prostitution was a social evil caused not only by the double standard of sexual morality but by the poverty which drove women on to the streets when they could find no other way of earning a living. Pappenheim did not entirely concur.

The Jewish population of Galicia was, indeed, at the time of Pappenheim's first visit, one of the poorest regions of Eastern Europe. Contemporary Jewish statistics put the number of unemployed Jews, six years later, as half the population of 800,000, among them some 39,000 unmarried women.[69] Pappenheim's aim was to encourage women's training and education, as well as to provide what today would be called shelters for women in need of care: girls who had been driven to prostitution, unmarried mothers, and orphans. But her analysis of the causes of Jewish prostitution went far beyond the theory of the double standard and the desperation bred of poverty.

Economic need, she wrote on her return, was not the dominant reason for widespread Jewish prostitution in Galicia. She maintained that there were prostitutes not only among the poor but in the apparently religiously observant middle classes as well. It was not the 'emancipated' women, 'infected' with modern ideas about sexual freedom, who had taken to selling their bodies, commented Pappenheim, in what appears to be a reply to the male communal leaders who blamed emancipation. Orthodox rituals had become empty, she argued, the content lost, so that even observant married women sold themselves for a little extra cash.

While arguing against the ossification of religious practice, Pappenheim also attacked the attitude towards women's sexuality which was at the very base of Jewish teaching. In Jewish law, *halacha*, and according to Jewish mysticism, *kabbala*, she wrote, sexual relations were only approved if they had a reproductive purpose. While Pappenheim revered motherhood, she attacked the thinking which focused on women's biological purpose alone and ignored their spiritual potential. For thousands of years, she wrote, the Jewish woman had been regarded only as a 'sexual receptacle', and no attention had been paid to love. Women had no part in the spiritual life of men, no chance of intellectual fulfilment or, for that matter, of sexual fulfilment. Thus it had become unimportant to whom the woman gave herself. Feelings and sexual responses alike, she wrote, had been blunted. Pappenheim observed that women's lives in Galicia were 'a desert'. She did not comment, as many Germans did, on women's industriousness in orthodox communities; she compared their domestic abilities unfavourably with those of German women. Girls in Galicia were physically and mentally lazy, she said, hanging around waiting for an arranged marriage, waiting to be sexually used. They needed teaching and employment.[70]

This astonishing indictment, the bitter core of her 1904 report, which was the result of her first foray into Eastern Europe, is difficult to evaluate. It was the result of her personal observations, though her assessment of the scale of Jewish traffic in women was borne out in the enquiries carried out by the Jewish committees in Germany and elsewhere in subsequent years.[71]

But her views on its cause, while they went far beyond any contemporary analysis of Jewish prostitution, were not to be repeated in Pappenheim's later speeches in Jewish and inter-national forums, presumably because they might have fanned anti-Semitism.[72] There, she stressed the economic and social causes of prostitution, as well as pointing out that discrimination against Jews also contributed to the trade in women.[73]

Speaking at the 1910 Jewish International Conference on the Traffic in Girls and Women in London, she explained her initial bewilderment that Jewish prostitution existed at all, as Jewish ethics were so bound up in family life. But she said she had witnessed traders in the dress of orthodox Jews strolling the city streets in Romania and Galicia on Sabbath afternoons looking for girls to recruit. Jewish women ran brothels, and in one city she would not name, her guides had pointed out well-known Jewish procuresses. Even the Jewish intelligentsia, she insisted, was involved, and in Cracow, Lemberg (Lvov), and Czernowitz there were brothels in Jewish quarters. Pappenheim blamed the poverty of Jews in Eastern Europe, the misuse of liberty, the slackening of parental authority, and assimilation. Nothing was said on this occasion about Jewish sexual concepts, but she challenged the rabbis to face the facts and to help the vigilante organisations as the Christian clergy did. Moreover, she called on Jewish women to take the lead in erasing the traffic, using 'intelligence and tact' when raising children. 'Thinking women', she said, 'should realise that the family was not only an individual group but part of the community' to which their duty was paramount.[74]

Pappenheim's criticism of the rabbinical view of women as sexual objects did not change with the passage of time. Thirty years later, she wrote that arranged, early marriage, which had survived in Eastern Europe among the orthodox, and the sexual ignorance of the bride were contributory causes to the deterioration in sexual morals. She described the sexual 'enlightenment' after the wedding of the ignorant bride by her mother, both in tears. 'Here, I believe, are to be seen atavistically in our time, the beginning (though not the deepest) of psychological and sexual practices which seem to us today crude mistakes and blunders: the white slave trade and pretended marriage. The frivolous and myopic way of arranging marriages without any sympathy, even without the basis of a marriage of convenience, break up in present day conditions—and girls and women are the sufferers.'[75]

Nevertheless, Pappenheim is at some pains to argue that the Jewish family traditions in themselves were not to blame, any more than the role of the marriage broker. Jewish society in Eastern Europe, she suggested, had simply not adapted itself to modern life: and this was the heart of the matter.

Pappenheim's campaign among Jews was twofold: she tried to persuade the rabbis and heads of communities in Eastern Europe to modify Jewish law and abandon obsolete practices, as well as to issue warnings to their congregations; and she advocated vocational training and domestic work, which she optimistically believed would provide an alternative to prostitution.[76] In Germany, in 1907, she herself founded a home for 'endangered or morally sick' Jewish girls, at Isenburg near Frankfurt. Here,

unmarried mothers and illegitimate children could find acceptance and care, and, in accordance with her ideas, were trained
in 'home economics', which meant that they could find work later
as domestic servants. This was in tune with the Frauenbund's
philosophy that the first step to women's equality was training
in work limited exclusively to housewifery, social work, and
childcare.[77] Such homes existed in England, but for Jews this
was the first such home on the continent of Europe. Pappenheim
directed Isenburg—unpaid—for twenty-nine years.

Unlike her colleague the tough-minded American Jewess Sadie
American, Pappenheim never admitted that domestic service, or
the exploitation of girls in industry, could seem far more destructive and terrifying to an unprotected young girl than life in a
brothel. Nor did she agree with Sadie American that prostitutes
could not be 'saved'. In this she resembled the non-Jewish
vigilantes who protested against the double standard of sexual
morality in late nineteenth and early twentieth-century Europe.
There is a note of romanticism is what she writes about beautiful
girls in brothels, notably in Salonika and in Alexandria; she also
recognised that prostitution was for some girls adventure, self-
assertion, and a gesture of defiance towards their families.[78]

The letters sent back from Pappenheim's second tour of
Eastern Europe in 1911–1912 indicate both the problems she had
with prominent Jews and her own difficulties in 'understanding'
Jewish prostitutes. On this trip, she tried to enlist the help of
community leaders and rabbis in Austro-Hungary, Bulgaria,
Greece, Poland, Turkey and its dependencies. Time and again
she was rebuffed by community leaders, both because they
refused to face their responsibilities and because they did not
want to negotiate with a woman or admit women on to their
welfare committees. In all cases she found Jewish women more
helpful, though she was shocked that 'respectable' women were
involved in amateur prostitution, like a certain 'Laura L', a
Romanian Jewess living in a Bulgarian city who ran a dubious
café chantant and who also headed the local Jewish charity.[79]

The men's reaction differed according to country. In Budapest
the secretary of the local Burial Society (an influential figure in

all Jewish communities) told Pappenheim that prostitution was 'completely outside his duties'; and a leading rabbi, chairman of a society for the protection of children (many of the prostitutes were under age), asserted that he was not interested in the matter and that 'he would not allow himself to be converted'.[80] The chief rabbi in Constantinople, where, according to Pappenheim, ninety per cent of local prostitutes were Jewish and the traffickers were almost all male Jews, knew that there was a synagogue patronised by traffickers but refused to close it down.[81] In Lodz, Poland, Pappenheim found a Hasidic rabbi prepared to warn his congregants of the dangers to women and girls from traffickers in his community.[82] But he seems to have been an exception.

A businessman in Salonika did not want to discuss the few thousand prostitutes. Pappenheim objected, for her part, to the community's reformist proposal: to employ thousands of ten-year-old children in factories.[83] In Adrianapole, Thrace, the local rabbi, who held the Ottoman title of Chacham Bashi, told her that he had a list of fourteen 'bad girls'. 'He promised a girl in Constantinople that if she were good for two years he would find a husband for her—for a fee. If the fourteen girls would not reform, he would punish them by publishing their photographs, cutting their braids, or writing on their foreheads with indelible ink.' Pappenheim reported: 'Though the Torah demands punishment, I pointed out that these were children ... he promised to give up this form of punishment.' Pappenheim thought this rabbi meant well but was sure the number of 'bad girls' was a hundred times greater than his estimate.[84] Only in Jerusalem, despite dire poverty, Pappenheim found no Jewish prostitutes since (though she did not care for the city) in the holy city 'piety outweighs depravity'.[85]

On her way back to Germany via Warsaw in 1912, writing to her little group of women subscribers in Germany, those colleagues who took the place, in her life, of family or intimate friends (and whom modern feminists would call a 'women's support network'), she made a rare admission of her personal loneliness. She was gratified, Pappenheim wrote, that her colleagues missed her, since 'I am not necessary. For nothing and to no one. This is not an accusation, probably it is all my own fault—only a fact. And this makes it easy for me to live like a nomad.' In expressing her nostalgia for her home in Frankfurt, she wrote, what she missed most poignantly was her collection of fine lace. Lace was part of a girl's trousseau, a sign of family wealth, of distinction; its delicacy suggested that it was only at some cost to herself that Pappenheim had chosen to face the facts of sexual squalor. It also hints at a reason for her single state. The letter continued: 'If I were not an enemy of all poetic comparisons, and if all such comparisons were not lame, I would say that our lives should also be made out of fine flawless material and be interwoven in a way which is sometimes simple and sometimes complex, sometimes aesthetic and sometimes ethical, but this is the only longing I have: to live such a life. I hate the clumsy fingers which disturb my beautiful planning and tear my threads or destroy them.'[86]

Pappenheim became a leading figure in the international organisations set up to counter the trade in women; she worked together with Catholics and Protestants and during her travels came into contact with women social workers of many different persuasions. Her letters and the records of international conferences indicate that, while involved in this work, she encountered growing anti–Semitism.

Within the German and Eastern European Jewish communities she had to combat rabbinical prejudice against women and the hostility of those who believed she was endangering Jews by her campaign; in the outside world, however, she had to fight on behalf of all Jews against those who eagerly seized on the facts of Jewish traffickers and prostitution in order to blacken Jewry as a whole.

The period of emigration, of World War I, and of economic depression—all of which encouraged prostitution—coincided with the rise of political anti-Semitism in its most virulent form. Both at the League of Nations and later in Nazi Germany, Pappenheim and her colleagues among the Jewish vigilantes hoped that their efforts to expose and curb the Jewish traffic in women and girls would head off calumny and anti-Semitic abuse. Conscious of the vulnerability of Jewish communities, and intensely self-critical, they believed that anti-Semitism was, at least in part, a rational phenomenon. But at the heart of that anti-Semitism which battened on Jewish prostitution were racial prejudices and phobias that had little to do with the facts about the traffickers and those who fought them. The Nazi sexual libel was that Jewish male traffickers dealt in innocent Aryan flesh. But the real tragedy was that, as Pappenheim pointed out, most of the traffickers, the girls, and the clients in the Eastern European trade were Jews.

'If we admit the existence of this traffic, our enemies decry us; if we deny it, they say we are trying to conceal it.'[87] This was how Bertha Pappenheim summed up the terrible dilemma facing the Jews in 1927. This was the year of the League of Nations' report on the traffic in women and girls, which earned world Jewry unwanted publicity. Nazism, meanwhile, was on the rise. The very efforts that the Jews had made to defend themselves against anti-Semitic slurs, exposing the extent of the Jewish traffic, rebounded on Jewry as a whole.

There were several reasons why this happened. Sexual phobias about Jews were as old as anti-Semitism. The Gentile attitude from the Middle Ages was that if Jewish prostitutes wanted to ply their trade with Gentile clients, they had to undergo conversion. Amazingly enough, this situation still prevailed in parts of Central Europe, even at the turn of the century.[88]

The fear of sexual 'pollution' combined with the fear of the foreigner or alien, and both were exploited ruthlessly by the Nazis. The Jewish emigration from Eastern to Western Europe amplified these fears. As early as 1892, even the impeccably liberal August Bebel, a Social Democrat deputy in the German Reichstag, alleged that Jewish girls from Eastern Europe were being baptised in Germany in order to become prostitutes and should be deported.[89] In Britain, the 1906 Aliens Act, which restricted immigration to those seeking political asylum, discouraged Jewish immigration thenceforth. Even in liberal Britain, aliens and foreigners (which also meant Jews) were suspected of including undesirable elements: the dreaded radicals in the East End, Yiddish-speaking revolutionaries, and finally Jewish pimps and prostitutes. There were very few of these in the community, but they were much publicised in the popular press.

Jewish leaders unwittingly abetted these fears. The Chief Rabbi, Herman Adler, and Claude Montefiore, one of the campaigners against the white slave traffic, both argued that any Jewish prostitutes were foreigners. Adler claimed that these women had been driven to prostitution by persecution. Montefiore said that 'they had not had the benefit of an English upbringing'.[90]

In 1913 a proposal was made at an interdenominational congress on the traffic to deport immigrant prostitutes from Britain. The question was hotly debated and opposed by the Jewish delegates, including Bertha Pappenheim.[91] In the United States, immigrant prostitutes were deported from 1910, and from 1918 alien anarchists could also be 'repatriated'.[92]

Bertha Pappenheim encountered anti-Semitism at each of her appearances in international congresses from 1904 onward. But participation in interdenominational groups was necessary for several reasons. Jewish communities were reluctant to expose the problem publicly and alone. Catholic and Protestant groups usually had easier access to the local police and to the courts. In England and in the United States, Jews who were fully represented in national institutions were prepared to play a public role in legislation against prostitution. In France, a courageous woman, Madame Simon, took up the issue, while the Jewish press remained silent. Throughout the 1890s the Dreyfus case was too sensitive an issue to risk more undesirable publicity for the Jews.

Jews worked together, therefore, with other religious groups at railway stations and at ports, where they intercepted girls travelling alone, warned them against cruising traffickers, and when possible tried to send them home. But Jews were also opposed to the repatriation of immigrants of their own faith, who were almost always fleeing persecution.

The anti-Semitism encountered by Pappenheim was sometimes

disguised as a desire to convert the prostitute. More often, it was open hostility. She describes contempt, anger, and slander against the Jews. But Pappenheim had the misgivings of a woman who had to fight both inside and outside her community. She repeats several times the accusation that Jewish parents were 'selling' their children, and she records it as confirmed in Lodz in May 1912 by a certain Frau B., who was an orthodox German Jewish social worker.[93] There is no explanation of what she means by 'selling'. Possibly she means that dubious characters bid for girls who were handed over on payment of the traditional sum by which the 'groom' ensured the future security of the 'bride'.

Pappenheim reported that there was no shelter or asylum in Europe for a Jewish prostitute, and compared this unfavourably with the situation for Protestant and Catholic girls. Christian girls, she was told, could go back to their native village, even after a sexual misadventure, and marry. Moreover, according to Pappenheim and her informants, unmarried mothers in the Jewish community had no chance of marriage.

When Pappenheim arrived in Czarist Russia in May 1912, she was horrified by what she called 'the unquestioning way in which the procurers are called JEWS. It's truly shocking. It would help ... if the Russian committee and some other people would get acquainted with me, a Jewish woman, who feels ashamed and tries to work against it.'[94]

When Pappenheim met an anti-Semitic Russian aristocrat, she could not convince her that Christian ethics had their foundation in Judaism. 'As to aesthetics, the adaptability and crookedness of our race, I had to be silent, for Countess B. was right. She could only see the product of our difficult history.' After visiting the countess's shelter for the homeless in Moscow, Pappenheim records, 'My thanks were sincere, though I knew that conventionally and politely I shook hands with an enemy.'[95]

After the First World War, the grinding poverty of the Jews of Eastern Europe and the new laws in the West restricting immigration made the problem of the traffic worse, as the traffickers, to evade restrictions, sent more girls to South America. It was at this stage that the newly established League of Nations set up a special commission to enquire into the international traffic in women and girls. 'Experts' sent out questionnaires, to states in Europe and America and to the voluntary organisations that had been trying to cope with the traffic. The Jewish voluntary organisations were not religious, though Jewish prostitutes were recognised as belonging to a separate community, defined ethnically rather than in terms of their faith. This gave them undue prominence. A number of governments either replied that they had no information, or merely acknowledged receipt of the questionnaire. These included the governments of a number of South American countries notorious as havens for the traffic: Argentina, Chile, and Cuba among them. On the other hand, the Jewish organisations which had been approached, anxious to clear their communities of the stain, responded eagerly, handing over all the information in their possession.[96] Consequently, the commission's summary of the information received gave the impression that the traffic was a specifically Jewish problem.

Historians have established that while Jewish traffickers were certainly prominent in the trade, in no country was the number of registered Jewish prostitutes disproportionate to the community as a whole.[97] This was not the picture which emerged in 1927. When the League report was published, its first section qualified as a profoundly anti-Semitic document because of the emphasis placed on Jewish participation in the trade—based on information provided by Jewish organisations. This was a disaster, and the report was bitterly condemned by Pappenheim herself.

The final and most terrible irony for Pappenheim was that with the rise of Nazism, the work that she had done was turned against her and other Jews. The Nazis made the Jewish role in the traffic a central feature of anti-Semitic propaganda. Julius Streicher's obscene publication *Der Stürmer* dedicated an entire number to the libel that Jewish pimps and traffickers were perverting, polluting, and corrupting innocent Aryan women. Pappenheim lived just long enough to witness the introduction of the Nuremberg Laws at the end of 1935, one of whose provisions was the prohibition of sexual contact between Gentiles and Jews, the so-called 'Racial Pollution' law.

Now an old woman, dying of liver cancer, Pappenheim's last excursion outside her home was to answer a summons by the Gestapo in the spring of 1936. One of the inmates of her home for girls at Isenburg had been overheard making an anti-Nazi remark, and Pappenheim had to explain this away. On her walk, she might have perceived on the walls of her native town, Frankfurt, a Nazi broadsheet which quoted from one of her own speeches against Jewish prostitution.[98]

The full story of what happened to the Isenburg home has never been revealed. The Nazis closed it down, and the fate of the girls is unknown.

It was probably fortunate for Pappenheim that she died shortly after her summons to the Gestapo. Thus she was not to witness the destruction of German Jewry and the end of what her friend Martin Buber called 'the thousand year symbiosis of German and Jewish culture'.

The traffic in Jewish women and girls came to an end only with the assimilation of the Jews into the middle classes of Europe and America, the complete end of emigration from Europe following the outbreak of the Second World War, and the destruction of European Jewry in the Holocaust.

'I NEED A VIOLENT STRIKE'

༄ۚৡ۫

Rose Pesotta and American Jewish Immigrant Unionists

In the spring of 1936 a Jewish woman union leader, Rose Pesotta, helped organise the first big strike at a mass production factory in the United States: the Goodyear tyre factory in Akron, Ohio. Pesotta had been loaned to the Congress of Industrial Organizations (CIO), the rebel wing of the American Federation of Labor (AFL), concerned with organising unskilled labour in mass industry, by the International Ladies' Garment Workers Union (ILGWU), the most durably socialist of American unions.

Pesotta, with three top CIO organisers, harangued the workers, defied the employers' hired roughnecks, and held the picket line. Her main task was to organise what were called the women's auxiliaries—not only the few women workers at the Goodyear plant but the more substantial number at the local union branch of the Firestone plant, and the wives, mothers, and girlfriends of the strikers. They brought hot food and clean clothing to the workers barricaded in the factory, drove off the 'scabs', and withstood police brutality. Pesotta, a handsome and spirited woman, led the singing to keep up their spirits, earning the nickname of 'the Rose of Akron'.[1]

Akron was the climax of Pesotta's personal fight for a new America. She was by far the most radical of the handful of Jewish women union leaders who left the factory bench for union work. An anarchist by conviction, she justified her participation in union activity to her comrades by arguing proudly that she, the active labour leader, represented the downtrodden better than those who handed out leaflets at street corners and disdained all organised movements. To her fellow unionists, she maintained that she was a 'propagandist' for a society in which industry would be a co-operative venture owned by the workers, not a 'peanut politician', one of the bureaucrats she despised.[2]

In the 1930s Pesotta was at the height of her career as paid labour organiser and, from 1934, sole woman on the ILGWU executive. In the thirty-odd years of that union's history, she was only the third woman to hold this office, and the first to make her mark.[3] She had worked since 1920 as a leader of women workers in the clothing industry, recruiting thousands of women who hitherto had remained outside the union, most of them immigrants but not Jews.[4]

A skilled and pugnacious organiser, by 1936 Pesotta had garnered experience not only in those parts of East Coast cities where the working class was Jewish but also in cities like Milwaukee and Seattle, where she complained that American-born dressmakers, '100 per cent daughters of ... American pioneers, members of bridge clubs, card clubs and lodges', had no sense of working-class solidarity.[5] She earned her promotion to the union executive with her successes in the big cities of the West Coast, where Mexican and Chinese women, bound by family and ethnic loyalties, had been afraid to rebel against their employers or to endanger their jobs by joining the union. She carried the union's message as far afield as Puerto Rico (whose primitive conditions reminded her of the market town in the Ukraine where she had spent her girlhood) and another anti-union stronghold, Montreal, where she tried to organise Catholic French Canadians.

The heroic days of the CIO strikes marked not only the climax but the turning point in Pesotta's life. Thereafter she became increasingly embittered by the Jewish male leadership's preference for men fieldworkers and for a token woman on the ILGWU executive—even though that woman was herself. Pesotta was enraged that while the vast majority of rank-and-file workers in the garment industry were women, their interests were defined and represented by men. Six years after the Akron strike, she retired to the factory bench as an ordinary 'operative' (worker in charge of a machine); and two years later she resigned from the executive.

Pesotta's personal letters suggest that the decision to retire at the height of her career had several motives. She was frustrated as the sole woman leader in a male-dominated union. She sensed that the revolutionary idealism she shared with the radical nucleus of Russian Jewish immigrants was on the wane, and that socialist ideas had failed to strike roots among the American working class. But what ultimately tipped the balance was the growing weariness and loneliness of a tough but emotionally vulnerable woman, most of whose life had been spent travelling from factory to factory in trains, living in grim lodging houses, standing for hours on public platforms, and picketing in all weathers. She often wrote longingly of the warm, friendly work room where she could sit at her machine, the substitute for a home. For Pesotta's marriages and love affairs had been as much of a battlefield as the public life in which, as one labour historian has noted, 'she took no shelter and asked no quarter'.[6]

When Pesotta arrived in America in 1913, with her grandmother as chaperone (her parents feared the traffickers who waylaid single girls), the 'revolution in the needle trades' was at its height. Between 1909 and 1920 Jewish girls led the rebellion against women's exploitation by factory owners and sub-contractors in the garment industry, and against conditions in the sweatshop which sapped their health and sometimes claimed their lives.

The ILGWU leadership, unlike that of most other American unions in the AFL, was made up of men who not only believed in improving working conditions and wages but who were socialist in their political outlook. The garment industry had been the first to defy the crafts and organise on a countrywide basis. Between 1910 and 1920 women who had organised by their own initiative made up most of the ILGWU membership, and formed one quarter of all women in America's unions during the second decade of the century. This was all the more remarkable because women's countrywide membership was so low at this period— only about six per cent of the total.[7]

So it was no coincidence that the CIO, at the time of the mass-production strikes, requested a woman from the New York garment industry to organise the rubber workers in the Ohio valley. Although the commitment of John L. Lewis, the CIO's leader, to radical change was dubious (as Pesotta already saw), he was determined to break up what remained of the traditional, craft-based structure of labour organisation in the mass-production industries—something which most socialists saw as a major obstacle to progress.

During the 1930s, both the CIO and the AFL tripled union membership, with twenty per cent of this increase made up of women.[8] But the labour activism of the 1930s proved a false dawn for socialists. Roosevelt's New Deal policies were to pre-empt their appeal to the American working class, and with the unions on a more solid footing from the mid-1930s, radicalism was disarmed. After the Second World War the CIO was to rejoin the AFL. Though socialist ideas persisted in Jewish labour organisations for somewhat longer than in labour circles in general, the Jewish woman radical was already becoming a rarity, more a reminder of the past than a herald of the future.[9]

As the majority of Jewish union women left factory work on marriage, and as the economic situation of the Jewish working class steadily improved, the 1930s also saw a decline in Jewish women's rank-and-file activities in the unions. Jewish women were never typical of the female working class as a whole in the United States. Though they were most militant during strikes, they were much less active in union activities on a permanent basis. This was not only because of male prejudice, but because Pesotta and the handful of Jewish union women like her were an exception in their dedication to labour activism.

Each of these women unionists, in her own way, was affected by the prevailing trend away from socialism in American labour movements. **Rose Schneiderman**, for many years head of the

Women's Trade Union League (WTUL) and subsequently a leading figure in labour circles under the Roosevelt administration, was by far the most important figure historically. Though she continued to call herself a socialist, she found her radical past an increasing embarrassment during her long tenure as head of the WTUL, whose campaign against the exploitation of working women was moral rather than political. Most of its major figures were affluent native-born Americans. Schneiderman opposed the Equal Rights Amendment, first proposed in 1923, not only for fear of undermining those benefits the women unionists had achieved but because she accepted the need for government patronage of women. She became the chief architect of protective legislation for women in the period of the New Deal.[10]

Leading Jewish unionists found work that was not politically controversial. **Pauline Newman** and **Fannia Cohn** dedicated themselves to improving the health and education, respectively, of the women in the unions. The women who had been symbols of Jewish women's militancy disappeared from the scene. **Clara Lemlich**, for instance, one of the most dramatic figures in the 'revolution', the young girl who had issued the legendary strike call, in Yiddish, in the dark days of 1909, retired from active life while she raised her children and re-emerged years later in the tiny communist camp, which had become a besieged refuge for American radicals.

There were a number of outstanding Jewish women among American socialists, chief among them **Theresa Malkiel**, who began her career as a union organiser in the 1890s, and **Rose Pastor Stokes**, who later became a leading figure in the Communist Party, but their involvement in union affairs was less important than their role as propagandists.[11]

Jews played a leading part in labour reform in America between the 1880s and the 1930s only partly because of the socialist ideas they brought from Eastern Europe. The garment workers' 'revolution' began at a meeting where the slogan was not 'Workers of the world, unite' but an old Jewish oath. A tradition of communal solidarity and a sense of class consciousness within the community made them activists, though the much vaunted 'ethic of social justice' did not extend to women. Jewish employers had no particular compassion for the women immigrant workers, and Jewish trade unionists were no more sympathetic to women's claim for equal consideration in the workplace than those labour leaders in America at large who feared both women's competition for jobs and their willingness to accept lower wages.

Where the rank and file of Jewish women workers were concerned, their experience of the American workplace influenced them in contradictory ways. The fact that they were exploited by male employers did not make them more feminist, in the American sense. Even for the politically conscious, a new sense of independence and opportunity, despite the problems, tempered their revolutionary zeal. There was no straightforward transfer of radical ideas from Russia to the United States. The American class structure, the development of American industry, and the libertarian environment all made such a transfer impossible.

In Eastern Europe, middle-class Jewish women had acted as teachers of socialism; skilled women workers had formed an important part in the leadership of the Bund. But in the United States, those middle-class (and mostly non-Jewish) women in the WTUL who encouraged the workers' revolution in the name of women's rights and solidarity across class barriers were part of a very different culture—they were career-activated feminists less bound by family or communal ties. In the Jewish context, distinguished middle-class American women—usually of German-Jewish parentage, like Lillian Wald, who founded the famous Henry Street settlement (on the lines of London's Toynbee Hall), Idah Rauh, and Belle Moscowitz, all of whom were active in social welfare legislation and strike organisation among the Jewish immigrant workers, and who supported the WTUL—had a different vision of the just society. They were in favour of protective legislation for women workers, even at the cost of excluding them from many occupations and reducing their wages. They shrank from any association with genuine radicals, those whom they could not patronise.

The Jewish seamstresses of Eastern Europe had belonged to

a working-class élite, proud of its skills. But in the United States, young girls, many scarcely out of childhood, who had not as yet gained experience at work, were funnelled into an industry which split up the process of dressmaking into a number of different tasks in the interests of speed and mass production.[12] If a girl wanted to acquire the composite skills which would earn her a higher wage, to become an 'operative' rather than a 'finisher', she had to show personal initiative and risk security by continually switching from one job to another. While some worked their way up in the trade, most girls wanted simply an easier work load, better working conditions and pay, and the prospect of an early marriage that would end their life as wage-earners altogether.

The third major difference was that in Eastern Europe the girls' rebellion was directed less against a capitalist than against an authoritarian regime, and for both this reason and that of tradition, they became involved in conflict with their parents. There, Jewish employers in most of the small workshops were scarcely better off than their employees, and the girl workers saw little chance of immediate change; they were all the more drawn to a radical and theoretical ideology. In the United States the employer, not the state, was the enemy. Wringing concessions from bosses whose concern was to cut costs to the minimum, at the girls' expense, satisfied all but the most radical.

In the new country, Jews, and families, clung together. Family obligations still dominated Jewish culture; the girls worked to help the family in the new country or to bring relations from the old to increase the family income, or to help pay for their brothers' education, not to achieve independence. Women who had ambitions outside the family looked beyond industry. Jewish women made up forty per cent of New York's night school pupils in 1910–1911; many were to emerge from the working class altogether and become teachers, social workers, or professionals.[13] Though they usually had the backing of the family when they went on strike (unlike, for instance, Italian or Chinese women), working for a wage ended at marriage, though wives might help husbands in the shop or take in lodgers.[14] The women union leaders were lone figures, too, in their willingness to remain single—the usual fate of women unionists, Jews or non-Jews alike.[15] Marriage caused the high turnover in the workplace and, consequently, in the ranks of unionised women. In the most militant New York trade union branch, Local 25, the work force changed every three years.[16] The Jewish women's 'revolution' of the early decades of the century was more a reaction against the specific working conditions the girls encountered on their arrival in America than a commitment to radical changes in the social, political, and economic system.

Unlike most of the leaders of the WTUL, the Jewish socialist union women had all done their stint on the factory bench or in the sweatshop. They were very close to the girls they represented; and they had felt the abuses by employers and the slights from union men in their own working lives.

All came to America, travelling steerage just before or after the turn of the century. Some, like Schneiderman and Pesotta, came to join a father or sister already at work. They arrived almost destitute; Newman's family had all their belongings stolen, including the family Bible in which the children's births were inscribed—so she never knew her birthday and adopted that of the Bolshevik revolution.[17] These women were scarcely out of childhood—and though they had fled the poverty and insecurity of Jewish life in the *shtetl* and the prospect of a marriage like that of their mothers, they were all to look back nostalgically at the security of family life. Only Malkiel managed to combine family life with union activities.

Schneiderman, Pesotta, and Newman all felt particularly close to their learned, pious fathers, who had encouraged them to sit in the *cheder* with the boys; Newman's father had even helped her to study the Talmud. But adolescence brought conflict for them all. Newman recalled that the segregation of women in the synagogue aroused her resentment, and her father's explanation did not satisfy her: 'In later years I often wondered whether this early observation conditioned me to resent and fight against all discriminations based on sex. I think it did.'[18]

All were rebels against Jewish women's fate in traditional society and their mother's lives of drudgery and childbearing. Schneiderman, whose father died shortly after their arrival in America, had wanted to become a teacher; her mother disapproved of factory work. She found that working as a cashier or hat-check girl, though more 'genteel' in American terms, was even more humiliating.[19] Pesotta left her hometown to escape an arranged marriage. Malkiel wrote of women as victims of 'the breeding beast', took a Jewish fellow socialist to task for praising women as 'instinctual, intuitive creatures' and looked forward to a socialist society in which 'women would cease to be idle candidates for marriage, children no longer a burden, and women would return to a primeval freedom'.[20]

When these older women unionists were young girls and began factory work, they were packed into crowded, airless rooms, into which they were locked for the entire day, save for trips to the lavatory, when their absence was timed. The custom of locking the girls in at work was partly responsible, with the absence of fire precautions, for the disaster of March 1911, when a fire broke out at the Triangle shirtwaist (blouse) factory (where Newman spent years of her working life). One hundred and forty-five women, mostly immigrants, lost their lives, either asphyxiated or killed by their leap from the upper windows of the ten-storey building. Other, less dramatic, 'rules' invented by employers also made the working day an ordeal.

The girls were fined (by having money deducted from their already meagre wages) on any pretext—for lateness, talking, laughing, spoiling material, losing a screw on a machine. The working day had no limits. In busy seasons it could last thirteen hours a day, seven days a week. Women's salaries were substantially lower than men's, not only when they were unskilled but even when they became operatives with the same abilities and responsibilities as men.[21] Male cutters and tailors dominated the trade. If skilled, the girls had to pay for use of their sewing machines and even for the thread they used. They could be hired and fired at will—sometimes even when, like Newman, they worked too fast or too efficiently, which might lead to demands for higher pay.[22]

Women workers were bullied and sexually harassed as a matter of routine, fondled and propositioned by supervisors and employers, and, when they worked alongside men, were deliberately subjected to conversation they found offensive. If they demonstrated or went on strike, they could be assaulted by hired thugs or prostitutes, arrested or brutalised by the police.[23]

In the 1890s there was no organisation to which they could turn for help. In New York, with the biggest concentration of immigrants, where many girls who had come to America ahead of their families rented a 'place in a bed' and a sheet in another family's tenement home, there was one charitable organisation available: the Clara De Hirsch home for working girls.[24] There were as yet no trade schools in which they could acquire the kind of skills which would improve their earning power. Middle-class Jewish social workers encouraged 'housewifery', not work in industry.

Vital as the girls' labour was to the community, the single girl remained as powerless as she had ever been in Jewish society, even now that she was the breadwinner—sometimes the only one in the family. The United Hebrew Trades, formed from the old *khevre* tradition of male craft industries, did not encourage or seek women's participation in the unions, and at first recruited them only for the 'seasonal' unions—those formed for a definite purpose after a strike.[25] Girls could and did join the male unions but were made to feel redundant; the union was a male precinct, with meetings held late at night, in public halls where a girl alone could easily feel uncomfortable.

Conditions in the garment industry, in which most Jewish girls worked, were not the worst. Rose Pastor Stokes rolled cigars in 'a suffocating effluvia [sic] of tobacco dust', in a shop where children under statutory working age like herself were hidden when inspectors called. 'The leaf tobacco in which we rolled our bunches was often so rotted, that we had to re-roll our "stogies" several times'—and pay was according to the number of cigars completed[26]. Rose Schneiderman, an ardent suffragist, gave this answer to a senator who told her that women would 'lose their charm' if they became voters. 'There was little charm in women working in foundries stripped to the waist or in laundries where they stood for 13 hours in terrible heat and steam with their hands in hot starch.'[27]

American women had begun unionising in the last decade of the nineteenth century, but the Jews in the garment industry were the first to organise the most dramatic and active protest against conditions at work. Malkiel, who immigrated in 1891, was among the founders of the Infant Cloak Makers Union of New York, the first organised group of women to demand and win recognition as a union from the United Hebrew Trades. The union did not survive long, but it encouraged groups of women workers to band together and join the union as a unit and to set up a 'local' or branch.[28] Schneiderman, who arrived in 1900, was sewing linings in hats by 1903 and got twenty-five women together in a 'local' of the United Cloth and Capmakers Union. Her energy and success in recruiting girls soon won her a place on its executive board, the first woman ever to hold such a position. Her friend and colleague, Pauline Newman, became the first female organiser with the ILGWU, which ultimately fielded a number of women unionists.

During the two decades which followed, Jewish girl workers had the financial and moral support of the Women's Trade Union League (WTUL), which handled publicity and organisation and raised funds to help the girls during their strikes. Together, the immigrant workers and the WTUL staged the first American industrial uprising: 30,000 workers from hundreds of firms came out in sympathy and protest against women's working conditions during the great Shirtwaist (blouse) makers strike in New York in 1909–1910, virtually paralysing the trade.[29] Middle-class and society women held benefits and lobbied for better conditions.

Some of the injustices in the garment industry at least were rectified by the Protocols of Peace drawn up from 1910 onward between the unions and the manufacturers. The Protocols set minimum wages, put an end to arbitary fines, and instituted health supervision, work security, and welfare benefits within the industry. But many manufacturers ignored the agreement (as the Triangle fire later proved), and all of them perpetuated the practice of paying women far less than men for equal work. Moreover, though such agreements were important beginnings, they were fragile, as Pesotta's career was to show, without the supervision and enforcement of concessions the employers had only granted under duress.[30]

Jewish unionists and American feminists were oddly paired. The idea that women could help one another across class barriers was only partially true. The middle-class women who staffed the WTUL were called 'allies', but their relationship with the immigrant women was often uneasy. Even more dubious was the patronage of society women and community leaders, whom Schneiderman called 'the mink brigade' and Newman saw as inspired by 'the instinct of charity rather than of unionism'.[31] However, the activities of the WTUL and their friends in society did help the immigrant girls learn and claim their rights and bridged the initial period during which they were too disorientated to organise on their own. Immigrant girls (including their leaders) arrived in the United States knowing not a word of English. Schneiderman recalled that the first union meetings had interpreters in German, Polish, Yiddish, and Italian.[32] It was only in the 1930s that Pesotta was able to write back to the unions that there was 'no worker now who did not understand the English of the brochures and leaflets—or pretend to', and she sent back those printed in Yiddish.[33]

Schneiderman optimistically argued that American girls' 'practicality' would offset the Jewish girls more 'idealistic' bent. But this idealism was linked to radicalism alien to America. **Fannia Cohn**, who became head of the ILGWU's education department, came to America, as she wrote 'in search of freedom rather than for economic advantages', having promised her family, who remained behind, that she would continue her studies in the new country. Unlike most girls, she had wealthy cousins who offered to support her while she continued with her studies. She refused. Coming, as she said from a 'revolutionary' background, she wanted to really understand the mind, the aspirations of the workers. In dedicating herself to the education of working girls, she tried to protect them against disillusion in the sweatshop, with its 'moral and antispiritual' influence, so different from the freedom they had expected.[34]

In Malkiel's (fictitious) *Diary of a Shirtwaist Striker*, a work of propaganda, she puts into the mouth of her narrator, an American 'Mary', admiration for the Jewish girls who seemed to have in their blood, 'like Jesus Christ ... the spirit of sacrifice'.[35] In real life, such admiration was often tempered by prejudice and hostility. Even inside the WTUL, which twice voted Schneiderman into the presidency, there was ethnic conflict and even covert anti-Semitism. American-born middle-class unionists argued, with some justice, that Jewish girls, however militant, were not permanent figures on the industrial scene, and they also feared their socialist ideas.

Tensions between Jewish unionists and other WTUL leaders, who wanted to direct their campaigns at American working girls rather than Jewish immigrants, came to a head in 1914 when Schneiderman was outvoted at election time—though she returned triumphantly to a prolonged tenure after the war. After a labour conference at the war's end she wrote: 'I am sick and tired of always having to be the butt between the radical and the conservative groups because of my difference of political opinions ... I am not a politician and never will be.'[36]

Jewish working girls' relations with the male leaders of the 'Jewish' unions were even more difficult. While Jewish women unionists were never fully accepted by the American feminists because of their (suspected or actual) 'radicalism', they were constantly put down by the Jewish male unionists for their self-assertion as women. Not only would the unions not back demands for equal pay; they sometimes denied even their own paid women organisers the same rates and status as men.

Newman broke with the ILGWU temporarily in 1912, when she was offered, as paid organiser, less than a man would have been given, and she made it clear that it was the principle, not the money, at stake.[37] A year later she found her niche as leading member of the ILGWU Joint Board of Sanitary Control, set up by the trade union and manufacturers to control standards at work.[38] Rose Schneiderman, working briefly with the ILGWU as an organiser in Boston in 1916, was replaced at the time of a big clothing strike by an inexperienced male organiser. She wrote angrily to the ILGWU president, Benjamin Schlesinger, that 'this leads me to believe that you have no confidence in me as an organiser of women or my ability to assume the responsibility that a strike of this size entails.'[39] Barely three years later, once again head of the WTUL, she represented all American women at a trade union conference in Europe, appointed by Frances Perkins of the US Department of Labor.[40]

Early in her career as a union organiser, Pesotta was told by Schlesinger to 'go home and get married'.[41] Schneiderman and Newman in their letters exchanged acid comments on male attitudes towards women in the 'Jewish' unions,[42] though Newman played down sexual harassment of women in the factories, on the grounds that wage agreements were a more important issue.[43]

Schneiderman saw herself as a champion of the American working woman, and she was rewarded during the Roosevelt National Recovery Administration, in 1933–1935, with the responsibility for drawing up the NRA 'codes'—which were intended to govern working conditions in all women's industrial jobs. Though the United States Supreme Court disqualified the NRA as unconstitutional in 1935, the Wagner Act of that year compelled employers to recognise the union to which their workers belonged and to bargain with it in any dispute over hours and wages.

Schneiderman was proud of her relationship with the White House and jubilant at her ability to prescribe working conditions to be enforced by the union leaders, for whom she now set standards. Yet, as the career of Rose Pesotta, youngest of the Jewish women unionists, shows, the struggle for women's union-isation and for fair treatment at work had barely begun.

Pesotta linked her social beliefs and her work in the union with her father's influence on her youth. Peisoty (the family name) was a pious Jew, a grain merchant; unlike most of the other Jews in Derazhnia, a Ukrainian market town most of whose citizens were Jews, he had served five years in the czar's artillery not only willingly but proudly. But in other ways he was unconventional, and Rose believed that he would have made a great social leader: 'Long before I heard of cooperative ventures, of Robert Owen or the Rochdale plan [the first weavers' cooperative in England, set up in 1844] my father launched a cooperative venture and bust a trust.'[44] The Jewish bakers in Dzhernia kept the prices of *matzoth* high every Passover. Peisoty was the treasurer of the local credit union, or *kasse*, and he decided that its members would bake their own *matzoth* and sell them more cheaply. After three years, the bakers caved in. But Peisoty was no match for his own daughter, who threatened suicide rather than face an arranged marriage at sixteen; and—though parting from her father grieved her—Rose sailed to join her sister in New York.

Her father, she later wrote, was her inspiration in her working life. But Pesotta's energies, her political ideas, and her early education were all acquired from women. Rose's mother was 'a businesswoman from the age of nine'—the bookkeeper in a flour, grain, and cereal store; she also led women in the synagogue, using *T'sena Ure'ena*. Her sister Esther, who belonged to a clandestine 'circle', introduced her to the subversive literature brought by fugitive Jewish activists, which she stored in the family attic. Rose received her general education from a city-bred Jewish girl who ran a local school; like the other Jewish women unionists, she was well read and taught herself English in America by reading translations of the Russian classics she knew so well.[45]

New York's Lower East Side was a Russian Jewish and socialist enclave; one of Pesotta's first experiences was watching the 1914 May Day parade. The aim of socialist reform was local and precise. The Triangle fire and the Shirtwaist strike were fresh in people's minds; Esther Peisoty had worked at the Triangle where two girls from Derazhnia had died.[46] In January 1913, shortly before Pesotta's arrival, seven thousand strikers in the white goods (lingerie) industry, organised by Schneiderman and supported belatedly by the WTUL, had won a reduced working day, an end to charges for machines and material, and a minimum wage, among other benefits.[47]

Determined to become an 'operative', Pesotta moved from one job to another, learning different skills. In 1913 there were no fewer than twenty-three separate components in factory dressmaking, from the tailoring and cutting, which was entirely a male sector, to the menial trimming, sorting, and cleaning of goods, which was almost entirely female. Intermediate skills like button-hole making and pressing were shared by both sexes. Blouse (shirtwaist) making, most of which was done at the sewing machine, was women's work.[48] Within a few years, Pesotta was a skilled worker and a union activist, elected to the executive of the ILGWU's Local 25. But these years were darkened by the sisters' complete loss of contact with their family during the First World War. When letters began arriving, in 1919, they learned that their father was dead—shot down in front of his wife by followers of the Ukrainian nationalist and anti-Semite Petlyura in the months following the revolution. Late in life Pesotta was to begin to write a fictionalised account of her family life in Russia, but it was never completed or published, for she could not bring herself to describe the scene of her father's death.[49]

In 1922 Pesotta won a union scholarship to attend a course in social science, organised by WTUL supporters at Bryn Mawr College, for two years running, and she also studied at Brookwood Labor College. This gave her a good grounding in labour history. At these courses, she first encountered American workers from the steel mills, coal mines, auto plants, and textile mills of the United States. 'I might proudly say that the pulse of the US beats in Bryn Mawr at this very moment,' she wrote to friends. But the Russian Jewish girl with her political consciousness was very critical of American women workers. Girls from the Tennessee mills, she reported, were 'timid' and knew little of the outside world; born racists, or, as she put it, 'true aristocrats of the South' they defended southern segregation when Pesotta criticised the oppression of the blacks. The northern girls she found more 'progressive', better informed. Faculty teachers, she observed, included 'would-be revolutionaries from good homes who wanted to be arrested so that it will stir public opinion'; Pesotta's experience of the police made her sceptical of this strategy, though she applauded the teachers' good will.[50]

During the 1920s, while Pesotta gained her basic experience in the trade and on the picket lines, she was twice married and divorced. Her surviving letters suggest that her ideal of freedom, in her personal as in her working life, admitted no compromise in marriage. She insisted that her second divorce was the result of 'ideological differences' with her communist husband, though she also hinted at his chronic infidelities ('none of her business'). As for a family, 'Personally, I would not use an innocent babe as an alibi,' she wrote to the wife of a man with whom she was having an affair, 'for nothing is more erroneous than this, and because of this I did not have any children to tie [a man] for life to myself.'[51]

Most immigrant anarchists were, as she was, followers of Kropotkin and Bakunin, with a vision of a future society based on voluntary and co-operative institutions. Few were capable of the violence which some anarchists believed inevitable if the world was to be changed. But in America all anarchists were believed to be terrorists, and often were punished merely for their beliefs.

Seven years after Pesotta's arrival in the United States, two illiterate Italian artisans, Sacco and Vanzetti, were unjustly convicted of murder and executed seven years after their conviction. Pesotta visited the Italians in prison, protested against their imprisonment, and kept up a correspondence until their execution in 1927.[52] She was unique as an anarchist in her determination to play an active role in American labour affairs. Anarchists denounced her for accepting a paid union job, and she was criticised by American socialists, who denied that an anarchist could contribute to labour reform. She defended herself, shortly after she began working as an ILGWU organiser, in a letter to

Hippolyte Havel, one of the Emma Goldman circle and editor of the anarchist journal *Freedom*.

Trade unions, she agreed, were capitalist like every other institution in America. But mocking another anarchist writer, she asked, 'Should we then grow lettuce and cabbages on some deserted farm pending the millennium?' Anarchism was a human creed, and the anarchists' place was among the workers, instead of sitting back and 'leaving the field to the Fascists'. Anarchists who fulminated and merely criticised 'lived on the labor of their brethren'; the true anarchist should work for reform and freedom, she insisted, not foster hatred and mistrust.[53]

So Pesotta set out to take the message of unionism to the great 'open shop' cities of the Pacific coast, where, defying injunctions brought by employers, police brutality, and hired scabs, she established union locals and badgered the officials concerned into enforcing compliance with the new industrial codes the Roosevelt administration had introduced.

During the first year of her work, between early 1933 and the spring of 1934, membership of the ILGWU rose from 50,000 to 200,000.[54] But the letters and reports Pesotta sent to local labour officials, colleagues, and the head of the ILGWU, David Dubinsky—a man she respected but with whom she tussled hard—show that she battled not only with the employers but with indifferent and fearful workers, lazy labour officials, and even her own union's leadership, which initially was reluctant to commit funds and send officials to cities whose names had become bywords for anti-unionism.

During the industrial upheaval following the slump of 1929, thousands of workers in the garment industry lost their jobs, and many moved to the West Coast, 'the land of sunshine and starvation wages,' as Pesotta called it in her reports to the ILGWU.

Los Angeles, to which Pesotta was sent as an educational organiser in mid-1933, was a notorious 'open shop' town, with hundreds of small employers, 'fly by night bosses', who would, she wrote, change premises rather than pay a living wage or employ workers on a permanent basis. Within months she had recruited a militant corps of workers prepared to strike for their rights—most of them Mexican immigrant girls who had been the easiest prey for the employers.

Pesotta knew Los Angeles well; she had worked there for two years as a skilled 'sample maker' but was summarily fired when the foreman found out that she was a union member. Now she was able to fight back, and throughout the autumn she kept Los Angeles employers on their toes. By September she was asking Dubinsky for financial help for a strike she was organising in the cloak (coat) industry.

Dubinsky was taken aback. 'I am overwhelmed by the speed by which you report the people in LA are working,' he replied. A cloak strike almost at the end of the season was 'a bit too much for us in the East'. Besides, wasn't she supposed to be concentrating on the dressmakers' shops?[55] Pesotta snapped back that the cloak strike would be a warning to all the employers in Los Angeles. It was the second largest group in the union, staffed by the Spanish Mexican dressmakers who, she believed, could be 'the backbone of the union on the West Coast'. She refused to back down. 'If I'd be dead as some of them [union officials] and they are as petrified as the forests of Arizona, I would never have undertaken that trip. Now, my dear President, you will have to come across with the help we need.'[56] Dubinsky came across, impressed not only by her determination but by the details she furnished in her reports of the abuses in the Los Angeles industry.

Pesotta's own style was uncompromising; when one employer suggested a 'selective' strike, Pesotta agreed, and suggested beginning with his firm.[57]

The manufacturers had argued with local labour officials that there was a dearth of skilled workers; Pesotta, after a thorough investigation, showed this was a hollow excuse for underpaying. The West Coast was teeming with skilled operatives who had come from all over America in the Depression, carrying with them either the benefit of experience in the trade in the East or training in the trade schools which had multiplied over the last few years (and which had not existed during Pesotta's own apprenticeship). One of the employers' stratagems was to take on such workers for brief periods, until the specific order was filled, and then dismiss them; this also meant that the employees never worked together for long enough to organise protest.

Another employers' trick was to employ 'housewives, grand-mothers and minors' prepared to work for pin money, since by now, as Pesotta pointed out, almost any woman could learn how to operate a Singer sewing machine. Little girls, she wrote, 'with the aid of high heels, heavy makeup and spit curls, passed the not so keen eyes of the foreman or forelady when that rush order had to be filled.'[58] At this time, thousands of skilled operatives were out of work.

Eventually, in November, when several hundred experienced dressmakers were locked out or discharged, two thousand workers in several factories staged a successful strike. Norman Thomas, the socialist leader, visited the pickets, and Pesotta handled the police. The girl workers arrested were so noisy that the matron of the local jail pleaded with her to bail them out rather than keep them all night. Flushed with success, Pesotta wanted the president to come and see for himself what was happening. 'My idea was to give [the employers] one shock after another, thus giving the more class conscious [workers] the opportunity to entrench themselves.' She also saw her task as that of reconciling American and Mexican workers by showing the union potential of the immigrant girls. American 'race conscious workers,' she said, 'had got a dose now that will last them a lifetime.'[59]

Pesotta sent personal reports not only to the ILGWU executive but to Max Danish, editor of the union newspaper *Justice*, very influential in socialist circles. She described the 'revolt against the sweatshop in the most modern buildings', against what she called the 'top floor walk down'. Skilled operatives seeking work would take the elevator to the top floor of a building where several dress manufacturers were housed and walk down, knocking on every door to ask for work, in the face of 'abuses, physical injury and unequal distribution [of work and wages]'. To Danish she confided not only her confrontations with employers but the prejudices she had to overcome among the American-born workers who 'hate Spaniards and Jews. All bosses to their opinion

[sic] are Jews and all Jews are bosses, hence they are doubly hated. The American element also despises Jews as bolsheviks.'[60] Pesotta's letters show that she loathed the Jewish employers just as violently as did her recruits, but she found that the communists in the union went beyond the class struggle when they encouraged anti-Semitism, undermined her work, and tried to hang on to the union's coat tails after successful strikes. It was the beginning of a period in which squabbles between socialists and communists in the garment union were to seriously damage its unity; yet in the following year, at a CIO convention, alarmed by the spread of Fascism in Europe, Pesotta opposed evicting the communists from the ILGWU lest this encourage their common enemy.[61]

'Three subcellars deep, where neither light nor air ever penetrate, where days and nights are spent under the dim light of an electric bulb, you will find ... factories hardly wide enough to allow people to walk through the narrow alleys between the sewing machines. Each machine is segregated from its neighbour with a wooden wall the size of a seated person—thus the Chinese are observing privacy even in the shop, and incidentally, keeping the girls from seeing or conversing with each other ... If such stables ... are allowed to exist under the present system of sanitation, health rules, etc., it is due to the secrecy of the Chinese.'[62]

Soon after her arrival in San Francisco in the hard winter of 1934 Pesotta sent this account of Chinese labour in the garment industry not to Dubinsky but to Max Danish at *Justice*. She wanted a published exposé of conditions in San Francisco—and Danish complied a few weeks later—because even she had to tread warily lest she set off 'Fong Wars' in Chinatown.[63] She could not infiltrate the Chinese sweatshops as she had the Los Angeles factories, because Chinese labour was not only a communal but a family affair. But she was reluctant to bring the abuses to the notice of the immigration authorities, as many of the Chinese were illegal immigrants. She turned instead to John O'Connell, the secretary of the Labor Central Council, who should have been concerned with women's welfare in the city; but she found that his chief fear was that if the Chinese factories were broken up, Chinese girls might compete with American girls for work. Pesotta later observed that it was only during the Second World War, when China was America's ally against Japan, that Chinese workers got a fair deal.[64]

Pesotta shuttled between San Francisco and Los Angeles, where she found that, barely three months after the cloakmakers' strike, the manufacturers were already violating the agreements she had drawn up. To the local NRA inspector, she pointed out that they evaded paying wages commensurate with the workers' skills by bringing in cleaners or examiners to do drapers' work, and were paying less skilled workers overtime rather than employ experienced operatives who were on the streets.[65] She kept the strike weapon in reserve at all times, to the dismay of the far less aggressive union officials working with her.

Her situation in ILGWU circles in Los Angeles was undermined by the fact that the official who represented the locals, Paul Berg, was her lover, a notorious womaniser who was as faithless a colleague as he was a husband. The secretary of the union, John Dyche, warned her that she could expect no support from him against her critics. 'Berg is not your friend; emotion is not friendship.'[66]

Pesotta tore furiously into Berg in letters from San Francisco. 'You are made of that stuff which I call OBEYS ORDERS. You will never use your own initiative, but want what the comrades will order. Oh hell.'[67] She soldiered on with or without Berg's support. In San Francisco she taught the Chinese girls she managed to attract to union headquarters the rudiments of solidarity. In Los Angeles she urged Mexican girls not to take work home and to insist on regular payment for every hour they worked. She sent back data to Rose Schneiderman for the drawing up of 'codes' for the industry in the West, and made hard bargains with the manufacturers. To her closest friends, she confided her feeling that the West Coast people, employers and rank-and-file union members alike, were 'the scum of the earth'; most of the unionists were 'cranks, leftists [communists] banished or sent to conquer the working class, old maids, women who had run away from their husbands'.[68] She praised only the Mexican girls, whom she found good union material, quicker to learn than blacks or Puerto Ricans, and she insisted on leaving Spanish Americans in control of union offices in both cities.[69] There were rare moments of despair in which she tired of standing up to ruthless employers and bullying inadequate officials and thought of asking Dubinsky to replace her with a man.[70]

In March 1934 Dubinsky responded to her request to send a union vice-president permanently to the West, praising her for the agreements she had won; she had, he wrote, 'almost conquered the Coast'.[71] At the annual ILGWU convention in June that year, Pesotta was voted vice-president of the union—a member of the executive, a decision-maker rather than an employee. It was a great achievement. But she felt that the promotion compromised her political aims. 'I feel I lost my independence', she wrote in her diary.[72]

Her first mission as vice-president was to Puerto Rico, which Rose Schneiderman had visited the previous year. Officially, the NRA codes were in operation, but, as Pesotta reported, 'The NRA is a washout here, as elsewhere ... they simply do not know what it is all about.'[73] Conditions in Puerto Rico were so primitive that, rather than trying to enforce the codes, Pesotta found herself functioning as a combined social worker and health visitor.

The workers from the slums of San Juan lived in shacks built on stilts over mud, with no plumbing; most of the dressmakers and their families suffered from hookworm, tropical anaemia, and malnutrition. Women who attended the meetings called by Pesotta sometimes fainted from hunger, and Pesotta—who had skipped the usual inoculations—washed in alcohol as a precaution against infection. Instead of teaching the women about labour laws, she set up classes in personal hygiene, birth control, and health care.[74] She did her best to argue the workers' case and to reinstate girls sacked during the Depression in factories run by the Syrian Jews, small traders who had made profits from the ignorant and illiterate women who worked for them. But she realised that the workers feared that enforcing the NRA codes in this environment would simply wreck the local handicrafts industry by pushing prices up and losing the market to cheaper and similar goods from Madeira or Ireland. 'Personally,' she wrote to Dubinsky, 'I would give them all the blessing to leave these people alone.'[75] To a friend she wrote that, though the anarchists had cold-shouldered her after her appointment to the union executive, 'I am still considering myself an anarchist, now organising the most exploited, most backward people on earth.'[76]

On returning to the United States, she accepted Schneiderman's invitation to Washington to confer with Ernest Gruening, the official in charge of Puerto Rico under the Roosevelt administration. She urged a birth control campaign and suggested bringing young Puerto Rican social workers to the States for training. But she knew that remedial measures alone could not stop the island's slide into destitution. Writing in 1944 of the further decline of the Puerto Rican economy, she blamed America for 'the tragic state of two million people'. Puerto Rico was 'a glaring example of the ills of imperialism', she wrote. America would do best to 'clean up the US doorstep', before getting further involved in world affairs.[77]

Straight from the heat of Puerto Rico, Pesotta went to work in the 'chill Oregon mists' which hung the following winter over Seattle; she soon caught a bronchial infection and harangued the garment workers with a camphorated towel wrapped round her head. Seattle had become the most conservative of American cities since the general strike of 1919. By 1935 it was what Pesotta called a 'union ghost town',[78] and 'the dullest city where it has ever been my pleasure to work'.[79] She soon had the city in an uproar.

The labour problems in Seattle were similar to those of Los Angeles; many skilled dressmakers were out of work, while the employers paid nominal wages to thirteen-year-old girls. But the mass of women workers in Seattle were indifferent. Pesotta mounted a systematic campaign of harassment of the employers. At first Dubinsky regarded Seattle as a lost cause, especially as Pesotta did not have the support of more than three factories. She wrote back angrily, 'We are not involved in "a couple of squabbles", it is war, class war if you please. The entire labor movement is watching this strike with apprehension; it is a test case for the entire movement. The Chamber of Commerce has linked us up with the waterfront unions, and anyone knowing Seattle will realise what that is.'[80] She rented a mimeograph machine and put out letters of warning to all the employers, reminding them of their obligations under the NRA codes. But she was also handicapped by the fact that the codes themselves were already coming under attack by American right-wingers. The local Chamber of Commerce was alarmed by her campaign and started investigating complaints that she was a foreign agitator. Seattle, as she had told Dubinsky, did not like outsiders.

Soon, a number of employers began dismissing those employees who they had discovered belonged to the union; this gave Pesotta the excuse she had been looking for, and she called out the workers of three dressmaking factories. The employers fought back; first they provided beds for the scabs brought in to replace the strikers, so that they did not have to run the picket lines Pesotta had set up. Then they brought in more non-union workers in buses and limousines, with guards riding shotgun. There was more solidarity among the employers than among the workers: a group of businessmen raised funds to counter 'communist agitation', offered the strikers money, and then raised their salaries by fifteen per cent.[81]

When a striker threw a tomato at a factory owner, the employers had Pesotta arrested. The Seattle manufacturers wanted her deported, but she produced the naturalisation papers which she carried with her at all times.

This time Pesotta was only partly successful. The cloakmakers received the rise in wages she had demanded, but her 'outsider' status was against her, and she knew it. She recommended to Dubinsky that he send 'an American or local person' to head the Seattle locals.

What made the winter months in Seattle even more of an ordeal were the repercussions of her continuing liaison with Berg. The affair was well known and, given Berg's notoriety with women, damaged her standing in the union. He was attacked by fellow unionists for 'immorality' and Pesotta's name was involved. 'Why have I so many enemies?' she asked, in her diaries. 'I have a right to love.'[82] But Pesotta was caught in the worst dilemma for a woman—sexually in thrall to a man she did not respect. Most of the male unionists were, like Berg, Jewish married men; most were domestically settled, but a few, married or not, were quite prepared to take what they could from lonely women unionists without committing themselves emotionally. Berg emerges from the letters as spiteful and coarse-grained. While he envied her freedom as a single woman, he could write: 'I think a woman more wholesome and natural when she is not altogether detached from the home ... a woman without a child looses [sic] a great deal of the beauty offered by the seriousness and kindliness of motherhood—did you ever think of it?'[83]

'I am alone. Only my interest in the work ... keeps me from going insane,' she wrote in her diary in 1935.[84] A new mission to Milwaukee at the end of 1935 helped her end the relationship with Berg. In this city she found the women more ready to risk dismissal by joining the union. (Her predecessor had got them to attend meetings by promising free samples of a new pudding).[85] Pesotta organised a strike at a plant where the management had violated signed agreements on pay and arbitration. One grievance the workers had was related to the principle of taking a fifteen-minute break every two hours.

Pesotta supported the claim: 'As a machine operator ... I refused to be geared to a machine like a robot. The best way to encourage production is to determine the causes of industrial fatigue and eliminate them at the source.' Satisfying work, she told the employers, and fair pay, would increase production.[86]

At the beginning of 1936 she was sent to Buffalo, in upstate New York. She had scarcely begun work when the call from the CIO reached the ILGWU. The Akron strike gave Pesotta a chance to take part in an uprising in America's chief industries; once more she could feel close to the country's heartbeat. But Akron was also to involve her in a new love affair, with a man who was her equal in terms of idealism and energy, yet who destroyed her last hope of a stable emotional life. She was now almost forty.

*

The CIO had been formed to bring the benefits of collective bargaining under the union banner to the largely unskilled workers of the mass-production industries. The Akron strike had begun when the management of the plant had summarily sacked seventy of the plants workers and, reneging on an earlier agreement, had restored a longer working day. The hundred and thirty-seven workers who protested were promptly dismissed too, but before long, rubber workers at two other major companies had sat down and occupied the factory. Others joined them, and eventually, for five weeks, 14,000 workers picketed the company's plants.[87]

The Congress of Industrial Organisations only recently formed under John L. Lewis, the mining leader, began operating at Akron at the end of January. The organisers were a quartet of seasoned activists now nicknamed the Four Horsemen for their teamwork and mobility.[88] Three belonged to the CIO; the fourth was Rose Pesotta.

Pesotta had heard Lewis speak at a labour convention in Atlantic City two years earlier, and was not among his admirers. 'I saw the man as a consistent conservative Republican, who might at any time support the Democrats if it meant gain for his organisation or fame for himself,'[89] a 'dictator' in his own field, who would 'flirt behind his shaggy brows' with the more radical organisers in the union when necessary, turning his back on them at other times.[90] When the great campaigns of 1936–1937 got under way, it was radicals like the Horsemen who came into their own. Pesotta was to note that during the following mass strike, Lewis himself did not even put in an appearance.[91]

As the strike went on, it became clear that company agents would pressure the strikers' women in order to break morale. Women were only a minority of the actual rubber workers, but their participation, and that of the workers' families, was crucial. In mid-February Pesotta was called in to organise the Women's Auxiliary, which worked in six-hour shifts, many remaining in the plant together with husbands or sons. The mood was defiant; as one woman told Pesotta: 'We got them unawares this time, before they had a chance to prepare gas bombs and barbed wire against us, and if they call the militia against us, why we will stick it out all the same.'[92] The plant was occupied by thousands of strikers, many, Pesotta noted, armed, 'hunters from mountain country'. The 'sit-down' strikers were to occupy Goodyear for a month, the women cooking—on stoves improvised from oil drums—and keeping up the spirits of the men who manned the pickets.

Pesotta was far, now, from the socialist Jewish garment workers with whom she had begun her organising career. Among the strikers were men and women of every political colour, and among the unskilled workers many were risking a precarious livelihood for principles they barely understood. Pesotta even noted a large number of deaf mutes, who had their own interpreter. The Ku Klux Klan, too, had followers at Akron. The strikers thought Pesotta Spanish or Italian, but she announced 'I'm a full blooded Hebrew', and met possible hostility head on: 'You probably thought all Jews were bankers, million-aires, exploiters, bloodsuckers. They're not. I'm a wage earner, like yourselves, and there are millions of Jews like me.'[93]

As the thousands of strikers could not all be accommodated in the plant, many bivouacked in shanties and shacks in the grounds. When the police tried to tear these down, the picketers prevented them. Every train arriving at the nearby station was checked out by the pickets for infiltrators; the railwaymen were sympathetic and helped. In this first great strike, publicity was all important. Pesotta had a movie camera and made a film in which all the strikers wanted to take part, and the strike organisers were interviewed in the longest broadcasts so far in labour history. Pesotta encouraged the workers, many of them new to union work, by telling them of the benefits won by strikes in the garment industry.

When, on March 21st, the employers finally agreed to the workers' conditions—a thirty-six-hour week for the toughest divisions, forty in others, a promise to stop sanctions against union members, and the right for shop committees to deal with foremen—the strikers staged a victory parade, the greatest celebration in Akron, Pesotta noted, since the Armistice. Pesotta and the three CIO men went out to drink and dance together.[94]

Two were working-class union men in their fifties: Adolph Germer, German born, who had worked in the mines from the age of eleven, and Leo Kryzycki, a lithographer from the steel workers' union. The third was a Harvard engineering graduate three years younger than Pesotta, Powers Hapgood. A socialist from a privileged family who had dedicated himself since graduation to studying labour problems at their source, Hapgood had worked as a miner in the Minnesota iron mines, as a railroad hand, as a teamster in Kansas, as a labourer in a Montana sugar beet factory, as a coal miner in Colorado and Pennsylvania, and in the coal mines of Wales, France, Germany, and Soviet Russia between 1924 and 1926. He was one of a small radical group in the miners' unions who constantly challenged John L. Lewis's leadership. In his union career in the 1930s he was committed to the nationalisation of the mines, had headed several strikes, and had been arrested a dozen times. His background and education made him articulate in committee rooms and during political campaigns (he had stood for governor of Indiana as a socialist in 1932), and his working-class experience had made him popular among the union rank and file. With the founding of the CIO in 1935 he had gone to work for John L. Lewis.[95]

Hapgood and Pesotta had first met nine years earlier, during the left-wing campaign to save Sacco and Vanzetti. Hapgood had been repeatedly jailed and even put in a mental hospital for his defence of the anarchists. Pesotta respected and liked him and his wife; he had been married for some years to Mary Donovan, a leading working-class Catholic trade unionist, and had two children. But Hapgood and Pesotta had never worked together; now, during the long shifts touring the picket lines at Akron, they became close, and found that despite their totally different origins they shared political ideals and sympathies. Hapgood fell passionately in love with Pesotta, and it was hard for her to resist. He was ardent, handsome, and a tested comrade in the struggle. He was also naïve, emotionally adolescent, and self-centred. Moreover, as Pesotta was to discover, his drinking before and after work with miners and labourers, in order to be accepted, had made him increasingly dependent on alcohol in moments of self-doubt and crisis.[96]

Pesotta tried to avoid seeing Hapgood, but their work brought them together constantly that year, both during strikes and at union conventions. As union leaders, the two met at the auto workers' convention, where she was the ILGWU delegate, then at the Pennsylvania steel workers' rally, where she was sent as a correspondent for *Justice*. She had a summer school engagement at a labour college when Hapgood was ill in a nearby hospital. At another convention, in New York in July, she made a last effort to resist her growing love for him, and asked Dubinsky to send her as far away as possible, to Montreal. But in the following month, the two met again at Akron and became lovers.[97]

Hapgood and Pesotta carried on their affair at intervals, thrown together on picket lines and then having to board trains that took them to union work in different parts of America. Hapgood deluged her with protestations of his love and admiration for his 'pal in the anticapitalist struggle'; her surviving letters (for he destroyed most on arrival, afraid for his union reputation) are more controlled, wry, sometimes angry. Her real defiance, despair or bitterness she confined to her diaries, or to letters never sent. 'Life has been rather cruel to me,' she wrote when the affair was just beginning. 'Every inch of space I had to fight for, if I wanted to win ... Because of that, each minute I enjoyed. My brief experience within the last few weeks were of the nature I knew [sic] will not culminate in permanent happiness. But the brief moments were an idyll.'[98]

It was clear from the outset that Hapgood would not leave Mary Donovan, his support during a stormy career, or his two children; nor did Pesotta expect it.[99] She tried to be frank with Donovan, who was a comrade, and sent her an initial apology and a resolution, inevitably broken, to behave more sensibly. Her anarchist beliefs in total freedom gave way to a very conventional sense of guilt towards Hapgood's family. 'I shall try to bury myself in my work,' she wrote Donovan. 'Now I need a violent strike or something to keep my thoughts away from myself.'[100] Hapgood sought the advice of Antoinette Konikow, Donovan's doctor, a worldly European who was a leading socialist; Konikow informed him that she had not expected his marriage to last beyond five years, and encouraged his affair, but warned him that a sexually free-living woman might have given him gonorrhea.[101] All this Hapgood faithfully related to Pesotta, who was shocked into an atavistic reaction. 'So you had misgivings all the time? ... Today is the Day of Atonement. The religious ask their God to forgive them their sins. I have sinned only before my own self and I shall not forgive myself for the weakness.'[102]

Hapgood's letters show that Donovan tried to accept the situation, as Konikow advised her to if she wanted to keep her husband, and she too turned back to union work, like Pesotta, in an attempt to suppress her jealousy. Hapgood, caught rather unhappily between 'two strong women' and unwilling to give up either, tried to rationalise his self-indulgence by quoting Havelock Ellis and Bertrand Russell on sex and marriage, to his wife and lover. Pesotta was unimpressed: 'Your explanation to Mary may have sounded logical to you and Bertrand Russell; but to Mary, the wife, mother and woman, it was a slap. I respect her for her dignity.'[103]

In Montreal, during that hard winter, Pesotta encountered stubborn opposition at work, chiefly from the Catholic church; in sermons in churches, preachers warned workers against Jews, radicals, and 'disruptive foreigners'. The local dress manufacturers guild split; one faction preferred the Catholic syndicate to the 'Jewish' union. The clergy urged Pesotta's deportation from Canada. In January she none the less reached a settlement for wage increases and improved conditions with the employers on behalf of the dressmakers she had recruited.[104] But in mid-campaign she was again sent to work with the CIO 'Horsemen', this time at the second great mass-production strike, in Flint, Michigan, which spread from a sit-down at two plants to the entire General Motors empire, affecting 140,000 employees and fifty per cent of its industries. The chief demand of the auto workers' union, the UAW, was that it be recognised as the exclusive bargaining agency for all General Motors employees. The manufacturers, determined not to yield, called in the police.[105] Pesotta described what followed as a 'miniature civil war', in which the workers were bombarded with tear gas. It lasted all night but ended with the workers still in control of the plant.[106]

This was only the first of several confrontations with the police in which women picketers, led by a worker's wife, Genora Johnson, fought side by side with the men. They called themselves the Women's Emergency Brigade, whose weapons were clubs, stove pokers, crowbars, and lead pipes. The Flint strike, like the Akron, ended in a victory for the workers. The General Motors management agreed to recognise the UAW and not to interfere with workers who joined the union.[107]

At Flint, fighting together, Pesotta and Hapgood enjoyed their happiest hours. But this was the last time they were to work side by side. From this moment on the couple found little stolen time to be together. When they met it was for a weekend between strikes, a few days when their itineraries crossed: in Washington at the beginning of 1937, and the following summer when he headed the United Shoe Workers' battle against the craft guilds in Massachusetts and she was working in Boston. When he was jailed for six months in Maine for ignoring a court injunction ending a strike, she—and his family—visited him, alternately, in jail. In December they had ten days together, but it was marred by his drinking. After this, Pesotta suffered intensely, 'dreaming what could have been ... wandering around alone without any hope of ever meeting you again as we did these past months.'[108]

The summer months had also provided her with the 'violent strike' she had hoped would distract her from unhappy love. In August 1937, while she organised women in the knitwear industry in Cleveland, she was attacked by four women hired by the union's enemies and slashed over the eye with a razor; the wound needed four stitches. Two weeks later, 'loyal Federal employees' blackened her other eye.[109]

Meanwhile, the strain on Hapgood of being 'needed by John L. Lewis in forty places at once', of seven years' non-stop work as a strike organiser during the most stormy period in American labour history, and of handling two reproachful women was telling. He was drinking heavily and had a 'breakdown' that landed him in the Massachusetts General Hospital in Boston. In May 1938 Pesotta wrote desperately: 'Leaving Boston on Thursday evening, with you stretched dead drunk on your bed, with people waiting in the lobby and me coming ... to excuse you because you were "in conference", was more than I could stand.' She warned him that she would break off the affair if he continued drinking.[110]

Hapgood took the pledge to try and mollify her but broke it repeatedly and became truculent and resentful as she distanced herself. Yet over the next few years, as their affair gradually subsided into a rueful, disillusioned friendship—by Pesotta's choice—they still exchanged reassuring letters on their shared political views. In 1940 Hapgood wrote to Pesotta: 'We never differ ... even though sometimes our respective problems and surroundings make us see some details a little differently.'[111] Both opposed the CIO's return to the AFL fold, and both doubted the wisdom of the American socialists' opposition to America's entry into the European war. Both continued to goad American workers to strike action: 'Today I picketed by land, sea and air,' Hapgood wrote in October 1940; and he congratulated her on a 'good, hard strike' in Los Angeles towards the end of 1941. But it was she who tired first, and by mid-war was scarcely troubling to answer his letters. Hapgood continued to work himself into the ground, disregarding his doctor's warnings, and died at the age of forty-nine of a heart attack, at the wheel of his car.[112]

Hapgood and Pesotta's frantic activity may have been linked to a growing realisation that their hopes for American socialism were illusory. The strikes at Akron and Flint, the earliest trials of strength of the CIO, were a landmark of American industrial and trade union history. But they were not a sign that the socialist movement, in the doldrums since the First World War, was gaining strength. For the workers, it was an encouragement to go on fighting for a share in their employers' profits, rather than to change the system.

Pesotta's final years as an organiser were spent patching holes

in the union blanket she had knitted herself. In the autumn of
1938 she wrote to a fellow anarchist, Mollie Steimer, that 'in
spite of the advantages of labour legislation, we still have to cope
with the old problems—scabs sleeping in factories, scabs escorted
by the police and thugs'.[113] In 1940 she was sent by the ILGWU
to California to investigate the anti-union trusts, and found a
slush fund that 'would have put Midas to shame'. Here, where
she had scored her greatest triumphs, twelve large corporations
and banks had raised half a million dollars to fight the unions.
Migrant workers were selling bootleg services, and piece workers
were earning starvation wages in garages, hovels, and back rooms.
Yet despite these setbacks, she noted the achievements: more
than half the local businesses were working under union conditions, and even the anti-trust funds in banks had been cobbled
together under conditions of secrecy, as so many of the depositors
were union men and women.[114]

By July of that year, Pesotta had already decided to resign her
position on the executive of the ILGWU. She realised that the
union already had it in mind to 'shelve' her for another 'only',
that is, token, woman. But she postponed the act because she
wanted to choose the moment herself.[115] She was bitter and angry
that she had not received personal recognition for her California
report, which was presented at the convention, in order not to
alienate hostile union officials in the locals. At Atlantic City, in
June 1942, she announced that she was leaving organising work
in mid-term and going back to the factory bench. She recognised
that since 1933, the 'liberal element' in America had enacted
'radical measures' for labour, and that her union had been in the
vanguard. But she complained of a lack of co-operation from the
executive—always excepting Dubinsky, to whom she paid a
special tribute. She accused the other union leaders of being as
'provincial, small and petty' as when they joined up and with
having 'eased her out' of the Pacific Coast in 1940. She argued
that they had never recognised the tenacity with which she had
founded and supported so many of the union's locals. All
Dubinsky would say was that he 'deplored the situation on the
West Coast', though later he expressed discomfort. Pesotta was

becoming an embarrassment to the union—too forthright, too radical, and a woman struggling alone against male cabals.[116]

If Pesotta's angry departure from ILGWU work, at the age of forty-five, indicated fatigue and disillusionment, a year back in the factory led to a more balanced summing up of the state of American labour. In January 1943 she wrote, in a rare letter to Hapgood, that, while there had recently been a work stoppage in the dressmakers' factories:

> there was nothing of the old times inspiring stoppages, when workers walked into strikers' halls, congregated there and listened to speeches ... My shop did not stop at all. People on the streets [asked] ... what it was all about, and none could give an answer, but refer them to read the press ... The case goes to the labor board, and meanwhile things will remain status quo.
>
> To me this was a great disappointment, and as I foresaw a year ago, that [sic] no longer will we be able to conduct organisation drives as of old ... we are entering a new era— the era of arbitration by disinterested individuals, mostly on government payroll, who will consider this sometimes as an unpleasant duty, while the workers will remain aloof, the leaders will disclaim any responsibility, and thus the old labor movement will die a natural death.
>
> But there is always a bright side to the picture. I am still in the shop, working now 8 hours a day ... and am enjoying good health. My pay envelope is steadily improving ... the season is beginning, and I hope to make up for less [sic] during the dull period.[117]

Rose Pesotta had become an American.

EPILOGUE

*Pesotta and Emma Goldman Write Letters on the Eve of
World War II*

Emma Goldman was the most extreme, the most extravagant, of all the Jewish women rebels. Her life was one long, indignant protest: as a Jewish girl from a traditional home, against her parents; as a woman, against marriage and unwanted pregnancies; as an anarchist, against the state; among anarchists, against puritanism and a blind dedication to a cause; as a libertarian, against both Fascist and Soviet tyrannies; to the end of her life, a pacifist who would not advocate war against either. Neither theorist nor politician, her message was her life—a life in which she refused to yield to any authority or to accept any compromise, whether in her public or personal life (which was anything but private).

Goldman's Russian childhood, in the 1870s, illustrated the negative side of the Jewish family: the domination of children by their parents, a family whose energies were cruelly inverted because of the hostility of the world outside. Goldman remembered that all members of her family were obsessively concerned with and for one another, but lacked real affection. Her parents' arranged marriage (her mother was a widow) was deeply unhappy. The children of the first marriage resented their stepfather, who had invested their mother's inheritance and lost it. Late in life, Goldman sympathetically attributed her father's vicious rages to the sexual frustration he suffered from her unresponsive mother;

but in her childhood Emma was his main victim. She was an unwanted female child who refused to conform to his idea of a Jewish girl's behaviour, longing for higher education and refusing an early marriage with a partner of his choice. Abraham Goldman emerges from her memories as an insensitive brute; yet she also loved and admired him—a love never reciprocated—and other relations described him as a man of some learning. He knew several languages and had been prevented from becoming a scholar or professional by Russian discrimination against Jews. Instead, he became a publican and small trader.[1]

Goldman's mother worked with her husband to help support the family, looked after their finances after emigration to America, and was active in philanthropic work in the Jewish community in upstate New York all her life. But she preferred her son to her daughters, and, in Emma's memory, lacked all sympathy for her aspirations and hated the evidence of her strong sexuality.

As a young girl, Goldman was expected to work for the family, and she was exploited by both her Russian employers and—on arrival in the United States—German Jewish employers, something she neither forgot nor forgave. Lonely and unhappy at home, she married a young fellow immigrant who proved not only impotent but unable to give her the intellectual companionship she needed. Goldman divorced him—against her parents' wishes—but later, clearly because of family pressures, remarried him. It was not until this second attempt to conform proved as useless as the first that she finally took her sewing machine and a handful of dollars and set out alone to defy the world.

It is notable that Goldman never related this bitter early life to her subsequent development as a rebel. She preferred to see herself as self-created, both as a woman and as an anarchist.[2] And within a few years, the small, stubborn, penniless immigrant girl was to become a symbol, in the United States, of red anarchy, terror, and a challenge to every American convention.

Goldman's career as a propagandist for rebellion began in the largely Jewish immigrant socialist and anarchist milieu of East Side New York, in strike organisations and demonstrations against the sweatshop conditions she had experienced herself. Working-class immigrants, both Jews and Italians, swelled the ranks of the anarchists; but women from Eastern Europe, most of whom were Jewish, made up thirty per cent of all anarchist women. Goldman was the best known; but there was also the courageous Mollie Steimer, who suffered long imprisonment and final deportation for her libertarian beliefs, and **Marie Ganz**, who, like Goldman and Manya Shochat, contemplated the assassination of a class enemy (in Ganz's case, John D. Rockefeller, on whose desk she left a message conveying her intentions).[3]

Goldman's conversion to anarchism was the direct result of her disillusionment with American life and her compassionate sympathy with others—immigrants, loners, and even criminals and prostitutes—on the fringes of American life. Every miscarriage of justice, from the execution of the Chicago anarchists in 1887 onward, seemed to her a sign of capitalist corruption. She carried her memories of the populists who had inspired her as a girl to America, and at first she clearly identified American big business with Czarism. Through her early association with Alexander Berkman, another Russian Jewish rebel, her first lover and lifelong comrade, she became the accomplice in his attempt on the life of the American steel baron Henry Clay Frick—for which he served fourteen years in jail. This was her one real involvement in would-be political violence, but it marked her for life.

Goldman went on to preach the doctrines of European anarchism to an American public unresponsive to her message but fascinated by her personality and her rhetoric. She argued that women should have the same sexual freedom as men; but she had nothing in common with American feminists. Her experience of American social welfare workers among working-class immigrants had convinced her that what they were doing was 'teaching girls to eat with a fork when they had no food' and instilling in them contempt for their own class. She was one of the most outspoken campaigners for birth control in America, but this was the result more of her work as a nurse and midwife among working-class women than of any feminist principle.

By 1901 Goldman was notorious enough to be arrested on suspicion of complicity in the assassination of President McKinley—merely because the deranged assassin had once heard her speak; but it was typical of her hatred for authority that she expressed sympathy for the assassin as well as an audacious willingness to nurse the dying President. She held to her pacifist beliefs even after America entered the war—unlike so many American feminists, who were pacifists only until America was involved—and by its end the American administration finally found a legal way of deporting her in 1918, together with Berkman, to post-revolutionary Russia.

What followed was probably the finest hour of her life. Despite her previous passionate defence of bolshevism, and the welcome she received from the Soviet leaders, she made it her business, with Berkman, to make a fact-finding tour of the Soviet Union which convinced them, ultimately, that the Bolshevik regime was a travesty of the revolutionary society in which they had believed. This was no easy decision, for it made them permanently homeless, and, but for the increasingly beleaguered anarchists of Europe, left them almost without allies on the left. What turned the scale for Berkman and Goldman was Lenin's massacre of the Kronstadt sailors who demanded the democracy they had been promised, and the communists' savage elimination of the anarchists who had helped them to power. At the end of 1921, the two ageing campaigners left Russia, hoping to rally liberal opinion against the Bolsheviks without providing ammunition to those who supported the Russian autocracy. It was a campaign as hopeless as the one they had formerly waged for anarchism in America.

In England, for instance, where left-wing intellectuals had supported the Russian revolution, only the formidable Rebecca West credited Goldman's reports. Goldman's dispute in 1925 with Bertrand Russell, who after much soul-searching decided that he could not attack bolshevism, was typical. She commented: 'The argument advanced by Mr Russell, that since there is no other political group of an advanced nature to take the place of the bolshevik government, he does not believe in the effectiveness of my work, seems to be out of keeping with the scholarly mind of a man like Mr Russell. What possible bearing can that have on the stand on behalf of some justice to the political victims of the [Bolshevik] government? But granted that Mr Russell's contribution is logical, does that mean that all liberty loving men and women outside Russia must supinely sit by while the bolsheviki are getting away with murder?'[4]

The last battle of Goldman's life was that on behalf of the doomed Spanish anarchists, among whom, in her sixties, she became a revered mother figure. It meant a late, and reluctant, compromise. All her life there had been an unresolved tension between Goldman's belief in a chosen élite that would propagate the message of utopian anarchism and the problematic unresponsiveness of the downtrodden masses. In Spain, where the anarchists had formed not only a labour organisation but also during the civil war a fighting force, the contradiction seemed resolved. However, the anarchists became involved in an alliance with the communists which Goldman reluctantly supported but which ultimately destroyed them. In 1936 she visited an experimental anarchist school on a mountain top in the Pyrenees, 'pushed and pulled' to the summit by her young Spanish friends, a final moment of optimism before the descent to the real and murderous world below. From then on, all she could do was to help as many anarchists as possible escape from Fascist Spain.

Perhaps because the United States had expended so much legal and administrative effort on getting rid of her, Goldman ended by believing in the subversive power attributed to her by American leaders from Theodore Roosevelt onward. In 1935 she wrote to Rose Pesotta, in one of her delightfully misspelled letters, that 'if Sasha [Berkman] and I had not been kicked out and we could have continued our work which was only begining to take on large dementions shortly before the [First World] war, Anarchsim would be known and the Communists would not now have the entire militant field.'[5]

Goldman was thirty years Pesotta's senior, and when their correspondence began, in 1934, it was because Pesotta sought Goldman's views on the failure of socialism in the United States.

Later that year, Pesotta met Goldman in Montreal—the nearest the old tigress could get to America—and after a long talk the two concluded that 'the youth was sadly neglected in [Goldman's] days, and that is why we [the American anarchists] are now an isolated group.'[6]

Up to the outbreak of war, Pesotta was to reiterate her doubts about anarchism, and Goldman to respond angrily, and sometimes in a tone of personal resentment. From Seattle, Pesotta wrote to Goldman of her own battle with vested interests on behalf of an unresponsive working class: 'What I would like to know, after forty years of your activities must I begin from the very, very beginning? ... What I cannot understand is this, forty years of propaganda and enlightenment meant nothing to these people? If you could see the literature, hear the radio speeches and the arguments advanced against us you would think that they were a hundred years behind the times.'[7]

Goldman wrote back reproaching Pesotta for having the audacity to compare their respective battles. Pesotta had a powerful union behind her, while she had fought alone. 'Its backing not only means material security while you serve it but also social and legal protection. I had nothing and no one when I began or even years after. I was dragged from pillar to post more in police station houses than in my bed. In the face of the densest ignorance that existed in America forty years ago. In places where there had never been a socialist even before me, let alone an anarchist.'[8]

But when Pesotta continued to express her concern that native-born American workers lacked class consciousness and would not take full advantage of the labour machine she had helped to build, Goldman sent an answer remarkable, and typical, for its combination of realism and utopian prophecy: she reminded Pesotta that in the United States there was no proletariat, in the European sense, and that until the Depression the American working class had been better off than many European middle-class people. She pointed out that the American trade unions had always tried to harmonise capital and labour, 'never a word about fundamental changes', and that the 'foreign element' (including the Jews) expounding radicalism had always been a minority. But she saw signs of hope. After fifteen years in exile, Goldman had just been allowed into America for a three-month tour to publicise her autobiography, *Living My Life*; she told Pesotta that she had witnessed a 'tremendous awakening'; in 'modern literature', the drama, social life, and 'among people of every layer in the country, the very things I propagated ... have now entered the lives of millions as a matter of course ... The intellectual and cultural advancement preceed [sic] the economic and not, as Marx would have it, the reverse.'[9]

Throughout the early Nazi period, Goldman was conscious that the anarchists were being crushed everywhere between the two forces of Fascism and communism; she anticipated a new world war, and sensed that she would not survive it. But she was determinedly blind to the probable fate of the Jews.

Pesotta, by contrast, was much concerned for the Jews, for whom she feared as she feared for her own family in Russia. Pesotta favoured Zionism. Not so Goldman, who sent her a copy of a letter setting out her own beliefs, in January 1939, just as refugees from Nazi Germany were refused entry to Europe and America; even their flight to Palestine was restricted. 'Not believing in the efficacy of nationalism does not mean that we remain "objective and cool" about the plight of the Jewish people. For myself, I can say that I feel it deeply, but I insist that it was the bounden duty of the Jews to fight for their rights and freedom and, in every country where they were born and raised, to help to create its culture and its civilisation. I fail to see the benefit that it will get by establishing a new state in Palestine with the same old feelings of nationalism and a state.' The Jews of Germany, she argued, had not banded together to counter anti-Semitism. 'Please do not think that I feel they are getting what they deserve—no, but I cannot close my eyes to the fact that the Jews have failed miserably to defend their own grounds. I insist further, that if Hitler had only persecuted the Polish Jews, he would have 90 per cent of the German Jews on his side, just as Mussolini had nearly all the Jews of Italy on his side. Alas, it is no good to be a coward.'[10]

Like Rosa Luxemburg, Goldman was not interested in 'special Jewish sorrows', maintaining, for instance, that the blacks were persecuted far more seriously than the Jews, but got less attention.[10] She had serious personal resentments against her own community: further, like most of the Jewish women anarchists, in both England and the United States, her sense of class divisions within Jewry was keener than any ethnic solidarity. Jewry's enemies made no such distinction.

On the very eve of war Pesotta and Goldman, with other anarchist and socialist friends in America, worked frantically to raise money for visas for Spanish and Jewish anarchists trapped in France at the outbreak of war. Goldman was concerned primarily with her anarchist comrades. Even when war had been declared, and when, according to Hitler's threat, the Jews were now at particular risk, what concerned her most was the fate of Arthur Bartoletti, an Italian fugitive from Fascism threatened with repatriation to Italy from Canada. Furious with Dubinsky's feeble response to her appeal for funds, Goldman's last letter to Pesotta, dated January 30, 1940, reminded her that the anarchists had contributed generously to Jewish rescue activities, and that she was 'ashamed' of the lack of Jewish support for other refugees, 'though I have never felt particularly Jewish'; it was the anarchists, after all, she wrote, who were Pesotta's own 'flesh and blood'.[11]

A month later, Goldman suffered a stroke in Toronto and died in May 1940. Pesotta worked on at her sewing machine and, when America entered the war in 1941, made uniforms for American women soldiers. After the war, through refugee organisations, she discovered that all save one of her Russian family had died in the war—two brothers had fought with the Red Army and the rest were deported and gassed by the Nazis. She wrote her second volume of memoirs as a tribute to the Jewish civilisation destroyed in the Holocaust; she also wrote a work of fiction, in the first person, as a *yeshiva* student who escapes his religious background to join the revolutionary cause. She supported American civil rights organisations and campaigned for the Israeli trade union federation, the Histadrut. Pesotta continued working until her terminal illness, and died in Florida in 1965.[12]

Goldman's life—from the influences of her early youth to her death exactly at the moment when the 'phoney war' became a world conflict—spanned the entire world of the Jewish women rebels. Her models, as a young girl, were the populist martyrs of the People's Will. She was concerned primarily with the fate of working women and mistrusted middle-class feminists, in whose activities she saw charity and philanthropy, but not the foundation of a more just society. She lived between two worlds— that of Czarist and revolutionary Russia, on the one hand, and America, which she never ceased to idealise for its innocence and energy, on the other. She was both teacher and working woman, believing that the masses would respond to the word. She advocated communal living as a model for the world at large, and had the courage to defend her beliefs even at physical danger to herself. So that, whether or not she recognised it, Goldman had much in common with the Jewish women radicals who had preceded her. In her final letters to Pesotta, Goldman touched on many of their concerns. Like Pesotta, she was primarily a propagandist, a missionary. Her insistence that 'intellectual and cultural advancement' must precede economic revolution was held by the Bundist women and was at the heart even of Frumkin's arguments. Like Luxemburg, Goldman believed that the danger of creating yet another nation state was more important than that threatening the Jewish people. Goldman propagated birth control, arguing that for too long women 'had kept their mouths shut and their wombs open'; but she pitied feminists who deliberately avoided sexual involvement. In her denunciation, as a Russian Jewess, of German Jewry, she underlined the tragic separation of the two Jewries of Europe, which Pappenheim had tried to bridge, and also her resentments of the class bias in Jewry, and among Jewish women.

In her personal life, Goldman flouted every Jewish principle; very probably, as she must have known the rules, in reaction against the repressive family life she experienced as a child and young woman. Perhaps unwittingly, she extorted a terrible revenge when, after the assassination of President McKinley, she was suspected of complicity: her father was ostracised by his community and banned from the synagogue. She asserted her sexual independence, refusing to be tied even to those lovers who wanted to make her into a wife and mother, gallantly conceding defeat when others left her, and in most cases retaining their friendship. Her recently discovered correspondence with Ben Reitman, the 'hobo' doctor, shows that she broke every Jewish taboo in her sexual behaviour;[13] and she chose, by avoiding an operation which would, as she tells it, also have improved her sexual life, to remain childless. But she insisted that her notion of free love did not mean promiscuity, and her most durable relationship remained that with Berkman, with whom she enjoyed a comradeship which, as she wrote to him late in both their lives, had outlasted their sexual estrangement and every other attachment.[14]

Like that of so many Jewish radicals, her attitude towards her fellow Jews was deeply ambivalent. In her autobiography, she recalls not only the support given her by the radical Jewish press but the appeals made to her to lend her energies and persuasive powers to supporting Jewish causes. She mentions, in particular, the efforts of Chaim Zhitlovsky, whom she describes as a 'social revolutionist and an ardent Judaist', whom she rebuffed by arguing (again like Luxemburg) that the whole world was her arena, that 'social injustice is not confined to my own race', though in her childhood she had seen herself as a 'Judith'.[15]

The reference is suggestive. Zhitlovsky and Goldman had much in common. He too was mercurial, ambitious, and widely influential before 1914, in Russian populist and Jewish socialist circles. He too believed in voluntaristic socialism and opposed the socio-historic and 'scientific' claims of Marxism. Above all he was an individualist. Zhitlovsky was one of the first radicals to try to define what being a Jew meant in the secular sense. But this, paradoxically, was the result of his early training (and suffering)—twelve years spent in Bible and Talmudic classes, which instilled in him a sense of Jewish identity, something Jewish radical women were to find only with difficulty, if at all.[16]

On one significant occasion Goldman acknowledged that her sphere of influence might have been too restricted for her ability to right wrongs. This was when, with Berkman, she toured post-revolutionary Russia in an attempt to see, for herself, exactly what was happening in her motherland. During these travels, despite all that she had heard of the pogroms, it was only by accident, when her train broke down in the Ukraine, that she and Berkman found themselves in a *shtetl* named Fastov, where four thousand Jews had been massacred and their women raped. The rabbis welcomed the two anarchist Jews, whom they believed had been sent by God. 'I was strangely stirred by the tragic scene in the poverty stricken synagogue in outraged and devastated Fastov. The Jews of America were more likely to answer their prayers, but, alas, neither I nor Sasha had access to them. It would have been too cruel to tell these people that in America we were considered Ahasverus. We could make known their great tragedy only to the radical labour world and to our own comrades.'[17]

Anarchism was a lost cause, and Goldman's life, today, has an antiquarian interest. She figures mainly in novels and documentaries seeking to recreate the lost age between the two world wars, and particularly the flirtation of the British and American intelligentsia with revolutionary ideas. Yet in her condemnation of bolshevism she towered over those American radicals, and English left-wing intellectuals, who for all their sophistication had a less keen understanding of the realities of revolutionary politics. She inhabits a kind of historical no–man's-land, and in this, too, she resembles the other Jewish women radicals, whose legacy was both controversial and contradictory.

In 1991 a British historian visiting Lvov saw workmen placing, by a street sign reading 'Rosa Luxemburg Street' another reading 'Cathedral Street'—as a guide to the coming change in the topography of the city.[18] Posterity has garbled Luxemburg's reputation. Forgotten for years after her death, she was then celebrated not only by the apparatchiks she despised and regimes she would have hated but in speeches, on street signs, and on postage stamps, by the most dictatorial of communist regimes; and by intellectual circles in the West she almost certainly would have disowned. Now, with the overthrow of Leninism, she again falls out of favour, precisely at a time when the primitive and sectarian nationalism she warned against ravages Eastern Europe.

Such ironies are typical of the fate of all the Jewish women rebels. The populists, who believed they represented the Russian people, died and were remembered as members of a martyred élite. Kuliscioff, who dedicated her life to the Italian working class and to the rights of women, is commemorated chiefly as Turati's partner. Frumkin was written out of both Bundist and communist history. Shochat became an anachronism in Jewish politics, even within her own lifetime. The end of Jewish prostitution came not as the result of Pappenheim's courageous rebellion but because of social changes in Jewry and the ravages of the Holocaust. Pesotta was rejected by the union she served and lost faith in the power of libertarian ideas to influence American life.

When these women's activities did have a lasting effect on the societies they lived in, it was in a manner startlingly different from that they anticipated. Goldman was a case in point. Like all the rebels, she exaggerated the power of her rhetoric. But though there was to be no revolution in America, civil liberties can arguably be said to have benefited by the challenge Goldman and others like her posed to the legal system and the concept of free speech in the United States. The trials and deportations of anarchists, including her friend Mollie Steimer, for instance, in the Abrams case of 1918, led great American jurists like Holmes and Brandeis to reconsider how far short the rhetoric of libertarians fell of a 'clear and present danger' to the Constitution.[19]

Again, if in the 1990s the vast majority of the hundreds of thousands of Jews leaving the Soviet Union for the Jewish state were totally ignorant of Jewish history and tradition, it was largely because of the success of the campaigns of Frumkin and her comrades in the Jewish Section. The woman who was probably best versed, of all the rebels, in Jewish tradition, and who looked forward to a secular Jewish 'nationality', helped create generations of Jews who could ask, on arrival in Israel, the meaning of the words 'bar mitzvah' and were ignorant of the customs observed at Jewish festivals. They had preserved just enough of their Jewish identity to seek reunion with other Jews, largely because Soviet society defined them as such.

In the last analysis, the most important legacy these women left is one which, because they have never been examined in the context of Jewish society and history, has not been recognised. Their efforts to create a new identity for themselves as women, in defiance of the norms of their own society, made them pioneers of women's liberation.

'I pitied [mother] but my sympathies were with father.' Jewish women's breach with the past, the refusal to be one more link in the golden chain and to follow their female ancestors into 'kosher beds' is most dramatically obvious in the change in mother–daughter relationships, and not in the rebellion against patriarchal standards alone.

This difference sets Jewish women apart from their non-Jewish radical counterparts in the Russian Empire, not only, as is obvious, from the peasant women who were little more than chattels, but also from the daughters of the Russian intelligentsia, who came from the (privileged or impoverished) nobility, and of the Russian merchant class. The ties between mothers and daughters, in the host society, were stronger, perhaps because the Russian male, of whatever class, had far more extensive rights over his women and was thus often more domineering and brutal than the Jewish husband and father.[20] Rabbinical law had set clear limits to these rights, and subjected them to constant reassessment in the rabbinical courts.

Jewish women thus did not usually band together against the men in the family; just as they did not enjoy, in compensation for the despotism of the Russian father, the feeling of innate moral superiority, linked with the option of chastity, encouraged in Christian theology. In the case of all the women discussed above, only Anna Kuliscioff's mother, encouraged by her radical daughters to abandon her husband altogether (an extreme case in any social group), had a strong moral and emotional tie to her daughter. This was possibly because—even in the context of the early populist Jewish girls—Kuliscioff appears to have come from the most assimilated and privileged background. Moreover, the 'despotism' of Anna Kuliscioff's father fell far short of that of non-Jewish fathers of the famous radicals.

However difficult the Jewish girls' relations with their fathers may have been, there is no indication in their memoirs that their relationships with their mothers influenced their intellectual and moral development. Mothers of Jewish radicals might look after their semi-abandoned grandchildren, bring chicken soup to their daughters in prison (like Bobrowskaya's mother) and elicit a pitying, irritated concern in their old age (as in the case of Luxemburg and Pesotta, who shared the care of her mother with her sister in her own lonely middle age). The primary concern of the Jewish radicals was to be as different from their own mothers as possible, even if it is clear that they inherited their mothers' practical energies. The managerial skills of radical women, both in the middle and working-class sectors, appears to have been inspired by their trading, peddling mothers and grandmothers. Such figures appear very frequently in the memoirs of the women surveyed.

The escape from the 'kosher beds', from early marriage, the rituals accompanying menstrual purity, the continual burden of childbirth, was particularly dramatic in the case of the women revolutionaries, living lives which discouraged not only family life and childbirth but frequently, even close emotional ties and a regular sexual life. Though women radicals had a reputation for promiscuity (usually because of libertarian manifestos written by men) their personal lives were sexually abstemious, because of the apprehension of unwanted pregnancies as well as an ethic which placed the revolutionary struggle before all personal ties. This ethic was as much a convenience for men seeking to evade commitment as a charter for women's freedom—as women like Luxemburg and Pesotta, like many non-Jewish radical women, were to find. But despite the rebellion against the marriage whose main justification was childbearing, the women's memoirs are full of the frankest expression of regret at the loss of motherhood (or in Kuliscioff's case, its joys). There is much evidence that these women knew how to avoid pregnancy and that when they became pregnant, it was the result of a conscious decision. When childless, they found various forms of compensation. Kuliscioff's early letters indicate that she believed to her sorrow that she could not bear children, longed for Costa's child, and once a mother, was able to break with him; and she was maternally protective of Turati—who identified her explicitly with his own mother. Luxemburg, denied the child she passionately wanted by Jogiches, was overwhelmingly maternal in her affair with the much younger Kostia Zetkin and was the 'mother' of her pet cat. Frumkin mothered both her own and other children, and her pupils. Even Manya Shochat, who neglected her children almost from birth, had not been able to resist the lure of motherhood. Pappenheim called the young social workers she trained her 'daughters'. Pesotta and Goldman deliberately avoided pregnancy; but Pesotta argues this was in order not to use a child to emotionally blackmail a father—a strange argument—and Goldman called herself Reitman's 'blue-eyed mommy' at moments of the frankest eroticism.

If the 'sympathies' of the radical Jewish women were primarily with their fathers, it was because of their fathers' intellectual interests. Whether the fathers were artisans reading their page of Gemara at the end of an exhausting working day, or middle-class *maskilim* struggling to get a foothold in the professions, their daughters eyed them enviously.

The sympathy was often mutual. If women were perennially barred from the religious world of learning, and from the Jewish élite, the *maskil* father very often encouraged his daughter's general education. This did not mean that he wanted her to leave the fold, but, on the contrary, that such an education would enable her to make a more advantageous marriage. Almost all the women whose lives are sketched here were given a good education, with the active approval of their fathers. Emma Goldman's memory of her father saying that all a girl needed was to know how to cut noodles fine and give a man plenty of children should not be allowed to obscure the fact that he also demanded good results from her at school and punished her when she did not produce them.

Moreover, in Jewish families it was very often the father himself who was his daughter's model—as in the very different cases of Manya Shochat, Rose Pesotta, and Aletta Jacobs. (Shochat even argues, in her memoir, that her penchant for conspiracy originated in an incident in which her father gave help to a peasant fugitive from Czarist justice and swore her to secrecy.)

Radical Jewish women were intensely class-conscious even before they were politically educated, and it is difficult to separate that from the differences they were able to note, in their own communities, between the wealthy merchant community, the artisan class, and the growing industrial working population. Their lack of sympathy for middle-class feminism, and their interest in the political education of the working class, may have stemmed as much from rebellion against their traditional role in maturity in their own community as from the anomalous composition of the Jewish working class, so unlike the Russian peasantry turned industrial working class. Esther Frumkin's diatribe against the fiction of Jewish solidarity (Klal Yisrael) was also a rebellion against the traditional role of middle-class women like herself, part of whose task was to organise *t'sedaka*, or charity, which kept the working class dependent on the generosity, approved by rabbinical law, of the merchant class.

Furthermore, the age-old class division within Jewry had, after the Enlightenment, become that between the largely impoverished, and far more orthodox, communities of Eastern Europe and the prosperous, and more assimilated, communities of the West. Esther Frumkin's opposition to a widely based Diaspora Yiddish culture reflects an awareness of this division, as does Bertha Pappenheim's ambivalent attitude to the Eastern European women she encountered on her travels. The same was true of the hostility between the libertarian Jewish feminists who belonged to the European middle class, and the anarchist or radical Jewish women who defied them; and between German Jewish women philanthropists and social workers in the United States and the militant women in the sweatshops. Their common Jewish origins, or the threat of anti-Semitism, was far less important than the class barriers which now separated them. It is in the light of this development that the hostility of a Rose Witcop or an Emma Goldman to the Jewish community at large must be seen.

In the final analysis, however, it was the Jewish women's desire to appropriate the world of ideas—hitherto, in their communal tradition, the world of men alone—and to build a new and egalitarian relationship with men that characterise them most strongly. It is also striking that they lent themselves most eagerly to the drive to educate the working class, and not just to arouse their political consciousness. Furthermore, they judged the acquisition of culture—literature, music, and art—to be as important in that education as class-consciousness or a knowledge of history and politics. This is surely to be attributed to the influence of the Enlightenment—either through their fathers, or because secular culture had always been more freely permitted to Jewish women than to men.

In Rosa Luxemburg's letters to Jogiches these two major ambitions—to experiment with ideas and to share life with a man on equal terms—coalesce most strikingly. The letters are full of the excitement at exercising her powerful mind, on the one hand, and the desire to share this excitement with Jogiches, on the other. She expects him, moreover, to reciprocate, and reproaches him when his own letters have only political, and no emotional, content. And she is well aware that such a relationship between men and women is a new departure: 'No couple on earth has the chance we have.'

The same theme is repeated explicitly in Kuliscioff's letters to Costa and Turati, in Pesotta's to Powers Hapgood, and in Goldman's letters and autobiography. The desire for equality with men on the intellectual and emotional plane together is implicit in the worldview of Frumkin and Shochat, just as its absence in traditional Jewish society is deplored by Bertha Pappenheim.

The intensity of the Jewish radical women's yearning for a share in the intellectual and spiritual life of men is difficult to explain without reference to their communal history. Perhaps this is why they meet with an ambivalent response from so many feminist writers, who see them as poised uncertainly between the feminine ideal of an earlier age and the contemporary model of the emancipated woman.

Like many other radical women of their time, the Jewish women did not put women's concerns before those of socialism; for they believed that only when social and economic inequalities were redressed would women come into their own. Nor did they always stand up for emotional independence. They were often passionately involved with men who could not accept them as equals, or who expected them to accept a double standard. They fought this with varying degrees of success. Some have been subjected to procrustean treatment by feminist historians in order to adapt their lives to contemporary values—emerging predictably mutilated. Franca Pieroni Bortolotti, the Italian feminist historian, has charged Kuliscioff with lacking the moral courage to put feminism before her socialist ideals.[21] Raya Dunayevskaya has tried to read into the life of Luxemburg a latent feminism for which there is not the slightest evidence.[22] Emma Goldman has been rediscovered by feminist writers, like Alix Kates Shulman, who celebrate her challenge to traditional female behaviour; but reproached by Dale Spender, for instance, for failing to 'indict male power in general' and for 'invoking the cult of true womanhood'.[23] Pesotta has been reprimanded, by the American labour historian Alice Kessler-Harris, for ignoring the importance of 'female bonding' and for relying on men for support—thus courting disaster in the union.[24]

Criticism along these lines—while rehearsing the old conflict between middle-class feminists and socialist women—misreads the historical context. With the exception of Pappenheim, too damaged in her youth to form any close ties whatever, the Jewish women radicals and rebels tried valiantly, and against enormous odds, to build a totally new emotional and sexual relationship with men. They certainly recognised—sometimes in anger, sometimes ruefully—that socialist comradeship did not exclude sexual injustice. In their emotional lives, as in their political careers, they refused compromise and maintained a devastating honesty with themselves which often put their male partners to shame.

If they were not feminists in their time, it was because in that time feminism meant, primarily, women's suffrage—which many of them supported but which they did not believe would automatically ensure a juster society or a fundamental change in the political scene, leading, for instance, to a less belligerent world. Developments between the wars proved them right.

They did not, it is true, see 'male supremacy' as the essential issue in their campaign for independence, and so did not believe that by associating uniquely with other women they would achieve greater equality. It is worth noting that Rosika Schwimmer, who cannot be faulted as a militant feminist and who could be bitterly sarcastic at male politicians' expense, led her campaign for women's suffrage in Hungary together with men, and opposed pacifism in the name of international motherhood. Feminists, at this period, held the belief that women's special qualities gave them the moral right to make political judgements. Kuliscioff, on trial in Milan in 1898, to gain the sympathy of the Italian people, argued that the interests of socialist women were those of the nation's mothers.[25]

The women rebels did not shun the battlefield between the sexes. They had the courage to commit themselves to loving, the fortitude to sustain injury, and the emotional depth to risk danger in their relationships with men. Witness Kuliscioff, tearing herself away from Costa despite her love for him; witness Luxemburg, who outgrew her dependence on Jogiches ('I am I, now I am free of Leo'); witness Pesotta, so much stronger than the man she loved, turning a disastrous love affair into a stable friendship; witness Goldman, who could write in her old age, with humour and resignation, 'It seems to be my fate to prepare my lovers for other women and then act as confidante of the women. The irony, eh?'[26]

All were women of ideas. Their rebellion was not the result of a whim or a thirst for adventure; it was governed by political and personal ideals which might not be fully realised but which were never abandoned.

They tried to evolve a new, difficult, but more rewarding way to live as a woman, despite moments of despair and doubt. Whether they succeeded or not, their belief in political and social change sustained them. It was an assertion of their individuality, a sense of their own intrinsic worth, over and above but not excluding their relationship with men. In this sense they were thoroughly modern.

In a moment of self-doubt, Pesotta wrote to Goldman: 'I find that something is wrong somewhere; we are either too far advanced or are lagging far behind. Which is it?'[27] The answer should have been, resoundingly, the first.

NOTES

INTRODUCTION

1. Cecilia Bobrowskaya, *Twenty Years in Underground Russia*, New York, 1934.
2. Elyohu Cherikover, 'Yidn-revolutsyonern in rusland in di 60-er un 70-er yorn' (Revolutionary Jews in Russia in the (18)60s and (18)70s), *Historishe Shriftn* III, Vilna and New York, 1939, pp.129–30 and 133–4 (Yiddish). Leonard Schapiro, in 'The Role of the Jews in the Russian Revolutionary Movement', *Slavonic and Eastern European Review* XL, 1961–62, also mentions women's conversion as his sole reference to their part in early Russian radicalism.
3. Saul Stampfer, 'Literacy amongst East European Jewry in the Modern Period: Context, Background and Implications', in *Transition and Change in Modern Jewish History: Essays in Honour of Shmuel Ettinger*, Jerusalem, 1987, Vol.1, pp.459–83 (Hebrew).
4. Anna Heller, 'Bletlech fun a Lebens-Geschichte', *Historishe Shriftn* III, op. cit. n.2, p.422 (Yiddish).
5. Israel Joshua Singer, *Of a World that is No More*, New York, 1970.
6. I.M. Rubinow, 'Economic Conditions of the Jews in Russia', *Bulletin of the US Bureau of Labor* 15, n.72, 1907; reprinted Arno Press New York, 1975, pp.523–5.
7. See Rose Glickman, *The Russian Factory Women; Workplace and Society, 1880–1914*, Berkeley and London, 1984. A comparison between the women portrayed by Glickman and those in Chapter 4 of this book is instructive.
8. Quoted in Zvi Y. Gitelman, *Jewish Nationality and Soviet Politics*, Princeton, 1972, pp.29–30.
9. Richard Stites, *The Women's Liberation Movement in Russia, Feminism, Nihilism and Bolshevism 1860–1930*, Princeton, 1978, p.150.
10. Glickman, op. cit. n.7.
11. Robert Wistrich, 'Rosa Luxemburg the Internationalist', in *Revolutionary Jews from Marx to Trotsky*, London, 1976, p.77.
12. Lily Bes, 'Fun eygene vegn'. Quoted by Norma Fain Pratt, in 'Culture and Radical Politics: Yiddish Women Writers in America, 1890–1940', in Scharf and Jensen, eds., *Decades of Discontent, The Women's Movement 1920–1940*, Westport, Conn., 1983, pp.136–7.

CHAPTER 1: A FOOTNOTE IN HISTORY

1. Grace Aguilar, *The Women of Israel, a Defence of Jewish Womanhood*, London, 1861; Nahida Remy, *The Jewish Woman*, Louise Mannheimer, tr., New York, 1895.
2. Jane Rendall, *The Origins of Modern Feminism*, London, 1985. See Chapter III: 'Evangelicalism and the Power of Women'.
3. Ibid. p.113.
4. Aguilar, *The Spirit of Judaism*, Isaac Leeser, ed., London, 1842, p.18.

5. Aguilar, *The Women of Israel*, op. cit. n.1, Introduction.
6. Ibid. p.377.
7. *Archives Israélites de France*, Vol.II, 1841, p.207, letter from Fanny Angel. See also editorial comment.
8. Yigael Yadin, *Bar Kochba*, London, 1971, pp.222–30, 233–41, 244–9, 251–2.
9. Bernadette Brooten, *Women Leaders in the Synagogue: Inscriptional Evidence and Background Issues*, Maine, 1982. See also Shaye J.D. Cohen, 'Women in the Synagogues of Antiquity', *Conservative Judaism* XXXIV, Nov./Dec. 1980.
10. S.D. Goitein, *A Mediterranean Society*, Vol.III, p.352. Goitein is rare among Jewish historians in that his range of interests extends to women, to whom he dedicates an entire section, 'The World of Women', in this volume.
11. Cecil Roth, *A History of the Jews in England*, Oxford, 1941, p.115; W.C. Jordan, 'Jews on top; women and the availability of consumption loans in Northern France in the mid 13th century,' *Jewish Journal of Sociology*, Vol.XXIX, 1978.
12. A.M. Haberman, 'Women writers, authors and printers', *Kiryat Sefer* XV, 1938, pp.373–6 (Hebrew).
13. Shlomo Simonsohn, *The History of the Jews in the Duchy of Mantua*, Tel Aviv/Jerusalem, 1977, p.585. See also Haberman, loc, cit. n.12; Howard Adelman, 'Rabbis and Reality; Public Activities of Jewish Women in Italy during the Renaissance and Catholic Restoration', in *Jewish History*, Haifa and Leiden, Vol.5, no.1, Spring 1991.
14. Shlomo Ashkenazi, *Ha'isha Be'aspeklariat Ha'yahadut*, Tel Aviv, 1979, Vol.I, Appendix (Tsiyunim) (Hebrew).
15. Tal Ilan, 'Notes on the Distribution of Jewish Women's Names in Palestine in the Second Temple and Mishnaic Periods', *Journal of Jewish Studies* 2, New York, 1989. S.D. Goitein, *A Mediterranean Society*, Vol.III, pp.315–19. See also, for comparison, Leopold Zunz, 'Namen der Juden', *Gesammelte Schriften* III, reprinted Hildesheim 1971.
16. Goitein, op. cit. n.15, p.355.
17. Shlomo Ashkenazi, 'Women Authors of Piyyutim, Tehinot and Prayers', in *Mahanayim* 109, 1967, pp. 75–82 (Hebrew); also Chava Weissler, 'The Religion of Traditional Ashkenazic Women: Some Methodological Issues', in *Association of Jewish Studies Review*, Vol.12, no.1., Spring 1987, pp.79–84; Weissler, 'The Traditional Piety of Ashkenazic Women', in Arthur Green, ed., *A History of Jewish Spirituality*, New York, 1990.
18. Ellen Schiff, *From Stereotype to Metaphor, the Jew in Contemporary Drama*, Albany, 1982, Introduction; Luce Klein, *Portrait de la Juive dans la littérature française*, Paris, 1970; P. Hildenfinger, 'La Figure de la Synagogue dans l'art du Moyen Age', *Revue des Etudes Juives* XLVII, p.187.
19. Shaye J.D. Cohen, 'The Origins of the Matrilineal Principle in Rabbinic Law', *Association of Jewish Studies Review*, Vol.X, no.1, Spring 1985, pp.19–53.
20. For an exhaustive examination of the creation myth and women, in the context of recent archaeological and anthropological research, see Carol Meyers, *Discovering Eve – Ancient Israelite Women in Context*, New York/Oxford, 1988. For the confusion between matrilineal and matriarchal see pp.37–9.
21. Ibid. Chapter 4.
22. Richard Elliott Friedman, *Who Wrote the Bible?*, London, 1988, pp.85–6. The speculation about the J version of creation is curious, since it was the P (priestly, definitely male) version which has God create man and woman together and the J version which has him produce Eve from Adam's rib as a 'help meet' (see Appendix, p.246). Harold Bloom, in *The Book of J*, New York, 1990, presents the

view that the entire version was written by a well-born woman.

23. Leonie J. Archer, 'The Role of Jewish Women in the Religion Ritual and Cult of Graeco-Roman Palestine', in Cameron and Kuhrt, eds., *Images of Women in Antiquity*, London and Sydney, 1983, p.274. Archer argues that this marked a transition from pre-exilic, Canaanite culture to a 'rigidly monotheistic' (and patriarchal) one.

24. S. Safrai, 'Religion in Everyday Life'; 'The Temple'; 'The Synagogue' in S. Safrai and M. Stern, eds., *Compendia Rarum Iudaicarum ad Novum Testamentum*, Amsterdam, sect.1, Vol.II, 1969, 793–833; 865–907; 908–44.

25. See Chana Safrai's forthcoming 'Women in the Temple', for the most detailed examination of this subject.

26. Salo W. Baron, *The Jewish Community*, New York, 1942, Vol.I, p.96.

27. B. Porten, *Archives from Elephantine; the Life of an Ancient Jewish Military Colony*, Berkeley, Los Angeles, 1968. See also Ze'ev Falk, 'Inheritance Laws of the Daughter and the Widow in the Mikra and Talmud' in *Tarbiz*, Vol.XXIII, no.1, Jerusalem, 1952 (Hebrew).

28. Judith Romney Wegner, *Chattel or Person? The Status of Women in the Mishnah*, New York and Oxford, 1988, pp.172, 196. Wegner argues ingeniously that the unmarried daughter over the age of twelve and a half also enjoyed these privileges in legal theory, and calls all three categories of women 'autonomous'. It seems to me extremely doubtful that young girls could ever exercise such privileges, and, as Wegner herself admits on p.174 in a caveat, all three categories were marginal members of Israelite society unless they were economically independent.

29. Shaye D. Cohen, 'Women in the Synagogues of Antiquity', in *Conservative Judaism* Vol. XXXIV, Nov./Dec. 1980; Shmuel Safrai, 'Was there a Women's Gallery in the Synagogue of Antiquity?', in *Tarbiz*, Vol. XXXII, 1963, p.329 (Hebrew). For an extensive account of the new system of education, which, however, makes no mention of women's exclusion, see S. Safrai, 'Elementary Education, its Religious and Social Significance in the Talmudic Period', in *Cahiers d'Histoire Mondiale*, Vol.XI, 1968.

30. Ibid.

31. See Brooten, op. cit. n.9.

32. Adin Steinsaltz, *Nashim Be Mikra* (Women in the Bible), Jerusalem, 1988, p.12 (Hebrew).

33. Bereshit Rabba, 18.2.

34. See references to the various biblical women in Louis Ginzberg, *The Legends of the Jews*, New York, 1909–38; Judith Plaskow, *Standing at Sinai; Judaism from a Feminist Perspective*, New York and San Francisco, 1990.

35. Sifrei Numbers (circa fourth-century exegesis) 99. B. Talmud, *Sotah*, 12a (quotations from the Babylonian (B) Talmud are taken from the 1930s Soncino edition, London).

36. Rashi II Kings 22.14–15 (commentary of Rabbi Solomon Yitzhaki of Troyes).

37. Megilla, B. Talmud, tractated *Moed*, 14a, b.

38. Ibid.

39. B. Talmud, *Yebamot* I, 103a, 103b; *Nazir*, 23a.

40. Talmud *Nazir*, 23a.

41. See Yosef Hayim Yerushalmi, *Zakhor, Jewish History and Jewish Memory*, Seattle and London, 1982, pp.17–18.

42. B. Talmud, *Sanhedrin*, 74a,b.

43. B. Talmud, *Sanhedrin*, 22a.

44. For a succinct apologetic for the Talmud's treatment of women, see Adin Steinsaltz, *The Essential Talmud*, New York, 1976, Chapters 17 and 18. Perhaps unconsciously,

Steinsaltz underlines the rabbinical view that women's piety is often regarded as hypocrisy.

45. Jacob Neusner, 'The Mishnaic System of Women', in *A History of The Mishnaic Law of Women*, Studies in Judaism in Late Antiquity, Leiden, 1980, pp.13–41 and 179–271.
46. Romney Wegner, op. cit. n.28. See also that note.
47. Judith Baskin, 'The Separation of Women in Rabbinic Judaism', in Y.Y. Haddad, ed. *Women, Religion and Social Change*, London, 1985.
48. L.M. Epstein, *Marriage Laws in the Bible and the Talmud*, London, 1942. Rachel Biale, *Women and Jewish Law*, New York, 1983, 80–3.
49. Falk, op. cit. n.27.
50. M.A. Friedman, *Ribui Nashim Be Yisrael* (Polygamy among the Jews), Jerusalem, 1984 (Hebrew), is the most recent and extensive study based on Geniza and Palestinian sources. See also: idem, *Jewish Marriage in Palestine, A Cairo Geniza Study*, New York and Tel Aviv, 1980; and Ze'ev Falk, *Jewish Matrimonial Law in the Middle Ages*, Oxford, 1966.
51. Falk, *Jewish Matrimonial Law*, op. cit. n.50. For the European influence, see also Rudolf Huebner, *A History of Germanic Private Law*, Boston, 1918, pp.603, 623–32.
52. B. Talmud, *Ketuboth* 59b.
53. See Louis Finkelstein, *Jewish Self Government in the Middle Ages*, New York, 1964, Note B. in Appendix, p.377 (The Legal Status of Women in German Jewry).
54. Ibid.
55. Goitein, op. cit. n.10. Vol.I, p.127, 'Professions of Women'.
56. Finkelstein, op. cit. n.53.
57. Samuel Morell, 'An Equal or a Ward; How Independent is a Married Woman according to Rabbinical Law?' in *Jewish Social Studies*, 40, Summer-Fall 1982, pp.189–210.
58. Ibid.
59. Ibid.
60. Talmud *Pesachim*, 49b.
61. B. Talmud, *Niddah*, 13a.
62. B. Talmud, *Ketuboth*, 61b.
63. B. Talmud, *Kiddushin*, 29b.
64. B. Talmud, *Ketuboth*, 62b.
65. See Rachel Biale, op. cit. n.48, p.239ff. B. Talmud, *Ketuboth*, 51b for the suggestion that women are aroused by rape; B. Talmud *Horayoth*, 13a argues that when both men and women are threatened by rape in captivity, men are to be ransomed before women—the reverse of the usual order.
66. B. Talmud, *Yebamoth* II, 63a.
67. See Rachel Biale, op. cit. n.48, pp.136–40 passim. Biale quotes medieval sources to make this point.
68. B. Talmud, *Ketuboth*, 62b.
69. See also *Ketuboth*, 12a, 13a, etc., for two of several examples that there is no purpose in meetings between men and women other than sex.
70. B. Talmud, *Kiddushin*, 70a. There is an echo of this in Corinthians 4:34.
71. L.M. Epstein, *Sex Laws and Customs in Judaism*, New York, 1948.
72. Rachel Biale, op. cit. n.48, p.141.
73. Gershom Scholem, *Major Trends in Jewish Mysticism*, New York, 1961, pp.37–8, 225–35.
74. Weissler, 'The Religion, etc.', op. cit. n.17, pp.88–9.

75. Ze'ev Falk, 'She Who Rebels against her Husband', *Sinai*, 49, 1961 (Hebrew). See also Morell, op. cit. n.57. Talmudic sages suggested that one way to deal with such a wife was to take a 'rival'.
76. Yalkut Shimoni (thirteenth-century anthology of biblical Midrashim), 964. Solomon Buber, *Midrash Mishlei*, Lemberg, 1893.
77. Deuteronomy 11:19; B. Talmud, *Kiddushin*, 29b.
78. Jerusalem Talmud *Sotah* 3.16.
79. B. Talmud, *Sotah*, 20a, b.
80. Shmuel Safrai, op. cit. n.29.
81. In B. Talmud, *Sotah*, 22a, a maiden who gives herself up to prayer is one of three who 'bring destruction upon the world'; and pious virgins are often as suspect as ascetic widows, both of whom are classed among *mevalei olam* (Steinsaltz, op. cit. n.44. Chapter 18) or idlers. As the gadabout widow is also condemned, it must have been difficult to be a widow whose conduct was beyond reproach.
82. Maimonides, *Sefer Hamada*, I, 15.
83. Rachel Biale, op. cit. n.48, pp.35–6.
84. Ibid. p.43.
85. See Mary R. Lefkowitz and Maureen B. Fant, *Women's Life in Greece and Rome*, London, 1982; and Sarah B. Pomeroy, *Goddesses, Whores, Wives and Slaves: Women in Classical Antiquity*, New York, 1975, for comparative material.
86. Chava Weissler, 'Women in Paradise', in *Tikkun*, Vol.2, no.2, pp.43–6 and 117–120 (English).
87. Ashkenazi, op. cit. n.17, pp.120–21.
88. See Ivan G. Marcus, 'Mothers, Martyrs and Moneymakers' in *Conservative Judaism*, Spring 1986, for the poem analysed.
89. A.M. Haberman, ed., *Sefer Gezerot Ashkenaz ve-Zarefat*, Jerusalem, 1945, p.34 (Hebrew). The prototype of the female martyr was Hannah, the Maccabean 'mother of seven sons' in Hellenistic times.
90. Salo W. Baron, 'The Jewish Community', New York, 1942, Vol. 2 *Education and Public Enlightenment*, pp.177ff.
91. Ibid.
92. Riccardo Calimani, *The Ghetto of Venice*, New York, 1987, pp.173–8.
93. B. Talmud, *Ketuboth*, 54b.
94. Jacob Ben Asher, *Even HaEzer* (medieval rabbinic code) 154.3.
95. Maimonides, Mishne Torah, Seder Nashim, Hilkhot Ishut, 13.11. Maimonides argues elsewhere that Jewish women had voluntarily imposed restrictions on themselves which had acquired the force of law with time. See Plaskow, op. cit. n.34, p.65.
96. Avraham Grossman, 'Medieval Rabbinic Views on Wife-Beating, 800–1300', *Jewish History*, Haifa and Leiden, Vol. 5, no.1, Spring 1991, pp.53–62.
97. Louis Finkelstein, ed., *The Jews*, 2, 1960, pp.1043–75.
98. Falk, op. cit. n.50.
99. L.M. Epstein, op. cit. n.71.
100. Ibid.
101. Gershon Hundert, 'Approaches to the History of the Jewish Family in Early Modern Poland-Lithuania', in Cohen and Hyman, eds., *The Jewish Family—Myths and Reality*, New York and London, 1986, p.23.
102. Jacob Katz, 'Family, Kinship and Marriage among Ashkenazim in the 16th–18th Centuries', *Jewish Journal of Sociology* 1 (1959), pp.4–22.
103. Ada Rapoport-Albert, 'On Women in Hasidism: S.A. Horodecky and the Maid of Ludmir Tradition', in *Jewish History; Essays in Honour of Chimen Abramsky*, London, 1988.

104. Chava Weissler, 'Woman as High Priest: A Kabbalistic Prayer in Yiddish for Lighting Sabbath Candles', in *Jewish History*, Haifa and Leiden, Vol. 5, no.1, Spring 1991, pp.9–26.
105. Max Weinreich, *History of the Yiddish Language*, Noble, tr., Chicago, 1980, pp.272–8.
106. *T'sena Ure'ena, The Classic Anthology of Torah Lore and Midrashic Comment*, New York, 1983, tr. from the Yiddish by M.S. Zakon, pp.364, 456, 907. (The three volumes are paged with consecutive numbers.)
107. Ibid. pp.99, 831.
108. Ibid. pp.154, 940.
109. Ibid. pp.364–5.
110. Ibid. p.456.
111. Ibid. p.403.
112. Ibid. p.36, and subsequently after each reference to the creation.
113. Ibid. pp.403, 419, 825 and at each mention of Satan.
114. Ibid. p.602.
115. Ibid. p.381.
116. Ibid. p.417.
117. Ibid. p.496.
118. *The Memoirs of Glueckel of Hameln*, Marvin Lowenthal, tr., New York, 1977.
119. Katz, op. cit. n.102.
120. *The Memoirs of Glueckel of Hameln*, p.2.
121. Ibid. p.241.
122. Ibid. pp.151–2.
123. Ibid. p.272.
124. Ibid. p.223.
125. Katz, op. cit. n.102.
126. Jacob Katz, 'Marriage and Sexual Life Among the Jews at the End of the Middle Ages', in *Zion* X (1944), pp.21–54 (Hebrew).
127. Ibid.
128. Paul Ritterband, ed., *Modern Jewish Fertility*, London, 1987. See articles by Steven Loewenstein on Bavaria, Paula Hyman on France. Barry Kosmin, 'Nuptiality and Fertility Patterns of British Jewry 1850–1980', in D.A. Coleman, ed., *Demography of Immigrants and Minority Groups in the United Kingdom*, London, 1982, with reference to the falling birthrate of the old Sephardi community in the mid century. For rabbinical attitudes to birth control, see David Feldman, *Marital Relations, Birth Control and Abortion in Jewish Law*, New York, 1974.
129. For a comprehensive survey of Jewish life in Russia at this time, see Salo W. Baron, *The Jews under Czars and Soviets*, New York, 1976, Chapters 6–8.
130. Yuri Suhl, *Ernestine Rose*, New York, 1970.
131. David Biale, 'Childhood, Marriage and the Family in the Eastern European Jewish Enlightenment', in Cohen and Hyman, eds., n.101. pp.45–61. For Czarist policy towards the Jews at this period, see Hans Rogger, *Jewish Policies and Right-Wing Politics in Imperial Russia*, London and Oxford, 1986.
132. Quoted in Biale, above.
133. Ibid.
134. Azriel Shochat, 'German Jewish Integration in Non Jewish Society in the early eighteenth century', in *Zion* XXI, NS 1956, pp.220–4 (Hebrew).
135. For a short account of the 'salon' women, see Michael A. Meyer, *The Origins of the Modern Jew: Jewish Identity and European Culture, 1749–1824*, London, 1968, pp.85–114. For a detailed portrait, see Deborah Hertz, *Jewish High Society in Old*

Regime Berlin, New Haven and London, 1988. See also Julius Carlebach, *The Forgotten Connection; Women and Jews in the Conflict between Enlightenment and Romanticism*, Leo Baeck Institute Yearbook XXIV, 1979.

136. Hertz, op. cit. n.135, pp.238–43.
137. D. Philipson, *The Reform Movement in Judaism*, New York, 1907, pp.219–20.
138. Pauline Wengeroff, *Memoiren eines Grossmutter*, Berlin, 1913, pp.100ff.
139. Puah Rakowski, *Lo Nichnati*, tr. from Yiddish to Hebrew by David Kalai, Tel Aviv, 1951.
140. Barbara Alpern Engel, *Mothers and Daughters; Women of the Intelligentsia in 19th-century Russia*, Cambridge and New York, 1983, pp.141–2, 154–5.
141. Compare, for instance, the peasant women turned factory women described in Rose Glickman, *The Russian Factory Woman: Workplace and Society 1880–1914*, Berkeley and London, 1984, pp.132ff and pp.241ff with the Jewish working-class women described in Chapters 4 and 7.
142. Engel, op. cit. n.140, p.5. The link between the religious female value system of Russian revolutionary women and their radical beliefs is one of the themes of this book. No such study has been written about Jewish women.
143. Translated by Adrienne Rich, quoted in Pratt, op. cit. n.12, p.135.

CHAPTER 2: SINGING FOR THE REVOLUTION

1. Franco Venturi, 'Anna Kuliscioff e la sua attività rivoluzionaria in Russia', in *Movimento Operaio*, 2, 1952, p.285.
2. Lev Deich, 'Anna Rozenstein Macarevich', in *Rol Yevreev v russkom revoliutsionnom dvizhenii* (The Role of the Jews in Russian Revolutionary History), Berlin, 1923, pp.217ff, p.218 (Russian). Hans Rogger, op. cit. Chapter 1, n. 131, p.12. Venturi asserts that Rozenstein was a convert to Russian Orthodoxy, but Deich, his source, who knew Kuliscioff personally from adolescence, makes no mention of a conversion, and includes Anna Kuliscioff among the Jews assembled in this book. As the records of the Jewish community of Simferopol disappeared during the Holocaust, there is no way of proving or disaproving Venturi's assertion. Anna Kuliscioff herself refused to discuss her family or early life in public, but her occasional references to Jews in her private letters are sympathetic. The Catholic Gavazzi family into which her daughter married were obviously embarrassed by Anna's Jewishness and one of their descendants has suggested that Kuliscioff became a Catholic on her deathbed (Mino Martelli, *Andrea Costa e Anna Kuliscioff*, Milan, 1980). Her own silence and apparent lack of interest in Jews is quite typical of her generation of Jewish women radicals.
3. E. Cherikover, 'Yidn-revolutsyonern in rusland in di 60-er un 70-er yorn', in *Historishe Shriftn* III, Vilna and New York, 1939, p.129 (Yiddish).
4. Ibid. p.130.
5. Ibid. p.134.
6. Barbara Alpern Engel, *Mothers and Daughters; Women of the Intelligentsia in 19th-century Russia*, Cambridge, 1983, p.71.
7. For a full discussion of non-Jewish women's motivation, see Barbara Alpern Engel, 'From Separatism to Socialism: Women in the Russian Revolutionary Movement of the 1870s', in Marilyn J. Boxer and Jean H. Quataert, eds., *Socialist Women European Socialist Feminism in the 19th and early 20th Centuries*, New York 1978.
8. Ze'ev Ivianski, *Mahapekha Ve'terror* (Revolution and Terror), Tel Aviv, 1989, pp.49–50 (Hebrew). E. Cherikover *Yehudim Be'itot Mahapekha; Ideologia Mahaphanit Ve'leumit bikerev Ha'yehudim Bi'russia Bi'shnot Ha'shivim Ve'hashmonim* (Jews in

Revolutionary Times; Revolutionary and Nationalist Ideology among the Russian Jews during the 1870s and 1880s), Tel Aviv, 1957, pp.366ff (Hebrew).

9. Richard Stites, *The Women's Liberation Movement in Russia; Feminism, Nihilism and Bolshevism, 1860–1930*, Princeton, 1978, Part III.

10. I.M. Rubinow, *Economic Conditions of the Jews in Russia*, 1907, reprinted New York, 1975, p.579. For the figures on women in the Mal'tsev prison, see Margaret Maxwell, *Narodniki Women: Russian women who sacrificed themselves for the dream of freedom*, New York and Oxford, 1990, p.219.

11. Venturi, op. cit. n.1, p.284.

12. Deich, op. cit. n.2, pp.153ff.

13. Ivianski, op. cit. n.8, p.50.

14. Simon Dubnow, *History of the Jews, in Russia and Poland*, Philadelphia, 1918, Vol.II, pp.348–53.

15. Stites, op. cit. n.9, p.169. See also Fanni Schvartsmann, *Moya Sudba*, Paris, 1964, pp.167ff for details of obstacles placed in the way of Jewish girl students under czarism.

16. Cherikover, op. cit. n.3, p.130.

17. Deich, op. cit, n.2, pp.18–28. For Epstein's liaison work, see n.22 below.

18. Vera Broido, *Apostles into Terrorists, Women in the Revolutionary Movement in the Russia of Alexander II*, London, 1978, p.102.

19. Ibid. p.110.

20. J.M. Meijer, *Knowledge and Revolution: The Russian Colony in Zurich, 1870–1873*, Assen, 1955, pp.69ff. Vera Zasulich, the daughter of the gentry who shot the czarist governor Trepov, is described thus: 'as voluble as she was in private conversation, she was so bashful that in a public meeting she rarely uttered a word'. (Maxwell, op. cit. n.10, p.34).

21. Alpern Engel, op. cit. n.6, p.137.

22. *Baderech*, Papers for the research of the Jewish workers' movement, no.4, pp.94–5, Givat Haviva, August 1969 (Hebrew).

23. Deich, op. cit. n.2, pp.165–74.

24. Venturi, op. cit. n.1, p.278.

25. Broido, op. cit. n.18, p.106.

26. Deich, op. cit. n.2, pp.138–49.

27. Barbara Alpern Engel, *Five Sisters; Women Against the Czar*, New York, 1975, p.185.

28. Broido, op. cit. n.18, p.201.

29. Ivianski, op. cit. n.8, pp.47, 61–3.

30. Boris Sawinkow, *Erinnerungen eines Terroristen*, Berlin, 1931, p.39. Albert Camus, *L'Homme révolté*, Paris, 1951, pp.210–11.

31. For the Old Believer female tradition, see James Billington, *Fire in the Minds of Men; Origins of the Revolutionary Faith*, London, 1980, p.495. (Billington mentions Ginsburg but not that she was Jewish and hence could not have inherited this belief.) 'Suffering' quote: Prescobia Ivanskaya, priest's daughter turned terrorist, on Brilliant: Ivianski, op. cit. n.8, p.268.

32. Maxwell, op. cit. n.10, pp.262 ff.

33. L. Salvatorelli and G. Mira, *Storia d'Italia nel periodo Fascista*, Milan, 1957, p.561.

34. *Anna Kuliscioff: Lettere d'amore a Andrea Costa, 1880–1909*, Milan, 1979. Introduction by Piero Albonetti.

35. Deich, op. cit. n.2. He also mentions that 'her rather thick lower lip betrayed her Jewishness.'

36. *Lettere d'amore*, op. cit. n.34, Costa to Kuliscioff from Perugia prison, December 11, 1880.

37. Ibid. Costa to Kuliscioff, November 25, 1880.
38. Venturi, op. cit. n.1.
39. For the basic details of her early life in Italy, see Nino Valeri, *Turati e la Kuliscioff*, Firenze, 1974, Chapter 2. Her formative years are scarcely mentioned in the discussion of her feminist and socialist views by Claire LaVigna, 'The Marxist Ambivalence Toward Women: Between Socialism and Feminism in the Italian Socialist Party' in Boxer and Quataert, eds., *Socialist Women*, New York, 1978, pp.146–82. Beverley Tanner Springer's short essay on Kuliscioff in Kern and Slaughter, eds., *European Women on the Left*, 1981, dates her birth inaccurately (1855 is the correct date given by Kuliscioff herself in a letter to Turati in the *Carteggio*, May 24, 1899); states that Kuliscioff 'left her anarchist ideas behind in Russia' (p.17) against the evidence in the letters to Costa; calls feminism 'the most integral part of her life' (p.19), ignoring the often caustic criticism by Kuliscioff of middle-class Italian feminists in the *Carteggio*; and expresses surprise at Kuliscioff's approval of maternity (p.24), ignoring its historical context.
40. *Critica Sociale*, September 16, 1893, article signed TK (Turati-Kuliscioff).
41. Martin Clark, *Modern Italy 1871–1982*, London and New York, 1984, p.77.
42. Anna Kuliscioff at her trial in Florence, 1879–80; quoted by Arduino Agnelli, 'La Kuliscioff e il socialismo internazionale', in *Anna Kuliscioff e l'Età del Riformismo; Atti del Convegno di Milano*, Dicembre 1976, p.5.
43. *Lettere d'amore*, n.34, Kuliscioff to Costa, October 14, 1880.
44. Ibid. Costa to Kuliscioff, November 25, and November 30, 1880.
45. Ibid. Kuliscioff to Costa, November 18, 1880.
46. Ibid. Kuliscioff to Costa, November 25, 1880.
47. Ibid. Kuliscioff to Costa, December 21, 1880.
48. Ibid. Kuliscioff to Costa, December 21, 1880 (evening).
49. Ibid. Kuliscioff to Costa, December 22, 1880.
50. Ibid. Kuliscioff to Costa, October 30, 1882 ('we can only live together as equals').
51. F. Turati-A. Kuliscioff, *Carteggio*, A. Schiavi, ed., Milan 1954–1978 (7 vols.).
52. Ibid. Kuliscioff to Turati, May 25, 1907.
53. Valeri, op. cit. n.39, p.22.
54. Lecture to Milan Philological Circle, 'Il Monopolio dell'Uomo' dated April 27, 1890, in *Anna Kuliscioff: In Memoria*, F. Turati, ed., Milan, 1926, p.213.
55. Philip Spenser di Scala, *Turati and the Dilemma of Italian Socialism*, Princeton, 1986, pp.19–20.
56. Ibid.
57. August Bebel, *Women and Socialism*, London, 1879. See Kuliscioff's tribute to Bebel, 'Per Augusto Bebel nel suo settantennio,' *Critica Sociale* 4, 1910.
58. Labriola to Engels, July 1, 1893, in K. Marx-F. Engels, *Corrispondenza con Italiani*, G. del Bo, ed., Milan, 1964.
59. The *Carteggio* indicates that while Kuliscioff frequently sided with Turati against Labriola's criticisms, and thought him too dour and dogmatic because he was a 'southerner', his radical ideology attracted her.
60. Valeri, op. cit. n.39, pp.36–43.
61. Ibid.
62. Kuliscioff to Engels, January 19, 1894, in *Corrispondenza con Italiani*, op. cit. n.58.
63. Ibid. Engels to Turati, January 29, 1894. Also in *Critica Sociale*, February 1, 1894.
64. Kuliscioff to Camillo Prampollini, quoted in Valeri, op. cit. n.39, p.56.
65. *Carteggio*, Turati to Kuliscioff, March 16, 1898.
66. Di Scala, op. cit. n.55, pp.64–5.
67. *Carteggio*, Kuliscioff letters of December 5 and 16, 1903, and March 22 and 23, 1911. See also Valeri, op. cit. pp.74, 90.

68. *Carteggio*, Kuliscioff to Turati, December 10, 1906.
69. *Carteggio*, Kuliscioff to Turati, April 3, 1899.
70. *Carteggio*, Kuliscioff to Turati, March 24, 1901.
71. *Carteggio*, Kuliscioff to Turati, August 14, 1901.
72. *Carteggio*, Kuliscioff to Turati, March 16, 1917.
73. *Carteggio*, Kuliscioff to Turati, January 15, 1918.
74. *Carteggio*, Kuliscioff to Turati, December 13, 1917.
75. 'Il Monopolio dell'Uomo', see n.54.
76. Richard Evans, *Comrades and Sisters: Feminism, Socialism and Pacifism in Europe 1870–1945*, Sussex and New York, 1987, pp.104–115.
77. Kuliscioff, 'Candidature Femminili', in *Critica Sociale* 11, 1892.
78. Ibid.
79. Kuliscioff, 'La Sanctità della Famiglia', in *Critica Sociale* 1, 1891.
80. Kuliscioff, 'Il Sentimentalismo nella questione femminile', in *Critica Sociale* 9, 1892.
81. Ibid, editorial footnote.
82. *Carteggio*, Kuliscioff to Turati, March 24, 1904.
83. *Carteggio*, Kuliscioff to Turati, February 10, 1913.
84. Kuliscioff, 'Alle donne italiane' (per le elezioni politiche 1897), in *Anna Kuliscioff: In Memoria*, op. cit. n.54, pp.267–78.
85. Doriana Guidici, 'Anna Kuliscioff e il movimento sindacale', in *Anna Kuliscioff e l'Età del Riformismo*, op. cit. n.42.
86. Kuliscioff, 'Il Voto alle Donne, Polemica in Famiglia', pamphlet made up of articles in *Critica Sociale* and addressed to Turati, collected in *Anna Kuliscioff: In Memoria*, op. cit, n.54 pp.282–95.
87. Kuliscioff, 'Per Il Suffragio Femminile, Donne Proletarie, a Voi!', pamphlet made up of articles from Kuliscioff's journal *Difesa della Lavoratrici* explaining the exclusion of women from the vote, collected in *Anna Kuliscioff: In Memoria*, op. cit. n.54, pp.313–40. The particular reference is on p.336.
88. Mussolini gave women the vote at local elections in the last year of Kuliscioff's life (1925); Clark, op. cit. n.41, p.276, describes this as 'a huge concession marred only by the fact that there were no more local elections'.
89. *Carteggio*, Kuliscioff to Turati, May 17, 1923.
90. *Carteggio*, Turati to Kuliscioff, March 13, 1913. In her letter of December 12, 1912 she anticipates the coming war.
91. *Carteggio*, Kuliscioff to Turati, February 6, 1913; here she urged Turati to rally the socialists to expel Mussolini from *Avanti!*
92. *Carteggio*, Kuliscioff to Turati, May 12, 1915.
93. *Carteggio*, discussion of revolution which begins Kuliscioff to Turati, March 16, 1917.
94. *Critica Sociale*, September 1, 1919, article signed TK (Turati/Kuliscioff).
95. *Carteggio*, Kuliscioff to Turati, February 25, 1920.
96. *Carteggio*, Kuliscioff to Turati, February 26, 1920.
97. *Carteggio*, Kuliscioff to Turati, February 28, 1920.
98. *Carteggio*, Turati to Kuliscioff, March 1, 1920.
99. Valeri, op. cit. n.39, p.136.
100. *Carteggio*, Turati to Kuliscioff, February 28, 1921.
101. *Carteggio*, Kuliscioff to Turati, November 24, 1922.
102. *Carteggio*, Kuliscioff to Turati, July 12, 1923.
103. *Carteggio*, Kuliscioff to Turati, June 19, 1924.
104. Salvatorelli and Mira, op. cit. n.33, p.561.

CHAPTER 3: EIGHT CANDLES ON THE CHRISTMAS TREE

1. J.P. Nettl's biography, *Rosa Luxemburg*, Oxford, 1966, remains the classic and most comprehensive portrait of Luxemburg in the context of international Marxism. But Nettl is notably unsympathetic to viewing Luxemburg as a Jew. Robert Wistrich's 'Rosa Luxemburg, the Internationalist', in *Revolutionary Jews from Marx to Trotsky*, London, 1976, attempts to deal with Luxemburg in the Jewish context.

2. F.L. Carsten, 'Freedom and Revolution; Rosa Luxemburg' in Leopold Labedz, ed., *Revisionism*, London, 1963, is a refreshingly non-doctrinaire view of Luxemburg in this context by a historian of modern European pacifism. Lelio Basso, in *Rosa Luxemburg: A Reappraisal*, London, 1975 makes this point in the Marxist context.

3. This was probably Luxemburg's most important contribution to Marxist theory. See Rosa Luxemburg, *The Accumulation of Capital*, with an analytical introduction by Joan Robinson, London, 1951.

4. For the 'European' thesis, see Hanna Arendt, 'Rosa Luxemburg' in *Men in Dark Times*, London, 1970.
   For a critical view of Luxemburg as a moralist, see George Lichtheim, 'Rosa Luxemburg', in *The Concept of Ideology and other essays*, New York, 1967.
   For further bibliographical reference on the continuing debate, see Richard Abraham, *Rosa Luxemburg, a Life for the International*, Oxford, 1989.

5. Wistrich, op. cit. p.91.

6. Abraham, op. cit. n.4. p.51.

7. Abraham Bick (Shauli), 'Nesher Ha'mahapekha' (The Eagle of the Revolution) in *Me'rosh Tsurim*, Jerusalem, 1972 (Hebrew). Jacob Talmon, *The Myth of the Nation and the Vision of Revolution: the Origins of Ideological Polarisation in the 20th Century*, Vol. III, London, 1978.

8. Raya Dunayevskaya, *Rosa Luxemburg, Women's Liberation and Marx's Philosophy of Revolution*, New Jersey and Sussex, 1981.

9. Memoirs by Luise Kautsky and Henriette Roland Holst van der Schalk (non-Jews); but in particular Paul Froelich, *Rosa Luxemburg, her Life and Work*, Fitzgerald, tr., London, 1940, who maintains that her home was a Western European 'oasis' in the 'rotting morass' of Eastern European traditional Jewry.

10. See Appendix to Elzbieta Ettinger, *Rosa Luxemburg, A Life*, London and New York, 1988.

11. Anna Luksenburg to Rosa Luxemburg, May 9, 1987. Ibid. p.294.

12. Ibid. p.27. See Froelich, op. cit. n.9, p.21, etc., for fictitious version.

13. Luxemburg to Mathilde Jacob, November 13, 1915. In Rosa Luxemburg, *Briefe*, Tokyo, 1972.

14. *T'sena Ure'ena*, op. cit. Chapter 1, n.106, p.533.

15. Luxemburg to Leo Jogiches, October 4, 1904, from prison in Zwickau, in Elzbieta Ettinger, ed., *Comrade and Lover, Rosa Luxemburg's Letters to Leo Jogiches*, London, 1981.

16. See Ettinger, op. cit. n.10, Appendix, passim.

17. See Dunayevskaya, op. cit. n.8, p.95.

18. See Rosa Luxemburg, *Letters*, Stephen Eric Bronner, ed., New York, 1966, especially the introduction by Henry Pachter, and for numerous illustrations. The 'female eroticism' quote is from the letter to Mathilde Jacob, in this collection, dated September 4, 1915.

19. See Ettinger, op. cit. n.10, Appendix, pp.311,316.

20. Rosa Luxemburg to Leo Jogiches, October 20, 1905. In *Comrade and Lover*, op. cit. n.15, p.152.

21. Luxemburg to Jogiches, August 2, 1899. Ibid. p.80.
22. Elias Luksenburg to Rosa Luxemburg, April 20, 1900; in Ettinger, op. cit. n.10, Appendix, p.323.
23. Luxemburg to Hans Diefenbach, from Breslau jail, August 27, 1917; in *Briefe an Freunde*, Kautsky, ed., Hamburg, 1950.
24. Ibid.
25. Luxemburg to Mathilde Wurm, February 16, 1917. Ibid. Luxemburg's indifference to Jewish ethnicity is particularly striking, given her particular interest in other communities with a long history (such as the Indians). Still more notable is the *approval* of contemporary scholars for this indifference. See article by Michel Löwy, and sole reference to Luxemburg's Jewishness in this context by Gilbert Badia, in *Rosa Luxemburg Aujourd'hui*, Vincennes, 1986.
26. Ettinger, op cit. n.10, p.10.
27. Ibid. pp.92,96.
28. See n.20 and Ettinger, n.10, passim.
29. See n.9.
30. Luxemburg to Jogiches, July 11, 1900; *Briefe*, Tokyo, n.13.
31. Luxemburg to Mathilde Jacob, December 13, 1917, *Briefe aus dem Gefangnis*, Berlin, 1922.
32. Luxemburg to Karl and Luise Kautsky, July 13, 1900, in *Letters*, op. cit. n.18.
33. See Ettinger, op. cit. n.10, Appendix, pp.303–5.
34. Ibid. p.94.
35. For reference to 'Heilige Nacht', see letter to Mathilde Jacob, July 9, 1916, in *Briefe*, Tokyo n.13. The 'eight candles' letter is dated only 'mid December, 1917', in *Briefe aus dem Gefangnis*, n.31.
36. Luxemburg to Sonya Liebknecht, January 15, 1917, in *Letters*, op. cit. n.18.
37. Luxemburg to Hans Diefenbach, from Wronke jail, March 5, 1917, in *Briefe an Freunde*, op. cit. n.23.
38. 'The Spirit of Russian Literature; Life of Korolenko', in Mary-Alice Waters, ed., *Rosa Luxemburg Speaks*, London, New York, Sydney, 1986, pp.360–1.
39. 'The Junius Pamphlet; the Crisis in German Social Democracy', ibid. p.261.
40. Ettinger, op. cit. n.10, p.15.
41. Ibid.
42. N.M. Gelber, 'The Warsaw Pogroms of 1881', in *He'Avar* X, 1963, pp. 106–23 (Hebrew).
43. Ettinger, op. cit. n.10, p.27.
44. Gelber, op. cit. n.42.
45. Ibid., Appendix, Brenner's letters.
46. For instance, in letters to Jogiches of June 24, 1898, April 1899, and October 13, 1905, referring to political enemies as 'hazer mit indyk (Polish)' (pig and turkey), the 'schrecklicher chutzpeh' (terrible cheek) of others, and 'partei Jude' and 'myszures' (lackey) character of others.
47. See essay by Israel Getzler (Martov's biographer) on Rosa Luxemburg in Eli Shaltiel, ed., *Yehudim bi'tnu'ot Mahapchaniot* (Jews in Revolutionary Movements), Jerusalem, 1983 (Hebrew).
48. M.K. Dziewanowski, *The Communist Party of Poland*, Cambridge Mass., 1959, pp.37ff, for relations between the Bund and other Polish socialist parties.
49. Wistrich, op. cit. n.1, p.81. Wistrich deals in some detail with Luxemburg's relationship to the Bund, though not with the 1905 argument with Jogiches.
50. Ibid.
51. Ettinger, op. cit. n.10, p.122.

52. Ettinger, op. cit. n.10, pp.125–6.
53. Hans Rogger, op. cit. Chapter 1. n.131, p.18.
54. *The National Question, Selected Writings by Rosa Luxemburg*, edited and with an introduction by Horace B. Davis, New York, 1976.
55. See Nettl, op. cit. n.1, Vol.II, Appendix on 'The National Question'.
56. Froelich, op. cit. n.9, p.21.
57. 'The National Question and Autonomy', in *The National Question*, op. cit. n.54, pp.109–10.
58. Ibid.
59. Ibid. pp.266–8.
60. Luxemburg to Mathilde Jacob, November 13, 1915. *Briefe*, Tokyo, op. cit. n.13.
61. See Salo W. Baron, *The Jews Under Czars and Soviets*, New York, 1976, pp.142ff.
62. Nettl, op. cit. n.1, pp.91–2
63. Chaim Arlosoroff, *Jewish People's Socialism*, written in 1919; summarised in Shlomo Avineri, *Arlosoroff*, London, 1989, Chapter 2.
64. Wistrich, op. cit. n.1, p.82 describes her as 'divorced' from the Jewish working class.
65. Ibid, p.83.
66. Edmund Silberner, 'Was Marx an anti-Semite?', in *Historia Judaica* II, Vol.I, 1949, pp.3–52.
67. *The National Question*. See n.54, p.110.
68. For a full discussion of this question, see Hal Draper and Anne G. Lipow, 'Marxist Women versus Bourgeois Feminism', *The Socialist Register*, 1976, pp.179–226.
69. See Chapter 2.
70. Luxemburg, 'Die Proletarierin', *Gesammelte Werke* 3, 411–12, Berlin, 1970–75.
71. See Evans, op. cit. Chapter 2 n.76.
72. See Draper and Lipow, op. cit. n.68, p.200.
73. Quoted in Abraham, op. cit. n.4, p.71.
74. Ibid. p.67.
75. 'Women's Suffrage and Class Struggle', in Dick Howard, ed., *Rosa Luxemburg: Selected Political Writings*, New York and London, 1971, pp.216–22. (Also published in Draper and Lipow, op. cit. n.68.)
76. Abraham, op. cit. n.4, p.24.
77. Luxemburg to Konrad Heinisch, dated December 1911, in Bronner, ed., *Letters*, op. cit. n.18.
78. 'Socialist Crisis in France', in *Rosa Luxemburg Speaks*, op. cit. n.38, pp.91–105.
79. Wistrich, op. cit. n.1, pp.84–5.
80. Ibid, p.85.
81. *Briefe an Karl und Luise Kautsky*, Luise Kautsky, ed., Berlin, 1923, p.181.
82. Luxemburg to Sonya Liebknecht, February 5, 1917, in Bronner, ed., *Letters*, op. cit. n.18.
83. Luxemburg to Adolf Geck, November 18, 1918, in Bronner, ed., *Letters*, op. cit. n.18.
84. In this article, published in the *Röte Fahne* on January 14, she accused the socialist leadership of having failed the masses, who would eventually accomplish the revolution.

CHAPTER 4: THE DOUBLE REBELLION

1. For a detailed analysis of the antireligious campaign, see M. Altschuler, *Between Nationalism and Communism: The Evsektsia in the Soviet Union 1918–1930*, Tel Aviv, 1980, pp.292–303 (Hebrew).
2. For the Evsektsia, see Altschuler, n.1, and Zvi Gitelman, *Jewish Nationality and Soviet Politics*, Princeton, 1972.
3. No biography or comprehensive study of Frumkin exists, nor is there a catalogue of her many articles in the Yiddish press. The main biographical articles and (premature) obituaries are mentioned in this chapter. The most extensive bibliographical reference is in Reizen, Zalmen, *Leksikon fun der yidisher literatur*, Vilna, 1926–9 (Yiddish), though it terminates a decade before the end of Frumkin's career. See also a brief entry in *Encyclopaedia Judaica*, Vol.7 p.914 (unaccountably under her pseudonym). Her work in Russian is signed Maria Y. Frumkina, and in Yiddish, usually by the first and last letters of her pseudonym: E-R.
4. Altschuler, op. cit. n.1, p.303.
5. Maria Y. Frumkina, *Doloi Ravvinov* (Down with the Rabbis!), Moscow, 1923 (Russian).
6. Ibid., pp.16–17. Quoted in Yaakov Leshchinsky, *Zvishen Leben on Toyt*, Vol.I, Vilna, 1930, p.81 (Yiddish).
7. Gitelman, op. cit. n.2, pp.457–8.
8. Ibid. p.309. Gitelman argues that the antireligious campaign 'thrust Frumkin into the limelight'. But in fact her abilities as an agitator and orator were already recognised by 1908, during her appearance at the Czernowitz Yiddish language conference. See n.62.
9. Henry J. Tobias, *The Jewish Bund in Russia: From its origins to 1905*, Stanford, 1972, pp.43–5. For its dissolution, which took place in March 1921 but was made retroactive to the last regular conference in 1920, see Gitelman, op. cit. n.2, pp.209–15.
10. Eva Broido, *Memoirs of a Revolutionary*, Vera Broido, tr., London, 1967. See also Vera Broido, *Lenin and the Mensheviks, The Persecution of Socialists under Bolshevism*, London, 1987, pp.104–5.
11. See the profiles of women in the biographical anthology *Doires Bundisten*, J.S. Herz, ed., New York, 1956.
12. See Abbott Gleason, *Young Russia*, New York, 1980, p.307.
13. For the synagogue politics, see Yehuda Erez, 'Tanach U'masoret Yehudit Bi'tnuat Ha'poalim Ha'yehudit' (Bible and Tradition in the Jewish Workers' Movement) in Moshe Mishkinsky, ed., *Ha'socialism ve T'nuat Ha'avodah Ha'Yehudit ba Mea Ha 19* (Jewish Socialism and the Jewish Labour Movement in the 19th Century), Jerusalem, 1975, pp.117–8 (Hebrew). For women, see Harriet Davis-Kram, 'The Story of the Sisters of the Bund', in *Contemporary Jewry*, Philadelphia, Vol.V, no.2, Fall/Winter 1980, p.28. The reference to the Mogilev guild of women tailors is in Ezra Mendelsohn, *Class Struggle in the Pale: The Formative Years of the Jewish Workers' Movement in Czarist Russia*, Cambridge, 1970, p.42. Alone among historians of the Jewish Labour movement, Mendelsohn stresses women's role.
14. The distinction between *khevre* and *kasse* is clearly made in Mendelsohn's article: 'The Russian Jewish Labour Movement and Others', in Mishkinsky, op. cit. n.13. The article (in English) points out the similarities between the Jewish artisan socialists and others in Europe. See also Mendelsohn's *Class Struggle*, etc., no.13, pp.61ff.
15. Tobias, op. cit. n.9. p.44.

16. Mendelsohn, op. cit. n.13, in Mishkinsky, ed., *Jewish Socialism*, etc, p.240.
17. Mendelsohn, *Class Struggle*, etc., op. cit. n.13, pp.17 and 154–5.
18. Ibid. pp.25–6.
19. For the 'circles', see Gitelman, op. cit. n.2, p.22. For comparison with the middle-class Russian, non-Jewish, women in feminist and Marxist groups which formed the 'circles' among Russian working-class women, compare the biographies in *Doires Bundisten* with Rose Glickman, *The Russian Factory Women; Workplace and Society, 1880–1914*, Berkeley and London, 1984, pp.227ff. Glickman concludes that 'neither populist women, who came directly out of the feminist ferment of the 1860s, nor Marxist women, who theoretically acknowledged the condition of working women, sought to involve them in the revolutionary struggle' (p.241).
20. *Doires Bundisten*, op. cit. n.11, p.130.
21. Jonathan Frankel, *Prophecy and Politics*, Cambridge, 1981, pp.185–7.
22. Saul Stampfer, 'Literacy amongst East European Jewry in the Modern Period: Context, Background and Implications' in *Transition & Change in Modern Jewish History: Essays in honour of Shmuel Ettinger*, Jerusalem, 1987. Vol.I, p.459–83 (Hebrew).
23. The quote is from: Esther Frumkin, 'Vi azoi mir hobn amol gelernt marksizm', in *Liebknechts dor*, no.1, January 1923 (Yiddish), quoted in Gitelman, op. cit. n.2, p.30. For comparison with Russian women workers, see Rose Glickman, op. cit. n.19.
24. Erez, op. cit. n.13, p.123.
25. Gitelman, op. cit. n.2, p.31.
26. Moshe Mishkinsky, ed., *Four Speeches by Jewish Workers on May Day 1892*, Hebrew University, Jerusalem, 1967 (Hebrew with Russian facsimile).
27. Ibid. Introduction.
28. Ibid.
29. Glickman, op. cit. n.19, pp.196–9.
30. Mendelsohn, op. cit. n.13.
31. Tobias, op. cit. n.9, p.71. The reference to her emigration and subsequent beliefs is from *Arkadi; Zamelbukh*, New York, 1942, p.90 (Yiddish).
32. Gitelman, op. cit. n.2, p.89. For the Brus'nev circles, see Glickman, op. cit. n.19, pp.171ff.
33. *Doires Bundisten*, op. cit. n.11, p.240.
34. Arkadi, *Zamelbukh*, op. cit. n.31, p.138.
35. *Doires Bundisten*, p.240.
36. Ibid. pp.228–31.
37. Anna Heller, 'Froyen Gestalten in Bund', *Unzer Tsayt*, 4, (7), New York, 1942 (Yiddish).
38. Ibid.
39. Anna Heller, 'Bletlech fun ein Lebensgeshikhte', in Cherikover, ed., *Historishe Shriftn* III, Vilna, 1938, pp.416–37 (Yiddish).
40. *Doires Bundisten*, pp.180–92.
41. Ibid, pp.243–7.
42. *Vestnik Bunta*, 1–2, 1904, p.23 (Russian).
43. *Doires Bundisten*, p.137.
44. E. Falkovich, 'Ester—der lebensveg fun der groiser revolutsyonern', *Falkstimme* (New York), Vol.20, Nos.1–6, 1965 (Yiddish). This article, in several instalments, is the most comprehensive survey of Frumkin's life, but it is hagiographical, omitting both her role in the dissolution of the Bund, and her nine years in the Jewish section of the Communist Party, almost entirely. Falkovich was a pupil of

Frumkin's at the 'Mairevnik' (the Jewish department of the University for the Minorities of the West), and a Russian Yiddish linguist.

45. 'E-R', 'Wer fertehheidikt em besten di interesen fun folk?' (Who best defends the interests of the Nation?), in *Di Velt* (Vilna), no. 70, 1906 (Yiddish).

46. Frankel, op. cit. no.21, pp.471–2.

47. Falkovich, op. cit. n.44.

48. Ibid.

49. See, for instance, 'E-R', 'Vegn natsyonaler ertsihung' (Jewish education and the people), in *Tsayt Fragn* 1 (Vilna), 1909 (Yiddish).

50. Falkovich, op. cit. n.44.

51. Frankel, op. cit. n.21, p.155. See also S.S. Harcave, 'The Jewish Question in the First Duma', *Jewish Social Studies* VI (1944), pp.155–76.

52. Falkovich, op. cit. n.44.

53. See, for instance, 'E-R', 'Di Yidisher Val Kamiteten unzer Klal Yisrael Palitik', *Di Velt*, Vilna, 1906 (Yiddish).

54. Frankel, op. cit. n.21.

55. See n.53.

56. Idem.

57. See Frumkin's articles above, nn.45, 53.

58. Idem.

59. See Gitelman, op. cit. n.2, p.60–62.

60. 'E-R', 'Tzu der frage vegen der Judisher Folkshul', Vilna, 1910 (Yiddish).

61. Gitelman, op. cit. n.2, pp.71–2. For Jewish labour statistics, see Frankel, op.cit. n.21, pp.143–4.

62. E.S. Goldsmith, *Architects of Yiddishism at the Beginning of the Twentieth Century: A Study in Jewish Cultural History*, Rutherford and London, 1976, Chapter 5, passim.

63. Ibid., p.237.

64. Ibid., p.215.

65. Ibid., pp.212–3.

66. Ibid., p.239.

67. Falkovich, op. cit. n.44.

68. This view is expressed in her article on Jewish education and the people, n.49.

69. Ibid. passim.

70. Gitelman, op. cit. n.2, p.58.

71. See n.60.

72. Ibid.

73. Ibid.

74. See Stampfer, op. cit. n.22. pp.477–9.

75. See n.60.

76. Gitelman, op. cit. n.2, p.87.

77. Falkovich, op. cit. n.44.

78. Altschuler, op. cit. n.1, p.98.

79. Falkovich, op. cit. n.44.

80. Gitelman, op. cit. n.2, pp.161,162.

81. Ibid. p.233.

82. Ibid. p.266–7.

83. Altschuler, n.1, pp.82–3.

84. Ibid.

85. Ibid, pp.87–8.

86. For an account of the settlement projects and their failure, see Gitelman, op. cit. n.2. pp.379–88.

87. 'Esther' in *Der Veker* (Minsk), January 12, 1919 (Yiddish).
88. 'E-R', in *Tsayt*, January 30, 1914, quoted in Frankel, op. cit. n.21 p.180 (Yiddish).
89. Gitelman, op. cit. n.2, p.191.
90. Altschuler, n.1, p.204.
91. *Doloi Ravvinov*, op. cit. n.5, p.40.
92. *Der Veker*, Minsk, quoted in Gitelman, op. cit. n.2, p.303.
93. For a discussion of the fate of the Yiddish folk school, see Gitelman, op. cit. n.2, pp.336–50.
94. Stampfer, op. cit. n.29, p.479.
95. See n.93.
96. Altschuler op. cit. n.1, p.203.
97. S.M. Schwartz, *Jews in the Soviet Union*, Syracuse, New York, 1951, pp.126–8.
98. See n.86.
99. Schwartz, op. cit. n.97, pp.122–3.
100. Falkovich, op. cit. n.44. Obituaries appeared prematurely in *Der Veker* (New York) on February 12 and December 1, 1938, by N. Kanin and D. Tcharny. The *Sovietishe Heimland* of August 1989 dates her death to 1938 and implies that she was shot.
101. Y. Leshchinsky, op. cit. n.6.

CHAPTER 5: A RADICAL IN TRANSIT

1. Manya Shochat, 'Hakolektiv', in *Divrei Hapoalot—Measef* (Working Women Speak; An Anthology), Tel Aviv, 1930 (Hebrew).
2. On her visit to the USA in 1922 she was confronted by hostile Bundists whose attacks she countered in the Yiddish press. See *Forverts*, New York, December 14, 1921 to February 7, 1922; and *Die Tsayt*, New York, April 20–24, 1922. The relevant documents are appended to the text in Ya'akov Goldstein, *Manya Vilbushevitz-Shochat, Her Revolutionary Leadership in Russia*, Haifa, 1991 (Hebrew).
3. Shlomo Shva, *Shevet Hanoazim* (The Daring Tribe), Tel Aviv, 1969 (Hebrew). This highly coloured account of the radical circle of the Shochats is based largely on the memories of the (mostly octogenarian) survivors.
4. For a view of Sejera from the perspective of early Jewish colonists and their patrons, see S. Schama, *Two Rothschilds and the Land of Israel*, London, 1978, pp.170–4.
5. For the brief-lived feminist labour movement see Dafna N. Izraeli, 'The Zionist Women's Movement in Palestine 1911–1927' in *Signs, A Journal of Women in Culture and Society*, 7, (1), 1981.
6. Portraits of such women based on interviews and archival material are to be found in Ruth Baki, *Le'hatchil Miberashit* (To Begin at the Beginning), Tel Aviv, 1988 (Hebrew). Memoirs of women pioneers are collected in B. Chabas, ed., *Ha'aliya Ha'shniya* (The Second Aliya), Tel Aviv, 1947 (Hebrew); Y. Harari, *Ha'isha ve'em Be'Eretz Yisrael* (Women and Mothers in Israel) (Hebrew) and in Katznelson-Shazar, ed., *The Plough Woman*, New York, 1975.
7. Izraeli op. cit., n.5, p.102.
8. Deborah Bernstein, 'The Plough Woman who Cried into the Pots; the position of women in the labour force in the Pre-State Israeli Society', in *Jewish Social Studies* 45, (1) pp.43–56. See also the same author's *The Struggle for Equality: Urban Women Workers in Pre-State Israeli Society*, New York and London, 1987, the sole authoritative work on the subject at this time (1990).
9. Z. Liberson, 'The Workers' Kitchen in Hadera' in Chabas, op. cit. n.6, pp.72–3.
10. Bernstein, op. cit., n.8 ('The Plough Woman, etc.').

11. Quoted in Bernstein, 'The Plough Woman', p.52.
12. 'Eshet Haver' (Worker's Wife), 1928, in *Divrei Hapoalot*, op. cit. n.1, pp.134–5 (Hebrew).
13. For discussion of 'workers' wives', who enjoyed membership privileges via their husbands to swell the union electorate rolls see Bernstein, op. cit. n.8 (*The Struggle*, etc.), pp.85–7 and 128–9.
14. Protocols of the First Zionist Congress, Basle, 1897.
15. Ada Maimon, *Le'orech Ha'derech* (Along the Way), Tel Aviv, 1972, p.105 (Hebrew).
16. David Vital, *Zionism, the Formative Years*, Oxford, 1982, pp.452–4, and Appendix, p.479, in which he analyses the composition of the Sixth Zionist Congress in 1903.
17. Maimon, op. cit. n.15, p.215.
18. 'Judith', in *Me'hayyenu* (Labour Legion journal), Vol.1, pp.47–9. Quoted in Bernstein, op. cit. n.8 ('*The Struggle*', etc.) pp.153–5.
19. Bernstein, op. cit. n.8, ('The Plough Woman', etc.), pp.50–52.
20. Z. Even Shoshan, *Toldot Tnuat Ha'poalim be'Eretz Yisrael* (The History of the Workers' Movement in Palestine), Tel Aviv, 1963, Vol.1, pp.208–9 (Hebrew).
21. 'R.K', 'Aharei Ve'idah' (After the Conference), in *Divrei Poalot*, op. cit. n.1, pp.57–9 (Hebrew). This was written after a farm workers' conference in the Galilee in 1914, in which the women workers had petitioned for a hearing, and ends 'we did not share in the conference because we did not share in the life.'
22. Bernstein, op. cit. n.8, ('*The Struggle*'), p.19.
23. Margalit Shilo, 'The Women's Farm at Kinneret, 1911–1917; a solution to the problem of the working woman in the Second Aliya', in *The Jerusalem Cathedra* (English edition), Jerusalem, 1981.
24. For the story of Pessia Abramson, see Baki, op. cit., n.6, pp.46–55.
25. Izraeli, op. cit. n.5.
26. Ibid., pp.110–11.
27. Ibid., p.106.
28. Arthur Ruppin, *Pirkei Hayy'ay* (Chapters of my Life), Tel Aviv, 1947, p.110 (Hebrew).
29. Shlomo Shva, op. cit. n.3, pp.20–22. Episodes such as these are repeated in the biography of Manya Shochat written by her friend Rachel Yanait Ben Zvi [*Manya Shochat*, Jerusalem, 1976 (Hebrew)]. This biography was largely dictated by Manya Shochat herself during old age; here, she condemns the balloon episode as pure adventurism. The sole scholarly work on Shochat's revolutionary career in Russia, and its repercussions in 1921–2 on her visit to the United States as part of a Histadrut delegation, is the monograph by Ya'akov Goldstein (n.2).
30. For Zubatov and Police Socialism, see Jeremiah Schneiderman, *Sergei Zubatov and Revolutionary Marxism; The Struggle for the Working Class in Tsarist Russia*, New York, 1976; Dimitry Pospeliovsky, *Russian Trade Unionism, Experiment or Provocation*, London, 1971; Moshe Mishkinsky, 'Ha'Socialism Ha'Mishtarti' (Police Socialism) in *Zion*, 25, 1960, pp.238–49 (Hebrew). All stress the leading part played by Manya Shochat in spreading the Zubatov gospel. Her own version (in *Die Tsayt*, see n.2, and in the Ben Zvi biography and Shva, n.3) is contradicted by the documentary evidence which she argued had been doctored. But even her own evidence indicates intensive collaboration with Zubatov. See Goldstein, op. cit., n.2, appendices.
31. Pospeliovsky, op. cit. n.30, pp.73.
32. Jonathan Frankel, *Prophecy and Politics*, Cambridge, 1980, p.172.
33. Pospeliovsky, op. cit. n.30, pp.89–92.
34. Ze'ev Ivianski, *Mahapekha Ve'terror* (Revolution and Terror), Tel Aviv, 1989 (Hebrew).

35. Mishkinsky, op. cit. n.30, p.243, adds that the Czarist officials behind Zubatov also thought a more benevolent policy towards the Jews would help the regime recruit loans from the West.

36. See letters from Manya to Zubatov first published in Moscow in 1918 and quoted in Pospeliovsky, op. cit. n.30, p.90. The letters were first published by D. Zaslavski, 'Zubatov i Mania Vilbushevitz' (Russian), *Byloe* 9 (3), 1918.

37. Pospeliovsky, op. cit. n.30, p.91.

38. Ibid.

39. Ibid. p.116.

40. Ibid. p.123.

41. See n.1. The same account appears in Manya Shochat's article 'Pirkei Bereishit' (Early Chapters) in *Me'hayyenu*, 1921–29, Vol.3, p.616.

42. Shva, op. cit., n.3, p.293.

43. Baki, op. cit. n.6, p.184 (interview with Manya Shochat's daughter Anna), for suicide attempts in the family. For Ben Gurion's relationship with Manya, see Shabtai Teveth, *Ben Gurion; The Burning Ground, 1886–1948*, pp.284–307, passim. Teveth's account of Manay Shochat's early life, pp.56–7, however, is inaccurate in almost all respects.

44. See Schama, op. cit. n.4, for an exhaustive analysis of the Rothschild enterprise based on JCA documents.

45. For a detailed survey of the Second Aliya blend of Marxism and Zionism, see 'The Revolutionary Ethos in Transition—Russian Jewish Youth in Palestine 1904–1914' in Jonathan Frankel, *Prophecy and Politics*, op. cit. n.32, pp.366–452.

46. See Anita Shapira, *Ha'maavak Hanichzav, Avodah Ivrit 1929–39* (The Futile Struggle: the Jewish Labour Controversy 1929–39), Tel Aviv, 1977 (Hebrew).

47. Shochat, op. cit. n.41.

48. See *Sefer Ha'Shomer*, Tel Aviv, 1957 (Hebrew), for the history of the defence movement as written by its participants. No critical history has been published.

49. Shochat, op. cit. n.41.

50. Rachel Yanait Ben Zvi, *Manya Shochat*, op. cit. n.29.

51. For the murder, see Ben Zvi; for the story of the second arms smuggling incident, see Shva, op. cit. n.3, p.153.

52. Shochat, op. cit. n.41.

53. For the 'Am Olam' co-operatives, see Frankel, op. cit. n.32.

54. Irma L. Lindheim, *Parallel Quest*, New York, 1962, pp.273–5. Lindheim was one of the American backers of the bi-national idea, who lived for years on one of the early collectives, and was perhaps the closest, among American Jews, to Manya's ideas.

55. Schama, op. cit. n.4, pp.170–4; Keyla Giladi, 'Ha'poelet Be'Sejera' (The Woman Worker in Sejera) in *Ish Ha'adama* (Man of the Soil), Tel Aviv, 1939—a volume dedicated to Krause (Hebrew); and a memoir of Krause by his daughter in Baki, op. cit. n.6, pp.171–9.

56. Schama, op. cit. n.4, pp.170–4; Shva, op. cit. n.3.

57. Shochat, op. cit. nn.1, 41.

58. Shifra Betzer, 'Im Ha'rishonim be'Um Juni u'Merhavia' (With the first settlers in Um Juni [Degania, the first kibbutz] and Merhavia) in Bracha Chabas, ed., op. cit. n.6 (Hebrew).

59. Shva, op. cit. n.3.

60. In 1912 this decision led to a mass walk-out of workers in Sejera. See Frankel, op. cit. n.32, p.426

61. See Baki interview with Manya's daughter, Anna, op. cit. n.43.

62. Shva, op. cit, n.3, p.153. He writes (presumably following the veterans' account of the Shomer's move to Kfar Tabor): 'Three girls ... went with them, and worked all morning to prepare a special meal, which they served apprehensively, and then appreciated the men's appetite.'
63. Ibid., p.214.
64. Ibid., pp.207–8.
65. Baki interview, op. cit. n.43.
66. Teveth, op. cit. n.43, p.301.
67. Ibid.
68. For the Labour Legion, see Anita Shapira, 'Hitpathuto Hapolitit shel Gdud Ha'avodah' (The Political Development of the Labour Legion) in *Baderech*, 4, 1969 (Hebrew); and Elkana Margalit, *Kibbutz, Hevra Ve'politica: Hagdud Ha'avodah al shem Yosef Trumpeldor, etc*, (Kibbutz, Society and Politics; the Labour Legion: a study of the radical and equalitarian tradition of the Labour Movement in Eretz Yisrael), Tel Aviv, 1980 (Hebrew).
69. 'Judith' in *Me'hayyenu*, see n.18 (Hebrew).
70. Bernstein, op. cit. n.8, ('The Struggle for Equality') describes women in the Labour Legion on pp.33–5.
71. Baki, interview with Anna Shochat, op. cit. n.43.
72. *Sefer Ha'Shomer*, pp.385–94 (Hebrew). Summarised in Ben Zvi, op. cit. n.29, pp.106–7. A much more objective picture is that of Goldstein, op. cit. n.2. Bloch-Blumenfeld's letter appears on p.109.
73. Teveth, op. cit. n.43.
74. The story is told most graphically in Shva, op. cit. n.3, p.319.
75. Teveth, op. cit. n.43, p.297. Israel Shochat, 'Shlichut Ba'derech', in *Sefer Ha'Shomer*, Tel Aviv, 1957 (Hebrew).
76. Teveth, op. cit. n.43, p.301.
77. Ibid. p.461.
78. Shapira, *Ha'maavak*, op. cit. n.46, pp.346–7.
79. Ben Zvi, op. cit. n.29, pp.135–7, where she reproduces a proposal for a 'League for Jewish–Arab Rapprochement', drawn up by Manya in 1921.
80. The list of 'friends' of Brith Shalom, including Manya Shochat's name, is in Aharon Kedar, *Brith Shalom*, Tel Aviv, 1980 (Hebrew).
81. For the Workers' Brotherhood, see *Ahvat Poalim: kovetz maamarim ha'mukdash le'birur sheelot ha'irgun ha'benleumi shel ha'poel be'Eretz Yisrael* (Workers' Brotherhood; essays dedicated to the question of the international organisation of Palestinian workers), Tel Aviv, June 1930 (Hebrew).
82. Letters quoted in Ben Zvi, op. cit. n.29, p.137.

CHAPTER 6: THE REBEL AS LACEMAKER

1. Bertha Pappenheim's life is sketched in Chapter 2 of Marion Kaplan, *The Jewish Feminist Movement in Germany*, Westport, 1979.

   There are two biographies: Dora Edinger, *Bertha Pappenheim*, Solel Congregation Illinois, 1966; Lucy Freeman, *The Story of Anna O*, New York, 1972. Edinger's biography is based on interviews with Pappenheim's colleagues and acquaintances, and also contains a selection of her letters and writings. Freeman's is a lavishly fictionalised version of the Breuer–Freud case history, with borrowings from Edinger.
2. For details of the complex labours of the prosperous German Jewish housewife in the early nineteenth century, see Fanny Lewald, *Meine Lebensgeschichte*, Vol.I, *Im*

Vaterhause, Berlin, 1871. These included the storage and preservation of food in bulk, needlework and tailoring, and the administration of a large staff.

3. Marion Kaplan, 'Priestess and Hausfrau; Women and Tradition in the German Jewish Family'; in Cohen and Hyman, eds., *The Jewish Family*, New York and London, 1986, pp. 62–81.

4. The statistics of German Jewish girls attendance in secondary schools (high) and the memoirs stressing family hostility to their education, suggest a contradiction. See Marion Kaplan, 'Family Structure and Jewish Women', in Mosse, Paucker and Rurup, eds., *Revolution and Evolution in German Jewish History*, Tübingen, 1981, p.194, n.11. Kaplan argues that Jewish and Gentile statistics on German female education should be compared 'before we attribute a thirst for knowledge to Jewish tradition'.

5. Sigmund Freud and Josef Breuer, *Studies in Hysteria*, London, 1991.

6. For retroactive psychoanalytical studies of Pappenheim's illness (or rather, critiques of the Freud/Breuer interpretation), see Rosenbaum and Muroff, eds., *Anna O: Fourteen Contemporary Reinterpretations*, New York and London, 1984.

7. Ernest Jones, *Freud*, London, 1953, Volume 1, p.245, footnote 4.

8. Pappenheim wrote several collections of stories, a play about women's rights, and a translation of Wollstonecraft's *A Vindication of the Rights of Women* under the male pseudonym of Paul Berthold, during the 1890s; in 1913 she published three short plays under her own name.

9. Elaine Showalter, *The Female Malady: Women, Madness and English Culture*, New York, 1985, pp.155–7. Showalter finds that 'Anna O' was 'very much like the frustrated intellectuals and rebellious New Women seen by English nerve specialists', but stresses the 'sympathetic and even admiring view' of Anna O by Freud and Breuer, compared with the dismissive attitude of the English specialists to their female patients.

10. Kaplan, op. cit. n.1, p.32.

11. Ibid. p.52, n.6.

12. Freud and Breuer, op. cit. n.5.

13. Pappenheim, *Sisyphus Arbeit, Reisebriefe aus den Jahren 1911 und 1912*, Leipzig, 1924. Letter dated May 13, 1911 from Jaffa.

14. Ibid. Letter dated May 10, 1912, from Warsaw.

15. 'The Jewish Girl', reprinted in Edinger, op. cit. n.1.

16. Quoted in Freeman, op. cit. n.1, p.151.

17. Kaplan, op. cit. n.1. p.44.

18. Linda Gordon Kuzmack, *Women's Cause; the Jewish Woman's Movement in England and the United States 1881–1933*, Ohio, 1990, pp.19–22.

19. P. Gartner Lloyd, *The Jewish Immigrants in England, 1870–1913*, Detroit, 1960, p.156.

20. Kuzmack, op. cit. n.18, pp.34–8 (Littman); Ellen M.Umansky, *Lily Montagu and the Advancement of Liberal Judaism: From Vision to Vocation*, New York and Toronto, 1983.

21. Eugene Black, *The Social Politics of Anglo Jewry, 1880–1920*, Oxford, 1988, Chapter 8: 'Independence and Communal Control: Women and Social Discipline'.

22. Kaplan, op. cit. n.1, p.68.

23. See entry in Hindle S. Hes, *Jewish Physicians in the Netherlands 1600–1940*, pp.81–2. Most material on Aletta Jacobs, including her autobiography (*Herrineringen*, reprinted The Hague, Holland, 1985, now in translation) is in Dutch. However, *Politics and Friendship: Letters from the International Woman Suffrage Alliance 1902–42*, Mineke Bosch and AnneMarie Kloosterman, eds., Ohio, 1990, has a selection of Jacobs' letters and informed editorial comment.

24. The women's peace movement during the First World War has been well documented. The earliest account is in Marie-Louise Degen *The History of the Women's Peace Party*, Maryland, 1939, which describes the American element; see also Gertrude Bussey and Margaret Tims, *Pioneers for Peace, The Women's International League for Peace and Freedom*, London, 1980. The most recent and lively account is Anne Wiltsher's *Most Dangerous Women, Feminist Peace Campaigners of the Great War*, London, Boston and Henley, 1985.
None, however, has consulted the official archives of the countries to which the women addressed their appeal.

25. The precise dates of the women's delegates' meetings with European heads of states are given in the useful memorandum 'Note by Edith Wynner' (Schwimmer's colleague and curator of her papers) in the Schwimmer–Lloyd Collection, New York Public Library Ms. dept, A 464. According to this list, Jane Addams, the American feminist leader, and Aletta Jacobs met the French Foreign Minister, Delcassé, on June 12, 1915. No record of the meeting exists in the Delcassé papers, or in the French Foreign Ministry records for that date. Mention of the women's deputations in the British archives are cursory. See FO 371/105842, dated 3/8/1915 ('Denial of Statement attributed to Sir Edward Grey by Miss Addams'); see also FO 371/2531/57730; and FO371/2510/116330. The Ford Peace Ship mission of the following year, by comparison, evoked a flurry of paperwork on the dangers of an alliance between US big business and suspected German 'agents' in the peace movement.

26. The French Foreign Ministry archive for this period indicates much concern about women strikers in the munitions factories; see Ministère des Affaires Etrangères; Guerre 1914–18; Correspondances. Dossier général vol. 57, 25/6/1915 for munitions strikes at Tarbes; and 13/7/1915, Henry Berenger to Commission de l'Armée, on 'blackmail' by women workers striking for higher pay.
    For the peace movement seen in the widest possible context, see 'Women's Peace, Men's War?' in Richard Evans, *Comrades and Sisters*, Sussex, 1987, pp.121–56. Evans points out that both middle-class feminists and socialist feminists in Germany and elsewhere failed to connect their peace activities with working women's discontents.

27. Proceedings of the International Congress of Women, The Hague, Holland, April 28, 29, 30, 1915, pp.128–9.

28. Schwimmer's role in the Women's Peace Movement is well documented in Wiltsher, op. cit., n.24. See also Wynner's entry in *Dictionary of American Biography*, Supplement 4, pp.724–8.

29. Schwimmer–Lloyd Collection, op. cit. n.25, Box E29.

30. See Wynner, op. cit. n.28; Schwimmer–Lloyd Collection, Boxes G1 and E1 for a full record of district courts and Supreme Court hearing of her citizenship case.

31. Jacobs, *Herrineringen*, op. cit. n.23, p.5.

32. Wynner, op. cit. n.28.

33. Jacobs to Schwimmer, January 1, 1906. Bosch, op. cit. n.23, p.65. See also editorial comment, p.33.

34. Schwimmer interviewed by Marion Weinstein in *The Day* (New York), January 10, 1915. For the ambivalent attitude of American feminists towards their Jewish members, see Elinor Lerner, 'American Feminism and the Jewish Question', in David E. Gerber, ed., *Anti Semitism in American History*, Illinois, 1986.

35. Richard Evans, *The Feminist Movement in Germany 1894–1933*, London, 1976, p.180.

36. Quoted in *Politics and Friendship*, op. cit. n.23, p.219.

37. Ibid., p.223. See Catt to Friends of Rosa Manus, July 10, 1942, ibid., pp.262–4.
38. Schwimmer to Mrs Ford (unsent?) September 29, 1927. Box E29, Schwimmer–Lloyd Coll., op. cit. n.25.
39. Lerner, op. cit. n.34, p.309.
40. Susannah Walter, 'Anarchism and Feminism Reconciled. The Life and Work of Rose Witcop, 1890–1932', unpublished Cambridge University undergraduate thesis, 1987. The following sketch is based on her research.
41. Rudolf Rocker, *The London Years*, London, 1956, p.99.
42. Walter, op. cit. n.40.
43. Witcop in *The Herald of Revolt* (London), December 1913.
44. Rose Witcop to Margaret Sanger, March 24, 1923. Quoted in Walter, op. cit. n.40.
45. For the British background to Witcop's work, see Angus McLaren, *Birth Control in 19th Century England*, London, 1978; McLaren mentions Aldred but not Witcop in the latter part of the book; Sheila Rowbotham, in *Hidden From History*, London, 1974, makes good the omission, as so many others.
46. Walter, op. cit. n.40.
47. For a concise definition of feminism in historical context, see Richard Evans' essay 'The Concept of Feminism; Notes for Practising Historians' in Joeres and Maynes, eds., *German Women in the Eighteenth and Nineteenth Centuries*, Indiana, 1986, pp.247–58.
48. Kaplan, op. cit., n.1, pp.147–9.
49. Ibid., p.151.
50. Black, op. cit. n.21, pp.83, 89, 225–6.
51. Edward Bristow, *Prostitution and Prejudice: The Jewish Fight against White Slavery 1870–1939*, Oxford, 1982.
52. Ibid., pp.305–8. See also 'Jewish Ritual Marriages', in *The Vigilance Record*, July/August 1930, pp.6–7.
53. Kaplan, op. cit. n.1, pp.115–17. Pappenheim estimated that in 1929 there were 20,000 *agunot* in Eastern Europe who were easy prey for the traffickers.
54. Among the Jewish journals which drew attention to Jewish prostitution and anti-Semitism were the *Jewish Chronicle* of London and the *Jewish Daily Forward* of New York; European Jewish publications were more cautious. Among the Jewish authors who wrote on the subject were Sholem Asch and Isaac Bashevis Singer. In Argentina, the Yiddish theatre and press dealt with the subject extensively: see Yehiel Sheintuch, 'Problems of Acculturation and Communal Solidarity among the Jews of Argentina', in *Sefer Dov Sadan*, Tel Aviv, 1977, pp.316, 325 (Hebrew).
55. According to Frauenbund publications, illegitimate Jewish children were often given to orphanages where they might be adopted by non-Jews (Kaplan, op. cit. n.1, p.134). Pappenheim reported that in Eastern Europe, while Christian peasant girls with children might marry, Jewish girls in this situation were ostracised. This seems to indicate another sign of disintegrating communities as such children, in earlier centuries, were sometimes taken care of by the community, and the women married off. See S. Simonsohn, *History of the Jews in the Duchy of Mantua*, Tel Aviv/Jerusalem, 1977, p.543.
56. Inaugurated in 1900. See Bristow, op. cit. n.51, p.123.
57. Kuzmack, op. cit. n.18, p.53.
58. Bristow, op. cit. n.51, pp.235ff.
59. Kaplan, op. cit. n.1, p.43.
60. Edinger, op. cit. n.1, p.85.
61. Ibid., p.86.
62. *Sisyphus Arbeit*, op. cit. n.13, p.164. I have used Edinger's translations in the

abbreviated versions of the letters published in her biography, though these sometimes miss the slightly malicious irony of the originals.

63. Pappenheim, 'The Jewish Woman', in Edinger, op. cit. n.1, quotes from pp.78 and 79.
64. Pappenheim, 'The Jewish Girl', in Edinger, op. cit. n.1, quotes from pp.86 and 90.
65. Pappenheim, 'The Jewish Woman', op. cit. n.1, p.83.
66. Quoted in Kaplan, op. cit. n.1. p.41.
67. Letter of May 6, 1910 from Lodz; in *Sisyphus Arbeit*, op. cit. n.13, pp.149–50.
68. Official report on the Jewish International Conference on the Traffic in Girls and Women, London, 1910. Pappenheim's address, p.149.
69. Bristow, op. cit. n.51, pp.91ff. The figures are taken from the contemporary reports of the Jewish Colonization Association (JCA).
70. Bertha Pappenheim, Dr Sara Rabinowitz, *Zur Lage der jüdischen Bevolkerung in Galizien*, Frankfurt am Main, 1904, pp.47–8.
71. See Bristow, op. cit. n.51, pp.118, 288ff; also Kaplan, op. cit. n.1, p.111.
72. See selection from proceedings of Jewish and International Congresses on the Traffic in Girls and Women from 1910, 1913 and 1924 published as an appendix to *Sisyphus Arbeit*.
73. Official Report on the Jewish International Conference on the Traffic in Girls and Women, London, 1910, Pappenheim's address on pp.145–54.
74. Ibid.
75. 'The Jewish Girl', op. cit. n.64, p.86.
76. See her 1910 address, op. cit. n.73.
77. Kaplan, op. cit. n.1. Isenburg is described on pp.134–5. It is not clear from this or other accounts how many of the unmarried mothers were actually prostitutes; Kaplan refers to 'delinquents and prostitutes'. Jewish prostitution in Germany was trivial compared to Eastern Europe or South America, and from the scattered references it appears that most of the Isenburg wards were immigrants. In thirty years Isenburg cared for only 1,500 girls.
78. Sadie American's views were made pungently at the 1910 Jewish conference, op. cit. n.73, pp.175–6. There is some discrepancy between the highly romantic version of Pappenheim's letter dated May 23, 1911, from Alexandria, describing her visit to an Arab brothel, as given in Edinger's biography, and that in the German version in *Sisyphus Arbeit*, pp.130–33, where the picture of Jewish child prostitution is far grimmer.
79. Letter written en route from Adrianopel [sic] to Salonika, March 29, 1911, *Sisyphus Arbeit*, p.34.
80. Letter from Budapest, March 9, 1911, ibid. p.12.
81. Letter from Constantinople, April 8, 1911, ibid. p.53.
82. Letter from Lodz, May 6, 1912, ibid. p.150.
83. Letter from Salonika, April 2, 1911, ibid. pp.42.
84. Letter from Salonika, April (dated 'Sunday'), ibid. pp.36–7.
85. Letters from Jerusalem dated May 4–6, 1911, ibid. pp.106–12.
86. Letter from Warsaw dated May 10, 1912, ibid. pp.160–1.
87. Bristow, op. cit. n.51, p.4.
88. Ibid., pp.1–20.
89. Ibid., p.251.
90. *National Vigilance Record*, London, July/August 1913.
91. Bristow, op. cit., n.51, pp.279–80.
92. Richard Polenberg, *Fighting Faiths*, New York, 1987, p.156, n.4
93. *Sisyphus Arbeit*. Letter from Lodz, May 4, 1912.

94. Ibid. Letter from St Petersburg, May 21, 1912.
95. Ibid. Letter from Moscow, May 27, 1912.
96. Experts report presented to the League of Nations Commission on the Traffic in Women and Children, 6th Session 1927, Part 1 (Fawcett Library, London, C.52, M52 .927. IV Box 106).
97. Bristow, op. cit. n.51, p.118.
98. Freeman, op. cit., n.1.

CHAPTER 7: 'I NEED A VIOLENT STRIKE'

1. Philip Foner, *Women and the American Labor Movement*, New York, 1979 pp.302–3. Rose Pesotta, *Bread upon the Waters*, New York, 1944, pp.195ff.
2. Rose Pesotta Collection, New York Public Library, Manuscript Division (henceforth R.P. Coll.) General Correspondence 1922–65. Rose Pesotta, September 30, 1933 to David Dubinsky; Rose Pesotta November 1934 to Anna Winocour; Rose Pesotta November 8, 1935 to Anna Winocour.
3. Fannia Cohn, head of ILGWU's educational department in the 1930s, had briefly preceded Pesotta on the union executive; Pesotta also mentions Molly Friedman, who had 'retired to raise a family' (*Bread upon the Waters*, op. cit., n.1, p.91).
4. Foner, op. cit. n.1., p.282.
5. Rose Pesotta to David Dubinsky, February 6, 1935, R.P. Coll.
6. Alice Kessler-Harris, 'Organising the Unorganisable; Three Jewish Women and their Union', in Cantor and Laurie, eds., *Class, Sex and the Woman Worker*, Westport, 1977, p.158.
7. Alice Kessler-Harris, 'Where are the Organised Women Workers?' in Cott & Pleck, eds., *A Heritage of her Own; toward a new social history of American women*, New York, 1979, pp.344, 356.
8. Alice Kessler-Harris, 'Rose Schneiderman and the Limits of Women's Trade Unionism', in Dubovsky and Van Tine, eds., *American Labor Leaders*, New York, 1986, p.179.
9. John H.M. Laslett, 'Socialism and American Trade Unions', in Laslett and Lipset, eds., *Failure of a Dream; Essays in the History of American Socialism*, California, 1974, pp.130–32.
10. The only biography of Schneiderman is Gary Ed Endelman, 'Solidarity Forever; Rose Schneiderman and the Women's Trade Union League', unpublished Delaware University Phd thesis, 1978. Schneiderman's autobiography, *All for One*, written with Lucy Goldthwaite, New York 1967, needs supplementation by reference to her papers, which are in the Tamiment Library, New York University.
11. For Malkiel, see Françoise Basch, 'The Socialist Party of America, the Woman Question and Theresa Serber Malkiel', in *Women in Culture and Politics; a century of change*, Indiana, 1986; and Sally Miller, 'From Sweatshop Worker to Labor Leader; Theresa Malkiel: a case study'; in *American Jewish History* 68, December 1978, pp.189–205. For Rose Pastor Stokes, see sketch in Marie Jo Buhle, *Women and American Socialism 1870–1920*, Urbana and London, 1981, pp.319–21. The Stokes papers in the Sterling Library, Yale, call for a detailed reappraisal of this interesting woman.
12. For an exhaustive account of the garment industry production line at the turn of the century and during the next two decades, see Susan A. Glenn, *Daughters of the Shtetl; Life and Labor in the Immigrant Generation*, New York, 1990, and especially Chapter 3, 'Unwritten laws'.
13. Baum, Hyman and Michel, eds., *The Jewish Woman in America*, New York, 1976,

p.129; Alice Kessler-Harris, *Out to Work, A History of Wage Earning Women in the United States*, New York, 1982, p.137; Glenn, op. cit. above, p.154.

14. Gerald Sorin, *The Prophetic Minority; American Jewish Immigrant Radicals, 1880–1920*, Indiana, 1985, pp.130, 136.

15. Ibid, pp.133–6. Kessler-Harris, op. cit. n.6. According to the *Biographical Dictionary of American Labor*, 2nd edition, 1984, only 21.8 per cent of women labour leaders were married in 1925, as compared with 56 per cent in 1946 and 57 per cent in 1976.

16. Glenn, op. cit. n.12, p.217.

17. Pauline Newman papers, MC324, in Schlesinger Library, Radcliffe College, Harvard: unpublished memoir, in Box 1, Folder 3, p.8.

18. Ibid, p.2.

19. Rose Schneiderman, *All for One*, op. cit. n.10.

20. Malkiel, 'Women and Freedom', Co Op Press, New York, 1915. See also Basch, op. cit. n.11, pp.347, 353.

21. Glenn, op. cit n.12, 'Gendered Earnings', pp.117–22.

22. Newman papers, op. cit. n.17. Box 6 Folder 109: 'Women's Garments and their Markers' (in the Twenties), unpublished memoir. See also Pesotta, 'A Garment Worker's Diary' (1920s–30s), unpublished memoir, Box 24, R.P. Coll.

23. *The Jewish Woman in America*, op. cit. n.13, pp.132–6; Glenn, op. cit. n.12., pp.145–8.

24. Miller, op. cit., n.11, p.191; Glenn, op. cit. n.12, p.62, and pp.60–63 for the problem of boarding.

25. Foner, op. cit. n.1, p.225.

26. Rose Pastor Stokes, 'Life Story'; unpublished autobiography in the Rose Pastor Stokes papers, Sterling Library, Yale.

27. Rose Schneiderman, *All for One*, op. cit. n.10, p.121.

28. See n.11.

29. Nancy Schrom Dye, *As Equals and as Sisters; Feminism and the Labour Movement and the Women's Trade Union League of New York*, New York, 1980: Chapter Four, 'Revolution in the Garment Trades 1909–1913' (pp.88–109). An earlier, contemporary account is that of Lewis Lorwin (Levine) *The Women Garment Workers*, New York, 1924. Estimates of the number of workers on strike vary from Lorwin's 20,000 to Dye's 30,000 (also see Dye, p.177).

30. Ibid. See also Linda Kuzmack, *Woman's Cause*, Ohio, 1990, pp.125–6. Kuzmack notes that when employers reneged on the Protocols, the Jewish labour administrator and social worker Belle Moskowitz resigned, 'effectively ending the implementation of the Protocols' (p.126). For the terms agreed on by the ILGWU perpetuating wage discrimination, see *The Jewish Woman in America*, op. cit., n.13 pp.146–7.

31. Pauline Newman to Rose Schneiderman, December 1, 1911. Rose Schneiderman papers, Tamiment Library, New York University, A94. See also Newman to Schneiderman July 26, 1912 on 'the cultural ladies'. Endelman, op. cit. n.10, p.80, notes that Schneiderman's ambivalence regarding society women revived in 1918 when she accused wealthy 'volunteers' of taking work from factory operatives; but (p.129) that by the 1920s she had more in common with wealthy reformers than with Jewish seamstresses.

32. Schneiderman, *All for One*, op. cit. n.10, p.97.

33. Rose Pesotta to Max Danish, December 15, 1933, R.P. Coll.

34. Quoted in Sorin, op. cit. n.14, p.140; later quotes from Glenn, op. cit. n.12, pp.180, 221.

35. Theresa Serber Malkiel, *The Diary of a Shirtwaist Striker*, New York, 1910.

36. Rose Schneiderman to Mary Anderson of the US Dept of Labor, August 1, 1919. Schneiderman papers, R3082, in Tamiment Library, New York University.
37. Kessler-Harris, op. cit. n.6, pp.152–3.
38. Ibid.
39. Rose Schneiderman to Benjamin Schlesinger, February 6, 1916; Schneiderman papers, op. cit. n.36.
40. Frances Perkins to Rose Schneiderman, March 7, 1919. Ibid.
41. Rose Pesotta to David Dubinsky, September 30, 1933. R.P. Coll.
42. For criticism of the 'Jewish' unions, see Pauline Newman to Rose Schneiderman, September 13, 1910. Schneiderman papers op. cit., Collection 18A. Pauline Newman to Rose Schneiderman, February 9, 1912, Ibid.
43. Pauline Newman to Rose Schneiderman, September 6, 1912. Newman papers, Schlesinger Library, op. cit. n.17, Box 5, Folder 78.
44. Rose Pesotta, *Days of Our Lives* (memoir of life in the *shtetl*), Boston, 1958.
45. Ibid.
46. Ibid.
47. Schrom Dye, op. cit. n.29, pp.99–100.
48. For details of women's work, see Glenn, op. cit n.12, p.112; for job changing as a technique of learning, ibid. pp.126–7.
49. 'Family Album', unpublished novel Ms. in R.P. Coll.
50. Rose Pesotta to 'My dearest Comrade', August 4, 1922. R.P. Coll.
51. Rose Pesotta to 'My dear New Yorker' (anonymous correspondent), January 16, 1934.
52. Rose Pesotta, Special Correspondence, Sacco and Vanzetti; Box 20, R.P. Coll.
53. Rose Pesotta to Hippolyte Havel, February 10, 1934. R.P. Coll.
54. Foner, op. cit. n.1, p.282.
55. David Dubinsky to Rose Pesotta, September 28, 1933. R.P. Coll.
56. Rose Pesotta to David Dubinsky, September 30, 1933. Ibid.
57. *Bread Upon the Waters*, op. cit. n.1, p.17.
58. Rose Pesotta to David Dubinsky, November 20, 1933. R.P. Coll.
59. Rose Pesotta to David Dubinsky, December 13, 1933. R.P. Coll.
60. Rose Pesotta to Max Danish, December 15, 1933.
61. *Bread Upon the Waters*, op. cit. n.1, p.235.
62. Rose Pesotta to Max Danish, March 14, 1934. R.P. Coll.
63. Rose Pesotta to Paul Berg, March 2, 1934; and to Max Danish, March 14, 1934. R.P. Coll.
64. *Bread Upon the Waters*, op. cit. n.1, pp.62ff.
65. Rose Pesotta to Charles Green, Code Observance Director, New York, March 28, 1934. R.P. Coll.
66. John Dyche to Rose Pesotta, February 5, 1934. Ibid.
67. Rose Pesotta to Paul Berg, February 7, 1934. Ibid.
68. Rose Pesotta to Rae Brandstein, April 9, 1934. Ibid.
69. Rose Pesotta to David Dubinsky, November 25 and December 13, 1934. Ibid.
70. Rose Pesotta to Israel Fineberg, February 25, 1934 and April 3, 1934 ('A MAN IS NEEDED HERE'). Ibid.
71. David Dubinsky to Rose Pesotta, March 21, 1934. Ibid.
72. Rose Pesotta Diary, June 9, 1934, Ibid.
73. Rose Pesotta to David Dubinsky, August 14, 1934.
74. *Bread Upon the Waters*, op. cit. n.1.
75. Rose Pesotta to David Dubinsky, July 22, 1934, R.P. Coll.
76. Rose Pesotta to Emil Olaj, September 10, 1934. Ibid.

77. *Bread Upon the Waters*, op. cit. n.1.
78. Ibid, pp.148ff. ('Seattle is a union ghost town').
79. Rose Pesotta to Eva Ehrlich, February 8, 1935, R.P. Coll.
80. Rose Pesotta to David Dubinsky, March 22, 1935. Ibid.
81. Rose Pesotta to David Dubinsky, May 21, 1935. Ibid.
82. Rose Pesotta Diary, January 21, 1936.
83. Paul Berg to Rose Pesotta, January 14, 1935. Ibid.
84. Ibid. undated. The diaries are often random jottings.
85. *Bread Upon the Waters*, op. cit. n.1. Chapter 18.
86. Ibid., p.189.
87. See Foner, op. cit. n.1.
88. *Labor Dictionary of Biography*, op. cit. n.15.
89. *Bread Upon the Waters*, op. cit. n.1, p. 179.
90. Rose Pesotta to David Dubinsky, February 22, 1937.
91. *Bread Upon the Waters*, op. cit. n.1, pp.195ff.
92. Ibid.
93. Ibid., p.217.
94. Ibid.
95. For further details on Germer, Kryzycki and Hapgood, see *Labor Dictionary of Biography*, op. cit. n.15, under separate entries.
96. Longshoremen, miners and other labourers drank heavily together during this period and 'one needed a very good excuse not to participate in this sociable glass on any occasion.' (Robert Montgomery, *The Fall of the House of Labor; The Workplace, the State and American Labor Activism 1865–1925*, Yale, 1989, p.89.)
97. The progress of the Pesotta–Hapgood love affair and friendship is charted in the Pesotta papers in Special Correspondence 1934–45; Letters 1936–45 Powers Hapgood to Pesotta. Most of the hundreds of letters are Hapgood's, with a few copies of letters from Pesotta. Hapgood's letters indicate his concern that the affair should become public knowledge as 'like all radicals, we are likely to be raided', and he asked her to destroy them.
98. Pesotta, note (unsent), on ILGWU Montreal paper, dated September 29, 1936. Ibid.
99. Powers Hapgood to Rose Pesotta, April 30, 1936. Ibid.
100. Rose Pesotta to Mary Donovan, September 22, 1936. Ibid.
101. Powers Hapgood to Rose Pesotta, September 24, 1936. Ibid.
102. Rose Pesotta to Powers Hapgood, September 26, 1936. Ibid.
103. Ibid.
104. Rose Pesotta to Powers Hapgood, March 31, 1937. Ibid. Rose Pesotta to David Dubinsky, April 12, 1937. Ibid. *Bread Upon the Waters*, op. cit. n.1, pp.261ff.
105. Foner, op. cit. n.1, pp.304–10.
106. *Bread Upon the Waters*, op. cit. n.1.
107. See n.105.
108. Rose Pesotta to Powers Hapgood, undated and unsent ('I will not mail this letter'), probably late 1937, R.P. Coll.
109. *Bread Upon the Waters*, op. cit. n.1.
110. Rose Pesotta to Powers Hapgood, May 21, 1938, R.P. Coll.
111. Powers Hapgood to Rose Pesotta, June 14, 1940.
112. Rose Pesotta, obituary of Powers Hapgood, R.P. Coll., Special Papers, Box 24 (several drafts).
113. Rose Pesotta to Mollie Steimer Flechine, September 23, 1938. Steimer was the courageous anarchist deported from the United States in 1921. Ibid.

114. Rose Pesotta, Report to National ILGWU Convention 1940. R.P. Coll. Ibid.
115. Rose Pesotta, Resignation speech (several drafts), 1940. Ibid.
116. Rose Pesotta, Report to the General Executive of the ILGWU, June 15, 1942. (Minutes of ILGWU General Executive meeting, June 15–19, 1942.) Ibid.
117. Rose Pesotta to Powers Hapgood, January 30, 1943. R.P. Coll.

EPILOGUE

1. For Goldman's life, see the biography by Richard Drinnon, *Rebel in Paradise*, Chicago, 1961, and Goldman's autobiography *Living My Life*, New York, 1931, reprinted London 1988 with a useful introduction by Sheila Rowbotham. See also *Red Emma Speaks: Selected Writings and Speeches by Emma Goldman*. Compiled and edited by Alix Kates Shulman, New York, 1972. Alice Wexler's *Emma Goldman; an Intimate Life*, London, 1984, adds little but the sexually intimate letters sent by Goldman to Ben Reitman. Wexler's book ends with Goldman's deportation to Russia in 1918 and thus omits the most important period of her political activities thereafter. Wexler does, however, contribute some interesting details about the Goldman family, including that on Abraham Goldman in my text under this footnote. (Wexler, p.7) See also Alix Kates Shulman, *To the Barricades: The Anarchist Life of Emma Goldman*, New York, 1971.
2. Drinnon, op. cit. n.1, pp.23–7.
3. Margaret Marshall, *Anarchist Women 1879–1920*, Philadelphia, 1981, p.119 for statistics of women's origins; pp.29–32 for Marie Ganz (who abandoned her anarchism when she married). For Steimer, see Richard Polenberg's *Fighting Faiths*, New York, 1989, passim.
4. Goldman to Harold Laski, January 9, 1925; in *Nowhere at Home; the Letters from Exile of Emma Goldman and Alexander Berkman*, eds., Richard and Anna Maria Drinnon, New York, 1975, pp.37–40. This collection of letters is in many ways more illuminating than Goldman's autobiography (which was also extensively edited by Berkman).
5. Emma Goldman to Rose Pesotta, August 31, 1935. Rose Pesotta Collection, New York Public Library Ms. division. Correspondence: Emma Goldman 1934–37.
6. Rose Pesotta to 'Dear Comrades', November 27, 1934, R.P. Coll.
7. Rose Pesotta to Emma Colton (Goldman), April 15, 1935. See n.4.
8. Emma Goldman to Rose Pesotta, June 26, 1935. Ibid.
9. See n.5.
10. Copy of letter sent to Mark (?), by Emma Goldman, January 30, 1939. Goldman habitually made carbon copies of her letters and distributed them among her comrades. R.P. Coll: letters and papers, 1927–40.
11. Emma Goldman to Rose Pesotta, November 25, 1939. Ibid.
12. Details of the fate of Pesotta's family are in a letter applying for an American visa for her surviving sister, dated April 30, 1946. R.P. Coll. Mss of her fictional works 'Family Album' and 'From my Left Hand Pocket' (written in a male persona) are in R.P. Coll., Boxes 24–36.
13. For details, see Wexler, op.cit. n.1, Chapter 10.
14. Emma Goldman to Alexander Berkman, May 2, 1927. In *Nowhere at Home*, op. cit. n.4, pp.194–5.
15. *Living my Life*, op. cit, n.1. (1988 edition) Vol.1, p.370.
16. For a description of Zhitlovsky, see Jonathan Frankel, *Prophecy and Politics*, Cambridge, 1981, pp.258ff.

17. *Living my Life*, op. cit, n.1. Vol.II, pp.822–4.
18. Martin Gilbert. A personal communication.
19. Richard Polenberg, op. cit. n.3, p.370.
20. See Barbara Alpern Engel, *Mothers and Daughters*, op. cit. Chapter 2, n.6.
21. Franca Pieroni Bortolotti, 'Anna Kuliscioff e la questione femminile', in *Anna Kuliscioff e l'Età del Riformismo; Atti del Convegno del Milano*, pp.104–40 and in particular pp.111, 113 and 133.
22. See Chapter 3 n.8.
23. Dale Spender, *Women of Ideas (and what men have done to them)* London, 1982–88, pp.497–507.
24. Alice Kessler-Harris, 'Organising the Unorganisable', etc., in Cantor and Laurie, eds., *Class, Sex and the Woman Worker*, Westport, 1977, pp.160–1.
25. 'Anna Kuliscioff e il processo del 1898', in F. Turati, ed., *Anna Kuliscioff: In Memoria*, Milan, 1926, p.78.
26. Emma Goldman to Henry Alsberg, June 27, 1930. In *Nowhere at Home*, op. cit. n.4, pp.162–3.
27. Rose Pesotta to Emma Goldman, March 3, 1934. R.P. Coll. Correspondence, Emma Goldman 1934–37.

INDEX